THE NEW PATERNALISM

THE NEW PATERNALISM

Supervisory Approaches to Poverty

Lawrence M. Mead
Editor

BROOKINGS INSTITUTION PRESS
Washington, D.C.

Library of Congress Cataloging-in-Publication Data

The new paternalism : supervisory approaches to poverty / Lawrence M. Mead, editor.
p. cm.
Includes bibliographical references and index.
ISBN 0-8157-5650-X (cloth : alk. paper). — ISBN 0-8157-5651-8 (pbk. : alk. paper)
1. Poor—Government policy—United States. 2. Public welfare—United States. 3. Paternalism—United States. 4. United States—Social policy—1993– I. Mead, Lawrence M.
HV95.N455 1997
362.5'8'0973—dc21 97-33742
CIP

9 8 7 6 5 4 3 2 1

The paper used in this publication meets the minimum requirements of the American National Standard for Information Sciences—Permanence of Paper for Printed Library Materials, ANSI Z39.48-1984

Typeset in Times Roman

Composition by Cynthia Stock
Silver Spring, Maryland

Printed by R. R. Donnelley & Sons Co.
Harrisonburg, Virginia

THE BROOKINGS INSTITUTION

The Brookings Institution is an independent organization devoted to nonpartisan research, education, and publication in economics, government, foreign policy, and the social sciences generally. Its principal purposes are to aid in the development of sound public policies and to promote public understanding of issues of national importance.

The Institution was founded on December 8, 1927, to merge the activities of the Institute for Government Research, founded in 1916, the Institute of Economics, founded in 1922, and the Robert Brookings Graduate School of Economics and Government, founded in 1924.

The Board of Trustees is responsible for the general administration of the Institution, while the immediate direction of the policies, program, and staff is vested in the President, assisted by an advisory committee of the officers and staff. The by-laws of the Institution state: "It is the function of the Trustees to make possible the conduct of scientific research, and publication, under the most favorable conditions, and to safeguard the independence of the research staff in the pursuit of their studies and in the publication of the results of such studies. It is not a part of their function to determine, control, or influence the conduct of particular investigations or the conclusions reached."

The President bears final responsibility for the decision to publish a manuscript as a Brookings book. In reaching his judgment on the competence, accuracy, and objectivity of each study, the President is advised by the director of the appropriate research program and weighs the views of a panel of expert outside readers who report to him in confidence on the quality of the work. Publication of a work signifies that it is deemed a competent treatment worthy of public consideration but does not imply endorsement of conclusions or recommendations.

The Institution maintains its position of neutrality on issues of public policy in order to safeguard the intellectual freedom of the staff. Hence interpretations or conclusions in Brookings publications should be understood to be solely those of the authors and should not be attributed to the Institution, to its trustees, officers, or other staff members, or to the organizations that support its research.

To Robin

Foreword

American social policy is becoming more paternalistic. Traditionally, social programs gave benefits to people, but recently government has sought to supervise the lives of poor people who become dependent on it, either through welfare or the criminal justice system. "Welfare reform" primarily means requiring aid recipients to work, while parallel efforts to set standards for client behavior have appeared in programs for child support enforcement, sheltering the homeless, drug rehabilitation, education, and criminal justice. In all these areas, the demand is that dependent people do something—such as work or remain in school or refrain from substance abuse—to get some benefit or avoid penalties. The movement reflects an idea that government cannot ameliorate poverty unless those it helps do more to help themselves and avoid trouble.

In this book Lawrence Mead and ten coauthors take the first sustained look at this trend. Surprisingly little research on paternalism has appeared, partly because most researchers have emphasized the economic aspects of programs rather than their administration, which is crucial to supervising clients. All the authors know government and public administration first-hand, and that is essential for appraising these highly structured programs. Indeed, most of them have been directly involved in the conception, implementation, or evaluation of the programs they write about.

Most of what is written about paternalism is about mandatory welfare work programs, and it focuses mainly on their economic effects. *The New Paternalism* reviews this evidence, but it also considers directive programs or experiments in the other policy areas, and it gives particular attention to administrative arrangements. Other chapters offer cross-cutting perspectives coming from public management and psychiatry, and a concluding chapter considers the political implications of paternalism.

The policy is highly controversial, because some people think it implies "blaming the victims" for social problems or signals an abandonment of government's commitment to the needy. However, directive programs have advanced because the public is alarmed about welfare and crime, and policymakers seek new ways to deal with them. The authors of this book are cautiously optimistic that paternalism can help overcome poverty, although it makes serious demands on government.

The editor would like to thank John J. DiIulio Jr., founding director of the Center for Public Management, and Thomas E. Mann, director of Governmental Studies, for agreeing to conduct this project at Brookings. All the authors benefited from comments made by their coauthors during two meetings at Brookings. In addition, Douglas Besharov of the American Enterprise Institute generously reviewed all the chapters, and his suggestions led to important improvements.

The editor also thanks staff members Carey Macdonald, Tara Ragone, Susan Stewart, and Cindy Terrels of the Center for Public Management and Governmental Studies. Jim Schneider edited the manuscript, Fred Dews and Kristen Lippert-Martin verified its factual content, Susan Dobson proofread it, and Charlotte Shane compiled the index.

Michael H. Armacost
President

September 1997
Washington, D.C.

Contents

1. The Rise of Paternalism 1
Lawrence M. Mead

2. Welfare Employment 39
Lawrence M. Mead

3. Paternalism, Teenage Pregnancy Prevention, and Teenage Parent Services 89
Rebecca A. Maynard

4. Paternalism, Child Support Enforcement, and Fragile Families 130
Ronald B. Mincy and Hillard Pouncy

5. Homeless Men in New York City: Toward Paternalism through Privatization 161
Thomas J. Main

6. Coerced Abstinence: A Neopaternalist Drug Policy Initiative 182
Mark A. R. Kleiman

7. Paternalism Goes to School 220
Chester E. Finn Jr.

8. Implementing a Paternalist Welfare-to-Work Program 248
Eugene Bardach

9. Poverty and Paternalism: A Psychiatric Viewpoint 279
George E. Vaillant

10. Psychological Factors in Poverty 305
Miles F. Shore

11. Paternalism, Democracy, and Bureaucracy 330
James Q. Wilson

Index 345

One

The Rise of Paternalism

Lawrence M. Mead

This book investigates an important trend in social policy. Increasingly, government is seeking to supervise the lives of poor citizens who are dependent on it, often in return for supporting them. The trend is most visible in welfare policy, where *welfare reform* usually means attempts to require adults receiving assistance to work or stay in school in return for aid. However, the trend can also be seen in policy toward the homeless, in which shelters more frequently set rules for their residents, and in education policy, in which states have instituted tougher standards for schoolchildren. Some drug programs test addicts for compliance, and the criminal justice system has experimented with closer monitoring of offenders subject to probation and parole. The movement in antipoverty policy in general, then, is toward *paternalism,* meaning the close supervision of the dependent.[1]

Paternalism transforms the way social programs and policies are conceived and implemented, yet it has received remarkably little attention from policy analysts and researchers. Most of the studies and articles that apply are about welfare programs, where the use of mandatory work is well advanced. But the studies of these programs focus on their economics and effects, not the administrative influences they use to produce their results, which are their defining feature. Even less research exists on directive programs in other policy areas.

I gratefully acknowledge helpful comments on the first draft from several of the other authors of this volume and from Douglas Besharov.

This book begins to fill that void. I and my coauthors hope to open the subject for further discussion, analysis, and research. In the rest of this chapter, I define paternalism, discuss the ways in which it is novel, give some reasons for its appearance, show how it changes the assumptions behind social policy, assess its pros and cons, and suggest why inquiry about it has been scant. Finally, I summarize the contributions of my coauthors.

What Paternalism Means

As the term is used in this book, *paternalism* means social policies aimed at the poor that attempt to reduce poverty and other social problems by directive and supervisory means. Programs based on these policies help the needy but also require that they meet certain behavioral requirements, which the programs enforce through close supervision. These measures assume that the people concerned need assistance but that they also need direction if they are to live constructively.

Paternalism is sometimes used to denote protective or directive policies aimed at the entire population. Government does many things for citizens to prevent them from hurting themselves that, if they were more self-reliant, they would do for themselves. It requires credit card companies to state their interest rates on unpaid balances, rather than trust consumers to divine the terms from the fine print. Automobile passengers are made to wear seat belts in most states, although self-interest should lead them to do so without prompting. Even social security is paternalist in the sense that it forces people to provide for their own retirement. Paternalism in this broad sense may be on the increase.

This book, however, is about supervisory policies directed toward the poor or disadvantaged, or at least members of these groups who become dependent on society. *The poor* initially denotes people falling below the federal poverty line, but this book concentrates on those who are long-term poor and the likeliest to be dependent. These include people, usually men, involved with the criminal justice system as well as those who rely on welfare programs. The authors also concentrate on the working-aged poor, meaning adults who are not elderly or disabled, and their children. The long-term, working-aged poor are not many, perhaps 5 percent of the population.[2] However, they have posed the toughest challenges for antipoverty policy, and they are the main objects of paternalism.

Traditional versus Paternalist Policy

Paternalism toward the poor may be best understood in contrast with nonpaternalist practices, what I will call traditional social policy. This way of dealing with poverty, which is by far the most common approach, has two main dimensions. The first is welfare programs, meaning cash and in-kind benefits, such as Temporary Assistance to Needy Families (TANF) and food stamps that alleviate need directly.[3] The main beneficiaries are poor families, mostly headed by single mothers. Aid is usually given on the basis of *entitlement,* that is, using income criteria and without behavioral requirements.[4] The second dimension is law enforcement policies, which are meant to deter antisocial behavior. The most important in an antipoverty context are criminal laws, antidrug ordinances, and child support requirements. Traditionally, enforcement operates by apprehending wrongdoers rather than trying to head off noncompliance before it occurs, other than through deterrence.

Established policy, in short, leaves people free to choose their own course in life. It assumes that the poor, like other people, will conform to the law and the interest of society. But they are free to do otherwise, and if they break the rules, government proceeds against them only after the fact. It seeks to forestall trouble only by threatening *eventual* sanctions.

Paternalist social policy changes both emphases. Compared with the traditional approach, paternalist welfare programs become more demanding. Instead of a philosophy of entitlement, they emphasize a social contract, meaning that recipients have to satisfy behavioral requirements, such as working or staying in school, as well as income rules to receive aid. This requires new administrative structures that supervise their activities. Meanwhile, law enforcement becomes more proactive. Instead of only apprehending offenders, it attempts to forestall wrongdoing. This, as with new benefit requirements, involves administrative structures that supervise the lives of past offenders to prevent further crime.

Changes in Goals

These contrasts imply two important changes in goals. First, paternalism puts more stress on enforcement than does traditional policy. By enforcement I mean action taken by society to secure compliance with values that are not themselves contentious. Much that government does, such as allowing or forbidding abortion, brings values into question, but the values served by paternalism—the work ethic or obedience to the law—are usually not disputed. Rather, the political issue is whether to *require* that people conform to the agreed values. Paternalists think norms should be obligatory, and they take steps to improve enforcement.

Policies that enforce must be directive. That is, they must tell the people obligated what they are supposed to do. Thus paternalism includes policies that make school attendance compulsory for children or require welfare recipients to work as a condition of receiving aid. It excludes programs that seek to influence behavior through benefits or opportunities without telling people what to do. Thus paying children to attend school or improving financial incentives for aid recipients to work might be effective, but these steps are not paternalist because they leave attendance or work as a choice. Nor are education and training programs for the disadvantaged paternalist if participation is voluntary. Nor are the services of social workers if the caregivers are nondirective toward their clients.

Second, paternalism asserts the authority to judge individual interests. Society claims the right to tell its dependents how to live, at least in some respects. Whereas traditional policy assumes clients will usually follow the interests of society but leaves them free to diverge, paternalism assumes they may not follow society's interests and seeks to prevent their divergence. Individuals' decisions about their own self-interest are not routinely deferred to. Rather, a harmony of interests is assumed: enforcing society's interest in good behavior is deemed to serve the individual's interest as well.

Without judging individual interests, policy may be directive, even coercive, but it is not paternalist. For example, forcing businessmen to obey environmental laws is not paternalist, because a divergence between the individual and society's interest is accepted. Society does not pretend that it is in the immediate, personal interest of businessmen not to pollute, although they share in the collective interest in avoiding pollution. Requiring children to be vaccinated, however, is paternalist because it assumes that the social and individual interest coincide. Society has decided that for children not to get their shots is not only harmful to others but self-defeating.

Paternalism thus violates John Stuart Mill's famous "harm" principle, according to which "the only purpose for which power can be rightfully exercised over any member of a civilized community, against his will, is to prevent harm to others."[5] The offense is not so much the coercion as the assumption that government can know and serve its clients' own interests better than they would themselves. That belief may seem unwarranted: if those subject to enforcement agreed with the ends served, they would do the right thing on their own. But this assertion assumes that behavior is consistent with intention. In fact, the clients of paternalism commonly do accept the values being enforced; especially, they express a desire to work.[6] However, they commonly fail to conform to these values in practice. Paternalism seeks to close that gap.

Social Contract and Supervision

The idea of a social contract in benefit programs should be seen as an enforcement device. Government can lock up criminals and exact child support without giving the men involved anything in return, just as it penalizes stockbrokers for violating the securities laws. Recently, many states have enacted laws penalizing parents for the misbehavior of their children.[7] Paternalist income programs, however, use the benefits on which people depend as a lever to ensure compliance. Access to welfare or shelter for the homeless then involves a bargain. Society says to the clients, in effect, "we will support you in need, but only if you behave in ways society routinely expects."[8]

Programs may be directive but voluntary. In this model, people who sign up face clear direction from program staff about good behavior, but there is no social contract. They do not have to enter to obtain income or shelter, and they are free to leave without threatening those benefits. One example is the Job Corps, an intensive federal education program for disadvantaged youth. Another is STRIVE, a private job placement program that instills compliant attitudes in trainees to improve retention in jobs. Both appear to achieve something, but because the clients can leave at little cost, it may not be by enforcing anything.[9] Whether such programs can be termed paternalist is unclear. It depends on how authoritative they really are.

The close supervision in paternalist programs is also an enforcement device. Because the clients are not presumed to follow their own interest well, staff must check up on them to be sure they fulfill their obligations. Misbehavior is not just punished; it is preempted by the oversight of authority figures, much as parents supervise their families. The administrative structure needed to do this is the most distinctive thing about paternalist programs.

A Return to the Past?

Paternalism is an effort to control the lifestyle of the poor. For this reason, some might argue that it is a throwback to a less enlightened past. But in important respects it is novel.

How Paternalism Is Old

As historians point out, concerns over the deservingness of the needy are as old as poverty itself, and efforts to reform the lives of recipients are as old as welfare. Current mandatory work programs in welfare recall the efforts to discipline the poor in British and American workhouses or the prisons or asylums that nineteenth-century social reformers thought could rehabilitate their inmates.[10]

The recent movement toward a more conformist social policy reflects cultural changes in society. Many people want to reverse trends toward permissiveness often associated with the 1960s and with such public policies as entitlement welfare, legalized abortion, and no-fault divorce. Perhaps the rate of divorce will decrease and churchgoing increase because of these pressures, which reflect the desire of aging baby boomers to leave a more wholesome society to their children.[11] The decline in smoking shows the culture's power to change behavior with little help from government once a practice is widely viewed as dangerous. As Alexis de Tocqueville noted, public opinion governs America in some ways more inexorably than government.

One interpretation of paternalism is simply that America is, indeed, returning to the past. In the nineteenth century, aid to the needy was often given grudgingly amid moralistic judgments. It was partly given by local governments, partly by churches and other nongovernmental bodies. Aid givers and social workers often demanded that recipients regiment their sexual lives or change their parenting of children as a condition of receiving help. Welfare funded by state and federal governments emerged only in this century, and only in the 1960s did aid to families with dependent children (AFDC), the principle federal-state family assistance program and predecessor of TANF, give up setting invidious conditions for receiving aid. Some might consider paternalism simply an attempt to restrict aid and restore behavioral rules.

An oscillation has occurred in antipoverty policy between compassion and control, between the urge simply to aid those in need and the desire to prevent patterns of life, especially unwed pregnancy and nonwork, that often help keep people poor. Thus, compared with the nineteenth century, aid policy during the 1930s was generous and unquestioning, since many people were destitute because of the Great Depression rather than their lifestyle. When times improved, welfare became more restrictive and moralistic, then expanded again in the 1960s and early 1970s as concerns over deservingness eased. Paternalism may be just the latest restrictive cycle.

How Paternalism Is New

But in two respects, each of them a legacy of the welfare rights movement of the 1960s, paternalism should be distinguished from earlier swings toward control. First, paternalism in welfare does not primarily involve attempts to restrict access to aid by tightening the eligibility rules. Quality control, or the policing of eligibility determination, has been a federal and state policy since the early 1970s, but recent efforts to reform AFDC have not emphasized eradicating fraud and abuse.[12] Welfare is tougher to qualify for today than it was a generation ago because states have allowed income eligibility levels to lag behind inflation, but again the trend predates the recent vogue for reform. Congress has not undone any of the Supreme Court decisions of the late 1960s and early 1970s that disallowed practices once often used to curb access to aid.[13] Nor are the behavioral requirements that the federal government and the states have added to welfare chiefly been aimed at family and sexual life. Mostly they address conduct outside the home, especially requirements to work or stay in school.

Paternalism in welfare has generally meant adding obligations to the earlier welfare rights, not undoing those rights. Responsibility for determining eligibility has not been restored to the discretionary control of social workers. Access to aid is still determined on a rule-based, largely nondiscretionary basis, but now society says that if a person draws aid, he or she must also comply with behavioral requirements such as looking for work. Both eligibility standards and behavioral rules tend to be set by legislative enactments that are highly public, not devolved to the invisible control of administrators. Such demands are less invidious than in the past because they do not depend on an individualized finding of fault. Dependent adults simply have to meet the same societal expectations as other people, and the standards are set politically on general grounds.[14] They become individualized only in applying the rules to particular instances, in which some caseworker discretion is unavoidable.

Of course, one may regard such stipulations as de facto restrictions in the eligibility rules because not all who might get aid manage to comply with them. It is also true, as I note in chapter 2, that work requirements do divert some people from accepting aid. Knowing they will have to work, some who would be eligible for welfare because their income is low enough decline to seek it. But demanding good behavior while on the rolls is still distinct from blocking access to welfare. Indeed, some common welfare changes, such as more generous financial incentives for those who work, have the effect of easing their access to welfare. Although one goal of reform is certainly to reduce the welfare rolls, the means is now more often to turn welfare into a work-based system than simply to shut the door to aid.

The other departure from the past is that today's paternalism is mostly government led. Before 1960 the main pressures the poor faced to conform were private. They stemmed from popular sentiment, churches, and philanthropic organizations that sought to promote education or moral improvement.[15] To the extent social control was governmental, it occurred mostly at the local level. Public schools and police, for example, tried to discipline the immigrants who flooded into the slums of eastern cities at the turn of the century. Today the funding and the authority for directive policies come primarily from public officials. In poor areas, government is trying to perform the ordering function it formerly left to private society. This partly reflects the collapse of voluntary social organizations in these neighborhoods and partly the general growth of government in the society. Also, much of the initiative is now federal. Washington mandated the work programs that are now part of welfare, and it has urged tougher standards in both education and law enforcement, although responsibility for administering these policy areas remains generally nonfederal.

A subtler distinction is that until the past few decades authoritative programs tended to be custodial. They established institutions such as mental hospitals or reformatories that took their inmates entirely out of society.

They concentrated on the insane, the criminal, and others who could be treated as exceptions to the general population. The current paternalism more often involves supervision within society. It seeks to direct the lives of people who continue to interact with other citizens as fellow workers or students. Where the older policies segregated the deviant, the current policies seek integration by inducing people to work or go to school more regularly.

These changes reflect a profound change in social politics. Until recent decades, poverty and welfare were seldom matters to be dealt with in Washington. Federal politics was dominated by disputes over federalism, economic policies, class, and race. The labor and civil rights movements raised questions that addressed economic status and equal opportunity, not poverty or dependency. Prohibition, the effort to outlaw alcoholic beverages in the 1920s and 1930s, is the only instance in which Washington tried to control the lifestyle of citizens directly, and it was abandoned as unworkable.

After 1960, however, poverty, especially in the inner cities, landed squarely on the national agenda. This partly reflected the urban riots of the 1960s and the sense that, after civil rights, urban poverty posed the greatest threat to national cohesion. Since the mid-1960s every president has had an antipoverty policy, and the claim of having defeated poverty or the failure to solve the problem has had much to do with the electoral fortunes of the political parties. And at the center of the poverty debate has been the vexed question of welfare. In sum, as poverty and dependency became more visible problems, measures to deal with them became more governmental and more federal. The heritage of the civil rights movement also helps explain why the chief goal of paternalism is to integrate rather than segregate the poor.

A Return to the Private Sector?

Although social policy has become the province of government, the trend since the early 1980s has been devolution of responsibility for dealing with it to lower levels of government. The trend was reinforced by the Personal Responsibility and Work Opportunity Reconciliation Act (PRWORA) of 1996, which replaced AFDC with TANF and devolved more control over the program to states and localities. Some fear that this, together with paternalism, may signal the coming privatization of welfare. The nation may once again entrust aid for the needy to private bodies and provide for only a limited governmental role.

Some conservatives advocate this devolution on the grounds that only the private sector can really cope with poverty. They argue that public aid is inevitably permissive because American politics is preoccupied with protecting rights, and it is inevitably inefficient because of the limitations of public bureaucracy. Perhaps only private schools can educate disadvantaged children successfully. Perhaps only churches and other community institutions can overcome poverty, because only they can help people while challenging them at a personal level to change their lives.[16] It is true that some private religious organizations such as the Salvation Army seem notably committed and effective at serving the poor.[17] It is also true that even when programs remain public, nonprofit bodies operating as contractors to government are often good at implementing directive policies because they can be authoritative and efficient. Several authors in this book incline to these views.

Most of us, however, think it unlikely and undesirable that antipoverty policy should be privatized. After all, one reason that public social policies arose in the Progressive and New Deal Eras was that private charity could not cope with the scale of urban poverty. The public now expects that the most destitute will be cared for, whether or not private aid is available, and for this a welfare state is indispensable. The practical question is how to change public programs so that they do more to promote self-regarding behaviors.

Community organizations outside government cannot do much to force the poor to follow a better lifestyle as long as public aid programs demand little. Nor do many of them want to do so. The private agencies, including church charities, that serve as contractors to welfare departments in American cities are as imbued with a rights orientation as government itself. Typically, they want to help the attractive, "deserving" poor such as children in need of foster care, not govern the less deserving adults. They tend to oppose paternalism. Churches, liberal or conservative, seem unwilling to seize the new opportunities to participate in welfare reform offered by PRWORA.[18]

If directive programs are to develop, therefore, they must be based mainly on government, whatever its limitations. Only government has the necessary resources. Only public officials, acting with the mandate of the people, can have the standing to impose functioning requirements and, if necessary, withdraw benefits to enforce them. Nongovernmental bodies can help implement such programs but are likely to be of secondary importance. Paternalism has been primarily a government operation and is likely to remain so.

Social policy may oscillate between the indulgent and the demanding, but an oscillation between the public and private sector is less clear. Despite devolution, the trend toward paternalism has not yet compromised public responsibility for the poor. Paternalism may take some inspiration from the private sector, but it is still government led. Indeed, it rests on recent developments in public administration. These include the expansion of contracting to implement programs and, above all, the automated management information systems that are essential to run supervisory programs. The new programs also draw on research and evaluation, much of it government funded, as the authors in this book make clear. In general, paternalism transcends the old opposition of the public and private sectors to create a new form of public provision for the poor.

One sign of this is that paternalism is distinct from the social policy traditionally favored by either the left or right in America. It is a conservative policy in that it focuses on changing how the poor live rather than on improving their benefits or opportunities. It seeks order rather than justice, and social critics might call it blaming the victim.[19] But paternalism is also a liberal policy because it is pro-government. Far from reducing the welfare state, as conservatives usually ask, paternalism expands it. Now social agencies attempt not only to help those in need but to reorganize their lives. Paternalism does not primarily mean a change in the scale of government, a traditional bone of partisan contention. Instead, it means a change in the character of government so that benefits are linked to functioning.

In this book the authors recognize that the subject of privatization is important, but they also soft-pedal it so that it will not detract from the main subject. They seek mainly to understand the origins, nature, and potential of paternalist programs themselves, whoever ends up running them.

Political Causes

Why has a turning toward paternalism arisen mainly in the past decade, more than thirty years after poverty became a national concern? Some of the reasons are political. In the 1960s when liberals proposed to expand welfare, the nation enjoyed the luxury of a balanced budget and steadily growing personal incomes. In the 1990s, however, it struggles with a budget deficit, and most Americans have seen little improvement in their real earnings in a generation. Thus one might attribute supervisory trends in part to scarcity. Telling the poor how to live may cost less than giving them more income or services. It may reduce the welfare rolls and thus the cost of poverty for the rest of the society. But paternalism also places new demands on government. It may be less costly than expanding welfare, but it is more costly than simply cutting access to aid. So budgetary concerns cannot be the whole explanation.

Another factor is the conservative tide in electoral politics. It is difficult to imagine supervisory measures developing at the hands of Democrats, who have traditionally favored a benefit-oriented welfare state. Meanwhile, Republicans have controlled the presidency most of the time since 1968. They took control of the Senate temporarily in 1980, then all of Congress in 1994. After Ronald Reagan won the White House in 1980, most new federal spending went to the military or the large middle-class entitlements, social security and medicare. Little, relatively speaking, went to antipoverty programs. It became unimaginable that the nation would again launch a costly, many-pronged assault on poverty such as Lyndon Johnson's Great Society. The Democrats who won the presidency after 1968—Jimmy Carter and Bill Clinton—still proposed welfare reforms with liberal aspects, but on social policy they stood well to the right of their own parties.

At the state level a comparable shift has occurred. Republican governors have advanced in numbers, and after the 1994 elections they controlled a large majority of statehouses. Some among them—Tommy Thompson in Wisconsin, John Engler in Michigan—made their names chiefly as welfare reformers favoring paternalist changes. Even large states known for liberalism have elected Republican governors—Pete Wilson in California, George Pataki in New York. They advocated both cuts in welfare benefits and tougher government expectations for welfare and homeless clients.

But electoral trends cannot totally explain paternalism. The traditional Republican approach to poverty was simply to cut back government programs and benefits and rely more on the private sector to generate opportunities for the downtrodden. Paternalism is a big-government form of conservatism, and this has caused some in the GOP to reject it. During the Bush presidency, James Pinkerton developed the idea of a "new paradigm" for social policy that would abolish centralized, bureaucratic social programs in favor of a dispersed system of incentives and choices. Rather than give benefits such as public education or child care to passive recipients, Pinkerton argued, we should empower them with vouchers to make their own choices among many providers, either public or private.[20] The perspective is similar to that of Newt Gingrich, House Speaker and chief Republican leader since 1994.

That sort of thinking warred with paternalism in the "Contract with America" that Republicans made their manifesto in the 1994 elections.[21] The result was PRWORA, the dramatic welfare reform that the Republican congressional majority forced on President Clinton in 1996. The new law stiffens work requirements in welfare programs; but it also cuts welfare benefits and coverage to save money and deter unwed pregnancy, and it devolves much control over assistance to the states. The GOP is still of two minds as to whether to use government to enforce values, which paternalism does, or simply to cut it back to free up American society.

A better political explanation for paternalism is the power of public opinion. Paternalism appears to be the social policy that most Americans prefer, to judge from polls about welfare and poverty. Political elites criticize government for being too large or too small, but the views of voters are more complex. People blame government for neglecting the needy, but they also blame the parents of poor families for bearing children out of wedlock and failing to work. The popular response to the problems of the inner city is neither to expand nor deny assistance by itself. People do not want poor families or the homeless simply subsidized, nor do they want them thrown onto the street.

Thus the electorate does not become polarized over whether the individual or society is responsible for poverty. Typically, it divides the responsibility. It wants more done to protect the vulnerable, but also wants far tougher requirements that the adult poor work and otherwise behave well in return for support. This explains why *social contract* is a popular rubric for welfare reform.[22] The combination of aid with requirements, of course, is exactly what directive programs attempt. The recent advance of these measures in welfare, education, and elsewhere represents the triumph of social opinion over political ideology.

The Social Problem

A further explanation for the appearance of paternalism is the change in the nature of the social problem. Poverty in the sense of low income is hardly new, and welfare and other antipoverty policies are longstanding. Yet until the 1960s, poverty and associated conditions were not a focus of national social policy. The center was held by issues of class and race. Workers in America, as in other countries, contended for union rights and for governmental protections, including benefit programs, against the insecurities of capitalism. Black Americans carried on a legal and then a political campaign to dismantle Jim Crow and other barriers to equal opportunity for minorities. Later, the feminist movement won fairer opportunity for women, and today the gay movement seeks equal recognition for homosexuals. These movements along with other issues such as the regulation of business and protection of the environment formed the identity of the two main parties around questions of how big or small the government should be. For in every case the chief question was whether government, especially the national government, should intervene in the society more or less than it had before.

Poverty, welfarism, and other social problems were not absent, yet they were subordinate to the quests for equal standing and equal opportunity pressed by social reform movements. In the 1930s, mass destitution was a spur to a vast expansion of relief and public employment programs. But it was assumed that need and dependency would decrease once the primary problems of control of the business cycle and protection against the marketplace were solved. When the crisis passed, relief and public jobs programs were cut back. The main antipoverty policy was not to be welfare but rather the new full-employment economic policies coupled with unemployment insurance and social security for those unable to work.[23]

Similarly, the civil rights movement reached its height in the early and middle 1960s, just when the nation awoke to poverty as a serious problem. At first, poverty was chiefly seen as a by-product of the historical disadvantage suffered by black Americans. The main cause of the urban riots, as the Kerner Commission said, was the division of America into "two societies, one black, one white—separate and unequal."[24] Achieve integration, it was widely believed, and social problems such as burgeoning welfare dependency and crime that disproportionately involved blacks would abate.

Unfortunately, this did not happen. The black middle class grew, but crime, dependency, and other distempers associated with poverty continued to escalate during the 1970s and 1980s, long after all the reform movements—except gay liberation—had achieved their major goals. Rates of serious crime, welfare dependency, and unwed childbearing soared (table 1-1). The percentage of the poor who worked decreased, and educational achievement as measured by precollege test scores fell.

Of course, the crime surge was partly due to the baby boom passing through its youth. The falling percentage of the poor who worked meant not so much that the same poor worked less but that most workers left poverty because of rising wages. College test scores fell in part because the college-bound population grew to include more disadvantaged students. Some trends showed improvement in the 1990s. But, after all caveats, the figures support the idea many people have that America is a less orderly, less well behaved place today than it was a generation or two ago.

Some would say that past reformism was insufficient, that poverty is still the by-product of larger societal problems. They point out that starting in the late 1970s the economy generated proportionally fewer well-paying jobs accessible to those with few skills than it did in the 1960s and that blacks still face discrimination in employment and housing. These impediments, some experts believe, can still account for the disarray of the inner cities.[25] Perhaps social reform of the traditional kind would still be the best way to ameliorate poverty.

But if wage stagnation has made it harder to enter the middle class, massive job creation has driven employment in the general population to the highest levels in history and attracted unskilled immigrants from around the world. And although some racial bias remains in America, it has steadily lessened since the beginning of the civil rights movement and is thus inverse to the intensification of poverty in the inner city. Once people thought that single mothers could not work because of their children, but today most are employed, including a large majority of those not on welfare.[26] Thus systemic conditions such as economic depression or Jim Crow no longer account for poverty in the clear-cut way they once seemed to. Experts with a broad view of the evidence conclude that societal barriers can today explain only part of the poverty problem.[27]

These trends elevated poverty and associated disorders to prominence in their own right, not only as aspects of other issues. The political basis for supporting policies to restore order is broader today than it was a century ago. Then the leaders of social control were mostly local notables offended

Table 1-1. U.S. Social Indicators, 1960–94

Percent unless otherwise specified

Indicator	*1960*	*1970*	*1980*	*1990*	*1994*
Serious crimes (millions)	3.364	8.050	13.408	14.476	13.992
Per 1,000 inhabitants	18.8	39.6	59.5	58.2	53.7
Heads of poor families with children under age 18 who worked	82	67	54	56	56
Worked full-year and full-time	43	28	17	17	19
Persons receiving AFDC (millions)	3.073	9.659	11.101	12.159	13.974
Per 1,000 resident population	17	47	49	49	54
Births to unmarried women as percent of all births	5	11	18	28	31
Average SAT scores (sum of verbal and mathematics)	975	948	890	891	901

Sources: Crime: Federal Bureau of Investigation, *Uniform Crime Reports for the United States, 1974* (Department of Justice, 1974), p. 55; and FBI, *Uniform Crime Reports for the United States, 1994* (Department of Justice, 1994), p. 58. Serious crimes include murder, nonnegligent manslaughter, forcible rape, robbery, aggravated assault, burglary, larceny or theft, and motor vehicle theft.

Work: 1960: Bureau of the Census, "Poverty in the United States, 1959 to 1968," *Current Population Reports,* series P-60, no. 68 (Department of Commerce, 1960), table 10; 1970; "Characteristics of the Low-Income Population, 1970," *Current Population Reports,* series P-60, no. 81 (1970), table 23. 1980: "Characteristics of the Population below the Poverty Level," *Current Population Reports,* series P-60, no. 133 (1980), table 26. 1990: "Poverty in the United States, 1990," *Current Population Reports,* series P-60, no. 175 (1990), table 19. 1993: *Current Population Survey* (March 1995), table 19.

Welfare: Figures drawn or calculated from Bureau of the Census, *Statistical Abstract of the United States 1981* (Department of Commerce, 1981), p. 343; and *Statistical Abstract of the United States 1996* (Department of Commerce, 1996), pp. 8, 381.

Births: Bureau of the Census, *Statistical Abstract of the United States 1981* (Department of Commerce, 1981), p. 65; and *Statistical Abstract of the United States 1996,* p. 79; and National Center for Health Statistics, *Monthly Vital Statistics Report,* vol. 44 (June 24, 1996, supplement), table 16.

SAT scores: Educational Testing Service. Data are for academic years ending in the indicated calendar year. These averages are for all who took the SAT, not only college-bound seniors.

by the immoralities of urban life, often linked to prostitution and drink. They wanted to clean up cities by outlawing vice and saloons, but the public was more tolerant.[28] Today, however, crime and drugs dominate some urban areas. Among the needy, female-headed families on welfare are much commoner and steady employment much rarer than during the era of social reform. Basic order and functioning, not only morals, are now at risk. Accordingly, tougher crime, welfare, and education policies enjoy strong support, which helps explain the attractiveness of paternalism.

Policy History

Experts and policymakers have also been driven toward paternalism by disappointment with traditional antipoverty policies. Throughout the 1960s and 1970s, government counted mainly on a rising GNP and increased work opportunities to reduce poverty. At the federal level and in many states, cash and in-kind transfers to low-income people grew markedly in coverage and generosity. Washington committed itself to maintaining full employment, in part as an antipoverty measure. Civil rights legislation abolished overt discrimination against minorities, and national education and training programs were instituted to increase the skills of the disadvantaged.

By these means and a beneficent economy the early years of the War on Poverty achieved much. Social security and disability programs sharply reduced poverty among the elderly and impaired. Growing and better-paid employment lifted most of the working poor above the poverty line. Laws against bias as well as personal effort brought many black students and workers high-paying jobs for the first time, expanding the black middle class. Between 1959 and 1973 the poverty rate fell from 22 to 11 percent of the population, and from 55 to 31 percent among blacks.[29]

But after the early 1970s, progress ground to a halt. The main reason was that as poverty declined among the employed and elderly, the nonworking but nonelderly poor became a larger part of the remaining poor population, and they have proved difficult to help. The adage that most of the poor are not of working age is no longer true (table 1-2). Between 1959 and 1995 the population in poverty first fell sharply and then slowly rose to almost the same level as before, but its composition changed markedly. The numbers and percentages of poor children and elderly poor fell while those

Table 1-2. U.S. Poverty Rates and Relative Poverty, by Age Group, 1959–95[a]

Percent unless otherwise specified

Age group	*1959*	*1970*	*1980*	*1990*	*1995*
All persons					
Number in poverty (millions)	39.49	25.42	29.27	33.59	36.43
Poverty rate	22.4	12.6	13.0	13.5	13.8
Younger than 18					
Number in poverty (millions)	17.55	10.44	11.54	13.43	14.67
Poverty rate	27.3	15.1	18.3	20.6	20.8
Age 18–64					
Number in poverty (millions)	16.46	10.19	13.86	16.50	18.44
Poverty rate	17.0	9.0	10.1	10.7	11.4
Age 65 and older					
Number in poverty (millions)	5.48	4.79	3.87	3.66	3.32
Poverty rate	35.2	24.6	15.7	12.2	10.5
All poor					
Younger than 18	44.0	41.0	39.0	40.0	40.0
Age 18–64	42.0	40.0	47.0	49.0	51.0
Age 65 and older	14.0	19.0	13.0	11.0	9.0

Source: Bureau of the Census, "Poverty in the United States: 1995," *Current Population Reports,* series P-60, no. 194 (Department of Commerce, 1996), tables C-1, C-2.

a. Figures may not add because of rounding.

of the working-aged poor grew. Between 1970 and 1995 the number of working-aged adults in poverty almost doubled to comprise more than half of all poor.

Although the poverty rate declined for every age group between 1959 and 1995, it fell least for the working-aged poor. The chief initial cause was that few of this group worked regularly. Between 1967 and 1984, when most of the change in the makeup of the poor occurred, the share of poor households with clearly employable heads increased from 37 to 47 percent, yet the share of poor family heads who worked year round fell from 20 to 15 percent.[30] Most poor under age eighteen are the children of adults with low earnings. Children and the working-aged poor comprised 91 percent of all poor in 1995. Thus today's poor live mostly in families connected to working-aged but nonworking adults.

For the working poor and elderly the main solutions to poverty could be narrowly economic—larger wages and pensions—because these groups were already working or were not expected to. Poor families and single people, however, often did not work despite society's work expectation or they bore children out of wedlock. Their poverty might have been reduced the same way it was among the elderly, by income transfers. Indeed, welfare reformers in the 1960s and 1970s proposed to liberalize AFDC to cover working-aged poor more generously. But the lifestyle problems of this group of poor raised questions of deservingness, and the liberal reform plans were rejected. Most members of Congress and voters insisted that poor parents show more work effort before government aided them.[31] That decision would later lead to the welfare work programs that I discuss in chapter 2.

Meanwhile, compensatory education and training programs tried to reduce poverty by improving the skills and wages of the younger poor, but they achieved only modest success. Evaluations establish that well-run family and skills programs can improve the prospects of children and trainees compared with those of peers who do not receive the services. The gains in employment and reductions in welfare dependency and crime often repay the costs to society. Advocates would have society spend more on such programs, and they have a case.[32] But the effects are not large enough to say that poverty and its problems would be solved.

Other problems linked to poverty also became worse during the 1970s and 1980s. Crime soared as gangs selling drugs took over ghetto areas. Substance abuse caused the collapse of many families, forcing the diversion of children into foster care. Homelessness mushroomed for reasons only loosely connected to economic or social conditions.[33] These trends made it insufficient to view poverty as a lack of income. The poverty of the inner city came to connote a broader breakdown of order. And it was difficult to imagine any program of the traditional, benefit-oriented kind that could restore order.

This was the context that generated paternalistic trends. In the 1980s serious supervisory programs appeared in welfare, and policies for aiding the homeless began to become more stringent. The 1980s were also the seedtime of the more structured teenage mother, criminal justice, and drug treatment programs discussed in later chapters. Although federal leadership was important in welfare matters, many of the reform initiatives came from localities, which are more responsible than Washington for maintaining order, or from private groups. Conditions forced state and local officials to abandon the conception of poverty as solely an economic condition sooner than policy analysts or experts who viewed the problem from inside the Beltway or the universities.

The originators of paternalism concluded that the lifestyle causes of poverty had to be addressed on their own terms. The implication was not necessarily that the poor were responsible for their own problems or that antipoverty programs had failed. It was rather that service and benefit programs alone could not defeat poverty when it was heavily linked to behavior. Even if government accepted responsibility for the poor, its clients had to work more regularly, stay in school, and avoid unwed pregnancy and crime if they were to progress. The onus for overcoming poverty had to be divided between them and society, just as the public insists.

Changed Assumptions

Paternalism, then, is a response to the limitations of traditional antipoverty policies. It also involves fundamental changes in the assumptions underlying social policymaking.

Policy as Administration

The traditional language of policy analysis, especially in Washington, is economic. Programs are understood in terms of budgets, benefits, and benefit reduction rates. They cost money, deliver some benefits to the poor, then "tax" these away (or begin to charge money for services) as the clients' incomes rise. Policy analysts devote close attention to the trade-off between cost and the adequacy of benefits and between the generosity of programs and the disincentives they create for the recipients to escape poverty on their own.

The stance of the economic policymaker toward the client is activist but reactive. The policymaker "invests" in the poor through benefits or services and waits for them to respond. Programs are supposed to widen the opportunities available to the disadvantaged, who then make decisions such as getting further education or going to work that lead them out of poverty. After programs are instituted, the policymaker evaluates the effects and adjusts the benefits or incentives accordingly. Policymaking is a scientific enterprise based on feedback about what works.

In paternalism, in contrast, programs are more proactive, and they are seen as administrative structures. They still cost money and provide benefits, but they also levy behavioral requirements. That implies a less passive view of what social policy does. Programs do not simply invest in people and await a response. Rather, administrators prescribe certain responses such as work and require the clients to conform. Programs are still reactive in that penalties are imposed if people fail to comply. But now the desired behavior is stipulated more clearly, and programs try to forestall noncompliance by close supervision of their clients. Only on this basis, as paternalism presumes, can programs enforce values and assert authority over the individual.

Traditionally, administration was considered a tool to deliver policies conceived in economic terms. Such are the problems of bureaucracy in America that some economists have advocated that administration be minimized by delivering social benefits through vouchers or market mechanisms.[34] Paternalism gives up that strategy, for now not only the delivery of benefits but *policy itself* is administrative. The goal is to supervise behavior, largely outside institutional walls, something that can only be done by routines where staff members check up on clients. No incentive or reward structure can suffice. Public management becomes a much more critical dimension of social policy than it had been before.

Is this too much to expect of bureaucracy? A common view has been that social programs are fated to fail because the social problems they face lack clear solutions, or they become tangled in implementation problems, or they lack goals specific enough to permit effective management.[35] But paternalism has given administrators new supervisory tactics, states are resolving some implementation problems in welfare and child support programs, and some reform programs do have specific goals. Welfare employment programs generally have some indicators of performance, such as participation and job entry rates, that managers can use to hold staff and clients accountable. Again, the potential for paternalism rests on the progress of public administration.

Obligations Rather Than Rights

Another departure from traditional social policy is that paternalism emphasizes the obligations of clients rather than their rights or needs. Traditional antipoverty policy is compensatory. It attempts to fill in the deficits of income and skills that the poor suffer because of disadvantaged backgrounds. The goal of policy is to remove limits and barriers, whether inner or outer. The spirit, as Isaiah 61:1 states, is to "bind up the brokenhearted, to proclaim liberty to the captives, and the opening of the prison to them that are bound."

Freedom is also the policy goal most consistent with American political culture. Of course, left and right differ in what they mean by the term. For liberals freedom is advanced by extending public benefits and protections to shield the poor from the pressures of society, while for conservatives freedom means cutting back government to reduce interference with the marketplace, which is seen as the engine of opportunity. Both those who see more government as the answer to poverty and those who want less are selling freedom in some form.

In contrast, paternalist programs emphasize obligations. The idea is that the poor need support, but they also require structure. And behavioral rules are to be enforced through government. The law enforcement side of social policy serves the freedom of others, but it also claims to serve the poor themselves. This is what makes it paternalist, not merely regulatory. To some extent, public programs must provide the boundaries for their clients that healthy families, churches, and other neighborhood institutions would provide if more of them existed in poor neighborhoods.

The implications are particularly momentous for racial minorities, who are overrepresented among the poor.[36] Understandably, federal policy toward these groups has emphasized the dismantling of barriers, because past denials of equal opportunity have been a crucial cause of their disadvantages. The application of paternalism to the nonwhite poor, therefore, can seem like a reversal, and for blacks even a return to slavery or Jim Crow. For some, that is enough reason to reject it. But paternalism is really a postracial social policy. It has arisen at a time when racial theories of poverty are less plausible than they have ever been. The traditional liberal view that discrimination by whites explains black inequality is rebuked by the persistence of serious black poverty in a society without formal discrimination. But racists' beliefs that blacks cannot compete in an open society are rebuked by the expansion of the black professional class. Today's poor and those who serve them are integrated, drawing elements from all racial groups.

The most important causes of black poverty appear to lie in the past, in the generations before the civil rights movement. The discouragement blacks derive from that history still undermines their performance, even though society has become more fair.[37] Because history cannot be undone, social policy must focus not on further measures to eradicate bias but on altering the patterns of life that prevent the poor of all races from improving themselves. That is a conclusion many black caregivers who serve the poor draw themselves.

Political discussions of freedom in America tend to define it as the absence of restraint. But people who live without limits soon sacrifice their own interests to immediate gratifications. To live effectively, people need personal restraint to achieve their own long-run goals. In this sense, obligation is the precondition of freedom. Those who would be free must first be bound. And if people have not been effectively bound by functioning families and neighborhoods in their formative years, government must attempt to provide limits later, imperfect though they must be.

Competence

Paternalism questions the assumption of individual efficacy that underlies traditional social policies, liberal or conservative. Established benefit and opportunity programs take it for granted that poor clients are as able as other people to take care of themselves; they just need a better chance to do it. Policymakers assume that clients can advance their own self-interest if not society's. Perhaps they now live in ways injurious to society, but these ways at least serve their interests. The point of policy is to alter the incentives and constraints so that the search for personal advantage serves the social interest also.

This premise, which I call the competence assumption, lies behind liberal measures to suppress discrimination, train the poor for better jobs, or reduce the financial disincentives when welfare recipients take jobs. The conviction is that if one opens up more jobs to the nonwhite, raises skills and wages, and "pays" the dependent to work, more poor adults will earn and escape poverty without further prompting because it is in their interest to do so.[38] Conservatives, for their part, consider government programs and regulations as the barriers. But their argument that the barriers must be abolished also makes an appeal to competence, for it assumes that once the dependent are denied support, they will work and support themselves for lack of alternatives. Belief in competence explains why traditional social policy left the poor free to make their own choices. If one believes self-interest will lead people to other-regarding actions, one need not enforce behavioral standards.

Unfortunately, policies based on incentives have not shown much power to alter the behavior of the poor. In particular, the effect of welfare incentives and disincentives on how many recipients work is remarkably small.[39] This is hardly surprising, since not working and bearing children out of wedlock, the behaviors that do the most to precipitate the poverty of the working-aged, are themselves contrary to self-interest as most people understand it. They cause poverty or make it worse. If self-interest were a sufficient motivation, living in poverty and being on welfare should themselves motivate people to avoid or leave those conditions. Government action would not be needed. Yet long-term poverty and welfare dependence are substantial problems.[40] Again, situational constraints are not enough to explain this.

An unorthodox lifestyle would still be consistent with competence if the poor rejected conventional employment and family life. But this too is false. As noted earlier, most poor people accept conventional values. The defining idea of the culture of poverty, as sociologists developed that concept in the 1960s, was not that the poor had unusual intentions but rather that the gap between their values and their lives was unusually wide.[41] That is still a good characterization of their predicament.

This is the setting that has made the personal competence of the poor an issue. Paternalist programs do not take competence for granted; neither do they dismiss it. To set requirements for clients demands more of them than policies of service and subsidy that make no demands. But it is less demanding than the traditional antigovernment policy of doing away with programs and leaving the poor to fend for themselves. Paternalism aims to provide the combination of aid and structure—what I call help and hassle—that it seems the seriously poor need.

Pros and Cons

How might one sum up the advantages and disadvantages of the paternalist trend? I do so here only in general terms. The other authors in this volume do so more concretely in their individual policy areas.

Advantages

I have already stated much of the case for paternalism. A way of dealing with poverty that enforces values and governs individuals reflects a conservative political climate but also an intensification of the problems of poverty and the shortcomings of traditional social policies. Administration, obligation, and competence are emphasized because in the light of experience they seem necessary to deal with entrenched poverty.

Concrete evidence about the effects of paternalism is limited but encouraging. As later chapters discuss in detail, evaluations and research suggest that programs that set clear standards for their clients usually perform better than programs that do not. Hard data are more abundant in areas of welfare, teenage pregnancy, and education that concern women and children than in areas such as child support and drug addiction that mainly deal with men. But the limited information that does exist on the results of programs for deadbeat dads and substance abusers is at least encouraging, and there are no indications that paternalism worsens outcomes.

The political advantages of paternalism are that it enforces values without abandoning government aid to the needy, both of which are priorities with the public. It is also moderate in terms of the ideological battle over the scale of government. It has involved some devolution of responsibilities to local government and greater reliance on the private sector. But the strategy is largely government led and in some ways expands the mission of the welfare state.

Disadvantages

By offering primarily benefits and opportunities to the needy, traditional antipoverty policy at least avoided doing direct harm. Paternalism is more ambitious. It presumes that government can govern as well as support lives. That involves levying behavioral standards as well as paying benefits, and to enforce standards, government must be willing to withdraw benefits. The risk of direct harm thus increases. The danger is that the wrong people could be subjected to requirements and too many people could be penalized. The harm done could outweigh any benefits the programs have.

These dangers have been minimized because paternalistic programs are still the exception. Paternalism has appeared only in contexts in which the clients are self-selected. People who end up on means-tested aid for long periods, in homeless shelters, or in drug rehabilitation very likely do have problems organizing their lives, and demands that they work or otherwise function are likely to be constructive. The same argument could not be made for the beneficiaries of social insurance programs, who typically have a work history. Despite paternalist trends in the culture, nobody proposes governing the elderly or disabled. However, even among welfare recipients or the homeless, there are some people who are only temporarily in difficulties; if they were punished, the net effect could be harmful. And even when enforcement is needed and sanctions are justified, the result is still a loss for the recipients.

What evidence there is does not suggest that the costs of sanctions outweigh the benefits of directive programs. If anything, programs enforcing work standards for welfare recipients, for which there are the most data, appear to reduce the incidence of sanctions (see chapter 2). On balance, it is hard to argue that paternalism produces net harm; most likely it reduces overall suffering by improving lifestyles. But the evidence at present is insufficient to be sure. And even if we knew that the balance was positive, applying sanctions still raises a political issue. Most of the suffering that occurs with traditional social policies occurs indirectly because dysfunctional behavior is not constrained. Paternalism may reduce injury on balance, but it produces *some* harm as the *direct* result of governmental action. That may be difficult to justify.

The greatest damage of paternalism may be to values. Even if the programs improve the lot of the poor, they do so in ways that some people will find demeaning. By assuming that recipients cannot be trusted to pursue their own interest, paternalism in effect treats adults like children. The offense is especially egregious in the case of black Americans. The insult is limited in that enforcement is confined to a small number of responsibilities, such as working and obeying the law, that are incumbent on all citizens. But again, for the nondependent the enforcement, the cost, comes largely through the private suasions of society, whereas for the dependent it comes through government, and many may find that unacceptable.

The advocates of paternalism reply: What is the alternative? Paternalism is justified by necessity. Merely helping people has not removed pervasive poverty. Government's priority should not be to keep its hands clean but to do what is necessary to integrate the seriously poor into the larger society. The assumptions of paternalism no doubt are demeaning, but the problems the poor have with working and other civilities are far more damaging to them. If—and it is a big if—paternalism can help overcome those problems, it will be justified.

How Long?

The greatest imponderable surrounding paternalism may be how long behavioral requirements would have to remain in effect in order to help reorder the society. It would be easier to reconcile them with the political culture if they could be presented as temporary or transitional. That is, they could help produce greater self-reliance among the poor. Then they could be dismantled as the nation returned to a social policy based on economics and opportunity.

It would be incautious to claim this. As mentioned, the advocates of previous social institutions, such as Victorian-era work houses and reformatories, thought they could transform the poor into upstanding citizens; none clearly succeeded. The consistent enforcement of rules can positively influence the behavior of deviant people, but when the controls are ended the effects seldom last. And control is much easier to assert in an institution than in the community, as the current paternalism largely attempts to do.[42]

This is hardly surprising, since—except for children—most clients enter paternalist programs when they are already adults. It is far tougher to change people at that stage than during their formative years. Social policy, like voluntary efforts at self-improvement, must confront psychological determination—the tendency of early experiences to dictate later life. This suggests that some of those who now function poorly will have to be subject to supervision indefinitely, or at least as long as they are involved in the welfare or criminal justice systems. The main payoff to behavioral rules might come in the next generation, when the children of the dependent would have a better chance to live autonomous lives.

On the other hand, society has always contained less functional people, yet crime and dependency were somehow much lower before 1960 than today. How did society accomplish that with little governmental paternalism? Perhaps because private forms of social control were more effective then than now. It is possible that public paternalism might help regenerate those informal controls, partly by involving community organizations in directive programs and partly by legitimizing the idea—in and outside government—that social norms can and should be enforced. Then paternalism in its public sense might not have to be permanent.

Why Little Is Known

Paternalist policies have been developing in welfare programs and other contexts for a decade, yet this book is the first the authors know of to attempt an assessment. One explanation is that the idea of telling the poor how to behave is very sensitive. It implies criticism of past policies on both right and left, and the reflex of most policy experts is to avoid the matter. If paternalist programs are discussed, the tendency is to elide their directive nature. In congressional debates over welfare, advocates of work requirements from both parties often claim that they are only offering new chances to the poor to get ahead, evading the fact that the programs can compel participation.[43] Policy analysts often treat mandatory work programs in welfare as no different, except in clientele, from other employment programs in which clients need not participate.

Even experts, however, have devoted little attention or research to paternalism. This partly reflects the conventions of the academic world, which discourage the focus on institutions that the study of paternalism requires. Most experts and analysts who deal with antipoverty policy have been economists, and their analysis of social policy emphasizes benefits and incentives rather than administration. This neglect, admittedly, reflects the wider culture. As James Q. Wilson remarked, "Only two groups of people deny that organization matters: economists and everybody else."[44]

More important, economists assume that the poor, like other people, are rational maximizers who act to advance their own self-interest if not society's. People may not fully realize their ends because of constraints, but they do the best they can in the circumstances. However, no science that assumes an invariant, optimizing mentality can deal well with the self-defeating aspects of the poverty lifestyle. Understanding dysfunction requires positing a more complex psychology, where people fail to do what they themselves desire and thus fail to exhaust the potential of their environment. Only on this basis can one take directive policies seriously, because their purpose is to close the gap between intention and action. The unreality of economic assumptions partly explains why, as analysts of poverty, economists have lost ground to sociologists and political scientists, who have a more complex view of motivation.[45]

Another reason paternalism is neglected is that the methods usually used to study poverty obscure the administrative aspects of programs. Much of the research on the poor is based on academic data bases such as the Panel Study of Income Dynamics (PSID) and the National Longitudinal Survey of Youth (NLSY). These data sets have the virtues of large size and representativeness, but they say little about the influence of programs on clients, other than the economic benefits provided. Variables are usually not included for the administrative means, such as work or child support requirements, that paternalist programs rely on to affect behavior. Thus analyses based on these data ignore the influence of these policies.[46]

There are evaluations that show the efficacy of programs. But the most definitive and influential use an experimental methodology that again conceals the effects of administration. Indicators such as earnings are contrasted for clients given a tested program and for a control group. Random assignment of eligible clients between the two groups obviates unmeasured differences among clients and thus makes the difference in results a valid estimate of a program's effect. However, the programs tested typically have multiple features and involve several activities, with some clients assigned to one and some another. The experiment cannot disaggregate the effect of one feature or activity, except in the few cases in which clients were randomly assigned among them. This makes it hard for evaluators to appraise the directive dimension of programs. Even if a mandatory program shows some effect, one cannot be sure that it did so *because* it was mandatory.[47]

To study paternalism, therefore, scholars have to use a less systematic combination of inferences from evaluation reports, field observation, and program reporting data. The authors in this volume all do this. In discussing whether and how paternalism works, judgment is unavoidable.

Filling the Void

Despite these limitations, this book aims to open a serious discussion of supervisory methods in antipoverty policy. Most of the chapters are about paternalism in specific areas of social policy. I have asked each of their authors to respond to four questions.

—What paternalistic programs or policies have appeared in a particular policy area?

—Explain why they have appeared. What are the underlying social, political, or policy developments?

—Assess paternalism in this area of policy. What do directive programs appear to have achieved, if anything?

—Project the potential of paternalism. What might such programs achieve in the future, with due weight given to cost, implementation, and other practical problems?

The authors of chapters on individual policy areas discuss the economic results of programs where there are data, but they pay special attention to the programs as institutions, to how they operate administratively. Three other chapters apply cross-cutting perspectives derived from public management or from clinical psychology.

As mentioned earlier, paternalism has both conservative and liberal aspects, and it makes parties and philosophies on both left and right uneasy. The approach is fresh enough so that views about it do not align well with the usual disputes among experts and policymakers over poverty. These include:

—The causes of poverty. Is it due to structural features of the society, a culture of poverty, or the personal shortcomings of the poor?

—Policy issues. Are antipoverty programs successful? Are equal opportunity policies effective? Is too little or too much being done for the poor?

—Control issues. Who ought to run social policy, Washington or localities, the public, nonprofit, or private sectors?

—Partisan issues. Are Republicans or Democrats, conservatives or liberals, best able to deal with poverty?

Paternalism assumes moderate or agnostic positions on these issues. Paternalists do not say that society is or is not responsible for poverty, only that structural causes alone cannot explain it. Programs that provide only benefits or only opportunities cannot eradicate it, so the lifestyle problems of the poor must be addressed in their own terms. Paternalism divides the responsibility for social solutions between society and the poor. Whether or how to set standards for dependent people are issues largely separate from traditional partisan questions about the scale of government and who should run social policy.

In the spirit of public opinion, which is impatient with partisanship, I have asked the authors to deemphasize these matters and concentrate on the reality and potential of paternalism. What have directive programs achieved and what might they contribute to a better antipoverty policy?

My own discussion of welfare employment programs in chapter 2 tackles the policy area in which paternalism is most advanced. For a decade or more, many states and localities have moved toward requiring that adults drawing welfare either work or prepare for work in return for support. That demand reflects the public will and the fact that not working is a major cause of family poverty. Besides, programs that attempt to promote work without requiring it show little impact, and evidence of a lack of jobs or other barriers is not strong enough to explain nonwork. Meanwhile, programs that require work show results. Many welfare recipients respond favorably to the structure they provide. To judge from leading programs, especially in Wisconsin, determined work enforcement could cut welfare rolls by half or more. To date, few people seem to have been harmed. However, little is known about the effects of diverting people from welfare through work requirements, and enforcing work requires political resolve and administrative ability that few states have.

In chapter 3 Rebecca Maynard appraises programs designed to forestall teenage pregnancy. She finds that unwed pregnancy imposes serious costs on young mothers and their children, contrary to the mothers' intentions. Public and private programs for preventing pregnancy have been ineffective. One reason seems to be that most of them have been voluntary and nondirective, providing services and benefits to teenagers without telling them how to behave. Programs that enforced participation and gave more direction performed better. Under the Personal Responsibility and Work Opportunity Reconciliation Act of 1996 (PRWORA), Maynard believes, only directive programs for young people are likely to have much future.

Most of the evaluations in social policy are of programs aimed at welfare mothers. The next three chapters take up programs aimed at disadvantaged men, who are often the fathers of families on welfare. Much less is known about the effectiveness of these programs. Yet the data and the policy history suggest that poor men also benefit from enforced behavioral standards. Programs that set norms show some potential to promote work and child support payments and deter substance abuse.

In chapter 4 Hillard Pouncy and Ron Mincy discuss government efforts to make absent fathers support their children, many of whom live on welfare. The authors dramatize the administrative nature of paternalism as they show how child support has progressed through several regimes. Although enforcement of support has toughened, this alone is not a solution for fathers who lack the earnings to contribute to their families. Thus experiments have arisen that try to enforce support payment while also helping the fathers work and get better jobs. Some local programs even attempt to reattach the father to his children and spouse. Child support programs, like welfare programs, have edged toward the paternalist combination of help and hassle, but from the opposite direction. Welfare was a benefit system that has lately added work or school obligations; child support is an enforcement system that has lately recognized a need to help fathers fulfill their obligations.

In chapter 5 Thomas Main discusses policy toward homeless men in New York City. There, unlike anywhere else in the nation, local government has recognized an entitlement to shelter for all who need it. Because shelter has been declared a right, the city originally could not condition access on behavior, and in the 1980s its shelters were unsavory. In recent years the city has found a way to set standards by privatizing much of the system. Now to get services beyond the minimum, the homeless must go to shelters run by nonprofit organizations, where they have to accept routines and standards such as abstinence from drugs in return for a bed. This has sharply improved order and amenity in the system, although whether the clients are individually helped must await evaluation. Main suggests that the idea that either government or the private sector must run directive programs is too restrictive. In this case the two ended up working together.

In chapter 6 Mark Kleiman discusses policies to deter drug addiction . Addiction causes adults to act dysfunctionally, which belies the assumption that they are competent to do what is best for themselves. But if government intervention seems called for, existing policy is punitive rather than effective. Society has tried to stigmatize drug taking and throw drug dealers in jail, but neither policy gives the immediate response addicts need to realize that drugs are self-destructive. Where incentives fail, administration must drive the message home. Drug courts have moved toward closer supervision of offenders, forcing them to accept treatment to avoid prison. Kleiman recommends "coerced abstinence" in which addicts on probation have to accept regular drug testing and are immediately incarcerated for short periods if they fail the tests. He shows on plausible assumptions that this policy would reduce drug usage and benefit society, but he also admits that implementing it would make serious political and bureaucratic demands. As in other policy areas, the price of progress is the reinvention of government.

In chapter 7 Chester Finn discusses education, in which paternalism has been longstanding and relatively noncontroversial. He contends that the public schools have weakened in part because they are less effectively paternalist than they once were. Official reports criticize a lack of educational standards, and research shows that the best way to improve student outcomes is strongly directed learning in which teachers set standards and follow up on students who fail to meet them. The educational establishment, however, prefers a progressive style in which children set their own pace and schools emphasize social inclusion rather than mastery of specific learning and skills. Businessmen and politicians are pressuring educators to accept national testing and standards and to allow parents more choice about which schools their children attend. Change is again politically difficult, however, because many parents are complacent about the problem and distrust any standards set from the center.

In chapter 8 Eugene Bardach addresses the management of paternalistic programs, with an emphasis on programs to get welfare recipients to work. The key to successful programs, he finds, is moral reasoning in the broadest sense. Managers must communicate a sense of mission, that work is possible for most participants, and staff must make this real to their clients. Case managers appeal mainly to their clients' own goals to motivate them, but participation requirements and sanctions are also needed to get some people to take work seriously. To perform, the organization, from executives on down, must agree about what is expected. The essence of management is to work through those norms and then hold staff and clients accountable for achieving them.

Because paternalist programs are prepared to override personal preferences and not to assume individual rationality, they inevitably bring the psychology of the poor into question. If the poor need more direction than the better-off, are they different in some way? This is a question that few policy analysts have asked, in part because the issues involved are immensely sensitive. Psychological inquiries have played almost no part in the national policy debate. But there is research bearing on the distinctive mental problems of poor and dependent adults. I asked two psychiatrists from Harvard Medical School to interpret it. Their medical perspective contrasts sharply with the impersonal economism of traditional policy analysis.

In chapter 9 George Vaillant seeks to explain why it is that structured programs that set behavioral standards appear to help many disadvantaged adults. To him, chronic poverty likely does reflect mental limitations, although social causes are also important. A mandatory program is like a coach that helps a client achieve his own goals. The goals must be meaningful to the subject, and the program must provide him with some substitute for the drug or alcohol abuse he is abandoning. Because they provide this, methadone and supervised parole programs for addicts outperform voluntary hospitalization or mere imprisonment. Self-help groups, or therapeutic communities such as Phoenix House, also substitute relationship for addiction.

In chapter 10 Miles Shore asks not why mandatory programs work but what the mental problems of the poor are in the broadest sense. Several large surveys have found that schizophrenia, severe depression, and other serious psychological impairments are heavily concentrated among low-income people. It is less clear whether mental illness causes poverty or vice versa, or whether unusual attitudes are associated with poverty or welfare dependence. Shore recommends that high-risk populations be screened for mental disorders and receive more treatment, especially for depression. Personality disorders other than mental illness, such as antisocial tendencies, are much harder to treat, and this is where paternalism may help most. The uncooperative can be forced to change, essentially, only by programs that leave them no alternative.

Finally, in chapter 11 James Q. Wilson places paternalism in the broad context of American politics. He finds that the strategy may be effective but stirs a profound ambivalence. Telling people how to live plainly conflicts with the important value of freedom. However, the voters fear that moral character is declining in America, and for that reason they may support paternalism. The partisan debate about how to resuscitate the inner cities reflects this ambivalence. It is difficult to create agencies able to govern people, especially when they are subject to constant legal and political challenges. Wilson thinks that private organizations have a better chance than government to successfully direct behavior. The ultimate problem is to reconcile a controlling welfare state with the public's belief that individuals should remain free to define their own lives, if necessary in defiance of society.

Overall, our conclusions are optimistic but cautious. Most of us think paternalism can make an important contribution to overcoming poverty. The trends toward supervision are too advanced and well grounded to be dismissed or ignored. At the same time, too little is known about concrete effects to allay all concern about harm. More study is needed. The limit to paternalism may be set most of all by the capacities of government. Supervisory programs are difficult to justify politically and to implement well, even when they clearly benefit the recipients and are popular with the public.

Notes

1. The term *paternalism* expresses no sexist intent. One could as well say *maternalism or parentalism* because as many women as men are involved in developing these policies and applying them at the local level. I prefer paternalism to the other terms because it is more understandable, and it is already widely used to characterize directive programs.

2. Isabel V. Sawhill, "The Underclass: An Overview," *Public Interest*, no. 96 (Summer 1989), pp. 4–6.

3. Social insurance programs such as social security that are aimed at the middle class also have powerful antipoverty effects, but they are not intended explicitly to eradicate poverty.

4. TANF, enacted in 1996, amended AFDC to end the federal entitlement to aid at the individual level. But TANF is still a (capped) entitlement to states, and at this writing I have not heard that any state has ended the individual entitlement at the state level. I use *entitlement* here not in the legal or budgetary sense but in the behavioral sense that aid is not conditioned on behavioral tests.

5. John Stuart Mill, "On Liberty," in John Stuart Mill, *The Philosophy of John Stuart Mill: Ethical, Political and Religious*, ed. Marshall Cohen (Modern Library, 1961), p. 197.

6. Leonard Goodwin, *Do the Poor Want to Work? A Social-Psychological Study of Work Orientations* (Brookings, 1972); and Goodwin, *Causes and Cures of Welfare: New Evidence on the Social Psychology of the Poor* (Lexington, Mass.: D. C. Heath, 1983).

7. Peter Applebome, "Parents Face Consequences as Children's Misdeeds Rise," *New York Times*, April 10, 1996, pp. A1, B8.

8. The linkage to aid is used as the basis of behavioral requirements in federal programs such as welfare because Washington lacks the constitutional authority to regulate client behavior without providing benefits, as it can businesses. See Lawrence M. Mead, *Beyond Entitlement: The Social Obligations of Citizenship* (Free Press, 1986), pp. 170–72. In principle, a social contract rationale need not itself be paternalist because the obligation imposed might only be a quid pro quo. That is, it might serve only society's interest and not the client's. Social contract is thus a more civic, self-respecting ground for directive policies than the utilitarian ground that they are good for people. In practice, however, social contract arguments tend to serve social values such as the work ethic that policymakers also think are in the clients' interests.

9. The Job Corps has done well in evaluations, and STRIVE was chosen by the General Accounting Office as a notably successful training program. See Laurie J. Bassi and Orley Ashenfelter, "The Effect of Direct Job Creation and Training Programs on

Low-Skilled Workers," in Sheldon H. Danziger and Daniel H. Weinberg, eds., *Fighting Poverty: What Works and What Doesn't* (Harvard University Press, 1986), pp. 142–43; and General Accounting Office, *Employment Training: Successful Projects Share Common Strategy* (1996).

10. Michael B. Katz, *In the Shadow of the Poorhouse: A Social History of Welfare in America* (Basic Books, 1986); and David J. Rothman, *The Discovery of the Asylum: Social Order and Disorder in the New Republic*, rev. ed. (Little, Brown, 1990).

11. Charles Murray, "The Partial Restoration of Traditional Society," *Public Interest*, no. 121 (Fall 1995), pp. 122–34.

12. An exception is New York City, where an Eligibility Verification Review program has recently helped reduce the welfare rolls.

13. The most important of these were *King* v. *Smith*, 392 U.S. 309 (1968), which invalidated "man in the house" rules, which forbade aid to single mothers with live-in partners; *Shapiro* v. *Thompson*, 394 U.S. 618 (1969), which disallowed residency requirements; and *Goldberg* v. *Kelly*, 397 U.S. 254 (1970), which required fair hearings before benefits could be terminated.

14. Mead, *Beyond Entitlement*, chap. 11.

15. James Q. Wilson, "Crime and American Culture," *Public Interest*, no. 70 (Winter 1983), pp. 22–48.

16. Marvin Olasky, *The Tragedy of American Compassion* (Washington: Regnery, 1992).

17. Sallie Tisdale, "Good Soldiers: Why Liberals Should Love the Salvation Army," *New Republic*, January 3, 1994, pp. 22–27.

18. PRWORA expanded the right of church organizations to participate in the program as service deliverers without giving up their religious identity. But few appear willing to do so. See Stanley W. Carlson-Thies, "'Don't Look to Us': The Negative Responses of the Churches to Welfare Reform," Center for Public Justice, Washington, February 1997.

19. William Ryan, *Blaming the Victim* (Pantheon, 1971).

20. Jason DeParle, "Point Man in Battle for G.O.P.'s Soul Doesn't Worry about Drawing Fire," *New York Times*, December 18, 1990, p. B12.

21. Ed Gillespie and Bob Schellhas, eds., *Contract with America: The Bold Plan by Rep. Newt Gingrich, Rep. Dick Armey and the House Republicans to Change the Nation* (Times Books, 1994), pp. 65–77.

22. For summaries of the relevant studies see Lawrence M. Mead, *The New Politics of Poverty: The Nonworking Poor in America* (Basic Books, 1992), pp. 57–61; and Mead, *Beyond Entitlement*, pp. 233–40. On elite attitudes see Mead, *Beyond Entitlement*, chaps. 8–9; and Steven Michael Teles, *Whose Welfare? AFDC and Elite Politics* (University Press of Kansas, 1996).

23. James T. Patterson, *America's Struggle against Poverty, 1900–1985* (Harvard University Press, 1986), chaps. 3–5.

24. U.S. National Advisory Commission on Civil Disorders (Kerner Commission), *Report of the National Advisory Commission on Civil Disorders* (Government Printing Office, March 1, 1968), p. 1.

25. William Julius Wilson, *The Truly Disadvantaged: The Inner City, the Underclass,*

and Public Policy (University of Chicago Press, 1987); Wilson, *When Work Disappears: The World of the New Urban Poor* (Knopf, 1996); and Douglas S. Massey and Nancy A. Denton, *American Apartheid: Segregation and the Making of the Underclass* (Harvard University Press, 1993).

26. Robert Moffitt, "Incentive Effects of the U.S. Welfare System: A Review," *Journal of Economic Literature*, vol. 30 (March 1992), pp. 11, 13; and Bureau of the Census, *Current Population Reports*, series P-60, no. 194 (Department of Commerce, 1996), table 3; and Bureau of the Census, *Current Population Survey* (Department of Commerce, March 1996), table 19.

27. Christopher Jencks, *Rethinking Social Policy: Race, Poverty, and the Underclass* (Harvard University Press, 1992); Lawrence M. Mead, "Poverty: How Little We Know," *Social Service Review*, vol. 68 (September 1994), pp. 322–50; and Isabel V. Sawhill, "Poverty in the U.S.: Why Is It So Persistent?" *Journal of Economic Literature*, vol. 26 (September 1988), pp. 1073–1119.

28. Paul S. Boyer, *Urban Masses and Moral Order in America, 1820–1920* (Harvard University Press, 1978).

29. Bureau of the Census, "Poverty in the United States: 1995," *Current Population Reports*, series P-60, no. 194 (Department of Commerce, 1996), table C-1.

30. Sheldon Danziger and Peter Gottschalk, "Work, Poverty, and the Working Poor: A Multifaceted Problem," *Monthly Labor Review*, vol. 109 (September 1986), pp. 17–21. This analysis defines employable heads narrowly to exclude the elderly, disabled, students, and women with children under age six.

31. Mead, *Beyond Entitlement*, chap. 5.

32. Marian Wright Edelman, *Families in Peril: An Agenda for Social Change* (Harvard University Press, 1987).

33. Martha R. Burt, *Over the Edge: The Growth of Homelessness in the 1980s* (Russell Sage Foundation, 1992).

34. Robert A. Levine, *Public Planning: Failure and Redirection* (Basic Books, 1972); and Charles L. Schultze, *The Public Use of Private Interest* (Brookings, 1977).

35. Jeffrey L. Pressman and Aaron Wildavsky, *Implementation: How Great Expectations in Washington Are Dashed in Oakland* (University of California Press, 1973); and James Q. Wilson, *Bureaucracy: What Government Agencies Do and Why They Do It* (Basic Books, 1989), pp. 168–71, 175.

36. In 1995, blacks comprised 13 percent of the public but 27 percent of the poor, and 29 percent of blacks were poor. The comparable figures for Hispanics were 11, 24, and 30 percent. See *Current Population Reports*, series P-60, no. 194, table 2. Among people poor for at least eight years out of ten, a majority are black; see Greg J. Duncan and others, *Years of Poverty, Years of Plenty: The Changing Economic Fortunes of American Workers and Families* (University of Michigan, Institute for Social Research, 1984), p. 49.

37. William Julius Wilson, *The Declining Significance of Race: Blacks and Changing American Institutions*, 2d ed. (University of Chicago Press, 1980); Roger Lane, "Black Philadelphia, Then and Now," *Public Interest*, no. 108 (Summer 1992), pp. 35–52; and Mead, *New Politics of Poverty*, chap. 7.

38. The opposition of some liberals to such paternalist requirements as work tests

expresses, however, a lesser view of competence, a fear that these demands may be beyond the capacity of the poor. A policy of entitlement, therefore, can reflect either a favorable or unfavorable view of competence.

39. Moffitt, "Incentive Effects," pp. 15–26, 40–42.

40. Although most people who enter poverty leave quickly, a fifth of those in poverty at a given time stay there more than seven years; see Peter Gottschalk, Sara McLanahan, and Gary Sandefur, "The Dynamics and Intergenerational Transmission of Poverty and Welfare Participation," in Sheldon H. Danziger, Gary D. Sandefur, and Daniel H. Weinberg, eds., *Confronting Poverty: Prescriptions for Change* (Russell Sage Foundation and Harvard University Press, 1994), p. 91. Forty-nine percent of spells on welfare end within two years, but 48 percent of spells in progress at a given time last ten years or more; see Mary Jo Bane and David T. Ellwood, *Welfare Realities: From Rhetoric to Reform* (Harvard University Press, 1994), pp. 31–32.

41. Daniel P. Moynihan, ed., *On Understanding Poverty: Perspectives from the Social Sciences* (Basic Books, 1969), chaps. 7–10.

42. James Q. Wilson and Richard J. Herrnstein, *Crime and Human Nature* (New York: Simon and Schuster, 1985), pp. 380-9.

43. Mead, *Beyond Entitlement*, pp. 221–22.

44. Wilson, *Bureaucracy*, pp. 23–24.

45. Some economists have tried to revise economic assumptions to make them more realistic. See Henry J. Aaron, "Distinguished Lecture on Economics in Government: Public Policy, Values, and Consciousness," *Journal of Economic Perspectives*, vol. 8 (Spring 1994), pp. 3–21; and Thomas C. Schelling, "Egonomics, or the Art of Self-Management," *American Economic Review*, vol. 68 (May 1978), pp. 290–94.

46. A few studies have added administrative indicators to the academic data. See, for example, Robert D. Plotnick, "Welfare and Out-of-Wedlock Childbearing: Evidence from the 1980s," *Journal of Marriage and the Family*, vol. 52 (August 1990), pp. 735–46.

47. Lawrence M. Mead, "Welfare Policy: The Administrative Frontier," *Journal of Policy Analysis and Management*, vol. 15 (Fall 1996), pp. 592–94.

Two

Welfare Employment

Lawrence M. Mead

Of all areas of social policy, employment of those who receive welfare exhibits the most visible trends toward paternalism. By welfare I mean chiefly aid to families with dependent children (AFDC), the national family assistance program run by localities with both federal and state funds. In 1996 Congress restructured AFDC and renamed it Temporary Assistance to Needy Families (TANF). *Welfare employment,* as I use the term here, means policies to move the adults on AFDC or TANF, most of them single mothers, into jobs.[1]

It is unclear how paternalist, in general, welfare employment programs are. Congress has never mandated that they be mandatory, let alone attempt the close supervision of clients connoted by the term *paternalism.* Local work programs vary greatly. Yet it is fair to say that the trend in these programs is toward paternalism. It has the hallmarks of that trend noted in chapter 1: there is a movement toward requiring work for adult recipients of welfare as a condition of aid. And in some localities, work policy has attempted the close supervision of recipients. The more ambitious welfare work programs are the most directive social programs yet developed. By examining them, one can explore why paternalism seems to work and what its potential may be.

This chapter briefly characterizes the trend toward the enforcement of work for welfare recipients and the reasons for it. It summarizes the favor-

I gratefully acknowledge comments on an earlier draft of this chapter from other contributors to this book and from Ron Haskins.

able evaluations of welfare work programs. It then examines the paternalist methods that have developed in the leading programs and the apparent reasons for their effect. It assesses the pros and cons of paternalism and the potential that approach might have if well implemented. My conclusion is favorable but guarded: mandatory work programs have considerable power to tame dependency, but they cannot overcome it entirely, they involve some risks to clients, and they make great demands on political and administrative institutions. At several junctures I refer to Wisconsin, a state that has used work programs to drive its welfare rolls down.

The Work Problem in Welfare

Whether welfare recipients must work is an issue for two main reasons. First, politics. When AFDC was first enacted as part of the Social Security Act of 1935, society expected mothers to stay home and raise children rather than work. AFDC provided support to needy single mothers so that they could do that, even though they lacked spouses to support them. But in the 1960s, mothers not on welfare began to work in large numbers, partly to capitalize on growing opportunities for women, but mainly to help keep family incomes ahead of inflation. The share of married women working or looking for work rose from 31 percent in 1960 to 61 percent in 1995. The comparable numbers for formerly married women with children were 56 and 75 percent.[2]

The percentage of women on welfare who worked was, however, much lower. When surveyed by the government in 1994, only 8 percent reported that they were working, even part time, a percentage that has changed little since the 1960s.[3] Research indicates that the actual level is higher. To avoid reductions in their grants, many mothers on aid earn money without telling officials. Perhaps half work at some time while on the rolls. But this effort is concentrated among the short-term recipients. Sustained work is rare among the longer-term recipients who dominate the rolls at any given time.[4] Although welfare mothers have a good deal of income they do not report, most of it comes from friends and family members, little from regular employment.[5] Because they work much less consistently than other mothers yet are dependent on the public, there is pressure from the public and elected officials for them to work more.

A second impetus toward work is simply that lack of employment causes

Table 2-1. Employment Status of Persons Age 16 and Older and Family Heads, by Income Level, 1995
Percent

Employment status	*All persons*	*All heads of families*	*Female heads of families*	*Heads of families with children under age 18*	
				All	*Female*
All income levels					
Worked at any time	70	78	67	89	73
Worked full year and full time[a]	44	57	42	66	44
Did not work	30	22	33	11	27
Income below poverty					
Worked at any time	41	52	46	58	49
Worked full year and full time[a]	10	19	13	21	14
Did not work	59	48	54	42	51

Source: Bureau of the Census, "Poverty in the United States: 1995," *Current Population Reports,* Series P-60, no. 194 (Department of Commerce 1996), table 3, and March 1996 *Current Population Survey,* table 19.

a. Full year means at least fifty weeks a year, full time at least thirty-five hours a week.

poverty. When families with children are poor, the immediate reason is usually that the parents are not employed. In 1995, for persons and family heads of several types, the share of the population that worked at some time in a year is 20 to 30 points higher than for the same group among the poor (table 2-1). The discrepancy is especially great for full-year, full-time work, where the incidence is at least three times as high among the general population as among the poor. Table 2-2 shows for the same groups that nonworkers have dramatically higher poverty rates. The highest rates—from half to three-quarters—are among nonworking family heads, the group that includes most welfare mothers.

Of course, more than work levels explain poverty. Even if they worked normal hours, welfare mothers would still be abnormally poor because most would earn below-average wages. Perhaps, as AFDC originally presumed, the mother s problem is her lack of a spouse rather than her own weak work effort. But single parenthood seems a less fundamental cause of poverty than nonwork simply because the fathers of many welfare families have

Table 2-2. Poverty Rates of Persons Age 16 and Older and Family Heads, by Employment Status, 1995
Percent

Employment status	*All persons*	*All heads of families*	*Female heads of families*	*Heads of families with children under age 18*	
				All	*Female*
All	11	11	32	16	42
Worked at any time	7	7	22	11	28
Worked full year and full time[a]	3	4	10	5	13
Did not work	22	23	54	61	78

Source: U.S. Department of Commerce, Bureau of the Census, *Current Population Reports,* Series P-60, no. 194 (Washington, D.C.: U.S. Government Printing Office, September 1996), table 3, and March 1996 *Current Population Survey,* table 19.

a. Full year means at least fifty weeks a year, full time at least thirty-five hours a week.

their own work problems. Most long-term welfare recipients are black, and among the black poor about two-thirds of female-headed families were poor before the parents separated as well as after, apparently because both parents had little earnings.[6]

By one estimate, between a third and three-quarters of welfare mothers could escape welfare if they worked half time or more, with a smaller proportion escaping poverty. How many would escape would depend on how many hours they worked, the availability of child support, and the cost of child care.[7] The benefits of employment are not only material. Freeing mothers from employment was originally supposed to benefit children, but recent evidence suggests that the children of a single mother usually do better if she works in school.[8] It thus appears that increasing the work levels on welfare is crucial to overcoming family poverty, although improved child support and perhaps other subsidies are also needed.

The Drive toward Enforcement

Thus policies to promote employment were inevitable.[9] They might have taken many forms. Congress first enacted welfare work programs in the early 1960s. These programs were voluntary, offering to help welfare mothers work without requiring them to do so.[10] But few welfare mothers participated or took jobs on their own. Accordingly, later programs applied increasing pressure to require participation and work.

The WIN Program

In 1967 Congress replaced the earlier programs with the Work Incentive program. WIN had authority to require welfare mothers, if employable, to participate in work or training or face a sanction, a reduction in their grants. The authority to judge who was employable, however, was left with local welfare departments. Because it was a time of exploding welfare rolls and liberal politics, the departments referred very few clients to WIN, and most of those who did participate went into education or training rather than jobs.

In 1971 an impatient Congress mandated that all mothers with children age six or older register with WIN as a condition of receiving aid. It also required that at least 15 percent of those eligible actually participate annually and that programs spend at a least a third of their money on putting clients in subsidized or government employment. But because of limited funding and a widespread reluctance to enforce work, only a minority even of the employable mothers ever participated in WIN, and the program had no discernible impact on the welfare rolls.

Already in the 1970s several states obtained special permission from Washington to run work programs more demanding than WIN. In 1981 Congress, under pressure from the Reagan administration, freed states to alter WIN, for instance by vesting control solely in the state welfare departments (WIN had been run jointly by the welfare and labor departments) or by assigning participants to work off their aid in unpaid government jobs. The favorable evaluation of some of these programs suggested that work programs could succeed if they demanded more of recipients and spent more on education, training, and support services such as child care.

JOBS and After

Partly because of these evaluations the Family Support Act (FSA) of 1988 replaced WIN with the more ambitious Job Opportunities and Basic

Skills Training Program (JOBS). The new law sharply raised participation standards by dropping from six years to three the age of a child that exempted the mother and requiring that 20 percent of the employable adults participate actively in JOBS each month by 1995. Given turnover on the rolls, this was a much tougher standard than WIN's 15 percent over a year. FSA's liberal side was that it raised funding for JOBS and required that recipients who had not finished high school go into education or training instead of immediate employment.

Although the new program was a bipartisan achievement, satisfaction with it was fleeting. Like WIN, JOBS had the misfortune to begin during a sharp increase in dependency. Between 1989 and 1994 the AFDC caseload jumped 30 percent.[11] The program was implemented unevenly because a recession crimped state budgets, and many states could not spend enough of their own money on it to draw down all the federal funding allowed to them.[12] Although enrollment in work programs grew, many of the participants, as in WIN, went back to school or into training rather than begin work. Liberals complained that the program was underfunded, conservatives that it did not really require work.

The vogue for experimentation at the local level persisted. FSA allowed states wide latitude to design their own work programs, and many continued to obtain waivers from Washington to design programs still tougher than JOBS. Some states curbed benefits. Others extended from employment into other areas of life the demand for good behavior in return for aid. Wisconsin, for instance, instituted "learnfare," a requirement that welfare parents keep their children in school on pain of grant reductions, and "bridefare," incentives and requirements meant to foster intact families. The Bush and Clinton administrations promoted these experiments on the theory that more would be learned about how to "end welfare as we know it."[13]

As an alternative to enforcing work on welfare, some liberal analysts proposed aid with a time limit. Families would have several years on the rolls to reorganize their lives. Then they would graduate from AFDC to work, perhaps part time, buttressed by improved child support, wage subsidies, guaranteed jobs if needed, and other measures designed to "make work pay." A better, less stigmatizing safety net could be created outside welfare than on it.[14] The Clinton administration advanced a welfare reform of this type in 1994. Its Work and Responsibility Act would have limited families to two years on AFDC without work. After that they would have had to take jobs to retain aid, but if they did there was no time limit on assistance, and jobs were guaranteed for those unable to find them.

PRWORA

The plan was derailed by the GOP victory in the congressional elections of 1994. In 1996 congressional Republicans forced Clinton to sign a more conservative reform that combined cuts in welfare with the toughest work requirements yet. Besides changing AFDC to Temporary Assistance to Needy Families (TANF), the Personal Responsibility and Work Opportunity Reconciliation Act of 1996 (PRWORA) capped welfare funding so that it was no longer an entitlement in the sense that benefits were guaranteed to all eligible people.[15] The law also limited families to five years on the rolls, with or without work, although states may exempt a fifth of their caseloads from the limit. States receive more control over welfare eligibility, including a right to deny aid to unwed mothers younger than age eighteen and children born on the rolls.

At the same time, the new law requires adult recipients to work within two years of accepting aid and demands that states move half of them into work activities by 2002. That level is more than twice the percentage JOBS was to have achieved in 1995. And the base for calculating participation is now normally all cases, not the half of them judged mandatory under JOBS, although states may exempt mothers with a child less than a year old. Thus PRWORA raises the work standard by something like four times. Just as important, *work activities* is defined to mean mainly actual work in regular or subsidized jobs, curbing the JOBS preference for education and training. Moreover, the hours of activity required to count as a participant rise from twenty a week, as in JOBS, to thirty by 2000.

On their face the participation targets look impossible because they are much tougher than any work program has achieved.[16] In the next year or two the thresholds may be achievable because states may count against them any percentage by which their caseloads decreased after 1995, and caseloads are currently falling. But after that, many states will have difficulty meeting the targets unless caseloads continue to fall. Much will hinge on how narrowly work activities are defined in regulations. The thirty-hour participation standard also looks ambitious.

States cannot ignore the work rules, for if they fail to satisfy them, they face cuts in their TANF grants of as much as 21 percent. In PRWORA there is no specific funding for work programs because the earlier allocation for JOBS was folded into the TANF block grant. By one estimate there is insufficient money in the act to implement the new work requirements, if one assumes the caseloads of 1995.[17] But states currently get more federal money per recipient than they did before, since allocations under the block grant presume the caseloads of 1995, which were higher than now.

The new law, like the Family Support Act of 1988 and earlier legislation, does not spell out how localities should promote welfare work. They may take a wide variety of approaches, provided only that they meet the participation targets. But it is highly unlikely that states could satisfy the new rules without mandating that the great majority of welfare adults join work programs. To this extent, national welfare policy is becoming paternalist.

Reasons for Enforcement

How does one explain this steady drift toward enforcement in welfare work policy? I mention here some of the factors cited in chapter 1, but applied to welfare. First, a more conservative political climate. In the 1960s and 1970s two presidents proposed to liberalize the welfare system. Richard Nixon's Family Assistance Plan (FAP) and Jimmy Carter's Program for Better Jobs and Income (PBJI) would have raised welfare benefits and extended coverage from the mostly female-headed families eligible for AFDC to wider populations of needy. After 1980, with more conservative presidents in office, Republicans expanding their power in Congress, and the budget heavily in deficit, such proposals became unimaginable.

A second factor is that the politics of welfare became less rights oriented. Before 1980 most federal officials viewed the welfare poor as disadvantaged and antipoverty policy as a means of easing their burdens. In the Reagan era, in contrast, the deservingness of recipients came under more question and welfare came to seem permissive. Politicians asserted that the poor might need aid, but they should do more to earn it, above all by working. The Family Support Act rested on an idea of a social contract, of requiring recipients to better themselves as a condition of aid.[18] Although PRWORA still expresses that sentiment in its work provisions, it also embodies a more traditional antigovernment conservatism in its cuts and block-granting of aid, the urge to "get welfare out of Washington."

The Limitations of Voluntary Policies

The trend toward toughness has more than political causes, however. Another explanation is policy history: Programs and policies that offered welfare mothers the chance to work but did not require them to do so did not cause many of them to take jobs and reduce their dependency.

In the same period when Congress began to enforce work, it attempted to induce work through new benefits. In 1962 it vastly expanded funding for social services provided as part of welfare. The idea was that if welfare provided more social workers to advise recipients, as well as more child care and other practical assistance, more recipients would move into work. But although spending on services expanded briskly, the growth in dependency continued unabated. To limit spending, Congress in 1974 separated the main services program from welfare, although social services continued to promote work as part of WIN and JOBS.

Another strategy was work incentives. Many economists, liberal and conservative, think that welfare adults fail to work mainly because of the disincentives set up by welfare itself. If the recipients have earnings, their grants are reduced by a like amount and they may be little better off than before. Reduce this "tax" on earnings, the argument goes, and more work should result. To improve work incentives, Congress in 1962 allowed recipients who worked to deduct work expenses such as child care from their earnings before grants were adjusted. In 1967 it allowed them also to deduct $30 of their earnings plus one-third of the remainder each month. Together, these allowances cut the benefit reduction rate due to earnings to 50 percent or less.[19] Work incentives are a nonpaternalist policy because they leave work as a choice.

Unfortunately, the percentage of those on welfare who worked hardly budged. The main effect of work incentives was to keep more recipients with earnings on the rolls, not to cause more nonworkers to take jobs. In response the Reagan administration in 1981 persuaded Congress to trim the incentives so as to cut most working recipients from the rolls and save money. Experts cautioned that stronger disincentives would reduce welfare work still further. But again, little effect resulted. Researchers find that welfare has some depressing effect on work effort, but most women on AFDC would work few hours even in the absence of welfare. Welfare work behavior simply does not respond greatly to incentives.[20]

Since 1962 Washington has also funded a succession of voluntary job training programs for people with few skills. In the 1970s it created as many as 750,000 jobs in government and nonprofit agencies for the jobless and disadvantaged, some of which went to welfare recipients, and it provided tax incentives for employers to hire the disadvantaged. The effects of all these policies were slight or unclear, to judge from evaluations. A fair conclusion is that voluntary measures may be worthwhile from a political or cost-benefit viewpoint, but none has yet had a sizable effect on the work problems of America's poor adults.[21]

One reason early evaluations of the training programs disappointed was methodological. The studies were not experimental, so there was doubt whether the clients receiving the tested program were really equivalent to the control clients to whom they were compared. Without a clear baseline, the effects of the programs remained uncertain.[22] However, a recent experimental assessment of the Job Training Partnership Act (JTPA), the current authorization for voluntary training, still found its effects to be weak at best. It increased the employment of adult clients by 2 or 3 percentage points and raised their earnings by about $550 a year. But out-of-school youth recorded losses of earnings and employment, probably because they worked less in order to participate in JTPA.[23]

To the extent voluntary programs construed the main poverty problem as low wages, they were misconceived. It is true that poor adults suffer from low earnings if they work. But the major reason they are poor usually is a lack of steady work at any wage. Typically, voluntary measures seek to raise wages, but they too readily take work effort for granted. When they have effects, it is not primarily by raising the wages their clients can earn but by motivating them to put in more hours at the low-paid jobs they can already get.[24]

The Search for Barriers

Liberal analysts contend that the reason the job programs achieve little is that their clients face an unyielding opportunity structure. They confront racial bias in hiring or a sheer lack of jobs or inadequate child care, among other problems, so that it is hardly surprising that they work little. But as noted in chapter 1, the evidence that barriers explain poverty is weak. Although people with few skills do face greater trouble in finding and holding on to work than do those with more skills, the differences are not great enough to explain the large difference in the percentage who work.[25]

The commonest argument for barriers appeals to economic restructuring. Since 1970 the decline of manufacturing employment has reduced the number of manual but well-paying jobs in the cities, while other jobs have moved to the suburbs or overseas. Allegedly, a mismatch has developed between urban jobseekers and the location or demands of jobs. Either jobless adults cannot reach jobs in the suburbs or the remaining city jobs demand more education than they have. The mismatch theory, first advanced in 1968, drew little research support in the 1970s and 1980s.[26] But as restructuring gathered pace in the 1990s, the evidence for it became somewhat stronger.

William Julius Wilson and others contend that this theory explains what is happening in the inner city. Wilson attributes poverty to many causes, including the desertion of the ghetto by the black middle class, the breakdown of the family, and a cultural milieu that subverts conventional values. But the chief force behind these social changes is economic change: a lack of jobs demoralizes poor men, who then beget children without accepting responsibility for them. Their partners go on welfare rather than marry them because they are unreliable breadwinners. From these fatherless families most of the other problems of the ghetto follow.[27]

The strongest evidence for mismatch suggests that commuting difficulties or deindustrialization may explain part of the work problems of black youth.[28] But the differences in commuting times seem too small for them to explain much.[29] Besides, other poor groups have work difficulties too. The poor themselves usually complain of a dearth of "good" jobs, not of all employment. In 1992 just 10 to 12 percent of poor adults working less than full year and full time, including female heads of families, said inability to find jobs was the main reason; ill health and school and family responsibilities were all more important.[30]

Mismatch explains decreases in the wages of the low-skilled better than it does nonwork. Factory jobs have been replaced in and around cities by a profusion of service positions that often pay less.[31] But low wages have also promoted massive job creation. Immigrants, legal and illegal, keep flocking to American cities and finding work, suggesting that at least poorly paid jobs are plentiful. A massive study mounted by William JuliusWilson in inner-city Chicago in the late 1980s failed to document that jobs were lacking there. It found, rather, that low-skilled immigrants worked at high levels in the same ghetto areas where poor blacks and Puerto Ricans worked at low levels.[32]

The limited evidence for mismatch does not mean that measures to expand opportunity cannot help increase the percentage of workers among the poor. It does imply, however, that the labor market is not an immediate obstacle to work-oriented welfare reform. Low-wage jobs, at least, seem to be fairly widely available to those seeking them. Even liberal economists conclude that to put many more welfare mothers to work should be possible, provided they enter the market gradually over several years.[33] That realization has freed welfare reformers to regard employment at least initially as a problem internal to the welfare system.

The Success of Mandatory Programs

The disappointing results of voluntary education and training programs contributed to the sense in the 1970s and early 1980s that nothing works, that the effect of any antipoverty program when evaluated was likely to be zero.[34] But programs that require work have already shown some success, and this fact is a key impetus behind the trend toward welfare paternalism.

The Manpower Demonstration Research Corporation Studies

The verdict that nothing works was reversed mainly by the mandatory work programs that developed in the 1980s following the Reagan reforms that freed states to modify WIN. Some of these programs were evaluated by the Manpower Demonstration Research Corporation (MDRC). The evaluations were experimental and therefore more convincing than most of the ones done on earlier work programs. MDRC went on to evaluate several JOBS programs developed under FSA. On average, the earnings and employment effects have not been large, but they are definite (table 2-3). The JTPA evaluation mentioned earlier showed slightly larger earnings gains from voluntary training for adults. But the welfare employment programs did not damage anyone's earnings, and the workers also achieved measurable reductions in welfare dependency. Most of the programs saved money for government within two to five years, since the welfare savings more than offset the cost of the new services. Thus the recipients and society usually experienced economic gains.[35]

The most successful of these programs showed effects much larger

Table 2-3. Average Results from Nine Main Manpower Demonstration Research Corporation Welfare Employment Evaluations

Impact	*Control mean*	*Experimental-control difference*	*Percent change*
Average annual earnings	1,992	329	16
Employed at end of final year (percent)	28.4	3.0	11
Average annual AFDC payments	2,409	–175	–7
On welfare at end of final year (percent)	55.2	–3.1	–6

Source: See appendix table 2A-1.

than any voluntary employment program has achieved. Table 2-4 shows the results achieved by three notable programs in California. The first San Diego program was a homegrown effort to put AFDC applicants to work, while the second, known as the Saturation Work Initiative Model (SWIM), was mounted with special federal funds. Riverside was the most successful county in MDRC's evaluation of six counties operating California's JOBS program, known as Greater Avenues for Independence (GAIN). Although not all welfare work programs perform this well, these results suggested that well-run programs could move welfare recipients into jobs. When the early San Diego results became known in the mid-1980s, they deeply impressed Congress and the research community. Along with the political appeal of social contract, they do much to explain why the Family Support Act aimed to expand welfare employment programs around the country.[36]

Effects and Implementation

The evaluations, furthermore, understate the results the programs could have if implementation improved. The experiments estimated effects by comparing average outcomes for *all* members of the experimental group with those for *all* members of the control group. Clients have been randomly allocated between the two groups, and it is only if all are included in the group averages that one can be certain the two groups are equivalent. But in fact only some of the experimental clients participate in the program; many do not show up to enroll or they drop out. Assuming that the

Table 2-4. Selected Manpower Demonstration Research Corporation Welfare Employment Program Evaluations, 1982–93

Study	*Outcome in final year*	*Control mean*	*Experi-mental-control difference*	*Percent change*
San Diego (1982–85) [a]	Average annual earnings	1,937	443	23
	Employed at end of final year (percent)	36.9	5.5	15
	Average annual AFDC payments	2,750	−226	−8
	On welfare at end of final year (percent)	47.9	−2.0	−4
San Diego SWIM (1985–87)	Average annual earnings	2,246	658	29
	Employed at end of final year (percent)	29.3	5.4	18
	Average annual AFDC payments	3,961	−553	−14
	On welfare at end of final year (percent)	58.7	−7.4	−13
Riverside GAIN (1988–93)	Average annual earnings	2,552	1,010	40
	Employed at end of final year (percent)	24.6	6.6	27
	Average annual AFDC payments	3,448	−584	−17
	On welfare at end of final year (percent)	45.8	−5.2	−11

Source: See appendix table 2A-1.
a. Results apply to AFDC applicants in job search–work experience.

program does any good, the estimate of effects is understated because a lot of people who never experienced the program are included in the experimental averages. In SWIM, for example, the average experimental client earned $2,903 in the program's second year, but since only 49 percent of the group worked during the year, the average employed participant earned about twice as much.[37]

Of course, it would be unfair to look only at the successful clients.

Among the controls, too, some clients worked and some did not. To compare averages for the entire groups is still a fair way to assess the program. But it is also clear that the effects of a work program should improve if the level of participation rises.[38]

Diversion

Evaluation results can capture only the effects programs have on clients who are in the program. They miss the tendency that tough work requirements might have to keep people off welfare entirely. Welfare work programs might either raise or lower the number on welfare. They might attract people onto welfare if they were good at training people for better jobs or keep them off if they were severe. By one estimate, full implementation of a mandatory program like JOBS might reduce the welfare caseload by as much as 25 percent.[39]

Wisconsin may well have brought that possibility to pass. The state has been reforming its welfare program for more than a decade.[40] It began introducing JOBS-like work requirements in AFDC in the middle 1980s. It then introduced JOBS, achieving participation rates far above those mandated by the law. In the 1990s it reoriented JOBS away from education and training and toward putting clients to work in available jobs. Between 1987 and 1994 it reduced its AFDC caseload by 23 percent, much more than any other state. Statistical analyses suggest that the fall resulted from both the state's favorable economy, which generated many jobs, and its demanding work programs, which drove many employable recipients off the rolls.[41]

From 1994 to 1996 the state instituted experimental work programs in selected counties to divert families from welfare. When people entered welfare offices to apply for aid, they were intercepted by staff who tried to persuade them to get a job immediately or seek help from relatives instead. They could still apply for aid, but then they were required to look for jobs while their applications were processed. If aid was approved and accepted, they were referred immediately to a work-oriented JOBS program, where again they would have to look for work. As of early 1996, recipients had to put in documented hours of activity to earn their welfare payment.

The effect was to accelerate a decline in dependency. According to state and local officials, counties with diversion policies sharply reduced their intake to the rolls. The caseload, which had already fallen 25 percent between January 1987 and the end of 1994, fell another 26 points by October 1996 for a 51 percent decline overall. Even Milwaukee's caseload, the largest and most troubled in the state, came down by a quarter overall, mostly after 1994.[42]

Wisconsin's ability to reduce dependency contrasted with the sharp increases in welfare rolls that occurred in most other states between 1989 and 1994. Although some of the credit goes to a tight labor market, the results imply that serious work enforcement might reduce dependency by more than the evaluations suggest. But as I note later, whether the social consequences are good is unclear.

The Effects of Paternalism

What reasons are there to credit these results to paternalism? Perhaps welfare work programs have their effects simply because they spend the money to serve recipients and provide them with new benefits, not because they enforce anything. Not long ago, most experts recommended a voluntary approach. Work programs could be effective, it was believed, only if they motivated recipients to participate by what they had to offer, without any mandate.[43]

Trends

Current evidence suggests that work programs must be mandatory to get the most impact. One reason to think so is that they have performed better as they have become more stringent. Few recipients volunteer to enter these programs. For the programs to reach those who are eligible, therefore, they have to require participation. More participants, in turn, leads to more recipients going to work.

The need to enforce participation became clear early in WIN. When the requirement that all adults on welfare must register with the program became effective in fiscal year 1973, the number of people getting jobs doubled over any previous year, then doubled again by fiscal 1977. Recorded case closures and grant reductions also rose sharply.[44] Because this was an era of little change in the welfare rolls and mediocre economic conditions, these gains must reflect improved performance by WIN. Increased funding gets part of the credit, but better enforcement was probably more important.[45]

JOBS raised participation levels further by being still more demanding. Whereas WIN served 145,632 recipients a year at its height in 1980, by 1994 JOBS served 445,415 every month, which is estimated to be more than six times the WIN level on an annual basis.[46] The growth of JOBS in percentage terms considerably outpaced the growth in welfare in the early 1990s because JOBS rules forced states to raise participation rates. And to do this they generally had to enforce participation. The payoff was that although WIN never demonstrated any effect on the welfare caseload, JOBS probably did restrain the growth in the rolls.[47]

Evaluation Results

Another reason to think that enforcement improves the effect of a program is that of the programs evaluated by MDRC the more demanding were generally the most successful. The three programs in table 2-4 were all notably tough about enforcing participation and job searches, compared to other work programs of their era. All followed up closely on participants to be sure they fulfilled their assignments, and all levied sanctions on nonparticipators without hesitation.

One reason enforcing participation improves performance is that it ensures that more clients in an experimental group receive what the program offers, so that the average effect is stronger. Another reason is that work programs have their greatest effect on clients whose participation is doubtful. Those who join without prompting tend to be the least disadvantaged, the ones who would get off welfare even without a program. Serving them produces little gain compared with counterparts in the control group. It is the more disadvantaged clients who produce most of a program's impact.[48] They, however, will seldom participate voluntarily. Programs must mandate participation to reach them and perform well.

The most effective programs emphasized high participation and participation in actual work or work search in preference to education or training. The national evaluation of JOBS, now being conducted by MDRC, provides the first direct test of a work-oriented strategy against an education-and-training strategy in welfare employment. This evaluation tests multiple treatments rather than a single program. The first approach stresses labor force attachment, or job search followed if necessary by an unpaid job or short-term training. The other emphasizes human capital development, or education and training in advance of work. The evaluators say that all the sequences enforce participation stringently, so differences there are not a factor. In preliminary results after two years, clients in labor force attachment recorded markedly larger gains in employment and earnings, and greater economies in welfare, than did clients in human capital development.[49]

Perhaps this is only because labor force attachment gets clients into jobs quickly while human capital development puts them in school where they have less chance to earn money in the short run. Perhaps the investment that human capital development makes in skills will eventually yield better jobs for clients. Among several 1980s programs evaluated by MDRC, one in Baltimore with a training emphasis recorded the largest earnings gains five years after the program, even larger than San Diego's SWIM.[50] And in MDRC's GAIN evaluation, although Riverside was generally superior, other counties oriented more to training and education began to show similar earnings gains by the third year of the program, perhaps because their attention to skills had begun to pay off.[51]

However, SWIM realized large savings in welfare while the Baltimore program achieved none, and Riverside clearly outperformed the other counties in the GAIN study in reducing the welfare rolls. The earnings gains in training-oriented programs appear not to translate well into welfare roll reductions, chiefly because the gains are concentrated among the more advantaged recipients who leave welfare quickly even without a program. These clients generate little welfare savings when compared to similar controls. Work-oriented programs are better able to shorten welfare stays.[52]

Willingness to enforce participation and work is the major feature that explains the superiority of a SWIM or Riverside. These programs were well-funded compared with some others studied by MDRC, but not as well funded as some of the training-oriented projects. SWIM spent $643 per client, whereas Baltimore spent $953.[53] In GAIN, Alameda and Los Angeles Counties spent much more per client than Riverside, mainly because they invested more heavily in education and training.[54] Yet SWIM and Riverside generally performed better and saved more money for government because of their ability to reduce welfare rolls. However, some portion of this superiority is due not to policy but to the well-run character of the San Diego and Riverside programs, a factor that I return to later.

How Paternalism Works

The next question is how mandatory programs produce their effects. What is it about levying a requirement to work that motivates recipients to get a job or leave welfare? Experimental evaluations can tell us little about this. They can tell if an entire program has an effect, but not what specific activities produced the result. To find out how a program operates, one has to use a combination of field research and program data analysis.[55]

Enforcing Participation and Work

Why do requirements cause recipients to participate and work when simply offering them the chance usually does not? Most staff of welfare employment programs I have interviewed say participation in a work program must be mandated to get recipients attention. Most adults on welfare would in principle like to work, but they are preoccupied with day-to-day survival. Few will make the effort to organize themselves for regular activity outside the home unless it is required.[56] Starting to work or look for a job must also be enforced, many staff members say, because recipients are often reluctant to seek work on their own. They may want to work, but they have usually failed to find or keep jobs before, especially good jobs, and they fear to try again. Many prefer education and training because it is less threatening. It postpones the day when they must reckon with the labor market. Meanwhile, remaining on welfare is secure.

Even with a mandate, programs find achieving participation and getting recipients to work is difficult. When summoned to enroll in a program, many recipients fail to appear. If they do enroll, they often disappear later when referred to a specific activity. Every time clients are referred thereafter, some drop out. The disadvantaged often respond to challenges with withdrawal. To obtain and maintain involvement, programs must get out the word that participation is not a formality. When first implemented, they often must reduce the grants of many recipients for nonparticipation until the word spreads that the program is serious.

Among the counties I studied in Wisconsin in 1994, Kenosha and Sheboygan were the toughest about enforcing participation and work requirements. Four others, including Dane (Madison) and Milwaukee, were more loosely run and emphasized education and training more than immediate employment. In a given month, Kenosha and Sheboygan had the highest rates of enrollment, that is the highest percentage of recipients referred to them who actually participated. They also had smaller proportions than average in unproductive holding statuses between activities. Because they were tough about enforcing job search, they had the largest proportions actually working—about 40 percent in regular or unpaid jobs. The effect of making expectations clear was not to repel the clients but to involve and motivate them.[57]

Enforcement and Performance

Involvement in turn promoted performance. During 1993 Kenosha and Sheboygan placed more than a quarter of all their clients (enrolled and nonenrolled) in jobs, and more than a third of recipients on the rolls were employed, percentages far higher than those of the four other counties. Yet all the counties were similar in the quality of jobs their participants obtained, as measured by wages and the share of job entrants who kept their jobs for 30 or 180 days. This was true even though the other counties concentrated on clients' getting good jobs by training them before placement. Kenosha appeared able to combine job quantity with quality by emphasizing a combination of work and remediation. Recipients were told to get a job—any job—and then they could train for a better job as well. This "work first" sequence reversed the order in most other counties in Wisconsin at this time and in the JOBS program nationally.[58]

One might suspect that Kenosha and Sheboygan performed well because their clients were unusually employable or their labor markets favorable, or the programs were better funded. But the association of enforcement with performance held up even controlling for these factors. I constructed statistical models to predict variations in the JOBS performance measures across all seventy-two Wisconsin counties in 1993. The proportions of a county's clients that entered jobs, worked while on welfare, or closed their cases was determined largely by the shares that enrolled, entered job search, or went through job readiness, a component that teaches the skills and motivation for job search. Demographic and economic conditions were secondary. Enforcing participation and work did not improve the quality of jobs clients obtained by much; that depended much more on a caseload's level of education or training. The program, however, substantially controlled whether its clients went to work in *some* job. Although Kenosha historically had extra funding, in 1993 funding differences among counties had almost no influence on their JOBS performance once other differences were controlled.[59]

Other statistical analyses of welfare employment performance show much the same result.[60] And, as mentioned earlier, the implementation of JOBS is linked to the decrease of the welfare caseload in Wisconsin. Between 1986 and 1994, counties that had more welfare clients in JOBS activities had a faster decrease in caseloads.[61] These analyses use statistical controls rather than experimentation to adjust for nonprogram influences, so those factors are not entirely excluded. But the conclusion that enforcement matters parallels the implication of the evaluations, so it is probably valid.

Sanctions

To perform well, then, work programs have to be demanding, and to be demanding they have to reduce or deny benefits to clients who do not cooperate. One might expect that tough work programs sanction a great many recipients, and that this is the price of their success. It is true that effective programs such as SWIM or the Riverside project are very willing to sanction, and they advertise this to their clients. Opponents of mandatory programs suspect that most of the savings they generate come from throwing people off the rolls.

The evidence suggests otherwise. Little of the savings the programs generate result from sanctions; getting people off welfare by other means is far more important.[62] The rate of sanctioning in mandatory programs has been low. In several programs studied by MDRC, it ranged from 2 to 12 percent of the clients.[63] The number at risk of a sanction can be much higher. In SWIM 80 percent of clients were out of compliance with the program at some point, and in Riverside the program began proceedings to sanction in 34 percent of cases. But the majority of the noncompliant produce reasons acceptable to the program, or they return to participation without a penalty. SWIM finally reduced grants in 12 percent of its cases, Riverside in 6 percent.[64]

In the evaluation results any link between sanction rates and performance is unclear.[65] In statistical analyses of program data, the association may actually be inverse. Local offices that sanction many clients place fewer people in jobs than those that sanction fewer clients. The reason appears to be that programs that have to throw the book at noncooperators have failed to exert authority in more effective and informal ways. Typically, they have failed to make expectations clear to clients in the beginning.[66] Kenosha and Sheboygan, despite the demands they made, sanctioned only 1 percent of their clients, a smaller proportion than the less demanding counties or the state average. And as Wisconsin induced other counties to adopt the Kenosha work-first model between 1993 and 1995, the sanctioning rate dropped for the state as a whole. Clarifying expectations seems to reduce noncompliance and thus occasions for sanctions.[67]

It is true that very demanding programs can produce higher than average sanction rates, particularly when demands on recipients are first raised, and these sanctions generate part of the welfare savings recorded.[68] But once expectations are clear, sanctions decrease. The same administrative capacity that makes the top programs good at enforcing participation and work, so that noncompliance can occur, also makes them good at getting dropouts back in the program, thus minimizing sanctions. Most people who leave welfare do so on their own, not because they are thrown off. In no documented case has a work program reduced the rolls primarily through sanctions, or even sought to do so, as against putting people to work.

It is of course possible that sanction rates will increase to unacceptable levels as work requirements become stronger under TANF. One may also think that some of those diverted from welfare by tough work policies are de facto sanctioned if the demands made of them seem unreasonable. But good evidence about the diverted is lacking. All one can say is that to date throwing people off welfare has had little to do with the successes of work enforcement.

Reform as Administration

The public tends to see welfare as a passive condition where recipients do little to better themselves. Determined work programs alter that image. In seven programs studied by MDRC, within nine to twelve months of registration 75 to 97 percent of the clients had satisfied the program's mandate in some way, if not by participating or going to work, then by accepting a sanction or leaving welfare.[69] In a Kenosha or Riverside, few clients can escape accountability to the program for long. In one remarkable program in Kearns, Utah, determined enforcement drove the rate of nonparticipation down to almost zero, and two-thirds of recipients were involved in work activities.[70]

Many of the academic studies suggest that welfare dependency is explained mostly by social and economic factors such as the clients lack of education or an absence of well-paying jobs. But although those influences are undeniable, there is usually room in the environment to increase work participation considerably. Officials find that at an operating level welfare reform is primarily an administrative problem. One can raise participation rates in work programs and employment if one obligates more adult recipients to participate, strengthens sanctions for nonparticipation, and deploys enough staff and support services to keep the clients involved.[71]

Welfare reform turns out to involve not so much a change in the formal policies of welfare as the reinvention of welfare administration. Local agencies must emphasize putting recipients to work and not be satisfied with their old mission, which was mainly to determine eligibility and pay out grant money accurately.[72] In practice that usually means not that the agencies change the culture of the eligibility operation, which is difficult, but that they build up the importance of JOBS.[73] Some programs reorient their existing personnel and routines to employment, while others contract work programs out to nongovernmental bodies, whom they hold accountable for results.[74] In Wisconsin the extent of contracting varies widely among the counties.

Case Management

Effective work programs do more than impose a requirement to participate and work. They implement it through staff members who monitor clients closely to be sure they fulfill their obligations. States running JOBS have invested in case managers to increase client involvement in the program and meet the participation mandates in FSA.[75] Such oversight is at the core of paternalism.

Help and Hassle

Analysts tend to view case managers in passive and economic terms, as a resource for clients. They are seen as brokers who arrange child care or transportation or other services clients need to participate, and this helping role is undeniably important. But effective programs also use case managers to resist the tendency of clients to avoid programs or withdraw from them. When recipients assigned to work programs fail to show for orientation or drop out after entering, case managers pursue them to find out what the problem is. They call them up, send them letters, go out and visit their homes, and if necessary begin proceedings to sanction. In leading programs this follow-up is relentless. Case managers help overcome obstacles such as a breakdown of services or a family crisis, but they also levy expectations, pointing to consequences if the expectations are not met. In strong programs they struggle persistently to get even troubled recipients into the program and keep them there.[76] At its best, like good parenting, case management combines help and hassle.

Personalized attention makes expectations clear and allows the demanding programs to reduce sanctions once they have increased participation to acceptable levels. Kenosha, for example, sanctioned only 1 percent of its clients in a given month, but it had 7 percent in reconciliation, a counseling process by which noncooperators reach agreement with the program and avoid sanctions.[77] Intense interaction between clients and staff is a feature of effective work programs.[78]

All by itself, simple contact between staff and the clients appears to energize clients. "Making them active, tracking them, not letting them sit there in limbo," this was what got people moving, one case manager in Sheboygan told me. Riverside's JOBS director remarked, "It's really simple: you've got to be all over every client like flypaper! Every day."[79] In top programs case managers claim to know what most of their clients are doing every day.

Observers might fear that case management could be personal in an invidious sense, that caseworkers might decide client obligations in the arbitrary way that was common before the welfare rights era began in the 1960s. They might demand on their own authority that clients change their lives—for instance, by avoiding men—if they are to get aid. In today's work programs, however, discretion is limited by program policies, which are much more explicit and detailed than they were forty years ago. Congress or state legislatures decide which groups of recipients have to do what. Staff discretion, while still important, is limited to applying those rules.

Nor is case management usually personal in a more supportive way. It is less costly than traditional social work, both personally and financially. It does not usually involve intimate involvement in the lives of clients. If it did, it would be too demanding for staff to sustain for long periods. It would lead to burnout.[80] Mainly, case management is rule enforcement. Staff members do have to relate to their clients as individuals, not as numbers, but mainly they check up on them. Just doing this appears to be strongly motivating.

Case management can extend beyond welfare into the workplace. Recipients who take jobs may leave them quickly and return to welfare. The reason often is that the people do not realize what is expected of them by employers. Some are fired for absenteeism or conflict with supervisors, others because of difficulties with child care or transportation. The Kearns program in Utah hired "extended" caseworkers to help solve former recipients problems on the job so that they did not return to welfare.[81] One originator of the idea is America Works, a proprietary firm that performs job placement for JOBS in New York and elsewhere.[82] This sort of innovation illustrates the creativity that nongovernmental contractors can sometimes bring to paternalistic programs.

Monitoring

Case managers need help to do their tracking. Some welfare employment programs invest in elaborate management information systems to follow the movements of their clients. They record the activities to which the participants are assigned, such as job search, government jobs, or education or training. They cannot determine whether the clients are actually pursuing these activities. To know that requires information from the staff, often employed by outside contractors, who are running those functions. This information is often relayed back to the case managers on paper or over the phone, outside the computer. Effective programs have well-tested arrangements for taking and reporting attendance. Some even use their own staff for the function, or pay others to perform it.

The monitoring systems are also essential for higher-level management. To hold their case managers accountable, supervisors need to know where clients are referred and how many get jobs or leave welfare. Analysis of the figures can suggest which activities are most productive. Senior executives have to be able to compare the performance of offices and report results to elected officials. Under PRWORA, states are supposed to track cases so that time limits can be enforced. But few if any have information systems able to perform all these tasks.

How Clients Respond

To welfare advocates, mandatory work appears severe. They charge that programs force or coerce recipients to work. On the other side, some conservative critics of welfare see little point in trying to enforce employment in the teeth of the disincentives to work that welfare generates. Better to abolish aid so that the employable have no alternative to working. Both viewpoints assume that the recipients have in some sense *chosen* not to work.

The Uses of Structure

When asked, however, most welfare recipients and other poor people say that they want to work. If they do not actually work, the reason is that the practical difficulties seem overwhelming, not that they reject the idea. Not working, in fact, causes them shame and discouragement, since they are not living by their own values.[83] This gap between intention and behavior is what makes work enforcement necessary. But acceptance of the work ethic also makes it possible. Mandatory work programs do not ask most people to do something alien to them.

The programs operate to close the gap between the norm and the welfare recipient's lifestyle. Without enforcement the recipients are free to avoid work because it is difficult. Mandatory programs instead place them in a situation where they get needed help to work, but they also have to work. They now *have* to do what they always wanted to do. The combination of help and hassle seems to promote employment better than either voluntary benefits or the denial of aid.

Most participants respond with gratitude, not resistance. In several of its evaluations MDRC did surveys of recipients required to work off their benefits in unpaid government jobs. This sort of assignment, commonly called workfare, is often seen as punitive because it requires the recipients to labor for nothing besides the grant they already receive.The vast majority of respondents in such slots understood work as mandatory, not voluntary. Yet in most cases a majority said they were satisfied to work rather than not work, and most felt better about receiving welfare as a result. Majorities also liked their jobs, believed they were treated like regular employees, and thought the experience would help them get a decent-paying job later. The one dissatisfaction was that, economically, most clients believed they gained less from their assignments than did the agencies they worked for; they would have preferred regular jobs.[84]

These responses indicate that the psychology of nonwork is not middle class. Better-off people generally behave according to their own intentions. If they do not do something, it is because they do not want to. They will resist anyone telling them to do otherwise. Middle-class analysts too readily assume poor people are equally consistent. If they do not work, we infer that they "choose" not to, given their situation. But for most welfare adults, nonwork is felt as a dilemma, not a choice. They want to work, yet most do not. When a work program enforces work, the majority see it as a help. Their problem is not to learn the value of a job but to align their lifestyle with work. This the program assists and requires them to do, and for that they are grateful.

Many welfare recipients seem to need pressure from the outside to achieve their own goals. They seem to be looking for structure. The idea of case managers monitoring people easily strikes the better-off as severe. They compare that relationship with authority to the warmer, more affirming relationships they have known. For the poor, however, supervision is often new and welcome. In their formative experiences, authority figures commonly treated them harshly and inconsistently. At least case managers generally seek the good of the client, a good he or she can recognize. Above all, they are consistent. They enforce a set of rules. They can be satisfied if a client obeys the rules. The situation gives the clients more sense of control than they have just living on welfare.

Thus most recipients respond favorably to oversight. It honors them with the assumption that their behavior matters. They take it as a form of caring. This is why attention from staff motivates. As one recipient described the people running her training program, "they don't want anyone to fail. . . . They're always keeping an eye on you. They're behind you pushing."[85] So involvement with the program is affirming, and the more the better. "Contact! . . . Once a week, twice a week, there's no such thing as too often," said one supervisor in Riverside. "It reminds them that you *care,* and that you're *watching.*"[86]

Diversion and Direction

The positive response to authority helps explain why diversion can be an effective way to reduce the welfare rolls. To suspicious observers, the idea of talking poor people out of welfare sounds like nothing more than closing the door to aid. It seems, again, to be a return to a discretionary and invidious style of welfare administration.

But as practiced in Wisconsin, diversion does not deny access. At least, it is not supposed to.[87] Rather, diversion staff are directive. They tell applicants that they *may* apply for aid, but they *ought* to get a job or help from families instead. They also tell them the obligations they will face if they go on aid. In response, many applicants avoid welfare. The directive stance is clearly motivating, although whether those who avoid welfare are really better off is much less clear.

The political climate surrounding welfare reform in Wisconsin is itself a form of direction. In advocating their reforms the governor and other officials declare publicly that in the future adults on welfare will be expected to function. This does not mean that all aid is denied. In September 1997 the state will institute a new welfare system called Wisconsin Works, or W-2, in which everyone will have to work at some level to get aid. The system is not ungenerous; it will also extend new health and child care subsidies to working poor. But the message is, you will have to work to get that aid. Public officials, in the name of society, are telling the poor how to live.

The poor respond, at least to the extent that many leave welfare. According to welfare officials in the state, the moment controversies began about Governor Tommy Thompson's "learnfare" proposal in 1987, recipients began leaving the rolls. That program was not even directed to reducing welfare, at least in the short run. Instead, it required that welfare parents keep their children in school as a condition of aid. But the message of responsibility could not be confined to it. Recipients even outside the program heard a call to be more self-reliant, and some left welfare. A similar dynamic may now be driving the caseload down nationwide. The AFDC rolls dropped 18 percent between March 1994 and October 1996, the sharpest fall since 1960.[88] Although one cause is an improving economy, another may be recent national debates about reform and the clear message of PRWORA that the days of entitlement are numbered.

The diversion effect that surrounds welfare reform poses problems for evaluating them because it becomes difficult to delimit a reform's influence to a specific program at a specific time. Recipients may respond to programs not meant for them. A reform may influence the rolls as soon as it is publicly discussed, long before it is enacted, let alone implemented. In Wisconsin, welfare reform has become an ongoing process in which the initiatives can no longer be separated from one another or from an overarching political direction. The governor proposes and the legislature enacts change after change. Some programs may be half-baked, but they are instituted anyway to keep the ball rolling. Each reinforces and is reinforced by a rhetoric of self-reliance. To assess such programs discretely or in narrowly economic terms is to miss the dynamic that drives them.

An Assessment of Paternalism

What are the pros and cons of the paternalistic approach to welfare employment? I apply the general arguments suggested in chapter 1 to the specific case of welfare. There are doubts because many recent state initiatives have not been well evaluated, and information is lacking on how diversion affects those potentially eligible for aid.

Advantages

The economic case for paternalism follows from the effects work programs achieve. As an approach to welfare reform, voluntary service-oriented programs can do well but mandatory programs oriented to actual work typically do better. The effects of such programs are likely to grow stronger as they are more fully implemented. They are a worthwhile investment.

Although many investments might be made in the poor, a virtue of welfare enforcement is that it directly addresses nonwork, the greatest economic problem of poor adults. And it does so in a way that does not immediately deny them all support. The combination of aid and work tests seems to do more for welfare-dependent people than either aid without expectations, the traditional liberal recommendation, or the denial of aid, favored by antigovernment conservatives. This combination is also politic. The voters want welfare adults to help themselves, but not at the cost of putting children at risk.[89] The only way to realize both goals is to enforce work *within* the welfare system.

Work enforcement is also more practicable than more ambitious social programs. Some advocates would have social service providers intervene deeply in families to deal with health and abuse problems and promote child development. Some such programs have shown good results experimentally.[90] But it is doubtful that they could be instituted widely because of the cost and the enormous demands they make for talented and committed staff. Paternalistic work programs have some of the same effect because of their directiveness, but are much cheaper. Because they stress work enforcement outside the family, they are more staffable and sustainable without burnout.

Disadvantages

One may say against work programs that they have not yet "ended welfare as we know it." Liberals complain that not enough recipients have been helped to work, conservatives that not enough have been required to work. It is still rarer for a welfare adult to be involved in an employment program than not, to be working than not. That has started to change in the states leading welfare reform, and it will have to change nationwide if PRWORA is implemented seriously. But the nation is a long way from realizing what the public wants: a working welfare system.

Welfare work programs also address only part of the employment problem. In general, they address the problems of women, not of men. Although some fathers are on TANF and subject to its requirements, the vast majority of clients are single mothers with children. Many go on welfare in the first place because the fathers of their children do not support them. But welfare work programs can obligate few of the fathers to work because few receive aid directly. Welfare makes an effort to establish paternity and collect child support, but the potential is limited, again because the fathers often have few earnings to contribute.

A better answer would be a work enforcement structure for disadvantaged fathers parallel to the one that has evolved for the mothers. Such a system might emerge from child support enforcement. Some localities are experimenting with offering disadvantaged fathers in arrears with their support payments another option besides going to jail: joining in a mandatory work program. The participation requirement makes most men pay up more effectively than the threat of incarceration, and gives the others some practical help with work (see chapter 4).

In addition, welfare work programs do not address the problem of unwed pregnancies that precipitates many welfare cases. Some conservatives argue that solving that problem is more important for welfare reform than putting the mothers to work.[91] But government has never found a surefire means of stopping unwed pregnancy. It knows something about how to enforce work, but almost nothing about how to confine childbearing to marriage. That is a major reason why welfare reform to date has stressed employment rather than changing the family.[92]

Doubts

Any assessment of welfare paternalism must remain incomplete because in some ways our information is limited. Most of what is known about the effects of welfare work programs comes from the MDRC evaluations, but these mostly date from the 1980s and cover only a handful of sites. MDRC has a national study of JOBS under way at several sites, but it is still unfinished.

The local leaders of reform have little incentive to worry about evaluation. Welfare experiments run under waivers of normal federal rules were supposed to provide for evaluations, but the designs tend to be too weak to tell very much.[93] PRWORA frees work programs from the need for waivers, so less local evaluation will occur in the future, although the bill also funds federal-level evaluation and monitoring.[94] In Wisconsin, some evaluations of the welfare work experiments have been unfavorable; others are incomplete.[95] The studies were undertaken to obtain waivers and have played little part in state decisionmaking. The caseload is currently falling in Wisconsin and most states, and as long as it is, officials will feel little pressure to evaluate to show results.

Even if the will to assess were stronger, however, wholesale change in welfare would pose difficulties for evaluators. When the system changes radically, effects can no longer be confined to those measurable by experiments. Change is driven by political dynamics, not by treatments that can be precisely demarcated and assessed. And much of the effect is to deter people from going on welfare, which occurs off the caseload where no conventional evaluation can read it. Because the decrease in caseloads seems to be caused in large part by diversion, the overall verdict on work requirements is unclear. One can only say, using the existing evaluations, that the effects on people already on welfare are probably beneficial.

One cannot say much about people who never go on welfare because of the requirements, or who leave it before they are obligated to participate.

The presumption must be that decreasing caseloads are good in themselves, that the diverted have found some other way to support themselves, but this is only a presumption. To estimate and assess diversion effects, evaluators must resort to nonexperimental methods such as statistical modeling of caseload changes or surveys of the effected populations.[96] Very little such research exists. The Urban Institute, with support from the Annie E. Casey Foundation and other grantors, is planning a large survey in twelve states in 1997 and again in 1999 to assess the effects of PRWORA. Wisconsin is planning an evaluation of W-2, and this too will probably be non-experimental.

In Wisconsin, census data suggest that child poverty rates rose during the 1980s.[97] The immediate cause probably was the explosive growth of urban poverty in Milwaukee, where ghetto areas expanded more sharply between 1970 and 1990 than in any other city.[98] Welfare reform was probably not responsible because until recently most of the decrease in caseloads occurred outside the city. Statistical analyses suggest that until about 1990 economic conditions were the main force reducing caseloads; it is after 1990 that work enforcement plays an important role.[99] It is thus unlikely that welfare reform in Wisconsin had adverse effects through 1994.

Since 1994, when more drastic work policies went into effect, the situation has been less clear. In Milwaukee, some community groups say demands that recipients document their hours of effort to get aid have increased homelessness. Officials admit that the new rules are driving people off welfare, but they say that most leaving the rolls have earnings.

The current decline in caseloads has aroused similar questions in many states. Somehow, a great many people are leaving welfare, and the question is what has happened to them. Preliminary inquiries focusing mainly on Iowa, Massachusetts, and Wisconsin suggest that the fortunes of families that lose benefits because of time limits or failure to cooperate with work programs are highly varied.[100] Some of these families report earnings, others do not; some gain income and some lose. Serious hardship appears to be rare because the loss of TANF is cushioned in most cases by other family income, including remaining public benefits such as food stamps and medicaid. Evidence about noneconomic effects on families must await the surveys mentioned earlier. Nevertheless, for the Wisconsin and national caseloads to fall by so much without clearer evidence of hardship is remarkable. Although the overall effects of work enforcement are unclear, the assessment at this point must be favorable.

Institutional Conditions

But can this kind of reform be widely emulated? The chief limit on welfare paternalism as a prescription may be that it is highly institutional. Some other ways of dealing with poverty, such as maintaining full employment, arouse little controversy. Still others, such as voluntary training, require little administration. Work enforcement, however, is inherently controversial, and it makes great demands on the bureaucracy.

Politics

In a political culture dedicated to freedom, the idea of making people work is inherently suspect. To levy such demands on recipients who are disadvantaged and, in most instances, nonwhite is even more explosive. Unease at this situation helped make all work tests until PRWORA half-hearted. Liberals would far rather help people work than require them to. Even conservatives, who do want to enforce work, would rather do so by reducing aid than by direct governmental requirements. Both sides prefer to make freedom their instrument, not obligation. If enforcement has gathered pace, it is only because leaders have realized that raising work levels is essential to integrating the poor, and that neither voluntary benefits nor simple cuts in welfare can accomplish that.[101] But this realization has taken thirty years to dawn, and consensus is still elusive.

To enforce work, these tensions must be resolved at both federal and lower levels. In Washington the differences were somewhat composed by the Family Support Act of 1988, which combined some new benefits with stronger work and child support rules. PRWORA is more conservative, and whether Congress and the Clinton administration can agree about implementing it remains to be seen. In the states, governors and legislatures must agree closely enough to set the details of work policy. The issues are sometimes delegated to the city or county level, where they are no less contentious.

In most urban states with big caseloads, agreement has failed. Democrats will not seriously enforce work, while Republicans refuse to pay for the services and bureaucracy needed for effective programs. Even though work programs with bite save money within a year or two, governments must invest up front, and that can be tough to justify when budgets are tight. The impasse over enforcement and costs is a big reason why, although caseloads are currently falling, the experience of welfare has changed little in New York, Massachusetts, Illinois, or most of California.

Bureaucracy

Welfare employment is very much an administered policy. Because it is paternalistic, it cannot simply set out new opportunities and incentives for welfare recipients. It must explicitly direct them to do things. That means calling large numbers in to enter programs and then supervising their movements and activities. To say that this takes case managers and reporting systems only suggests the complexities. As noted earlier, welfare must change to focus on employment as strongly as it has on accurate claims payments. These burdens must be shouldered by a bureaucracy that, in many localities, has endured popular scorn and drawn few talented employees for decades. For public managers and staffs it is a tall order.

The public pressure to change welfare is too strong to ignore, yet few states are equal to the political and administrative challenges. Something must be done, yet the disagreements and operational problems are too much to do it seriously. The outcome is often ephemeral reforms in which governors announce initiatives and nothing happens. Either the proposals die in the legislature or in Washington (assuming waivers of normal federal rules are needed). Or if approved, they fizzle out amid bureaucratic compromise and incapacity. Some states such as New Jersey have seen several such reforms. Welfare in most places remains a flaccid bureaucracy that pays out money to most recipients while expecting little of them in return.[102]

Exemplary Cases

Where welfare really changes, the locality typically has unusual political and bureaucratic resources. One reason pathbreaking welfare programs appeared early in San Diego was that the city was too conservative for its policies to arouse much local opposition. It also had skilled administrators with experience running previous employment programs.[103] In Riverside the key to change was a talented welfare director with strong local support who built an outstanding organization. Riverside GAIN is suffused with the work mission, and everyone involved—staff and contractors as well as clients—is accountable for performance.[104]

Wisconsin, another exemplar, began with unusual political consensus. The state has an ambitious government with a tradition of generosity and innovation in social policy, yet its political culture is oriented more to obligations than rights. This ethos motivates Democrats to support enforcing work in welfare, as they seldom do in other urban states, while Republicans accept a governmental approach to reform rather than just trying to cut welfare. Although Tommy Thompson, the current Republican governor, is the leader of reform, change predates his election in 1986 and has drawn support from both parties.[105] Leadership is also strong at the local level, where a number of counties and private groups have undertaken reform initiatives on their own.

Impatience for quick results has weakened national antipoverty policy. American wars on poverty tend to be abandoned before they have a chance to succeed.[106] But in Wisconsin a consensus to reform welfare was reached in the mid-1980s and has lasted ever since. Far from fading, the will to change has grown. The state is planning, with little dissent, to implement the radical W-2 in September 1997. Although the new system will deny aid to the nonworking, it will also create large numbers of subsidized jobs to be sure that recipients willing to work can do so.

Above all, Wisconsin has a superlative bureaucracy, a legacy of the Progressive Era and the state s good-government tradition. Public service draws talented people who willingly shoulder the special problems of running complex work programs. Although in other states welfare often shuns innovation, in Wisconsin counties compete to run experimental reform programs launched by the Thompson administration. Contracting to private and nonprofit organizations is only one form of innovation. Although I estimate that the state has saved $68 million on welfare reform, this is entirely due to the sharp decline in the caseload since 1986. The state has spent millions on work programs, and much of that investment has gone into the bureaucracy itself.[107]

The result of these resources is that reform actually happens. Wisconsin is not unusual in what the governor or other politicians say about welfare. Rather, it is unusual in its capacity to execute, to deliver change. The implementation of JOBS and its later evolution altered palpably how recipients were treated at the local level. As the program refocused between 1993 and 1995 from remediation to a work-first strategy, its administration tightened and the assignment of clients changed dramatically throughout the state toward job search and actual work.[108] As the state prepares for W-2, the share of clients subject to serious participation and work demands grows month by month. New routines have been implemented at a rate that counts as the speed of light for bureaucratic change. Driven by administrative muscle as well as the economy, the caseload continues to fall.

Can other states do what these localities have done? In the short term, probably not. Therefore paternalistic welfare reform cannot come quickly. Before welfare can be changed on a wide scale, this part of government must be reinvented. A greater political consensus for change must form, and significant investments and reforms must occur in the bureaucracy, especially at the state and local level.

The Potential of Welfare Paternalism

But assume that government's capacity can or will expand. What might paternalism in welfare eventually achieve?

The New Welfare Reform

Any answer must make some assumption about the effects of PRWORA. The new law turns over much more control of welfare to states while holding them accountable to much stiffer work requirements. Some believe that this will set off a race to the bottom as states compete to cut benefits and taxes so as to sell themselves to business.[109] But even before the reform, states controlled benefit levels in AFDC, and although those levels have declined in the past generation, variation among states remains enormous and has not narrowed.[110] To date, most states are spending new money on reforms rather than cutting benefits.[111]

If change occurs, the chief impetus will instead be the demanding new work rules. As mentioned earlier, whether they can be implemented as written is doubtful. Funding may be insufficient. But the recent decrease in caseloads narrows the funding gap and, under the act, reduces the work participation thresholds states must meet. States may evade the new standards by using TANF to support only the most employable families, who can meet the rules, and using their own funds to support other cases. Or they might accept a fiscal penalty instead of struggling to meet the standards. Congress might ease the rules or suspend fiscal sanctions if many states did this. But the political pressure to enforce work is potent both in Washington and the states. Efforts to employ recipients will likely intensify, even if the new standards are not fully met.

Caseload Reduction

If and only if this happens will PRWORA become a vehicle for an expanded paternalism in welfare. States will find that they cannot raise the percentage of clients who work unless they supervise recipients to enforce work and also drive the most employable off the rolls. The effects, at least in caseload reduction, might then greatly exceed those suggested by the evaluations. Enforcement might trigger in many states the kind of deflation of the rolls seen in Wisconsin.

How much might the caseloads fall? Between January 1987 and October 1996 many smaller rural counties in Wisconsin reduced their caseloads by more than 80 percent. Milwaukee's 25 percent decrease is remarkable for a major city.[112] In the typical state the potential reduction through work enforcement would fall somewhere in between—toward the high end in a rural area, the low end in an urban one. It is a wide range, with much depending on political resolution and administrative quality.

Other factors would be economic conditions and the employability of the clients. Although job availability is not a major constraint at current welfare work levels, it would become so if caseloads shrank rapidly, debouching many recipients into the job market in a short period. Over a longer period the greater limitation is not jobs but the employability of the recipients. Even if hiring of low-skilled workers remains active, what share of the current recipients lack the capacity to work? Estimates suggest a fifth or a quarter, but it is difficult to know as long as these people are mixed among many more employable recipients.[113] In Wisconsin, where the caseload has already shrunk by a half, the state estimates that more than half the remaining recipients will be able to work in regular jobs, perhaps with some subsidy, once W-2 is fully implemented.[114]

If welfare rolls decrease, will the percentage of recipients who work increase? In evaluations to date, work programs have typically produced more notable gains in employment than they did reductions in dependency.

The main reason probably is that the work gains accrue chiefly to short-term recipients whose stay on welfare is brief in any event.[115] But if states attempt to enforce work stringently, I expect that caseload reductions will come to exceed employment gains. Faced with new requirements, many families will leave welfare, but only some of them will work regularly, the rest relying on support from relatives or other informal sources, as many do now. The weight of reform bears chiefly on TANF. Families might leave it and rely on other welfare, such as Supplemental Security Income and food stamps, where work requirements are less developed. For these reasons the gap between the proportions of workers who are poor and nonpoor will be narrowed but not eliminated.[116] To close it further, additional steps would be needed to enforce work, especially among men not on welfare.

Reducing caseloads will not be to end welfare because the more the rolls shrink the less employable the remaining recipients become. In Wisconsin, even counties that are the toughest about work have begun to doubt whether the families still on the rolls can work. Perhaps forms of community service short of actual work are needed to structure the lives of people too impaired for regular employment. These adults would be obligated to function in some ways, but not to work for pay or support themselves.[117]

With the caseload reduced, welfare could be reprogrammed to concentrate aid on the families who need help the most. As one example, Grant County, Wisconsin, enforces work stringently, but it also invests heavily in intensive social services to assist the most battered families. Thus the effect of shrinking welfare rolls might finally be to deemphasize the work approach to reform and to bring back an emphasis on traditional social work. It stands to reason that once the employable are off the rolls, the focus of welfare reform can no longer be employment.

The potential of paternalistic work programs to reduce dependency is clear. By this means, welfare can be much reduced, if not eliminated. But doubts remain about the overall effects on the poor. Larger doubts loom about the ability of many localities to enact and implement serious work requirements. If PRWORA imposes radical change, the questions are likely to grow larger before they are answered.

Table 2A-1. Main Manpower Demonstration Research Corporation Welfare Employment Program Evaluations, 1982–93

Dollars unless otherwise specified

Study	*Outcome in final year*	*Control mean*	*Experimental-control difference*	*Percent change*
Arkansas	Average annual earnings	1,085	337	31
	Employed at end of final year (percent)	18.3	6.2	34
	Average annual AFDC payments	910	−168	−18
	On welfare at end of final year (percent)	40.1	−7.3	−18
Baltimore	Average annual earnings	2,989	511	17
	Employed at end of final year (percent)	40.3	0.4	1
	Average annual AFDC payments	1,815	−31	−2
	On welfare at end of final year (percent)	48.4	−0.2	0
California GAIN	Average annual earnings	2,523	636	25
	Employed at end of final year (percent)	24.1	4.5	19
	Average annual AFDC payments	4,163	−331	−8
	On welfare at end of final year (percent)	55.5	−3.0	−5
Riverside GAIN	Average annual earnings	2,552	1,010	40
	Employed at end of final year (percent)	24.6	6.6	27
	Average annual AFDC payments	3,448	−584	−17
	On welfare at end of final year (percent)	45.8	−5.2	−11

Table 2A-1 (*continued*)

Study	*Outcome in final year*	*Control mean*	*Experi-mental-control difference*	*Percent change*
Cook County (job search/ work experience)	Average annual earnings	1,217	10	1
	Employed at end of final year (percent)	21.4	1.3	6
	Average annual AFDC payments	3,146	–40	–1
	On welfare at end of final year (percent)	80.8	–1.9	–2
Florida	Average annual earnings	3,138	80	3
	Employed at end of final year (percent)	37.8	0.4	1
	Average annual AFDC payments	1,945	–113	–6
	On welfare at end of final year (percent)	53.6	–2.4	–4
San Diego (job search/ work experience)	Average annual earnings	1,937	443	23
	Employed at end of final year (percent)	36.9	5.5	15
	Average annual AFDC payments	2,750	–226	–8
	On welfare at end of final year (percent)	47.9	–2.0	-4
San Diego SWIM	Average annual earnings	2,246	658	29
	Employed at end of final year (percent)	29.3	5.4	18
	Average annual AFDC payments	3,961	–553	–14
	On welfare at end of final year (percent)	58.7	–7.4	–13
Virginia	Average annual earnings	2,356	268	11
	Employed at end of final year (percent)	34.1	4.6	13
	Average annual AFDC payments	1,295	–111	–9
	On welfare at end of final year (percent)	39.3	–2.6	–7

Table 2A-1 (*continued*)

Study	*Outcome in final year*	*Control mean*	*Experimental-control difference*	*Percent change*
West Virginia	Average annual earnings	435	16	4
	Employed at end of final year (percent)	13.1	−1.0	−8
	Average annual AFDC payments	1,692	0	0
	On welfare at end of final year (percent)	72.5	−1.5	−2
Averages (excludes Riverside)	Average annual earnings	1,992	329	16
	Employed at end of final year (percent)	28.4	3.0	11
	Average annual AFDC payments	2,409	−175	−7
	On welfare at end of final year (percent)	55.2	−3.1	−6

Note: Studies are weighted equally. Results are for AFDC, not AFDC-UP, and are for the last full year of the evaluations, which varied from one to three years in follow-up. "Percentage change" means the absolute effect as a percentage of the control-group mean. Averages for the percentage changes are means of the individual percentage change figures, not calculated from the averages of the control means and experimental-control differences.

Sources: Judith M. Gueron and Edward Pauly, with Cameran M. Lougy, *From Welfare to Work* (New York: Russell Sage, 1991), pp. 142–4; James J. Kemple, Daniel Friedlander, and Veronica Fellerath, *Florida's Project Independence: Benefits, Costs, and Two-Year Impacts of Florida's JOBS Program* (New York: Manpower Demonstration Research Corp., 1995), p. ES-16; and James Riccio, Daniel Friedlander, and Stephen Freedman, *GAIN: Benefits, Costs, and Three-Year Impacts of a Welfare-to-Work Program* (New York: Manpower Demonstration Research Corp., 1994), pp. 120, 122.

Notes

1. I ignore work policies in other aid programs such as food stamps because they are less developed and the AFDC-TANF requirements take precedence for recipients subject to them.

2. Bureau of the Census, *Statistical Abstract of the United States, 1996* (Department of Commerce, 1996), p. 400.

3. Between 1969 and 1979 reported work levels ran from 15 to 16 percent, but the higher figures reflected the fact that AFDC eligibility rules allowed more working mothers to participate before 1981 than after. See House Committee on Ways and Means, *1996 Green Book: Background Material and Data on Programs within the Jurisdiction of the Committee on Ways and Means* (Government Printing Office, 1996), p. 474.

4. Kathleen Mullan Harris, "Work and Welfare among Single Mothers in Poverty," *American Journal of Sociology*, vol. 99 (September 1993), pp. 329–31.

5. According to one study of 214 welfare mothers, 63 percent of their income came from welfare, 18 percent from contributions from family and friends, and 15 percent from earnings, most of it unreported. See Kathryn J. Edin, "The Myths of Dependence and Self-Sufficiency: Women, Welfare, and Low-Wage Work," *Focus*, vol. 17 (Fall-Winter 1995), pp. 1–9.

6. Female headship much more often precipitates poverty among whites. See Mary Jo Bane, "Household Composition and Poverty," in Sheldon H. Danziger and Daniel H. Weinberg, eds., *Fighting Poverty: What Works and What Doesn't* (Harvard University Press, 1986), pp. 220–27; and James P. Smith, "Poverty and the Family," in Gary D. Sandefur and Marta Tienda, eds., *Divided Opportunities: Minorities, Poverty, and Social Policy* (Plenum Press, 1988), chap. 6.

7. Charles Michalopoulos and Irwin Garfinkel, "Reducing the Welfare Dependence and Poverty of Single Mothers by Means of Earnings and Child Support: Wishful Thinking and Realistic Possibility," Institute for Research on Poverty, University of Wisconsin, August 1989.

8. Irwin Garfinkel and Sara S. McLanahan, *Single Mothers and Their Children: A New American Dilemma* (Washington: Urban Institute Press, 1986), pp. 34–37; Deborah Lowe Vandell and Janaki Ramanan, "Effects of Early and Recent Maternal Employment on Children from Low-Income Families," *Child Development.*, vol. 63 (August 1992), pp. 938–49. I survey the evidence on how requiring mothers to work might affect children in "Welfare Reform and Children," in Edward F. Zigler, Sharon Lynn Kagan, and Nancy W. Hall, eds., *Children, Families, and Government: Preparing for the Twenty-first Century* (Cambridge University Press, 1996), chap. 4.

9. The following discussion draws upon Lawrence M. Mead, *Beyond Entitlement: The Social Obligations of Citizenship* (Free Press, 1986), pp. 121–26; and Mead, *The New Politics of Poverty: The Nonworking Poor in America* (Basic Books, 1992), chap. 9.

10. These included the Community Work and Training Act of 1962 and the Work Experience and Training program of 1964, which was part of the Economic Opportunity Act that launched Lyndon Johnson's War on Poverty.

11. House Committee on Ways and Means, *1996 Green Book*, p. 467.

12. Jan L. Hagen and Irene Lurie, *Implementing JOBS: Progress and Promise* (University of New York at Albany, Nelson A. Rockefeller Institute of Government, August 1994).

13. Lawrence M. Mead, "The New Paternalism: How Should Congress Respond?" *Public Welfare*, vol. 50 (Spring 1992), pp. 14–17; and Michael Wiseman, "Welfare Reform in the States: The Bush Legacy," *Focus*, vol. 15 (Spring 1993), pp. 18–36.

14. Task Force on Poverty and Welfare, *A New Social Contract: Rethinking the Nature and Purpose of Public Assistance* (State of New York, December 1986), chap. 4; and David T. Ellwood, *Poor Support: Poverty in the American Family* (Basic Books, 1988), chaps. 4–5.

15. TANF is now an entitlement to states and has funds capped at $16.4 billion a year. Thus, like other entitlements, it is still not subject to cuts through the normal budgeting process.

16. SWIM achieved 52 percent on a monthly basis, but only if a wide range of activities were included and participation required only one day of activity a month. See Gayle Hamilton, *Interim Report on the Saturation Work Initiative Model in San Diego* (New York: Manpower Demonstration Research Corp., August 1988), chap. 7. Kenosha, Wisconsin, achieved more than 60 percent by this measure and 50 percent by the measure used in JOBS. See Michael Wiseman, "Sample Family Support Act Job Opportunity and Basic Skills Training (JOBS) Participation Data (Revised)," University of Wisconsin–Madison, La Follette Institute of Public Affairs, November 24, 1991.

17. Congressional Budget Office, "Federal Budgetary Implications of the Personal Responsibility and Work Opportunity Reconciliation Act of 1996," CBO memorandum, December 1996.

18. Mead, *Beyond Entitlement*, chaps. 3–5; and Mead, *New Politics of Poverty*, chap. 9.

19. Thomas Fraker, Robert Moffitt, and Douglas Wolf, "Effective Tax Rates and Guarantees in the AFDC Program, 1967–1982," *Journal of Human Resources*, vol. 20 (Spring 1985), pp. 251–63.

20. Robert Moffitt, "Incentive Effects of the U.S. Welfare System: A Review," *Journal of Economic Literature*, vol. 30 (March 1992), pp. 15–19.

21. Laurie J. Bassi and Orley Ashenfelter, "The Effect of Direct Job Creation and Training Programs on Low-Skilled Workers," in Danziger and Weinberg, eds., *Fighting Poverty*, chap. 6; Gary Burtless, "The Effect of Reform on Employment, Earnings, and Income," in Phoebe H. Cottingham and David T. Ellwood, eds., *Welfare Policy for the 1990s* (Harvard University Press, 1989), chap. 4; and Rebecca M. Blank, "The Employment Strategy: Public Policies to Increase Work and Earnings," in Sheldon H. Danziger, Gary D. Sandefur, and Daniel H. Weinberg, eds., *Confronting Poverty: Prescriptions for Change* (Russell Sage Foundation and Harvard University Press, 1994), chap. 7.

22. In an experiment a sample of eligible people is randomly distributed between a experimental group that receives the new program and a control group that does not. Random allocation ensures that the two groups are equivalent in measured and unmeasured ways so that any difference in outcomes is attributable to the program. Several evaluations were done of the Comprehensive Employment and Training Act (CETA), the main federal training structure between 1973 and 1982, but because they were

nonexperimental, the effects of the program remained unclear, although they were definitely small. See Burt S. Barnow, "The Impact of CETA Programs on Earnings: A Review of the Literature," *Journal of Human Resources*, vol. 22 (Spring 1987), pp. 157–93.

23. Howard S. Bloom and others, *The National JTPA Study: Title II-A Impacts on Earnings and Employment at 18 Months* (Bethesda, Md.: Abt Associates, May 1992).

24. Gary Burtless, "Manpower Policies for the Disadvantaged: What Works?" *Brookings Review*, vol. 3 (Fall 1984), pp. 18–22.

25. See chapter 1, notes 26 and 27. The following discussion summarizes Mead, *New Politics of Poverty*, chaps. 4–6.

26. The seminal paper was John Kain, "Housing Segregation, Negro Employment, and Metropolitan Decentralization," *Quarterly Journal of Economics*, vol. 82 (May 1968), pp. 175–97. For reviews of the evidence, see Christopher Jencks and Susan E. Mayer, "Residential Segregation, Job Proximity, and Black Job Opportunities," in Laurence E. Lynn Jr. and Michael G. H. McGeary, eds., *Inner-City Poverty in the United States* (Washington: National Academy Press, 1990), chap. 5; and Harry J. Holzer, "The Spatial Mismatch Hypothesis: What Has the Evidence Shown?" *Urban Studies*, vol. 28 (February 1991), pp. 105–22.

27. William Julius Wilson, *The Truly Disadvantaged: The Inner City, the Underclass, and Public Policy* (University of Chicago Press, 1987); and Wilson, *When Work Disappears: The World of the New Urban Poor* (Knopf, 1996).

28. Keith R. Ihlanfeldt and David L. Sjoquist, "Job Accessibility and Racial Differences in Youth Employment Rates," *American Economic Review*, vol. 80 (March 1990), pp. 267–76; and John Bound and Harry J. Holzer, "Industrial Shifts, Skills Levels, and the Labor Market for White and Black Males," *Review of Economics and Statistics*, vol. 75 (August 1993), pp. 387–96.

29. On average in 1990, workers from both high- and low-poverty areas took virtually the same time to commute to their jobs—twenty-three minutes. The greatest difference, found in the Northeast and Chicago, was about five minutes. See Paul A. Jargowsky, *Poverty and Place: Ghettos, Barrios, and the American City* (Russell Sage, 1997), pp. 105–06.

30. Bureau of the Census, "Poverty in the United States: 1992," *Current Population Reports*, series P-60, no. 185 (Department of Commerce, 1993), p. 89.

31. Frank Levy and Richard J. Murnane, "U.S. Earnings Levels and Earnings Inequality: A Review of Recent Trends and Proposed Explanations," *Journal of Economic Literature*, vol. 30 (September 1992), pp. 1333–81. But Levy and Murnane find that deindustrialization explains only a small part of the trends, which remain largely mysterious.

32. Ninety-three percent of Mexican fathers aged 18–44 were employed, compared with 82 percent of whites, 76 percent of Puerto Ricans, and 66 percent of blacks. Robert Aponte, "Ethnicity and Male Employment in the Inner City: A Test of Two Theories," paper prepared for the Chicago Urban Poverty and Family Life Conference, Social Science Research Council, University of Chicago, October 1991.

33. Rebecca M. Blank, "Outlook for the U.S. Labor Market and Prospects for Low-Wage Entry Jobs," and Gary Burtless, "Employment Prospects of Welfare Mothers," in Demetra Smith Nightingale and Robert H. Haveman, eds., *The Work Alterna-*

tive: Welfare Reform and the Realities of the Job Market (Washington: Urban Institute Press, 1995), pp. 33–69, 71–106.

34. James E. Prather and Frank K. Gibson, "The Failure of Social Programs," *Public Administration Review*, vol. 37 (September-October 1977), pp. 556–64; and Peter H. Rossi, "The Iron Law of Evaluation and Other Metallic Rules," in Joann L. Miller and Michael Lewis, eds., *Research in Social Problems and Public Policy*, vol. 4 (Greenwich, Conn.: JAI Press, 1987), pp. 3–20.

35. Judith M. Gueron and Edward Pauly, with Cameran M. Lougy, *From Welfare to Work* (Russell Sage Foundation, 1991), chap. 4.

36. Michael Wiseman, ed., "Research and Policy: A Symposium on the Family Support Act of 1988," *Journal of Policy Analysis and Management*, vol. 10 (Fall 1991), pp. 588–666.

37. Gueron and Pauly, *From Welfare to Work*, p. 145.

38. David Greenberg and Michael Wiseman, "What Did the OBRA Demonstrations Do?" in Charles F. Manski and Irwin Garfinkel, eds., *Evaluating Welfare and Training Programs*, (Harvard University Press, 1992), pp. 39–40, 45–46.

39. Robert A. Moffitt, "The Effect of Employment and Training Programs on Entry and Exit from the Welfare Caseload," *Journal of Policy Analysis and Management*, vol. 15 (Winter 1996), pp. 32–50.

40. The following draws on Lawrence M. Mead, "The New Paternalism in Action: Welfare Reform in Wisconsin," Milwaukee, Wisconsin Policy Research Institute, January 1995; and Mead, "The Decline of Welfare in Wisconsin," Milwaukee, Wisconsin Policy Research Institute, March 1996.

41. These analyses, reported in Mead, "Decline of Welfare," pp. 17–22, include a time series of the statewide caseload trend and a cross-sectional analyses of caseload decline across the seventy-two Wisconsin counties. For a qualitative analysis with similar conclusions, see Michael Wiseman, "State Strategies for Welfare Reform: The Wisconsin Story," *Journal of Policy Analysis and Management*, vol. 15 (Fall 1996), pp. 515–46.

42. Calculated from monthly caseload data from the Wisconsin Department of Health and Social Services. The 25 percent statewide figure differs slightly from the 23 percent mentioned earlier because the latter is based on annual data from the U.S. Administration for Children and Families.

43. Laurence E. Lynn Jr., ed., "Symposium: The Craft of Public Management," *Journal of Policy Analysis and Management*, vol. 8 (Spring 1989), pp. 284–306.

44. In 1978 the Department of Labor informed Congress that "the 1971 amendments made an almost immediate impact in fiscal 1973, the first year they took affect, when WIN registrants obtained nearly 137,000 jobs—more than twice as many as in the previous year. Placements have continued to rise, even during the recession, and totaled more than 276,000 jobs in fiscal 1977." Between fiscal 1973 and 1977 the number of families leaving welfare because of WIN rose from 34,000 to 136,000 while the number reducing their grants because of earnings rose from 31,000 to 135,000. See *Welfare Reform Proposals*, Hearings before the Subcommittee on Public Assistance of the Senate Finance Committee, 95 Cong. 2 sess. (Government Printing Office, 1978), pp. 350, 474.

45. In fiscal 1969 WIN spent less than a third of its budget for lack of clients. See *Family Assistance Act of 1970*, Hearings before the Senate Committee on Finance, 91 Cong. 2 sess. (GPO, 1970), p. 134.

46. The Department of Health and Human Services estimates that the unduplicated count of JOBS participants over a year is more than two times the monthly average. Thus the monthly JOBS figure of 445,415 translates to more than 890,830 on an annual basis, or more than six times WIN's annual figure of 145,632. See Irene Lurie, "A Lesson from the JOBS Program: Reforming Welfare Must Be Both Dazzling and Dull," *Journal of Policy Analysis and Management*, vol. 15 (Fall 1996), pp. 577–78. Although the AFDC caseload grew from 10.6 million to 14.2 million, or 34 percent, between 1980 and 1994, this accounts for only a small part of the growth in welfare work enrollments. Caseload figures are from Committee on Ways and Means, *1996 Green Book*, p. 467.

47. States with high and growing participation levels in JOBS suffered less welfare growth during 1989–93. See Mead, "Decline of Welfare," pp. 14–17.

48. Daniel Friedlander, *Subgroup Impacts and Performance Indicators for Selected Welfare Employment Programs* (New York: Manpower Demonstration Research Corp., August 1988).

49. Stephen Freedman and Daniel Friedlander, *The JOBS Evaluation: Early Findings on Program Impacts in Three Sites* (New York: Manpower Demonstration Research Corp., July 1995).

50. Daniel Friedlander and Gary Burtless, *Five Years After: The Long-Term Effects of Welfare-to-Work Programs* (Russell Sage Foundation, 1995). One reason SWIM's effects faded was that it was dismantled after two years. Recipients who had participated in it could return to welfare without fear of facing the same regime, as Friedlander and Burtless themselves suggest (p. 146).

51. James Riccio, Daniel Friedlander, and Stephen Freedman, *GAIN: Benefits, Costs, and Three-Year Impacts of a Welfare-to-Work Program* (New York: Manpower Demonstration Research Corp., September 1994), pp. 270, 292–93.

52. Friedlander and Burtless, *Five Years After*, pp. 78–87, 194–95.

53. Gueron and Pauly, *From Welfare to Work*, p. 256.

54. Riccio, Friedlander, and Freedman, *GAIN*, chap. 3.

55. Lawrence M. Mead, "Welfare Policy: The Administrative Frontier," *Journal of Policy Analysis and Management*, vol. 15 (Fall 1996), pp. 592–98.

56. This view is shared by most but not all caseworkers in these programs. See General Accounting Office, *Work and Welfare: Analysis of AFDC Employment Programs in Four States* (1988), pp. 34–37.

57. Mead, "New Paternalism in Action," pp. 18–22.

58. Ibid., pp. 22–26.

59. Lawrence M. Mead, "Optimizing JOBS: Evaluation Versus Administration," *Public Administration Review*, vol. 57 (March-April 1997), pp. 6–9; and Mead, "Decline of Welfare," p. 26.

60. See Lawrence M. Mead, "Expectations and Welfare Work: WIN in New York City," *Policy Studies Review*, vol. 2 (May 1983), pp. 648–62; Mead, "Expectations and Welfare Work: WIN in New York State," *Polity*, vol. 18 (Winter 1985), pp. 224–52; and Mead, "The Potential for Work Enforcement: A Study of WIN," *Journal of Policy Analysis*

and Management, vol. 7 (Winter 1988), pp. 264–88. For a parallel analysis in Massachusetts, see Paul J. Provencher, "Welfare Recipients and Employment: The Influence of the Attitudes of Case Managers and Other Factors on Program Performance in Local Welfare Offices," Ph.D. dissertation, Brandeis University, August 1989.

61. Mead, "Decline of Welfare," pp. 19–23. Again there are some other statistical analyses to the same effect. See Bradley R. Schiller and C. Nielson Brasher, "Workfare in the 1980s: Successes and Limits," *Policy Studies Review*, vol. 9 (Summer 1990), pp. 665–80; Valerie Englander and Fred Englander, "Workfare in New Jersey: A Five Year Assessment," *Policy Studies Review*, vol. 5 (August 1985), pp. 33–41; and C. Nielsen Brasher, "Workfare in Ohio: Political and Socioeconomic Climate and Program Impact," *Policy Studies Journal*, vol. 22 (Autumn 1994), pp. 514–27.

62. Friedlander and Burtless, *Five Years After*, pp. 27, 33, 77, 87, 149.

63. Gueron and Pauly, *From Welfare to Work*, pp. 130–31. Later MDRC studies in California and Florida, not covered in Gueron and Pauly, fell within the same range.

64. Hamilton, *Interim Report*, pp. 133–35, 138–39; and Riccio, Friedlander, and Freedman, *GAIN*, pp. 59–61.

65. Gueron and Pauly, *From Welfare to Work*, p. 184.

66. Mead, "New Paternalism in Action," pp. 21, 30; Mead, "WIN in New York City," p. 659; and Mead, "WIN in New York State," pp. 237–38. At the state level, however, sanctioning is positively linked to performance, probably because it is linked to overall implementation levels; see Mead, "Potential for Work Enforcement," pp. 271–73.

67. Mead, "New Paternalism," p. 22; and Mead, "Decline of Welfare," pp. 12–13. One caveat is that the JOBS enrollment rate fell for the state between 1993 and 1995. Some of those who might have been sanctioned may have left welfare on their own.

68. Instances would include Cook County, which sanctioned 12 percent and probably gained some of its welfare savings this way; SWIM, which realized unusual welfare savings in two-parent cases, perhaps because of sanctioning; and Fond du Lac, Wisc., where the sanction rate jumped sharply to 10 percent after Work Not Welfare was instituted. See Gueron and Pauly, *From Welfare to Work*, p. 184; Gayle Hamilton and Daniel Friedlander, *Final Report on the Saturation Work Initiative Model in San Diego* (New York: Manpower Demonstration Research Corp., November 1989), p. 79; and Mead, "Decline of Welfare," p. 12.

69. Gueron and Pauly, *From Welfare to Work*, pp. 133–34. This is the concept that MDRC calls "coverage."

70. LaDonna A. Pavetti and Amy-Ellen Duke, *Increasing Participation in Work and Work-Related Activities: Lessons from Five State Welfare Reform Demonstration Projects, Final Report*, volume 2: *Site Visit Summaries* (Washington: Urban Institute, September 1995), p. 149.

71. LaDonna A. Pavetti, Pamela Holcomb, and Amy-Ellen Duke, *Increasing Participation in Work and Work-Related Activities: Lessons from Five State Welfare Reform Demonstration Projects, Final Report*, vol. 1: *Summary Report* (Washington: Urban Institute, September 1995).

72. Mary Jo Bane and David T. Ellwood, *Welfare Realities: From Rhetoric to Reform* (Harvard University Press, 1994), chap. 1.

73. Pavetti, Holcomb, and Duke, *Increasing Participation*, vol. 1, chap. 7.

74. Eugene Bardach, *Improving the Productivity of JOBS Programs* (New York: Manpower Demonstration Research Corp., 1993), chap. 3.

75. Jan L. Hagen and Irene Lurie, *Implementing JOBS: Case Management Services* (State University of New York at Albany, Rockefeller Institute of Government, July 1994).

76. For an account of such efforts in Kearns, Utah, see Pavetti and Duke, *Increasing Participation*, vol. 2, pp. 116–40.

77. Calculated from program data from the Wisconsin Department of Health and Social Services.

78. Mark Lincoln Chadwin, John J. Mitchell, and Demetra Smith Nightingale, "Reforming Welfare: Lessons from the WIN Experience," *Public Administration Review*, vol. 41 (May-June 1981), pp. 375–76.

79. Bardach, *Improving the Productivity of JOBS Programs*, p. 19.

80. Christina Maslach, "Burned Out," *Human Behavior*, vol. 5 (September 1976), pp. 16–22.

81. Pavetti and Duke, *Increasing Participation*, vol. 2, pp. 126, 130.

82. Joe Klein, "Shepherds of the Inner City," *Newsweek*, April 18, 1994, p. 28.

83. Leonard Goodwin, *Do the Poor Want to Work? A Social-Psychological Study of Work Orientations* (Brookings, 1972).

84. Gueron and Pauly, *From Welfare to Work*, p. 166, summarizes these results. For more detail, see Thomas Brock, David Butler, and David Long, "Unpaid Work Experience for Welfare Recipients: Findings and Lessons from MDRC Research," Manpower Demonstration Research Corp., New York, September 1993, table 5. The one instance where a majority was dissatisfied to be working for benefits was in Chicago.

85. Lisa W. Foderaro, "Leaving Welfare Behind by Degrees," *New York Times*, September 16, 1990, p. 38.

86. Bardach, *Improving the Productivity of JOBS Programs*, pp. 18–19.

87. A question raised by students of street-level bureaucracy is how far one can believe what welfare managers say about program operations. Perhaps welfare administration is more punitive in practice than in its professed policies. See Michael Lipsky, "Bureaucratic Disentitlement in Social Welfare Programs," *Social Service Review*, vol. 58 (March 1984), pp. 3–27. One solution I use to that problem is to interview confidentially at all levels of programs; I generally find what executives say consistent with what line-level staff say. Another check is to compare what administrators say against how clients are actually assigned, as indicated by program reporting data. Again, I generally find correspondence.

88. Jason DeParle, "A Sharp Decrease in Welfare Cases Is Gathering Speed," *New York Times*, February 2, 1997, pp. 1, 18.

89. Mead, *Beyond Entitlement*, pp. 233–40; and Mead, *New Politics of Poverty*, pp. 57–63.

90. Lisbeth B. Schorr with Daniel Schorr, *Within Our Reach: Breaking the Cycle of Disadvantage* (Doubleday, 1988).

91. Charles Murray, "What To Do about Welfare," *Commentary*, vol. 98 (December 1994), pp. 27–29, 32–33; and James Q. Wilson, "Welfare Reform and Character Development," *City Journal*, vol. 5 (Winter 1995), pp. 61–62.

92. There is evidence that work enforcement, among other mandates attached to welfare, reduces the incidence of pregnancy out of wedlock. See Robert D. Plotnick, "Welfare and Out-of-Wedlock Childbearing: Evidence from the 1980s," *Journal of Marriage and the Family*. vol. 52 (August 1990), pp. 735–46. But work requirements have never been sold on this basis.

93. Michael Wiseman, "Welfare Reform in the States."

94. The need for waivers and thus for evaluations of them remains only in programs such as food stamps and medicaid in which federal standards are more specific. PRWORA provides $25 million a year for research and monitoring of welfare reform by the Department of Health and Human Services and the Bureau of the Census.

95. John Pawasarat and Lois M. Quinn, "Wisconsin Welfare Employment Experiments: An Evaluation of the WEJT and CWEP Programs," University of Wisconsin-Milwaukee, Employment and Training Institute, September 1993.

96. For discussions of the methodological problems, see Manski and Garfinkel, eds., *Evaluating Welfare and Training Programs*, esp. chaps. 6–7. One survey in Michigan following a cut in the program found that former general assistance recipients suffered from serious health and employment problems. But how far these were caused by the cut is unclear, and general assistance serves a very disadvantaged population, less functional on average than welfare mothers. See Sandra K. Danziger and Sherrie Kossoudji, "What Happened to General Assistance Recipients in Michigan?" *Focus*, vol. 16 (Winter 1994–95), pp. 32–34.

97. Current Population Survey data, however, suggest that poverty rates may have declined. See Thomas J. Corbett, "Welfare Reform in Wisconsin: The Rhetoric and the Reality," in Donald F. Norris and Lyke Thompson, eds., *The Politics of Welfare Reform* (Thousand Oaks, Calif.: Sage, 1995), pp. 47, 52 note 37.

98. Jargowsky, *Poverty and Place*, pp. 49–57, 81–82.

99. Mead, "Decline of Welfare," pp. 21–22.

100. Thomas M. Fraker and others, *Iowa's Limited Benefit Plan: Summary Report* (Princeton, N.J.: Mathematica Policy Research, 1997); and General Accounting Office, *Welfare Reform: States' Early Experiences With Benefit Termination* (1997). Fraker and others found that 40 percent of terminated families in Iowa emerged with higher income, 49 percent with lower, and 11 percent with no change. On average families gained $13 a month (pp. 8–9).

101. Mead, *Beyond Entitlement*, chaps. 8–11.

102. Norris and Thompson, eds., *Politics of Welfare Reform*; and Richard P. Nathan, *Turning Promises into Performance: The Management Challenge of Implementing Workfare* (Columbia University Press, 1993).

103. Hamilton, *Interim Report*, pp. 15–17.

104. Bardach, *Improving the Productivity of JOBS Programs*; and Riccio, Holcomb, and Duke, *GAIN*, chaps. 2, 8.

105. Corbett, "Welfare Reform in Wisconsin"; Wiseman, "State Strategies for Welfare Reform"; and Paul E. Peterson and Mark C. Rom, *Welfare Magnets: A New Case for a National Standard* (Brookings, 1990), chap. 2.

106. Hugh Heclo, "Poverty Politics," in Danziger, Sandefur, and Weinberg, eds., *Confronting Poverty*, chap. 15.

107. Mead, "Decline of Welfare," pp. 27–29.

108. The proportion of clients in a given month assigned to inactive status dropped from 30 to 20 percent, the proportion in job search doubled from 4 to 8 percent, and the proportion in unpaid workfare jobs jumped from 1 to 5 percent. See Mead, "Decline of Welfare," pp. 11–12.

109. Paul E. Peterson, *The Price of Federalism* (Brookings, 1995), chap. 5.

110. Peter T. Kilborn, "Welfare All Over the Map," *New York Times*, December 8, 1996, p. E3; and Peterson and Rom, *Welfare Magnets*, pp. 6–13.

111. Jason DeParle, "U.S. Welfare System Dies as State Programs Emerge," *New York Times*, June 30, 1997, p. A1.

112. Figures are from the Wisconsin Department of Health and Social Services.

113. Rebecca A. Maynard, "Subsidized Employment and Non–Labor Market Alternatives for Welfare Recipients," in Nightingale and Haveman, eds., *Work Alternative*, pp. 114–15; and Judith M. Gueron, "A Research Context for Welfare Reform," *Journal of Policy Analysis and Management*, vol. 15 (Fall 1996), p. 555. These estimates sound consistent with the experience of the most intensive local programs, such as the ones in Grant County, Wisconsin, and Kearns, Utah. See Mead, "Decline of Welfare," pp. 9–10; and Pavetti and Duke, *Increasing Participation*, vol. 2, pp. 127.

114. Wiseman, "State Strategies for Welfare Reform," p. 533.

115. Friedlander and Burtless, *Five Years After*, pp. 78–80, 194–95

116. According to Fraker and others, *Iowa's Limited Benefit Plan,* pp. 8–9, 53 percent of families losing benefits in Iowa recorded employment afterward, while 47 percent did not.

117. Toby Herr, Robert Halpern, and Aimée Conrad, *Changing What Counts: Rethinking the Journey Out of Welfare* (Northwestern University, Center for Urban Affairs and Policy Research, April 1991).

Three

Paternalism, Teenage Pregnancy Prevention, and Teenage Parent Services

Rebecca A. Maynard

Teenage pregnancy and parenting are among the nation's greatest tragedies because of the burdens they impose on future generations. With the sharp increases in out-of-wedlock childbearing and a persistently high abortion rate, an especially strong link has emerged between teenage parenthood, long-term welfare dependence, and poor outcomes for children. The growth in the rate of out-of-wedlock childbearing, in turn, has paralleled expansions of the federal welfare safety net. At this juncture, there is substantial research to challenge the wisdom of past programs designed to prevent teenage pregnancy or to mitigate its consequences. Those programs were usually voluntary, nondirective, and focused on providing economic support. Their limitations suggest that more paternalistic policies linking public support for teenage parents and their children to specific parental and child behaviors would better serve both these families and society as a whole.

These conclusions are derived from two strands of empirical research. One is studies of child and adolescent development, which identify teenage pregnancy and parenthood as examples of the types of irrational behaviors common among adolescents, particularly those with inadequate external sources of behavioral controls. Teenagers do not intend to get pregnant and begin families at young ages. Moreover, doing so is at odds with their stated values. Yet more than 1 million become pregnant each year and just over half of those getting pregnant give birth. These statistics have worsened in the past few decades despite increased efforts to educate youths about sex and family planning and to increase both the availability and reliability of contraceptives.

The second strand of research has investigated the common features of the few effective pregnancy prevention or parenting policies and programs for teenagers. Those that have shown promise clearly state values, maintain specific behavioral requirements, and impose sanctions for failure to fulfill requirements.

This chapter first discusses the conflict between the values and actions of teenagers for teenage mothers and the implications of the half million births to teenagers each year for their children and for taxpayers. I then discuss public policies aimed at reducing teenage pregnancy and parenthood and the results. The chapter then examines in greater detail the practical lessons from the past two decades of policy and program evaluation research and assesses the current trend toward highly paternalistic social welfare policies. Not only are more paternalistic policies crucial to maintaining public support for social programs such as welfare, but they also offer the most promise for preventing teenage pregnancy and mitigating adverse consequences when it does occur.

Conflicts between Teenagers' Values and Actions

Each year more than a million teenage women in the United States become pregnant, 88 percent of them unintentionally.[1] More than 500,000 of them give birth, more than three-fourths of them for the first time. Teenage pregnancy and parenting are, of course, not new phenomena in the United States, but the face of this problem has changed dramatically in the past thirty years. Most notably, births occurring out of wedlock have risen from less than 30 percent of all teenage births in 1950 to more than 70 percent today. Indeed, only 18 percent of all teenage pregnancies end in the formation of traditional two-parent families.[2]

The increase in the incidence of these births has been accompanied by a steady decline in economic status and a corresponding increase in welfare dependence among teenage parents. More than three-fourths of teenagers giving birth out of wedlock end up on welfare for an average of eight to ten years.[3] Most will be living in poverty ten years after their first child is born.

Teenagers are still children. As a group, those who unintentionally get pregnant and begin parenthood at a young age signal their inability to make decisions that are in their own best interests, the best interests of their children, and the best interests of society. Despite the rapid growth of school- and community-based health and education programs focused on adolescent and reproductive health, more teenagers are having sex at younger ages. And despite greater use of contraception and the availability of more effective means of contraception, the incidence of unprotected sex and the failure rates of contraception remain unacceptably high. As a result, the rate of teenage pregnancy remains unacceptably high.

Teenagers' poor judgment has been compounded by social policies that enable those who bear children in their teenage years to continue to make poor decisions. The federal social safety net provided by AFDC, food stamps, and medicaid has traditionally guaranteed teenage mothers basic economic security. The laissez-faire attitudes in this country toward fathers' responsibilities have enabled fathers of children born to teenage mothers, most of whom are not themselves teenagers, to escape responsibility.[4]

Pregnancies Are Unplanned

The vast majority of the million-plus teenage pregnancies occurring each year are not planned but result from unprotected sex or contraceptive failure. In the words of young mothers who participated in a federal welfare demonstration program: "I didn't plan it, and then again, I kind of knew that it was going to happen because I wasn't like really taking the pills like I was supposed to. I couldn't remember every day to take the pill. And, I still don't." "I really don't want to take time off . . . right now. . . . But, I'm allergic to birth control pills." "My boyfriend thinks [the pills have] something in there killing him."[5]

At the same time that teenagers are becoming sexually active at increasingly younger ages, they are intentionally getting married at increasingly older ages (figure 3-1). These changing goals no doubt contributed to their greater awareness and use of contraceptives. For example, in 1982 only 48 percent of teenagers used contraceptives during their first intercourse, but by 1988 the rate had risen to 65 percent.[6] This increase in contraceptive use had not, however, been sufficient to keep increased sexual activity from raising teenage pregnancy and birthrates.

Figure 3-1. Sexual Activity and Marriage Rates among Teenagers, 1960–93

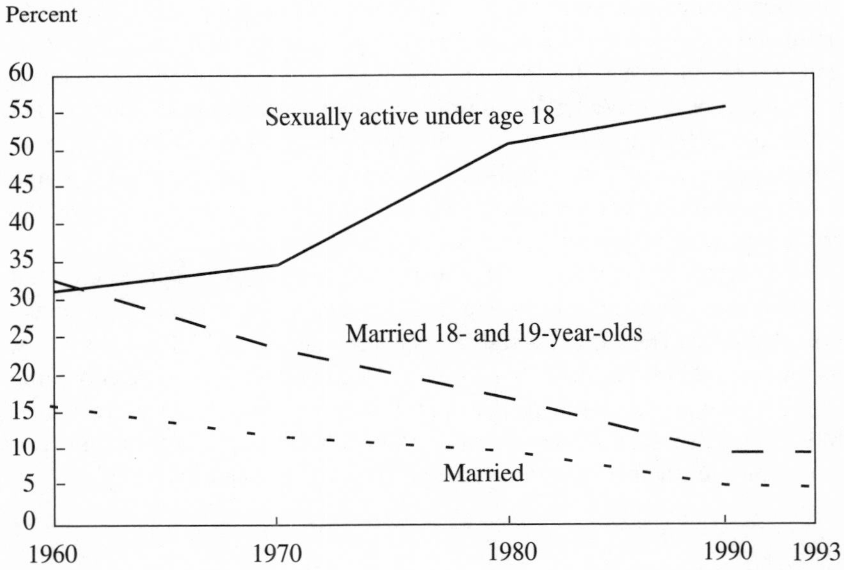

Source: Alan Gutmacher Institute, *Sex and America's Teenagers* (New York, 1994).

The most troubling aspect of the unplanned pregnancies is that more than 40 percent end in abortions, which pose both physical and mental health risks to the teenagers and financial burdens for them, their families, and society. In fact, many teenage mothers have had one or more unplanned pregnancies terminated through abortion before having their first baby.[7]

Dreams and Realities for Teenage Mothers and Their Children

As a group teenage mothers are no less excited about their newborns than are older mothers. And their goals for themselves and their children mirror those of the general population. They want to be good mothers and provide a good life for their children: "I have to get out of here. I can't stand it. No matter where you turn, all you see is this guy and that guy try'n to sell drugs. I don't want my son to grow up with them. Sometimes little boys let other people influence them, and I don't want him to be growing up thinking that that's something tha' he has to do to make money." They want good jobs for themselves: "I think mothers should work. For one thing, your child gets to learn how to be with other children. And they learn to do little things that maybe you don't have time to teach them at home. So I think she should work, even just to help the child out a little." And they want supportive relationships with male partners, although many reject marriage as a short-term goal because they believe that married men can be too controlling or are not stable providers for themselves and their children. "When you're single it's better. They [the men] treat you so much better when you're not married, you know. . . . When you're single, it's honey this and honey that. When you're married, do this, do that."

Most also are adamant that they want no more children in the foreseeable future. As one said, "I just want to get into school and to work. I really don't want to take time off for no more children right now. I'm not ready for it now. When I have my own place, a full-time job, but not right now." Another added, "It's different when you don't know, when you don't have a kid. . . . I know how hard it is with one. How in the world would you make it with two?" Yet teenage mothers fail miserably in achieving these goals. They, their children, and the fathers of their children all suffer from early parenting decisions—the children most of all.

In general, children of teenage mothers exhibit worse health, greater use of medical care, greater poverty, and poorer school performance than their counterparts born to older mothers. Young parenthood itself is responsible for most of these disadvantages. For example, in 1987, 28 percent of former teenage mothers age 21 to 33 were poor compared with 7 percent of the women who had their first baby at age 20 or older. Only 43 percent of this difference is attributable to the fact that the teenage mothers came from more disadvantaged backgrounds.[8]

The troubles for children of teenage mothers begin before birth and continue into adulthood. Even after controlling for differences in backgrounds, the offspring of young teenage mothers have a 50 percent higher probability of having a low birthweight and subsequently having poorer health as compared with those born to women who begin parenting in their early twenties.[9] The consequences of slightly older childbearing are similar in scope, if somewhat less severe. Despite having more health problems, children of teenage mothers, particularly young teenage mothers, get less medical care than if their mother delayed childbearing a few years.[10] They also do much worse in school. They are 50 percent more likely to repeat a grade, perform much worse on standardized tests, and have a much lower rate of school completion.[11]

In part these poor development and educational results may be related to the children's much higher rates of abuse and neglect. There are 110 reported incidents of abuse and neglect per 1,000 families headed by a woman who had her first child before the age of 18, compared with less than half that number among children born to mothers in their young twenties.[12] The results are only marginally better for children whose mothers delay childbearing until 18 or 19 years of age.

Not surprisingly, adolescent childbearing also contributes to the high rate of crime among sons and to the repetition of the cycle of teenage parenting. All else equal, simply being born to a mother younger than 17 rather than 21 increases by 13 percent (from 9.1 to 10.3 percent) the likelihood a male child will end up in prison and increases by 20 percent (from 13 to 16 percent) the probability that a female child will herself become a teenage mother.[13]

Unquestionably, those teenagers who get pregnant tend to have poor life prospects regardless of whether they become teenage parents.[14] Still, the added complications of being a young parent, especially a parent before age 18, further disadvantages these young teenagers in ways that may undermine their efficacy as parents. For example, less than 35 percent of teenagers who begin their families before age 18 ever complete high school, compared with 85 percent of those who delay childbearing. Nearly half of this difference is caused directly by the young teenage parenting. Young teenage mothers also spend 60 percent more time as a single parent, thus shifting a disproportionate share of childrearing responsibility to the mothers and depriving the children of the benefits of two parents in the household.[15]

As a group the fathers of children born to teenage mothers bear little of the cost of adolescent childbearing compared to the mothers.[16] Most are not themselves teenagers when they father children and less than 30 percent of them marry the teenage mothers of their children. The more than 70 percent who are absent fathers pay less than $800 annually for child support. Indeed, only a minority formally acknowledge their fatherhood, and fewer than half of those make regular child support payments.[17]

Spillover Costs for Taxpayers and Society

Unlike many life choices that primarily affect the individual, teenage pregnancy and childbearing affect the whole of society. Society pays for about 400,000 abortions for teenagers each year. It bears an even larger cost of teenage childbearing. One recent study estimated conservatively that childbearing by women under the age of 18 costs nearly $9 billion dollars annually, $7 billion of which is paid directly by the taxpayers.[18] Including the costs of childbearing by 18 and 19 year-olds raises these figures by at least 75 percent. Thus the economic rationale for stronger public policies against teenage pregnancy is clear. And this ignores the intangible gains from minimizing the affront to social values represented by unwed pregnancy and abortion.

Teenage Sex, Pregnancy, and Parenting Behavior

In the past three decades the United States has witnessed trends in teenage behavior that would seem to invite more paternalistic social policies. Before 1970 premarital sex was openly discouraged, and those "found out" by getting pregnant faced social sanctions from their peers, adults in their families, and their communities. At the same time, contraceptives were not readily accessible to teenagers, and those methods available (primarily condoms and foams or jellies) tended to be less effective than many of today's options. Abortions were widely illegal. And public assistance was essentially nonexistent for teenage-parent families. Only 27 percent of teenagers were sexually active before age 18, and only 61 percent were sexually active by age 20.[19] Although teenage pregnancy and birthrates were high by historical standards, the vast majority of the pregnancies occurred among 18 and 19 year olds who gave birth rather than having an abortion and who married the fathers of their children.[20]

In the 1970s there were marked improvements in contraceptive technologies and in the accessibility of contraceptives to young people. Abortions were legalized in 1973, although they were still not easily available in many parts of the country and among lower socioeconomic groups. The rate of teenage sexual activity increased dramatically: most teenagers were becoming sexually active before their eighteenth birthday.[21] At the same time, teenagers increased their rate of contraceptive use, and they more than doubled their rate of abortion, from 19 per 1,000 teenage girls to 43 per 1,000 by the end of the decade. As a result, the teenage birthrate approached its all-time low of about 50 per 1,000 women age 15 to 19, and the age at first marriage continued to edge up, reaching 22 by the end of the decade.

But the rate of births to unwed mothers steadily rose: by 1980 they accounted for 48 percent of all teenage births. The majority of these mothers turned to AFDC for support. This dramatic rise resulted in a steady increase in the number of out-of-wedlock teenage births despite the decline in the overall teenage birthrate.

The Policy Context

During the 1960s AFDC, which had primarily served divorced and widowed women, began primarily serving never-married mothers and their children. The 1970s marked the start of a new wave in social services; public assistance was more widely available and social service providers promoted empowerment among poor women, particularly poor single mothers. In the 1980s social services adopted a deficit model for service planning and delivery in which teenagers were seen as helpless clients in need of additional resources. Income and social support programs expanded their eligibility criteria and generosity, many of them assuming the qualities of entitlement programs. Between 1984 and 1991 funding for family planning services increased by 41 percent, outpacing the growth in the number of clients, which increased by only 31 percent.[22]

The 1980s also witnessed an explosion of programs serving the reproductive health needs of teenagers, often through health clinics located in or near schools, as well as an array of programs to support teenage parents as parents and enable them to continue their education.[23] Many large comprehensive high schools instituted special programs for teenage parents, often with on-site day care for the babies. Throughout the country there was also a rapid increase in the number of community programs to meet the social, health, economic, and educational needs of teenage parents and their children. Initially the programs were supported primarily through private funds. But by the end of the 1980s many were incorporated into state and local welfare programs. Indeed, the Family Support Act of 1988 mandated that states serve teenage parents on AFDC who have not completed high school as a priority group in their Job Opportunities and Basic Skills Training (JOBS) programs.[24]

By the middle of the 1980s teenage pregnancy rates and birthrates had stabilized, but the rate of out-of-wedlock births among teenagers continued to rise and by 1990 had reached 70 percent.[25]

Currently, the United States has entered a period of public policy that psychologists might characterize as codependency. Policies enable teenagers to continue to bear children and suffer few social or economic sanctions. Despite myriad welfare reform initiatives throughout the country, most states still allow teenage parents to qualify for AFDC with only modest reciprocal demands or none. In the Family Support Act, Congress gave states authority to mandate school attendance or serious employment efforts by teenage parents. Yet eight years later most states still had not acted aggressively on this authority.[26] Only a small minority of unwed teenage mothers enforce the establishment paternity and child support payments on the fathers of their babies. In addition, current policies do little to address the high rates of rape and incest that have occurred among pregnant and parenting teenagers, especially those who give birth before age 16.[27] Finally, policies do nothing to hold the schools accountable for their lack of success with pregnant and parenting teenagers, even those states such as Florida, Ohio, and Wisconsin that have "learnfare" programs.

Incentives and Welfare

Nevertheless, conservatives' views that the welfare system itself promotes teenage pregnancy and parenthood have at best weak support, at least within the range of plans states implemented before passage of the Personal Responsibility and Work Opportunity Reconciliation Act of 1996.[28] There is little connection between trends in real welfare benefits and the trends in teenage pregnancy rates and birthrates. Similarly, there is little correlation between states' teenage pregnancy and birthrates and the generosity of their welfare benefits. Instead, during periods when benefits have eroded, the rates have tended to increase and vice versa.[29]

Nor are changes in welfare incentives a clear answer to preventing teenage pregnancies. More than twenty states have implemented family caps, which end the practice of increasing welfare benefits if families have additional children. In taking this action states are sending a clear message that it is not acceptable for people to have children they cannot support. States are not, however, explicitly imposing penalties or social sanctions on those who bear additional children while on welfare. The states thus are not being truly paternalistic. Study findings are consistent with the fact that family caps impose only modest financial penalties and social sanctions for having more children while on welfare. The early results from the New Jersey Fed Wed program, begun in 1994, show little or no effect on the fertility of welfare recipients (adults and teenagers together) compared with that of control groups.[30]

Pregnancy Prevention Efforts

In the past decade many program and policy initiatives have sought to encourage teenagers to delay sexual activity and prevent unplanned pregnancies. Most of the more than $600 million in annual expenditures for fertility control flow through a few national programs: medicaid, the Title X Family Planning program, the Maternal and Child Health Services Block Grant, and the Social Services Block Grant. Hundreds of other programs throughout the country also seek to reduce the incidence of teenage pregnancy. These include programs with a primary goal of promoting abstinence, "safe sex," or both. They also include programs with a much broader focus on the social and educational needs of particular groups of at-risk and disadvantaged youth, including those who have dropped out of school or who are likely to do so and those who live in low-income families and in poor neighborhoods. Finally, the programs include school-based initiatives to provide sex education and adolescent health services.

Although the efforts have been many and scholarly studies are replete with descriptions, the programs have produced few answers as to how to reduce the incidence of teenage childbearing or improve outcomes for teenage mothers and their children. The base for judging the efficacy of various intervention strategies is a relatively small number of demonstration and community service programs. Still, the results suggest that the most successful programs have been those that were most directive or authoritative and sent the clearest messages about right and wrong.

National Programs Providing Family Planning Services

The millions of dollars of federal money spent on family planning and reproductive health has lowered rates of infant and neonatal death, decreased fertility rates among low-income women at high risk of tightly spaced births, and reduced the incidence of low birthweight babies.[31] Although there is no evidence that these funds have reduced teenage pregnancy rates, they may reduce the teenage birthrates by increasing the rates of abortion.[32] The research also shows that sexually active teenagers are somewhat less likely to use contraceptives at their first intercourse if they live in a community with relatively high welfare benefits, perhaps reflecting the greater likelihood that areas with such benefits also may offer teenagers greater access to abortions.[33]

Demonstration and Service Programs

The limited research on demonstration and service programs covers strategies ranging from promoting abstinence to providing full-service adolescent health education (with abstinence training) in conjunction with social and health services, sometimes including dispensing of contraceptives and counseling about options (table 3A-1). The most promising prevention programs are clear about which values they promote. They also offer ways to resist peer pressure to engage in sex and teach youths how to use contraceptives effectively after they become sexually active. Simply promoting abstinence does not seem especially effective, at least judging from current research. Neither Project Taking Charge, which combined abstinence education and vocational education, nor the Success Express school- and community-based abstinence initiative successfully promoted abstinence among middle school students.[34]

Programs providing only sex education, without the focus on abstinence (Teenage Talk, Group Cognitive Behavior Curriculum, and Facts and Feelings, for example) have in some cases increased knowledge of contraceptive options and contraceptive use. But they have not succeeded in delaying the onset of sexual activity.[35] But programs that combine values training with sex education have shown some success. For example, the Teenage Services Program based on the Postponing Sexual Involvement model, which combines abstinence training with sex education and contraceptive education, has shown evidence of delaying the onset of sexual activity among younger teenagers and increasing contraceptive use among those who are sexually active.[36]

Programs that combine education and family planning services through school- or community-based health clinics generally have not been effective in reducing teenage pregnancy and birthrates. Research has highlighted only a few programs with documented promise for reducing sexual activity rates, increasing contraceptive use among those who are sexually active, and reducing overall pregnancy rates. A recent review of research on school-based and school-linked health services concluded, "To date, the published literature does not provide any good evidence indicating whether programs focusing only upon abstinence either do or do not delay the onset of intercourse or reduce the frequency of intercourse . . . [or whether] school-based or school-linked reproductive health services, either by themselves or in addition to education programs, significantly decrease pregnancy or birthrates."[37]

Only one of the programs studied, the Self-Center, a full-service health education and counseling program offered through a community-based, school-linked health clinic, showed signs of delaying sexual involvement and improving contraceptive use.[38] It also appears that compared with the other program models, this one placed greater emphasis on values and used a more directive approach in helping teenagers make wiser choices.

The Quantum Opportunities program, a mentoring and enrichment program for at-risk high school students that emphasizes values and opportunities associated with staying and doing well in school, appears to have had dramatic effects on the teenage pregnancy rate in one of its four sites, a result that will be reexamined in a larger-scale replication study.[39] This successful site also appeared to be the most structured and paternalistic, providing greater levels of contact between program staff and students, as well as the most structured peer and mentor support components. In contrast, programs such as the Summer Training and Education program, which combined family planning education with summer employment in a voluntary and highly supportive setting, promoted improved knowledge about contraception but have not affected pregnancy and birth outcomes among teenagers.[40]

There is some promise that programs taking a more holistic approach to dealing with the social, economic, and educational needs of teenagers from at-risk families will reduce their pregnancy rates and birthrates. One of the best known, the Children's Aid Society Teenage Pregnancy Primary Prevention program in New York, offers strong reproductive health education and counseling in the context of comprehensively addressing the needs of teenagers from disadvantaged backgrounds. The program not only attempts to deal with the economic and social environments of the youths, but it also devotes considerable effort to building strong social values and decisionmaking skills that emphasize long-range goals. Although a descriptive assessment of program outcomes is encouraging, there has not yet been a rigorous evaluation of its effectiveness in preventing teenage pregnancy and parenting.[41]

Programs for Teenage Parents

There have been rigorous tests of only a few programs that target teenagers who already are mothers by simultaneously attempting to reduce the incidence of repeat pregnancies, increase the likelihood of high school completion and moving into higher education, and promote employment. After more than a decade of research, observers have discovered no magic formula. None of the eight methodologically sound evaluations of such programs covered in this review points to a model program for future policies.[42] But together these studies enrich our understanding of the problems and suggest the potential of directive programs.

These eight programs represent four strategies for addressing the needs of teenage parents, albeit with overlapping features (table 3A-2). Two are youth employment and training programs that served, but did not specifically target, significant numbers of teenage parents.

—JOBSTART. This thirteen-site demonstration of education, vocational training, and support services for disadvantaged young school dropouts operated between 1985 and 1988. During this time it served about 2,000 youths between the ages of 17 and 21. About one-fourth were teenage parents. The program was evaluated using an experimental design.[43]

—Job Corps. A federally funded program offering intensive education, training, and social services to at-risk 16- to 22-year-old school dropouts from disadvantaged backgrounds. Most Job Corps services are provided in residential centers. Job Corps centers were the focus of the most recent completed evaluation of the program conducted in the late 1970s and early 1980s. Only a small percentage of corps members (but relatively large absolute numbers) were teenage parents. The subsample of young parents for the evaluation consisted of 1,008 young women. The evaluators used a matched comparison sample study design.[44]

Two programs were comprehensive education and training programs targeted on teenage parents exclusively.

—New Chance. This national demonstration of small-scale, intensive, and comprehensive service programs offered education, training, and social support services for teenage parents on welfare who had dropped out of school. Programs operated in sixteen locations in ten states between 1989 and 1992 offering services to about 1,400 young mothers for up to eighteen months. The evaluation used an experimental design.[45]

—Project Redirection. This was a four-site demonstration of comprehensive services for parents age 17 or younger. The programs, which served about 300 young mothers between 1980 and 1981, were operated by community-based organizations offering education, training, mentoring, job placement, child care, family planning, and parenting training. The evaluation used a comparison-site design.[46]

Two of the programs were welfare-based education and employment programs directing mandatory education and job preparation services to teenage parent welfare recipients.

—Ohio Learning, Earning and Parenting (LEAP). This ongoing program is designed to keep teenage parent welfare recipients in school through a system of financial incentives and penalties. Some counties offer special support services to facilitate staying in school, but most provide only minimal case management services. LEAP has been evaluated using an experimental design.[47]

—Teenage Parent Welfare Demonstration. This was a large-scale field test of a change in welfare programs for first-time teenage parents. The programs required teenagers to participate in self-sufficiency-oriented activities to receive the maximum welfare grant. They also provided them with case management as well as education, training, employment, and social support services. More than 3,000 young mothers received services between 1987 and early 1991. The programs were evaluated using an experimental design.[48]

Finally, two programs focused on health and were targeted at first-time parents, many of whom were teenagers.

—Teenage Parent Health Care Program. This was an intensive health-focused intervention for mothers younger than 17 and their infants. It provided intensive case management by trained social workers for up to eighteen months after delivery. The program served about 120 mothers and infants in the late 1980s. The demonstration was evaluated using an experimental design.[49]

—Elmira Nurse Home Visiting Program. This was a demonstration of nurse home visitation services for socially disadvantaged women bearing their first child. The program served 400 women, 47 percent of whom were teenagers. It was evaluated using an experimental design.[50]

These programs ranged in cost from a few dollars per person per service month (Ohio LEAP) to more than $1,500 per service month (New Chance) (table 3A-2). They not only included programs serving very small portions of the teenage parent population (Job Start, Job Corps, New Chance, Project Redirection, and the two health-focused interventions), but also those serving the universe of teenage mothers going onto welfare (Ohio LEAP and the Teenage Parent Welfare Demonstration).

The Need for Mandatoriness

For years, the prevailing view among policymakers and social service deliverers alike was to prefer voluntary programs. The idea was that public resources should be reserved for the "most motivated," who were also presumed to benefit most. But today the trend is to mandate participation. This shift in emphasis arose in part from the frustration of taxpayers who were increasingly concerned about rising welfare expenditures and in part from the ineffectiveness of unstructured programs. These forces led to the first serious testing of paternalistic policies that establish general expectations: for example, that all welfare recipients should participate in work-oriented effort or that teenage parents who have not completed high school should attend school full-time despite their parenting responsibilities.

The evidence from these trials suggests that levying such expectations is constructive for teenage mothers and their children. First, experience from the two major field tests of mandatory programs for teenage parents, the Teenage Parent Welfare Demonstration and Ohio's LEAP, demonstrates clearly that most teenage parents will not participate voluntarily in any type of education or training program. For example, of the 89 percent of recipients who participated as required in the Teenage Parent Welfare Demonstration, just under half did so after they received their first notice from the welfare department informing them of their obligation to report to the program. Another 42 percent participated after the notification by the welfare department that their grants were about to be cut by 50 percent on average if they did not report. Finally, about 7 percent participated only after their welfare grants had been reduced.[51]

Similar experience with front-end participation occurred in Ohio's LEAP program, which offered a $62 a month bonus if the recipient complied with school attendance and performance standards, and a $62 a month penalty if she did not (mediocre performance meant no adjustment). Less than 10 percent of the teenagers in Ohio's LEAP program were unaffected by the policy, and more than half of the teenagers received at least one sanction. Indeed, the program's effects were large and consistently significant only in the site that made the greatest use of sanctions (68 percent of all teenagers versus only 56 percent in the other sites).[52]

In contrast, New Chance, which offered many more services but in which participation was voluntary, had enormous difficulty filling small programs even in areas that had large numbers of teenagers giving birth monthly. Participation patterns among the volunteers in these programs may look similar to those of the Teenage Parent Welfare Demonstration and the other more mandatory programs, with an average participation level of 4 hours a week (300 hours over eighteen months).[53] But the mandatory programs achieved this level for a much greater share of those eligible.[54]

Program Effects

These programs differ widely in the teenage parents they target, program size, intensity and mix of services, setting, and cost. Three larger demonstrations—New Chance, Ohio's LEAP, and the Teenage Parent Welfare Demonstration—allow the examination of variations in effectiveness in the same program across sites and the features that might explain them.

EMPLOYMENT-RELATED OUTCOMES. Employment-related outcomes for teenage-parent populations served by these programs tended to be poor, whether or not the teenagers participated in the programs. Between one-fifth and one-third of participants engaged in any type of job training after enrolling in the programs. Between 20 and 60 percent of the young mothers were employed at some time following their program experience (the higher rates were in sites with longer follow-ups). Average earnings were less than $300 a month and were as low as $76 a month in one demonstration (New Chance), largely because of the low employment rates and part-time nature of the jobs. Not surprisingly, given the alternative of welfare support, wages among those employed tended to average $5 to $6 an hour.

The seven programs for which employment-related outcomes were measured show at best modest results, and the effects varied considerably across programs (table 3-1). In three of the four programs—New Chance, Project Redirection, and the Teenage Parent Welfare Demonstration—that

Table 3-1. Estimated Employment-Related Outcomes of Seven Welfare Programs

Percent of control/comparison group mean unless otherwise specified

Program	*Job training*	*Employment*	*Monthly earnings (1995 dollars)*
Estimated program impact			
Job Start	n.a.	0.4	7.5
Job Corps	n.a.	–40.5[a]	–44.4[a]
New Chance	48.0[a]	–4.9	–33.4
Ohio Learnfare	–9.3	20.0[b]	7.6
Project Redirection	12.4	15.1	51.5[b]
Teenage Parent Welfare Demonstration	18.6[a]	11.8[a]	20.0[a]
Elmira Nurse Home Visiting Program	n.a.	46.8	n.a.
Participant group mean			
Job Start	n.a.	49.1	260
Job Corps	n.a.	40.0[c]	448
New Chance	0.3	42.6	85
Ohio Learnfare	17.5	33.2	143
Project Redirection	21.8	60.1	436
Teenage Parent Welfare Demonstration	26.8	48.2	108
Elmira Nurse Home Visiting	n.a.	21.0[d]	n.a.

Sources: See appendix table 3A-1. Data for the Job Start evaluation pertain to four years after sample enrollment; for Job Corps to four years after enrollment; for New Chance to eighteen months after enrollment; for Ohio Learnfare to three years after enrollment; for Project Redirection to five years after enrollment; for the Teenage Parent Welfare Demonstration to two years after enrollment; for the Teenage Parent Health Care Demonstration to eighteen months after enrollment; and for the Elmira Nurse Home Visiting Demonstration to forty-six months after enrollment.

n.a. Not available.

a. Statistically significant at the 5 percent level.

b. Statistically significant at the 10 percent level.

c. Percent of weeks.

d. Percent of months.

provided job training services and evaluated participants' job skills, training outcomes showed some evidence of increased training rates among participants relative to controls. The gains were especially large and statistically significant for New Chance and the Teenage Parent Welfare Demonstration (48 and 19 percent higher rates of training, respectively, among participants relative to controls). Only participants in Ohio LEAP had lower rates than those in a control group, presumably because of their younger ages and the emphasis on their attending school.

The gains in job training in Project Redirection and the Teenage Parent Welfare Demonstration were accompanied by net increases in employment and earnings. Ohio LEAP also led to modest (20 percent) increases in employment and, although not statistically significant, the point estimate of the employment increase for the Elmira Nurse Home Visiting Program is large (47 percent over forty-six months). None of the remaining three programs led to increases in employment. Indeed, participation in Job Corps led to large (40 to 44 percent), statistically significant reductions in employment and earnings.[55]

EDUCATION-RELATED OUTCOMES. In general the programs were successful in promoting increased school attendance and even degree attainment. All except the two health-focused ones and Job Corps increased high school enrollment. New Chance increased enrollment by 85 percent, from 18 to 33 percent of possible school weeks over an eighteen-month follow-up period (table 3-2).[56]

Four of the programs, including Job Corps, significantly increased the percentage who earned a general educational development certificate or a high school diploma, but mainly a GED. Interestingly, the increase in school enrollment among participants in Ohio's Learnfare did not translate into higher rates of school completion or GED attainment three years after enrollment. And the increased enrollment and degree attainment in New Chance and the Teenage Parent Welfare Demonstration did not translate into higher measured basic skills. This finding is consistent with the results of California's welfare JOBS program, Greater Avenues for Independence, in which there was no correspondence between effects on GED attainment and increased measured basic skills. The GAIN results also showed no correspondence between earnings gains and either GED attainment or measured basic skills.[57]

FERTILITY OUTCOMES. Rates of repeat pregnancies soon after a first birth are very high among teenage parents, especially those on welfare. Recognizing that additional pregnancies and births would interfere with education and employment goals, all programs except the two focused on youth employment devoted considerable resources to helping the young mothers

Table 3-2. Estimated Education-Related Outcomes of Seven Welfare Programs

Percent of control/comparison group mean unless otherwise specified

Program	*High school enroll-ment*	*Received diploma/ GED*	*Received GED*	*Measured basic skills*
Estimated program impact				
Job Start	n.a.	57.3[a]	67.1[a]	n.a.
Job Corps	–80.3[a, b]	666.7[a]	n.a.	n.a.
New Chance	84.9[a]	43.7[a]	74.9[a]	< 0.1
Ohio Learnfare	15.5[a, c]	6.6	32.1	n.a.
Project Redirection	16.7	0.1	n.a.	n.a.
Teenage Parent Welfare Demonstration	42.0[d]	4.0[e]	19.2	< 0.1
Teenage Parent Health Care	< –0.1	n.a.	n.a.	n.a.
Elmira Nurse Home Visiting	–45.2[d]	n.a.	n.a.	n.a.
Participant group mean				
Job Start	n.a.	42.0	39.1	n.a.
Job Corps	6.6[f]	6.3[f]	n.a.	n.a.
New Chance	33.0[f]	43.1	36.8	7.8
Ohio Learnfare	67.4	34.0	11.1	n.a.
Project Redirection	18.6	48.3	n.a.	n.a.
Teenage Parent Welfare Demonstration	41.6	48.4	5.7	8.1[g]
Teenage Parent Health Care	55.6	n.a.	n.a.	n.a.
Elmira Nurse Home Visiting	62.0[d]	n.a.	n.a.	n.a.

Sources: See table 3-1.
n.a. Not available.
a. Statistically significant at the 5 percent level.
b. Months 0–6 after enrollment.
c. Continued through tenth month postpartum.
d. Measured in grade equivalent scores.
e. Statistically significant at the 10 percent level.
f. Percent of time.
g. Measured 18 months after enrollment.

control their fertility by offering family planning services and counseling as part of the basic intervention.

Still, repeat pregnancy rates were higher than 50 percent in all but one of the programs that measured them. In the Teenage Parent Health Care

Demonstration the rate was 28 percent over eighteen months. Pregnancy rates increased significantly among participants in the Job Start and the New Chance demonstrations relative to rates among those in control groups (by 13 and 8 percent, respectively). Only the two health-focused programs were successful in reducing the repeat pregnancy rates (table 3-3). The Teenage Parent Health Care Demonstration reduced the repeat pregnancy rate by an estimated 57 percent, and the Elmira Home Visiting Demonstration reduced the rate by 43 percent. One theory about the greater effectiveness of these programs is that nurses are trained to follow strict service delivery protocols and to be much more direct than welfare caseworkers in their dealings with clients. The nurse home visitors in these programs may simply have been more willing to tell clients to use birth control and to follow up to ensure they were not only using contraceptives but using them correctly.

For New Chance participants the abortion rate also increased sufficiently to offset the higher pregnancy rate, suggesting that the program may have empowered the young mothers to engage in unprotected sex without the threat of an unplanned birth (table 3-3). In contrast, in Project Redirection and the Teenage Parent Welfare Demonstration, the abortion rate declined sufficiently to show increases in the birthrates among program participants, even though the repeat pregnancy rates had not increased significantly. For the Teenage Parent Welfare Demonstration at least, this result may stem from the program's overt policy against abortion counseling. Participants in Ohio LEAP had higher birthrates than control group counterparts, but the difference was not statistically significant.

Variations in Programs and Effects

One of the most troubling findings from this review of the evidence on program effectiveness is that the results vary significantly among sites participating in the same demonstration, supposedly implementing the same model, and generally having access to similar levels of demonstration or program resources. The pattern of site differences in three of the demonstrations suggests that a key to effectiveness in delaying repeat pregnancies is delivering a consistent message about expectations for the teenagers. The most striking example was in New Chance, where average expenditures for services ranged from $17,000 per participant to $4,400, even though, theoretically, sites had access to similar levels of resources. The impact estimates are even more variable, with little to no correlation between program costs and efficacy. At the other extreme the Teenage Parent Welfare Dem-

Table 3-3. Estimated Fertility-Related Outcomes of Seven Welfare Programs

Percent of control/comparison group mean

Program	*Pregnancies*	*Abortions*	*Births*
Estimated program impact			
Job Start	12.7[a]	n.a.	17.1[a]
New Chance	7.5[b]	34.2[a]	8.4
Ohio Learnfare	n.a.	n.a.	4.3
Project Redirection	n.a.	–41.5[b]	20.0[a]
Teenage Parent Welfare Demonstration	0.1	–16.9	6.6[b]
Teenage Parent Health Care	–57.1[a]	n.a.	n.a.
Elmira Nurse Home Visiting	–43.1[a]	n.a.	n.a.
Participant group mean			
Job Start	76.1	n.a.	67.8
New Chance	57.0	14.9	28.4
Ohio Learnfare	n.a.	n.a.	26.7
Project Redirection	3.3	0.3	2.4
Teenage Parent Welfare Demonstration	1.0	0.16	0.64
Teenage Parent Health Care	28.0	n.a.	n.a.
Elmira Nurse Home Visiting	0.7	n.a.	n.a.

Sources: See table 3-1.
n.a. Not available.
a. Statistically significant at the 5 percent level.
b. Statistically significant at the 10 percent level.

onstration had a more consistent and prescriptive model of services, lower cost and cost variance, and generally qualitatively similar results across sites.

New Chance

Schooling results for New Chance participants generally were positive. However, estimates range from no effect in Detroit to more than a 24 percentage point increase in GED or high school diploma attainment in Inglewood, Minneapolis, Pittsburgh, and San Jose. The results of the demonstration are much more mixed, however, if judged by effects on the fertility and earnings of the young mothers. Of the sixteen sites, Denver and Salem increased earnings or reduced the incidence of repeat pregnancies or both. The programs in Allentown, Detroit, and Portland experienced large increases in the rates of repeat pregnancies or significant reductions in earnings or both. San Jose had large reductions in the rate of repeat pregnancies but witnessed large earnings losses.

Explanations for these variations range from the way programs were implemented to how they were targeted. For example, the San Jose program, which increased school completion rates and reduced pregnancy rates but decreased earnings, emphasized education for non–high school graduates in connection with the California welfare JOBS program (GAIN). Participants were enrolled in both New Chance and GAIN.[58] As a result, the young mothers had access to welfare services and also may have had stronger incentives to participate in New Chance and the GAIN education services, thus delaying employment.

The Denver program that increased school completion and earnings was tightly linked to the local job training program operating under the Job Training Partnership Act, which may account for its stronger education and employment focus. The JTPA program in Denver also seemed to have fairly strict attendance policies.

Both the Denver and the San Jose programs had more intensive family planning components than most others, which possibly accounts for their greater effectiveness in preventing pregnancy. New Chance general program guidelines called for one group session each month on family planning, but the Denver program scheduled four each month and the San Jose program two.[59]

Weak implementation and a lack of emphasis on values training are likely explanations for the three sites that performed especially poorly. One of the sites moved a long distance from its client population midway through the demonstration period. In addition, these programs tended to celebrate rather than to sanction pregnancies and births. Many seem to have emphasized teenage empowerment without the complement of strong social values training.

Ohio's LEAP

In most counties the learnfare policy consisted simply of monetary incentives and penalties. In Cleveland and Cleveland East, however, financial incentives were complemented with case management and social support services, much like those offered in the Teenage Parent Welfare Demonstration. All of the positive results of LEAP were concentrated in Cleveland and Cleveland East. None of the sites that simply modified the benefit policy to account for teenage parents' school attendance and performance resulted in measurable changes in behavior. This suggests that the paternalistic actions of case managers, who reinforced the signals sent by the change in benefit policy, were essential to improving the behavior of the teenagers.

The Teenage Parent Welfare Demonstration

Results of the Teenage Parent Welfare Demonstration were somewhat more consistant across sites than were those of New Chance or LEAP. All of the sites showed modest estimated increases in employment and earnings and reductions in welfare benefits.[60] None had significant effects on pregnancy rates, and the effects on educational attainment were positive for two sites and negative for the third.

Likely explanations for the greater consistency relative to the New Chance programs are the clear participation requirements and program accountability. The federal project staff held the programs accountable for keeping young mothers in the demonstration actively engaged in some activity pursuant to employment (school, work, job training, or an activity preparatory to one of these). If a young mother chronically failed to meet this obligation, program staff were required to issue a request for a reduction of more than $150 a month in her welfare grant. The staff members were strongly motivated to work with the clients to avoid the imposition of sanctions; the clients were motivated to maintain their participation for similar reasons.[61]

Program Effects and Levels of Coercion

The Teenage Parent Welfare Demonstration offers a unique look at how applying different levels of enforcement of the program's participation requirements might affect its effectiveness. Activity rates differed somewhat among the demonstration participants who enrolled under varying degrees of coercion. Those coming in voluntarily were active 37 percent of the following two years. Those coming in after being threatened with sanctions were active 32 percent of the time. Those coming in only after receiving a financial sanction were active 29 percent of the time.

Yet from a policy perspective, what is important is whether the program was differentially effective for those who came in more or less voluntarily. The effects of the program were roughly similar for all groups of participants, regardless of the level of coercion needed to get them in (table 3-4). Where there were differences in effects, those who were least likely to come into the program on their own tended to do relatively better than those requiring less coercion.[62] Teenagers who came into the program only after being sanctioned had employment rates two years later that were more than twice those of their control group counterparts. Those who came in

Table 3-4. Estimated Effects of the Teenage Parent Welfare Demonstration, by Level of Encouragement to Enroll in Program

Percent unless otherwise specified

	Level of encouragement		
Outcome	*Routine call-in*	*Follow-up with no sanction*	*Sanction*
Estimated effects of the new welfare regime			
Time active	7.6[a]	6.4[b]	6.1[c]
Employed month 24	6.9[a]	6.2[b]	38.1[c]
Monthly earnings[d]	24.6[a]	25.8[e]	31.0[f]
AFDC benefits month 24[d]	−16.0[a]	−16.0[e]	−20.9[c]
Repeat pregnancy, all sites	5.1	2.5	. . .
Repeat pregnancy, Camden	−14.6[b]	3.0	. . .
Participant group means			
Time active	37.1	32.2	28.7
Employed month 24	40.8	35.8	62.5
Monthly earnings[d]	176	158	131
AFDC benefits month 24[d]	302	306	312
Repeat pregnancy, all sites	67.1	74.6	. . .
Repeat pregnancy, Camden	77.4	77.5	. . .
Number in sample	2,637	2,258	380

Source: Follow-up surveys administered an average of 28 months after sample intake.

a. Statistically significant at the 10 percent level, two-tailed test.

b. Statistically significant at the 5 percent level, two-tailed test.

c. The difference for the routine call-in and sanction groups combined is statistically significant at the 5 percent level.

d. 1995 dollars.

e. The difference is nearly statistically significant at the 10 percent level.

f. The difference for the routine call-in and sanction groups combined is statistically significant at the 10 percent level.

under less coercion experienced much more modest gains. The program achieved beneficial effects for many more clients than it would have had it been less demanding.

A part of the explanation for the comparable success rates across groups is the effect of participation mandates on operational practice. The sanction policy altered significantly the accountability of the case managers to the clients and, consequently, their attention to the clients' needs.[63] Case managers were accountable for helping all the young mothers meet their participation requirements. Failing to help meant that they might have to request a grant reduction for the mother. Although at first the caseworkers considered the policy punitive and attempted to ignore it, they quickly came to appreciate its power in gaining access to the mothers and creating clear expectations for them.

The clients had not generally known such consistency in message and expectations in any part of their lives, and they responded well. They reported that they considered the participation requirements fair, particularly since case managers and support services were available to assist them in overcoming real and perceived barriers. But for a large portion of them to comply with the requirements, they first needed to be convinced that the stated consequences of noncooperation were real.

> The first time they sent me a letter, I looked at it and threw it away. The second time, I looked at it and threw it away again. And then they cut my check, and I said, "uh, oh, I'd better go." I was like, "Oh, my goodness, these people really mean business. And I'd better go down there and see what this is all about."
>
> At first I didn't go. They used to send me letters and call me. I still wouldn't go. And then they sent this man [a case manager] out to my house. And I was like, I'll go and see what it is all about. Then the first time I went I didn't like it because they would ask me little personal questions. Then after I did that I never came back, and they came out to my house again and called. "Could you please come to the program." And I finally went, and then after that I went and I liked it then. I really liked it then.

Program participation requirements seem, however, to have been generally ineffective in helping to prevent repeat pregnancies and births. The program reduced rates of pregnancies and births in one site, had no effect in a second, and increased rates in the third. In considering the outcomes according to the extent of voluntarism among the participants, the researchers found that in the more successful site the program had large deterrent effects among those who responded on first call-in, but not among those requiring more coercive efforts to enter the program. Yet in the site where pregnancy rates increased among the program group relative to a no-service control group, the adverse effects were concentrated among those who came into the program voluntarily. Program staff suggested the following possible explanation for the perverse results.

> Our key to family planning was case manager counseling to reinforce the information presented in the up-front workshops. Case managers generally focused their attention on the "difficult, less compliant" cases. Their emphasis with the more voluntary participants was on building independence and on encouraging the mothers whom they judged to be least likely to have a repeat pregnancy to take charge of their lives and strive for independence. We more or less expected them to be compliant and follow the family planning advice provided in the workshops. We paid much more attention to reinforcing the messages of the workshops with the less cooperative clients and those who had exhibited less compliant behavior in the past.

After learning of these results the program staff realized that family planning needed to be emphasized with all participants. This is consistent with the fact that the more successful site offered a richer, six-week family planning workshop for all clients and had smaller overall caseloads, thus permitting staff to provide relatively intensive case management for all clients, regardless of the extent of voluntarism in participation.

Discussion and Conclusion

Now more than ever, the United States needs to consider much more paternalistic policies to address the problems of teenage pregnancy and parenting. At a political level the policies are essential to maintain public support for services. Taxpayers are simply no longer willing to provide unconditional assistance to the poor and disadvantaged. More important, however, paternalistic policies seem to offer the best hope to deter teenage pregnancy and thereby protect teenagers and their children from increasingly restrictive welfare policies.

The rich array of social support services available to teenage parents in the past is fast disappearing. The future will have more limited economic support, which may not include cash assistance particularly for young teenage mothers. Schools are becoming less willing to provide special services for teenage parents. Health care services are increasingly being offered to poor families through more paternalistic managed care systems. And under the current welfare reform policies, there will be greater competition for the already scarce community services that in the past have helped teenage parents cope.[64]

The silver lining in the current wave of welfare reforms is that this may be the setting in which, out of necessity, we discover more successful policies for reducing teenage pregnancy. Among the reasons for optimism are, first, there is now scientific evidence that the consequences of teenage pregnancy and childbirth are at odds with the long-run goals of the teenagers themselves and with the short- and long-run welfare of the nation. The teenagers' decisions are based, at best, on calculations of the likely benefits and rewards of sex or childbearing that are too short term. Second, experience with both prevention and social service programs suggests that the more paternalistic programs tend to outperform programs aimed at empowerment. Or, put another way, the clearer a program is about the behavioral response it expects and will reward, the more likely it will succeed. Third, clarity of expectations, boundaries, and consistency are elements of successful policies and also qualities that build social competence and economic independence in adolescents and young adults.[65]

In designing policies we should keep in mind that marginal changes in economic incentives will have little or no effect on either teenage pregnancy rates or birthrates; that simple programs teaching how babies are made, preaching abstinence, or providing universal access to contraceptives will not appreciably lower the teenage pregnancy rate; that teenage parents most in need of assistance are unlikely to walk into a volunteer program in search of help; and that full-service programs alone will not significantly improve outcomes for them.

The evidence suggests that future policies and programs should emphasize multipronged strategies that are much more paternalistic, strategies that emphasize prevention, establish behavioral expectations not unlike those expected of adult parents, and propound clear consequences for not fulfilling the behavioral expectations.

Table 3A-1. Selected Programs Aimed at Teenage Pregnancy Prevention, by Primary Focus of Intervention

Program focus and project	*Setting*	*Study design*	*Duration of intervention*	*Sample size*	*Program effects*
Abstinence programs					
Project Taking Charge (7th graders and their parents)	2-site, school-based program	Experimental design (randomly selected classrooms)	6-week program	91	No change in values or the likelihood of being sexually active after six months
Success Express (middle schoolers)	10-site school and community-based program	Quasi-experimental design (pretest-posttest)	6-week program	848	Effects on sexual activity ambiguous
Sex education					
Facts and Feelings (7th and 8th graders)	2 urban school districts and 2 rural counties in Utah	Experimental design	6-unit video curriculum	548	No effects on sexual intentions or behaviors after 12 months
Teen Talk (13–19-year-olds)	7-site community prevention program in Calif. and Texas	Experimental design	8–12 hour curriculum	1,288	No significant effect on teenage pregnancies. Increased knowledge of contraception options
Group Cognitive Behavior Curriculum (14–18-year-olds)	Community health center in Minn.	Experimental design	8 two-hour sessions	107	Lower rates of unprotected sex among males. Results decayed over 1-year follow-up for males

Sex education, abstinence, and safe sex					
Postponing Sexual Involvement (8th graders)	School-based program in Georgia	Quasi-experimental design (comparison schools)	10 classes	536	Decreased pregnancy rates by 12th grade. Delay in onset of sexual activity
Reducing the Risk (9th and 10th graders)	13 high schools in Calif.	Quasi-experimental design (comparison classrooms)	3 weeks, 15 classes	758	No effect on pregnancy rates
Education and family planning services					
Self-Center Program (middle and high school students)	2 schools and community health clinic in Md.	Quasi-experimental design (comparison schools)	Up to 3 years	3,944	Decrease in pregnancy rates among older teens. Increase in contraceptive use. Delay in becoming sexually active
School-Based Health Clinics (high school students)	Schools in 6 states	Comparison schools and before and after comparison of school-level outcomes	Ongoing	7,033	No change in pregnancy rates. No change in rates of sexual activity or contraceptive use
St. Paul School-Based Health Clinics (high school students)	6 schools in St. Paul	Before and after comparison of school-level outcomes	Ongoing	. . .	No evidence of effect of clinics on pregnancy and birth rates

Table 3A-1 (*continued*)

Program focus and project	*Setting*	*Study design*	*Duration of intervention*	*Sample size*	*Program effects*
Employment and education programs with prevention services					
Summer training and education (14–15-year-olds)	5 communities	Experimental design	Summer	4,800	No effects on pregnancy rates. Increased rates of reported use of contraceptives
Quantum Opportunities Program (9th graders)	4 communities	Experimental design	4 years	216	Decrease in pregnancy rates in one of the four cities

Source: Table draws on program summaries in Brown and Eisenberg (1995) and Moore, Sugland, Blumenthal et al. (1995), as well as primary information sources reported in table 3A-3.

Table 3A-2. Selected Programs Serving Teenage Parents

Program	*Setting*	*Cost (1995 dollars)*	*Study design*	*Sample size*
Youth employment and training programs				
Job Start	13 community-based organizations, vocational schools, and Job Corps programs	$1,073 a month (5.9 months)	Random assignment	508[a]
Job Corps	78 Job Corps centers	$1,256 a month	Matched comparison sample	1,008[a]
Comprehensive education and training programs for teenage parents				
New Chance	16 community-based organizations, PICS, and schools	$1,706 a month (6 months)	Random assignment	2,088
Project Redirection	4 community-based organizations	$475 a month	Comparison sites	277
Welfare-based education and training programs				
Ohio LEAP	County welfare program	$47.00 per eligibility month	Random assignment	4,225
Teen Parent Welfare Demonstration	Welfare offices in 3 cities	$244 a month (9 months a year)	Random assignment	5,297
Health-focused programs				
Teenage Parent Health Care Program	Urban community health center	n.a. (probably high)	Random assignment	243
Elmira Nurse Home Visiting Program	Rural community health center	n.a. (probably high)	Random assignment	51[a]

Source: See table 3A-3. Data for the Job Start evaluation pertain to four years after sample enrollment; for Job Corps to four years after enrollment; for New Chance to 18 months after enrollment; for Project Redirection to five years after enrollment; for Ohio Learnfare to three years after enrollment; for the Teen Parent Welfare Demonstration to two years after enrollment; for the Teen Parent Health Care Demonstration to 18 months after enrollment; and for the Elmira Nurse Home Visiting Demonstration to 46 months after enrollment.

n.a. Not available.

a. Teenage mother subsample.

Table 3A-3. Sources of Evaluation Data, Impact Estimates, and Costs

Program	*Sources*
Prevention initiatives	
Project Taking Charge	S. R. Jorgensen, V. Potts, and B. Camp, "Project Taking Charge: Six-Month Follow-up of a Pregnancy Prevention Program for Early Adolescents," *Family Relations*, vol. 42 (October 1993), pp. 401–06
Success Express	F. S. Christopher and M. Roosa, "An Evaluation of an Adolescent Pregnancy Prevention Program: Is 'Just Say No' Enough?" *Family Relations*, vol. 39 (January 1990), pp. 68–72
Facts and Feelings	B. C. Miller and others, eds., *Preventing Adolescent Pregnancy: Model Programs and Evaluations* (Newbury Park, Calif.: Sage Publications, 1992) B. C. Miller and others, "Impact Evaluation of Facts and Feelings: A Home-Based Video Sex Education," *Family Relations*, vol. 42 (October 1993), pp. 392–400
Teen Talk	M. Eisen and G. Zellman, "A Health Beliefs Field Experiment," in B. Miller and others, eds., *Preventing Adolescent Pregnancy* (Newbury Park, Calif.: Sage Publications, 1992) M. G. Eisen, M. G. Zellman, and A. McAlister, "A Health Belief Model—Social Learning Theory Approach to Adolescents' Fertility Control: Findings from a Controlled Field Trial," *Health Education Quarterly*, vol. 19, no. 2 (1992), pp. 249–62
Group Cognitive Behavior Curriculum	L. D. Gilchrist and S. Schinke, "Coping with Contraception: Cognitive and Behavioral Methods with Adolescents," *Cognitive Therapy and Research,* vol. 7 (October 1983), pp. 379–88
Postponing Sexual Involvement	M. Howard, " Delaying the Start of Intercourse among Adolescents," *Adolescent Medicine: State of the Art Reviews,* vol. 3, no. 2 (1992), pp. 181–93 M. Howard and J. B. McCabe, "Helping Teenagers Postpone Sexual Involvement," *Family Planning Perspectives,* vol. 22 (January 1990), pp. 21–26

Program	*Sources*
Reducing the Risk	R. P. Barth and others, "Enhancing Social and Cognitive Skills," in Miller and others, eds., *Preventing Adolescent Pregnancy* D. Kirby and others, "Reducing the Risk: Impact of a New Curriculum on Sexual Risk Taking," *Family Planning Perspectives,* vol. 23 (1991), pp. 253–63
Self-Center	L. Zabin, "Addressing Adolescent Sexual Behavior and Childbearing: Self-Esteem or Social Change?" *Women's Health Issues,* vol. 4, no. 2 (1994), pp. 92–97 L. Zabin, "School-Linked Reproductive Health Services: The Johns Hopkins Program," in Miller and others, eds., *Preventing Adolescent Pregnancy* L. Zabin and others, "The Baltimore Pregnancy Prevention Program for Urban Teenagers: How Did It Work?" *Family Planning Perspectives*, vol. 20, no. 4 (1988), pp. 182–87
Girls Incorporated	L. T. Postrado and H. Nicholson, "Effectiveness in Delaying the Initiation of Sexual Intercourse of Girls Aged 12–14: Two Components of the Girls Incorporated Preventing Adolescent Pregnancy Program," *Youth and Society*, vol. 23 (March 1992), pp. 356–79
St. Paul school-based health clinics	D. Kirby and others, "The Effects of School-Based Health Clinics in St. Paul on Schoolwide Birthrates," *Family Planning Perspectives,* vol. 25, no. 1 (1993), pp. 12–16
School-based health clinics	D. Kirby, C. Waszak, and J. Ziegler, "Six School-Based Clinics: Their Reproductive Health Services and Impact on Sexual Behavior," *Family Planning Perspectives*, vol. 23 (1991), pp. 6–16
Summer Training and Education Program	G. Walker and F. Vilella-Velez, "Anatomy of a Demonstration: The Summer Training and Education Program (STEP) from Pilot through Replication and Postprogram Impacts," Philadelphia: Public/Private Ventures, 1992

Table 3A-3 (*continued*)

Program	*Sources*
Quantum Opportunities Program	A. Hahn and others, "The Quantum Opportunities Demonstration," Brandeis University, 1994
Programs serving teenage parents	
Job Start	G. Cave and others, "JOB START: Final Report on a Program for School Dropouts," New York: Manpower Demonstration Research Corp., 1993
Job Corps	C. Mallar and others, "Evaluation of the Economic Impact of the Job Corps Program: Third Follow-up Report," Princeton, N.J.: Mathematica Policy Research, 1982
Ohio LEAP	D. Long and others, "LEAP: Three-Year Impacts of Ohio's Welfare Initiative to Improve School Attendance among Teenage Parents: Ohio's Learning, Earning, and Parenting Program, " New York: Manpower Demonstration Research Corp., 1996
	D. Bloom and others, "LEAP: Interim Findings on a Welfare Initiative to Improve School Attendance among Teenage Parents: Ohio's Learning, Earning, and Parenting Program," New York: Manpower Demonstration Research Corp., 1993
New Chance	J. Quint and others, "New Chance: Interim Findings on a Comprehensive Program for Disadvantaged Young Mothers and Their Children," New York: Manpower Demonstration Research Corp., 1994
Project Redirection	D. Polit and C. White, "The Lives of Young, Disadvantaged Mothers: The Five-Year Follow-up of the Project Redirection Sample," Saratoga Springs, N.Y.: Humanalysis, 1988
Teenage Parent Welfare Demonstration	R. Maynard, ed., "Building Self-Sufficiency among Welfare-Dependent Teenage Parents," Princeton, N.J.: Mathematica Policy Research, 1993
	R. Maynard, W. Nicholson, and A. Rangarajan, "Breaking the Cycle of Poverty: The Effectiveness of Mandatory Services for Welfare-Dependent Teenage Parents," Princeton, N.J.: Mathematica Policy Research, 1993

Program	*Sources*
Teenage Parent Welfare Demonstration (*continued*)	A. Hershey and M. Silverberg, "Program Cost of the Teenage Parent Demonstration," Princeton, N.J.: Mathematica Policy Research, 1993 R. Maynard and A. Rangarajan, "Contraceptive Use and Repeat Pregnancies among Welfare-Dependent Teenage Mothers," *Family Planning Perspectives*, vol. 26 (September-October 1994), pp. 198–205
Teenage Parent Health Care Program	A. O'Sullivan and B. Jacobsen, "A Randomized Trial of a Health Care Program for First-Time Adolescent Mothers and Their Infants," *Nursing Research,* vol. 41, no. 4 (1992), pp. 210–15
Elmira Nurse Home Visiting Program	D. Olds and others, "Improving the Life-Course Development of Socially Disadvantaged Mothers: A Randomized Trial of Nurse Home Visitation," *American Journal of Public Health,* vol. 78 (November 1988), pp. 1436–45

Notes

1. Kristen Moore, *Facts at a Glance* (Washington: Child Trends, 1996); and U.S. Bureau of the Census, "Fertility of American Women: June 1994," *Current Population Reports*, Series P-20, no. 482 (Department of Commerce, 1995), table 4.

2. Susan McElroy and Kristen Moore, "Trends Over Time in Teenage Childbreating," in Rebecca A. Maynard, ed., *Kids Having Kids: Economic Costs and Social Consequences of Teen Pregnancy* (Washington: Urban Institue Press, 1997), pp. 40–45.

3. David T. Ellwood, *Poor Support: Poverty in the American Family* (Basic Books, 1988); and Jon Jacobson and Rebecca A. Maynard, "Unwed Mothers and Long-term Welfare Dependency," in *Addressing Illegitimacy: Welfare Reform Options for Congress* (Washington: American Enterprise Institute, 1993).

4. Only 40 percent of the fathers of children born to teenage mothers are themselves teenagers. Twenty six percent are six or more years older than the mothers. Alan Guttmacher Institute, *Sex and America's Teenagers* (New York, 1994), figures 41 and 42.

5. Unless otherwise noted, all quotations in this chapter are from the teenage parents who participated in the Teenage Parent Welfare Demonstration sponsored by the Department of Health and Human Services in the late 1980s and evaluated by Mathematica Policy Research, Inc. Denise Polit, *Barriers to Self-Sufficiency and Avenues to Success among Teenage Mothers* (Princeton, N.J.: Mathematica Policy Research, 1992); and Rebecca A. Maynard, prepared statement, *Teen Parents and Welfare Reform*, Hearing before the Senate Committee on Finance, 104 Cong. 1 sess. (Government Printing Office, 1995).

6. This reflects primarily an increase in condom use. Alan Guttmacher Institute, *Sex and America's Teenagers*, figure 27.

7. Philip Gleason and others, "Service Needs and Use of Welfare-Dependent Teenage Parents," report PR93-17, Mathematica Policy Research, Princeton, N.J., February, 1993; and Janet Quint and others, *New Chance: Interim Findings on a Comprehensive Program for Disadvantaged Young Mothers and Their Children* (New York: Manpower Demonstration Research Corp., 1994).

8. Alan Guttmacher Institute, *Sex and America's Teenagers*, figure 52.

9. Kristin A. Moore, Donna R. Morrison, and Angela D. Greene, "Effects on the Children Born to Adolescent Mothers," in Maynard, ed., *Kids Having Kids*, pp. 145–80.

10. Barbara Wolfe and Maria Perozek, "Teen Children's Health and Health Care Use," in Maynard, ed., *Kids Having Kids*, pp. 181–203.

11. Moore, Morrison, and Greene, "Effects on the Children."

12. Robert M. Goerge and Bong Joo Lee, "Abuse and Neglect of the Children," in Maynard, ed., *Kids Having Kids*, p. 211.

13. Jeffrey Grogger, "Incarceration-Related Costs of Early Childbearing," in Maynard, ed., *Kids Having Kids,* pp. 240–44; and Robert H. Haveman, Barbara Wolfe, and Elaine Peterson, "Children of Early Childbearers as Young Adults," in *Kids Having Kids*, chap. 9 (figures in text derive from weighed estimates in table 9.6, panel 1).

14. Arline Geronimus, "Mothers of Invention," *Nation*, August 12, 1996, pp. 6–7.; and V. Joseph Hotz, Susan W. McElroy, and Seth G. Sanders, "The Impact of Teenage

Childbearing on the Mothers and the Consequences of Those Impacts for Government," in Maynard, ed., *Kids Having Kids,* pp. 55–94.

15. These estimates of direct effects are based on a methodology that controls for possible selection effects better than has been possible in most previous studies. The authors used teenagers who miscarried and so had a forced (somewhat random) delay in the timing of the first birth as the control group. Hotz, McElroy, and Sanders, "Impacts of Teenage Childbearing," pp. 58–61.

16. Michael J. Brien and Robert J. Willis, "Costs and Consequences for the Fathers," in Maynard, ed., *Kids Having Kids,* pp. 95–143.

17. Rebecca A. Maynard, "The Costs of Adolescent Childbearing," in Maynard, ed., *Kids Having Kids,* pp. 328–29, 336; Congressional Budget Office, *Sources of Support for Adolescent Mothers* (1990); and Rebecca A. Maynard, Anu Rangarajan, and Reuben Snipper, "To Sanction or Not: Are We Shortchanging Welfare Recipients through Laissez-Faire Attitudes toward Participation in Employment-Related Activities?" paper prepared for the Association for Public Policy Analysis and Management meeting, Washington, October 1993.

18. These are lower-bound estimates that take account of only the costs that are directly attributable to early childbearing. They measure the costs relative to delaying childbearing until age 20 or 21, still lower than the average age at first birth, and they do not include all costs. For example, these estimates include the higher health care costs for the children, but not for the parents; the foster care costs associated with higher placement rates, but not the protective services devoted to family preservation or reunification; and the construction and operation costs of prisons associated with the higher incarceration rates of the older male children of teenage parents, but not the other costs associated with elevated crime rates. So too, they omit the higher educational costs resulting from the greater incidence of health and developmental problems among children born to teenage parents, and such social costs as those associated with the high rates of poverty, single parenthood, and school failure. See Maynard, "Cost of Adolescent Childbearing."

19. Alan Guttmacher Institute, *Sex and America's Teenagers*, figure 12.

20. Susan W. McElroy and Kristin A. Moore, "Trends over Time in Teenage Pregnancy and Childbearing: The Critical Changes," in Maynard, ed., *Kids Having Kids*, figures 2.9 and 2.11.

21. Alan Guttmacher Institute, *Sex and America's Teenagers*, figure 10.

22. Leighton Ku, Freya L. Sonenstein, and Joseph H. Pleck, "Neighborhood, Family, and Work: Influences on the Premarital Behaviors of Adolescent Males," *Social Forces*, vol. 72 (December 1993), pp. 479–503; and Sarah S. Brown and Leon Eisenberg, eds., *The Best Intentions: Unintended Pregnancy and the Well-Being of Children and Families* (Washington: National Academy Press, 1995), p. 141.

23. Joy G. Dryfoos, *Adolescents at Risk: Prevalence and Prevention* (Oxford University Press, 1990).

24. Sheila Smith, ed., *Two Generation Programs for Families in Poverty: A New Intervention Strategy,* Advances in Applied Developmental Psychology, vol. 9 (Norwood, N.J.: Ablex Publishing, 1995).

25. McElroy and Moore, "Trends over Time," figure 2.3.

26. Jan L. Hagen and Irene Lurie, "Implementing JOBS: Progress and Promise," Nelson A. Rockefeller Institute of Government, Albany, 1994.

27. Debra Boyer and David Fine, "Sexual Abuse as a Factor in Adolescent Pregnancy and Maltreatment," *Family Planning Perspectives*, vol. 24 (January–February 1992), pp. 4–19; and Peggy Roper and Gregory Weeks, "Child Abuse, Teenageage Pregnancy, and Welfare Dependency: Is There a Link?" Washington State Institute for Public Policy, Evergreen State College, October 1993.

28. Robert Haveman and Barbara Wolfe, *Succeeding Generations: On the Effects of Investments in Children* (Russell Sage Foundation, 1994); Greg J. Duncan and Saul D. Hoffman, "Welfare Benefits, Economic Opportunities, and Out-of-Wedlock Births among Black Teenage Girls," *Demography*, vol. 27 (November 1990), pp. 519–35; Haveman, Wolfe, and Peterson "Children of Early Childbearers as Young Adults"; Shelly Lundberg and Robert D. Plotnik, "Adolescent and Premarital Childbearing: Do Economic Incentives Matter?" *Journal of Labor Economics*, vol. 13 (April 1995), pp. 177–200; and Shelly Lundberg and Robert D. Plotnick, "Effects of State Welfare, Abortion and Family Planning Policies on Premarital Childbearing among White Adolescents," *Family Planning Perspectives*, vol. 22 (November-December 1990), pp. 246–51.

29. Maynard, prepared statement, *Teen Parents and Welfare Reform*, Hearing; and Kristin Anderson Moore, Donna R. Morrison, and Dana A. Glei, "Welfare and Adolescent Sex: The Effects of Family History, Benefit Levels, and Community Context," *Journal of Family and Economic Lives,* vol. 16 (Fall 1995).

30. This finding is consistent with research showing that there is no relationship between the proportions of female teenagers who are sexually active and state welfare benefit levels relative to average communitywide incomes. Michael J. Camasso and others, "New Jersey's Family Cap Experiment," paper prepared for the Conference on Addressing Illegitimacy, American Enterprise Institute, Washington, September 1995); and June O'Neill, Baruch College, expert testimony in *C.K.* v. *Shalala*, USDC, D.NJ, Civil Action no. 93-5354, 1994.

31. Hope Corman, Theodore J. Joyce, and Michael Grossman, "Birth Outcome Production Function in the United States," *Journal of Human Resources*, vol. 22 (Summer 1987), pp. 339–60; and Kenneth J. Meier and Deborah R. McFarlane, "State Family Planning and Abortion Expenditures: Their Effect on Public Health," *American Journal of Public Health*, vol. 84 (September 1994), pp. 1468–72.

32. Kristin A. Moore and others, "State Variation in Rates of Adolescent Pregnancy and Childbearing," Child Trends, Washington, 1994.

33. One study reported only small positive relationships between welfare generosity and out-of-wedlock teenage births for whites and none for other racial-ethnic groups. However, the effects related to state family planning policies appear to be much greater. Not only is funding for family planning inversely related to teenage pregnancy rates, but funding for abortion is directly correlated with the likelihood that pregnancies end in abortion. States that made funding available for abortion also were more supportive of abortions. Lundberg and Plotnick, "Effects of State Welfare, Abortion and Family Planning Polices," pp. 246–51; Haveman and Wolfe, *Succeeding Generations*; and Moore, Morrison, and Glei, *Welfare and Adolescent Sex.*

34. Stephen R. Jorgensen, "Project Taking Charge: An Evaluation of an Adolescent

Pregnancy Prevention Program," *Family Relations*, vol. 40 (October 1991), pp. 373–80; Jorgensen, "Project Taking Charge: Six-Month Follow-up of a Pregnancy Prevention Program for Early Adolescents," *Family Relations*, vol. 42 (October 1993), pp. 401–06; Mark W. Roosa and F. Scott Christopher, "A Response to Thiel and McBride: Scientific Criticism or Obscurantism?" *Family Relations*, vol. 41 (October 1992), pp. 468–69; Roosa and Christopher, "Evaluation of an Abstinence-Only Adolescent Pregnancy Prevention Program: A Replication," *Family Relations*, vol. 39 (October 1990), pp. 363–67; and Karen S. Thiel and Dennis McBride, "Comments on an Evaluation of an Abstinence-Only Adolescent Pregnancy Program," *Family Relations*, vol. 41 (October 1992), pp. 465–67.

35. Brent C. Miller and others, "Pregnancy Prevention Programs, Impact Evaluation of Facts and Feelings: A Home-Based Video Sex Education Curriculum," *Family Relations*, vol. 42 (October 1993), pp. 392–400.; Marvin Eisen, Gail L. Zellman, and Alfred L. McAlister, "A Health Belief Model—Social Learning Theory Approach to Adolescents' Fertility Control: Findings from a Controlled Field Trial," *Health Education Quarterly*, vol. 19 (Summer 1992), pp. 249–62; Eisen, Zellman, and McAllister,"Evaluating the Impact of a Theory-Based Sexuality and Contraceptive Education Program," *Family Planning Perspectives*, vol. 22 (November–December 1990), pp. 261–71; Eisen and Zellman, "A Health Beliefs Field Experiment," in B. C. Miller and others, eds., *Preventing Adolescent Pregnancy: Model Programs and Evaluations* (Newbury Park, Calif.: Sage Publications, 1992); Lewayne D. Gilchrist and Steven Paul Schinke, "Coping with Contraception: Cognitive and Behavioral Methods with Adolescents," *Cognitive Therapy and Research*, vol. 7 (October 1983), pp. 379–88; and Schinke, Betty J. Blythe, and Gilchrist, "Cognitive-Behavioral Prevention of Adolescent Pregnancy," *Journal of Counseling Psychology*, vol. 28 (September 1981), pp. 451–54.

36. Marion Howard, "Postponing Sexual Involvement among Adolescents: An Alternative Approach to Prevention of Sexually Transmitted Diseases," *Journal of Adolescent Health Care*, vol. 6 (July 1985), pp. 271–27; Howard, "Delaying the Start of Intercourse among Adolescents," *Adolescent Medicine: State of the Art Reviews*, vol. 3 (June 1992), pp. 181–93; and Howard and Judith B. McCabe, "Helping Teenagers Postpone Sexual Involvement," *Family Planning Perspectives*, vol. 22 (January–February 1990), pp. 21–26.

37. Douglas Kirby and others, "School-Based Programs to Reduce Sexual Risk Behaviors: A Review of Effectiveness," *Public Health Reports,* vol. 109 (May–June 1994), pp. 339–60.

38. Laurie S. Zabin and others, "The Baltimore Pregnancy Prevention Program for Urban Teenagers: What Did it Cost?" *Family Planning Perspectives*, vol. 20 (July-August 1988), pp. 188–92; Zabin and others, "The Baltimore Pregnancy Prevention Program for Urban Teenagers: How Did It Work?" *Family Planning Perspectives*, vol. 20 (July-August 1988), pp. 182–87; and Zabin and others, "Dependency in Urban Black Families Following the Birth of an Adolescent's Child," *Journal of Marriage and the Family*, vol. 54 (August 1992), pp. 496–507.

39. Andrew Hahn with Tom Leavitt and Paul Aaron, *Evaluation of the Quantum Opportunities Program (QOP): Did the Program Work? A Report on the Post Secondary Outcomes and Cost-effectiveness of the QOP Program (1989–1993)* (Brandeis University, 1994).

40. Gary Walker and Frances Vilella-Velez, "Anatomy of a Demonstration: The Summer Training and Education Program (STEP) from Pilot through Replication and Postprogram Impacts," Public/Private Ventures, Philadelphia, 1992.

41. Susan Philliber, *Carrera/Dempsey Replication Programs: 1993–94 Summary of Client Characteristics and Outcomes* (Accord, N.Y.: Philliber Research Associates, 1995).

42. Although a number of other programs for teenage parents have been evaluated, the evaluations were more seriously flawed than the weakest of those in this list. Besides, including them would not change the quality the conclusions.

43. George Cave and others, *JOBSTART: Final Report on a Program for School Dropouts* (New York: Manpower Demonstration Research Corp., 1993).

44. Charles Mallar and others, *Evaluation of the Economic Impact of the Job Corps Program: Third Follow-up Report* (Princeton, N.J.: Mathematica Policy Research, 1982).

45. Janet Quint, *New Chance: Interim Findings on a Comprehensive Program for Disadvantaged Young Mothers and Their Children* (New York: Manpower Demonstration Research Corp., 1994); and Quint, Babara Fink, and Sharon Rowser, "New Chance: Implementing a Comprehensive Program for Disadvantaged Young Mothers and Their Children," Manpower Demonstration Research Corp., New York, December 1991.

46. Denise F. Polit and Cozette M. White, *The Lives of Young Disadvantaged Mothers: The Five-Year Follow-up of the Project Redirection Sample* (Saratoga Springs, N.Y.: Humanalysis, 1988).

47. Dan Bloom and others, *LEAP: Interim Findings on a Welfare Initiative to Improve School Attendance among Teenage Parents* (New York: Manpower Demonstration Research Corp., 1993); and David Long and others, "LEAP: Three-Year Impacts of Ohio's Welfare Initative to Improve School Attendance among Teenage Parents," Manpower Demonstration Research Corp., New York, April 1996.

48. Rebecca A. Maynard, ed., *Building Self-Sufficiency among Welfare-Dependent Teenage Parents: Lessons from the Teenage Parent Demonstration* (Princeton, N.J.: Mathematica Policy Research, 1993).

49. Ann O'Sullivan and Barbara Jacobsen, "A Randomization Trial of a Health Care Program for First-time Adolescent Mothers and their Infants," *Nursing Research*, vol. 41 (July-August 1992), pp. 210–15.

50. David L. Olds and others, "Improving the Life-Course Development of Socially Disadvantaged Mothers: A Randomized Trial of Nurse Home Visitation," *American Journal of Public Health*, vol. 78 (November 1988), pp. 1436–45.

51. Eleven percent of the teenagers required to participate in the program never did so, primarily because they had other means of support and so left welfare rather than participate.

52. Long and others, "LEAP: Three-Year Impacts," pp. 26–30.

53. Quint, *New Chance: Interim Findings*, pp. 58–61.

54. Most of the New Chance programs had difficulty filling their modest-size programs (generally 100 teenage parents a year). In its Chicago site, for example, New Chance had difficulty enrolling 100 teenage parents annually in a catchment area where, each month, more than 150 teenagers have their first child and go onto welfare.

55. Some have speculated that these decreases in employment and earnings may stem from the residential nature of the Job Corps, which takes young mothers out of their communities during the service period. However, the program did succeed in increasing the earnings of men in the residential programs. So it seems likely that this is not the explanation.

56. Participation in and completion of education programs varied widely among teenage mothers in the eight programs. Very few Job Corps participants were in regular high schools because the program did not offer this option. But a large proportion of those in Ohio Learnfare were in school, presumably because there were financial penalties of $62 or more a month for nonenrollment.

57. One possible explanation for the low correspondence of GED attainment and improvement of basic skills is that the basic skills tests are too unreliable at the low ends of the performance distribution to pick up gains that may have occurred. Elena Cohen and others, "Welfare Reform and Literacy: Are We Making the Connection?" background briefing report for the Family Impact Seminar, Washington; and National Center on Adult Literacy, University of Pennsylvania, June 1994.

58. Quint, Fink, and Rowser, "New Chance: Implementing a Comprehensive Program."

59. Ibid., table 6.2.

60. The estimated effects on earnings are statistically significant only for the Chicago site. Those for welfare and school enrollment are significant for all sites. However, the effects on educational attainment are significant only in the two sites where the estimates were positive. Maynard, Rangarajan, and Snipper, "To Sanction or Not."

61. Ibid.

62. Ibid.

63. Alan M. Hershey and Rebecca A. Maynard, "Designing and Implementing Services for Welfare Dependent Teenage Parents: Lessons from the DHHS/OFA-Sponsored Teenage Parent Demonstration," *Education, Training and Service Programs for Disadvantaged Teens*, Hearing before the Subcommittee on Human Resources of the House Committee on Ways and Means, March 6, 1992; and Maynard, ed., *Building Self-Sufficiency*.

64. Dryfoos, *Adolescents at Risk*; and Congressional Budget Office, *Sources of Support for Adolescent Mothers*.

65. Marilyn Benoit, "Instrinsic Psychological Issues in Teenage Pregnancy," paper prepared for the Seminar on Programs for Unwed Teen Mothers, American Enterprise Institute, Washington, 1994; Judith S. Musick, "The Psychological and Developmental Dimensions of Adolescent Pregnancy and Parenting: An Interventionist's Perspective," Rockefeller Foundation, New York, December 1987; and S. Shirley Feldman and Glen R. Elliott, *At the Threshold: The Developing Adolescent* (Harvard University Press, 1990).

Four

Paternalism, Child Support Enforcement, and Fragile Families

Ronald B. Mincy
and Hillard Pouncy

Child support enforcement means efforts by society to cause parents separated from their families to help support their children. This challenge is often the other side, the noncustodial parent's (usually fathers) side, of the welfare problem. And just as enforcement can promote employment among single parents on welfare, so a paternalistic structure can encourage work by the fathers of their children. It is not enough, experience has proven, simply to crack down on "deadbeat dads." Disadvantaged fathers also need help to pay their judgments. And at its frontier, child support policy actually can help strengthen fragile families.

In the 1990s some major demonstrations and state pilot programs showed that stronger child support enforcement strategies can work. These strategies feature interagency coordination among public welfare, child

We wish to thank editor Lawrence Mead for helpful comments and useful changes to the manuscript. We thank the National Practitioners Network, particularly Gerry Hamilton, Ed Pitt and Joe Jones, for their time, advice, and suggestions. David Arnaudo, Daniel Ash, Donald Bieniewicz, Richard Byrd, John Caskey, Kirk Harris, Michael Henry, Jeff Johnson, Stuart Miller, Elaine Sorenson, and Robert Williams patiently and repeatedly rehearsed us on how child support enforcement really works.

support enforcement, employment training, and community-based fatherhood groups. If done well, such efforts yield better support enforcement for fathers who can afford to pay and for those who currently cannot. The programs also seem effective at helping young, never-married fathers build stronger relationships with their children.

The changes in child support enforcement between the nineteenth century and the provisions of the 1996 welfare reform act have been dramatic.[1] In the nineteenth century, enforcement took place only after a marriage dissolved; now it may occur before marriage and birth.[2] Then enforcement was exclusively the province of state and local governments; today the federal government establishes standards and common practices. Then enforcement depended entirely on the custodial parent, who was required to sue for the support promised by the noncustodial parent in their divorce and separation agreement—the public enforcement of private contracts. Now child support agencies can chase deadbeat dads across state lines and hunt them down using federal and state databases.

In the nation's early years most of those involved in child support cases were not poor; now the problem driving innovation is how to achieve better enforcement for low-income fathers, in part as compensation for the welfare paid to their families. Programs such as Wisconsin's Children First help impoverished nonresident parents find work or training so they can afford to pay their child support obligations. And more recently, some community groups seek to build on this structure to reunite families.[3]

Child support enforcement thus shares features with other areas of social policy in which paternalism has developed. It expands the role of government and unites governmental authority and resources with the innovation of nongovernmental organizations. And it poses serious challenges to social institutions, public and private.

This chapter appraises paternalist child support policies aimed at poor men who do not reside with their children. After providing background on child support policy and the diversity of noncustodial fathers, it describes the evolution of child support through various administrative regimes. At each stage, support enforcement has improved, but there have also been limitations, and the effort to overcome them has driven the system toward a yet more complex regime. How successful are the recent, most ambitious child support programs? From limited evidence it is fair to call the results uncertain but encouraging.

Overview

In the five years following his 1992 divorce, Jeffrey Nichols, a commodities and precious metals investment adviser, could have regularly topped the child support enforcement community's ten most wanted list. He crossed three state lines and briefly lived in Canada to avoid the federal authorities who were trying to serve him with court orders. The amount he owed his former wife for support of their three children reached $642,550, constituting the nation's largest deadbeat dad case. His child support charges averaged $13,300 a month. After he was arrested in Vermont in 1995 he spent 114 days in a New York jail on contempt charges before reaching an agreement on a payment plan. He now sells Avon products door to door to support his children from his first marriage and two adopted children from a second marriage. His case is the most dramatic example of the effectiveness of the 1992 Child Support Recovery Act, which makes it a crime to cross state lines to avoid paying child support.[4]

If the Nichols case were typical, child support enforcement would be a fairly simple problem, even with tracking down the father. In 1991, of almost 10 million custodial mothers with children younger than 21 years, 56 percent had child support rights and an agreement that they would receive child support payments. Of these 5.5 million women, 4.9 million were entitled to receive support payments. The rest had awards that were no longer in force because, for example, the noncustodial father had died or the children had grown past the age of eligibility. Of those 4.9 million eligible women, 52 percent received the full amount of their child support awards.

But another 24 percent received less than they were owed, and 24 percent received no payment at all. The $13,300 monthly that Jeffrey Nichols was supposed to pay for three children ($4,400 per child per month) was more than four times higher than the entire 1991 yearly amount ($3,011) collected by the average custodial parent.[5] To be sure, we are comparing Nichols's judgment to actual payments, which are sometimes partial. But the contrast highlights the difference between expensive private divorce settlements and what child support provides the average mother.

The real problem in child support is not tracking down affluent deadbeats but the fact that most noncustodial fathers pay so much less. In a recent report Elaine Sorenson of the Urban Institute estimates that if Nichols and all other noncustodial fathers had paid Wisconsin standard child support rates, they would have generated between $44 and $48 billion in child support revenues in 1994.[6] In 1994 actual child support collections totaled $14 billion–$15 billion, leaving a widely reported $30 billion–$34 billion child support gap.[7] Approximately $17 billion of those missing funds represent nonreimbursed welfare costs, so that if all noncustodial parents of AFDC children paid their full judgments, half the estimated child support enforcement gap would be erased.[8] Recovering that money was one object of the recent welfare reform effort in Washington.[9]

Of the $14 billion–$15 billion paid in 1994, $9.9 billion was collected through public child support enforcement and the remaining $4 billion–$5 billion privately, the way Jeffrey Nichols might normally have paid child support. Federal, state, and local officials collected $3.81 ($9.9 billion total) for every dollar spent administering the child support enforcement system ($2.6 billion). Of that $9.9 billion, $7.3 billion was passed through to custodial parents.[10]

In 1995, child support enforcement services collected $2.7 billion from the noncustodial parents of children on AFDC. Of this, $0.4 billion passed through to AFDC parents. The rest was distributed among federal and state governments to recoup welfare costs.[11] On the basis of such returns and federal incentive payments, some states earn significant "program savings" off child support enforcement, even after they have paid its expenses. Some child support administrators informally call these savings a profit. This profit goes into a general fund to be used at a state's discretion. In 1994 California showed a $115 million profit, New York $46 million, and Pennsylvania $34 million, although some states "lost" money.[12]

In a case like Jeffrey Nichols's, such incentives are enough to motivate successful enforcement. Nichols owes and acknowledges the obligation. He once had the resources to pay, and child support enforcement (CSE) services know his name and address, social security number, the name and address of his most recent employer or place of work, names of friends and relatives, and organizations to which he belongs. In addition, state locators can look for him in telephone directories, motor vehicle registries, tax files, and employment data. The state also can ask the Federal Parent Locator Service for assistance and use its access to the Social Security Administration, Internal Revenue Service, Selective Service System, Department of Defense, Department of Veterans' Affairs, and National Personnel Records Center. Nichols has significant resources with which to flee and fight arrest, but the resources of the states and the federal government are vastly greater. For him the state's sanctions were effective and credible, and after a lengthy effort to avoid payment he capitulated.

Unfortunately, straightforward agency "profit" may not be enough to increase compliance and collection rates among low-income, young, noncustodial fathers.[13] The situation of these men is much more complicated than Nichols's. Few low-income fathers legally acknowledge their children. They are the most marginalized men in society, and they fail to pay child support as part of a larger pattern of detachment. Although they have fewer resources with which to flee, their legal and social footprints are also smaller. CSE and welfare agencies often cannot track them. The sanctions that won Nichols's compliance are not credible for these men. As welfare fathers, many are poorly motivated to pay because they know their payments go to the state to reimburse aid to their families; in most cases only $50 a month is passed through to the mother.

But she too may be reluctant to cooperate with CSE. One recent study reported that "Only a handful of mothers . . . cooperated with the child support enforcement agency, even though sizable numbers were in contact with the fathers of their children and many received support from them. Even those who received modest informal support from the fathers, however, generally felt it was in their best interest to resist cooperation with the enforcement agency."[14]

Unlike Jeffrey Nichols, young, low-income, noncustodial fathers are likely to be in a relationship with their children's mother that is unresolved. Nichols and his first wife had a relationship and ended it—resolved it by contractual settlement. Each attempted to make an adult commitment to the other. When that failed, all that was left was a requirement to honor the divorce contract and work out what would happen to the children. The young, low-income nonresident fathers involved in fragile families are often in relationships that could either wither away or result in more pregnancies. But such relationships may also become more stable and committed, leading to marriage. Among this population, there is both a need for support enforcement and a need to build families.[15]

In its fullest sense, then, CSE policy has three related but not necessarily complementary goals: traditional child support enforcement for marital births, enhanced child support enforcement for nonmarital births, and family building. Traditional and enhanced child support affect different populations. Traditional support involves previously married nonresident parents, usually fathers, who have already established paternity. Enhanced child support usually involves unwed fathers who may not have established paternity and whose ability to pay is unclear.

Enhanced child support and family building are complementary when fathers seek both to provide child support and become involved with their children.[16] But the fathers may be antagonistic when enhanced child support exposes them to risks that drive them away from building a family.[17] What if a father decides to acknowledge paternity and accept a child support judgment but cannot find work? Then his child support debt will grow, worsening his poverty. Being the good father then has a price that may be unsupportable. In these cases mere enforcement may drive fathers away. There is a need for a program structure that links obligations to benefits, that helps the father and by that means helps tie him to the family.

That is where paternalism comes in. But the advantage to government of pursuing such fathers is a lot less immediate than it was in the case of Nichols. Although some money may be saved, the real benefit lies in rebuilding young, unwed low-income families so that fewer instances of absent parenthood and welfare dependency occur in the first place. That is a long-term process in which both government and community organizations must be involved.

Diversity among Nonresident Father Populations

Mary Jo Bane and David Ellwood contended that an understanding of the diversity of the AFDC population should precede welfare reform. They showed that although most spells on welfare are short, most cases on the rolls at a given time are long term. Almost half of the long-term recipients will spend at least ten years on welfare. Policymakers, the researchers concluded, should devote greatest attention and resources to the long-term cases.[18] Ronald Mincy and Elaine Sorenson have taken the first steps toward understanding the diversity of young, unwed, noncustodial fathers. They not only asked who does and does not pay child support, but also who can and cannot pay.[19]

The noncustodial population is diverse. Twenty-two percent of all noncustodial fathers are currently married for the first time but have nonresident children outside marriage. Another 25 percent have remarried and have noncustodial children outside those marriages. The largest group (35 percent) are divorced fathers who do not remarry, and the smallest group

(18 percent) have never been married. The marital status of nonresident fathers is highly correlated with their ability to pay. Among all fathers, those who have divorced and remarried have average annual incomes of $28,572 (in 1990 dollars). Previously married fathers who have not remarried earn, on average, $22,530. Fathers who never married average only $9,016.[20]

Thus the original focus of child support enforcement policy on divorced fathers makes sense because most divorced fathers can afford to pay support. Divorce typically results in a significant drop in the living standards of mothers and children, but an increase in the living standards of the fathers.[21] Increasing collections among divorced fathers can improve the well-being of mothers and children without impoverishing the fathers. At the opposite end of the spectrum, however, many young, never-married fathers live very close to the poverty line, especially if one ignores the income of family members with whom they sometimes live.[22] Therefore, efforts to increase collections among them may increase the well-being of mothers and children while driving the young fathers further into poverty.

Mincy and Sorenson developed a four-part typology of young noncustodial fathers (table 4-1) using data from the 1990 Survey of Income and Program Participation.[23] Thirty-three percent paid child support and 67 percent did not. Most of the payers were able to do so; they could afford to pay support because they were not poor. Three percent of those who paid, however, were "poor payers" who paid support even though they were poor. One-third of young noncustodial fathers were able nonpayers and one-third were poor nonpayers, for whom paying would have meant squeezing blood from a turnip.

Table 4-1. Share of Young Noncustodial Fathers Who Make Child Support Payments, by Ability to Pay, 1995

Percent

	Able to pay	*Unable to pay*	*Total*
Payers	30	3	33
Nonpayers	34	33	67
Total	64	36	100

Source: Ronald B. Mincy and Elaine Sorenson, "Deadbeats and Turnips in Child Support Reform," *Journal of Policy Analysis and Management* (forthcoming). Figures differ slightly from those in Mincy and Sorenson because of rounding.

The challenges to the child support enforcement system differ according to the group being discussed. Ideally, the courts and enforcement services would apply traditional enforcement to the 34 percent who can afford to pay but like Jeffrey Nichols do not. The courts and services could apply enhanced enforcement to the 36 percent who are too poor to pay. In addition, they could refer some part of this group, especially those who have never married, to family building. But this assumes that the institutions know not only who has not paid support, but who among them can and cannot pay. Thus the problem of child support is a problem of knowledge as well as a problem of enforcement.

This explains much of the institutional change that has occurred in the child support system. As the system moved from a focus primarily on middle- and upper-income divorced and separated nonresident parents to a focus on lower incomes and marital as well as nonmarital births, it evolved through three regimes.[24] A fourth may be emerging. The regimes' strategies have differed, but they have been more complementary than contradictory. Mostly, each has built on the preceding regime, seeking to transcend it with a more complete system.

The Self-Administered Regime

For more than two centuries before 1975, state governments controlled the main child support enforcement instrument, the divorce laws.[25] It was assumed that child support payments would arise from private agreements made between parents at the time of divorce or separation. If the absent parent did not pay, enforcement required that the custodial parent, usually the mother, bring suit against the noncustodial parent for breach of the agreement. In this sense the process was administered by the mother. Because of its expense, only middle- and upper-income parents could make use of it. And because the policy relied on a previous divorce or separation agreement, unwed parents were not covered.

The court's intervention ended fairly quickly if the custodial parent lost interest or had too few resources to sustain her suit. Intervention might also cease if the couple reached a new agreement or the noncustodial parent began paying. In cases in which the custodial parent persisted and the noncustodial parent still refused to pay, the ultimate punishment for default was jail.

One objection to the system was that outcomes were grossly unequal. Most nonresident parents who avoided paying support incurred no punishment, but in zealous localities thousands went to jail. That is still widely true.[26] Another drawback was that the mother received little help from government in seeing that the laws were enforced. Finally, the system did not cover the children of unwed mothers, and births out of wedlock have increased rapidly in recent decades. Only 5 percent of births occurred out of wedlock in 1960, but by 1993 the rate was 31 percent.[27] The trend reflected other deep-seated social changes, including diminishing incomes and declining marriage rates.[28]

But the salient political objection was that unpaid child support came to be perceived as an important cause of the rapid growth in welfare dependency in the 1960s and 1970s. When first enacted in 1935, family welfare was designed to support widows. Their share in the caseload shrank rapidly, until by 1995 only 2 percent of welfare mothers were widows while 27 percent were divorced or separated and 56 percent were unwed. Yet in 1980 only 5 percent of AFDC payments were reimbursed from child support, and by 1995 the figure was still only 14 percent.[29]

The Child Support Enforcement Regime

The attempt to help mothers get more money from their children's fathers motivated greater government involvement in support enforcement. As early as 1950, amendments to the Social Security Act required state welfare agencies to notify law enforcement officials of abandoned children on AFDC, and further amendments in 1967 mandated that states establish paternity and obtain child support for children on AFDC. Both provisions were poorly enforced and widely ignored.

Title IV (D)

Senator Russell B. Long of Louisiana helped launch a new child support enforcement regime when he and others persuaded Congress to enact the 1975 Title IV (D) amendments to the Social Security Act. The law established the Federal Office of Child Support Enforcement (OCSE) and required states to set up their own enforcement agencies. CSE programs are generously funded by Washington, which pays two-thirds of their costs (90 percent for information processing) and also provides incentive payments to promote collections.

Most states placed their child support programs within comprehensive human service agencies that also administered the AFDC program.[30] These are the agencies that helped track down Jeffrey Nichols. In 1984 further amendments tried to relieve state courts of their burdens by allowing "judge surrogates" to handle the routine elements of cases. Although the CSE system was motivated chiefly by the welfare problem, it is in principle available to nonwelfare custodial parents who need help with support collection. The 1988 Family Support Act pushed states to establish paternity for all children under age 18.[31] The federal government reimburses states for 90 percent of the costs of laboratory tests in contested cases.

The Title IV (D) regime triggered enforcement sooner and extended it longer. Because the CSE agencies were supposed to enforce support against noncustodial parents of AFDC children, they did not wait for a divorce or separation agreement as under the earlier regime. And once identified, noncustodial parents of AFDC children remained under the program's scrutiny as long as their children remained on AFDC, whether the parents paid or not. Once mandated, their payments accrued independently of their circumstances.

Some results have been dramatic. Child support collected under Title IV(D) increased by 214 percent between 1978 and 1991, the number of absent parents located grew by 468 percent, and the number of paternities established rose 325 percent (table 4-2). But the regime has been less successful

Table 4-2. Title IV(D) Program Collections, Parents Located, and Paternities Established, 1978, 1991

Measures of effectiveness	*1978*	*1991*	*Percent change 1978–91*
Total collections (billions of 1991 dollars)	2.2	6.9	214
Parents located (thousands)	454	2,577	468
Paternities established (thousands)	111	472	325
Awards established (thousands)	15	1,022	224

Source: House Committee on Ways and Means, *1996 Green Book: Background Material, and Data on Programs within the Jurisdiction of the Committee on Ways and Means* (Government Printing Office, 1996), p. 581.

than it appears. The increases have been from a low base, and Title IV(D) is only part of the child support system. The total amount of support collected from all sources has remained flat. The proportion of owed support that was actually received grew only from 64 to 68 percent between 1978 and 1991, and in constant dollars the amount paid rose only from $8.9 billion to $11.2 billion a year. The gap is still enormous: even in 1991 barely a quarter of custodial mothers received all the child support due to them.[32]

The Paternity Problem

The Achilles heel of child support enforcement has turned out to be establishing paternity. Top-down enforcement works only when a father is legally identified and a support order is in place. In theory, state law and the CSE system can fix paternity on a man without his involvement, but it is much easier to do so if he cooperates. Many disadvantaged parents do not cooperate. This is why in 1991 only 27 percent of never-married custodial parents had child support orders, in contrast with 73 percent of divorced and 46 percent of separated mothers. Only 24 percent of poor mothers—much the same population—received any child support at all.[33]

Never-married mothers are particularly likely to live on welfare. Welfare mothers are supposed to identify the fathers of their children as a condition of aid, but it is difficult for the system to contradict them if they disclaim knowledge. In 1985, as an incentive to cooperate, mothers were allowed to keep $50 a month net of any reduction in their grants if any support was collected, but even this has had little effect. Some AFDC mothers believe that establishing paternity will jeopardize whatever informal payments the father does provide. Some do not want contact with the absent father. Others believe that involvement with CSE would break up a relationship with the child's father.[34] Accordingly, only 24 percent of never-married mothers on AFDC had paternity established for any of their children.[35]

A second problem, alluded to earlier, is that enforcement institutions have a difficult time determining whether a father is able to pay support or whether he is making a good faith effort to do so. When young, unwed, noncustodial fathers come before family courts because of nonpayment and claim they are too poor to pay, judges have little basis for disputing them. How do they know if the father is working off the books? In the terms used above, the regime has had difficulty differentiating between poor and able nonpayers. Lawrence Mead captured this dilemma for judges in Wisconsin:

> Of all delinquent noncustodial parents, [poor men] are the most disadvantaged. They are the toughest to get to pay because they are the hardest to locate and have the least to lose by not paying. Traditionally, local courts deal with such fathers in a punitive but ineffective manner. Child support lawyers find them and bring them before family court charged with nonpayment. Judges tell them to get a job and pay, but there is little supervision to see that they do so. When, on further nonpayment, they are hauled back into court, they can claim that they could not get a job, and a judge hesitates to hold them in contempt.[36]

The judge can of course order the father to make a "purge payment"—a one-time lump sum payment to clear his cumulative child support backlog—that he clearly can pay, but paying it does not establish what he can really do. Nor does the order prevent him absconding as soon as he is out of court. The result is that judges have few effective enforcement mechanisms for coping with poor nonpayers and eventually lose them. Faced with these dilemmas, the CSE regime often puts a low priority on collecting from fathers who appear indigent, even though this was a primary reason for setting up the system in the first place.[37]

The official response to these difficulties has been to bear down harder. It is much less controversial to crack down on deadbeat dads than it is to require welfare mothers to work. Every welfare reform for twenty years has included provisions turning up the pressure on nonpaying fathers. Legislation in 1984 required that states set a uniform scale for assessing child support judgments on fathers, so that judges would not be too easy on them, and the Family Support Act of 1988 mandated that effective in 1994 judgments be deducted from the wages of fathers, whether they were delinquent or not. The law also mandated that states establish paternity in 50 percent of cases involving welfare or Title IV(D), and the 1996 welfare reform (P.L. 104-193) raised this to 90 percent.[38] These mandates are goals, and states are rewarded for showing progress toward them.

No doubt, the process of establishing paternity can be improved. It is known that unwed fathers spend more time with their partners soon after children are born than they do later, so this is the best time to get them to acknowledge paternity. Massachusetts and New Jersey have used private contractors to implement and monitor paternity establishment in hospitals. Title IV(D) agents, who were normally involved in securing compliance, were replaced by hospital workers who counseled never-married parents on the merits of voluntarily registering the child's father. In Massachusetts the state's voluntary paternity acknowledgment rates reached 75 percent; New Jersey's reached 71 percent.[39] These achievements have allowed both states to satisfy federal requirements.[40]

But 81 percent of unmarried fathers who voluntarily acknowledged paternity were employed.[41] This suggests that this nondirective, voluntary establishment of paternity enlists mainly nonpoor men—the able payers. They are the most confident that they can satisfy the obligation they accept. How does one entice the more disadvantaged fathers, who are less confident?

The central weakness of CSE is the attempt to exact support through law enforcement without coming to terms with the noncustodial parents. When confronting poor nonpayers and their small social footprints, that is not good enough. To improve support enforcement, something must be done to address these fathers' needs. This will also help achieve the goals of the CSE regime because by addressing the fathers' needs we will also learn what the fathers can and cannot pay.

The Paternalist Regime

These realizations lie behind the tentative emergence of a third structure for support enforcement, one even more ambitious than CSE. So far, this regime exists only in experimental programs, both public and private, but they resemble one another enough to suggest a common pedigree. Probably programs like this will account for most of the innovation in the way child support enforcement affects unwed low-income families in the immediate future.

The fundamental idea behind the paternalist system is that child support must be enhanced. To establish paternity and achieve payment, it is not enough to enforce. It is not enough to throw the book at absent fathers. Enough of them are poor nonpayers, in Mincy and Sorenson's term, that they simply cannot pay unless something more is done to help them. The lure of that something is also what may persuade them to accept the travails of the enforcement system in the first place. The paternalist system does not reject CSE but seeks to build on it.

The paternalist experiments all offer services to nonpaying fathers that they do not routinely receive now. These include conventional employment and training services, support groups, and mediation services to help them resolve conflicts with custodial parents. Most important, the programs may offer fathers some relief from their child support obligations while they participate. And they must participate to obtain this relief. Otherwise they will sent back to the court where, as before, they face a Hobson's choice between paying up and prison. The attempt to link benefits to participation is one of the things that makes these programs paternalist. The other is the staff supervision they entail.

To institute a mandatory program for fathers also helps solve the information problem the courts face in enforcing support orders. Judges cannot verify whether a man is really poor or whether he looks for work in good faith. But they can verify whether he shows up at a program and attends regularly as ordered. That is an obligation he cannot evade. As a result, the program is more effective in enforcing his obligations than the apparently tougher threat of jail. The participation requirement conflicts deliberately with off-the-books jobs. It thus smokes out hidden income, inducing more fathers to pay up than court appearances do. And for those that cannot pay it helps to train and place them in work so they may be able to pay in the future. The participation obligation thus serves as a proxy for support payment. It falls between the unfruitful extremes of payment and no payment that were all the system could offer previously.

Children First

In 1987 Wisconsin launched an innovative program to help sort out who among the young and unwed can pay their child support and who cannot. [42] Children First was implemented in Fond du Lac and Racine Counties in 1990 and later expanded to cover much of the state. Currently it operates in twenty-three Wisconsin counties; in 1994 it served 1,221 noncustodial parents.

The program is aimed at men who are in arrears in their child support, have low incomes, are underemployed, and have no obvious reason not to work.[43] Most participants are single, and half of these say they have never married. Almost half have high school diplomas and almost a third have some training beyond high school. Typically, after a child support enforcement officer identifies a nonresident parent of an AFDC child, the client appears before a family court commissioner. If he is underemployed or poor, the commissioner may enroll him in Children First. The father can avoid the program only if he pays his judgment for three consecutive months. An early state accounting said that 77 percent of those referred to the program fulfilled their obligation by paying their judgments, which showed the program's power to expose denied income. Only 23 percent entered the program.[44]

Once he has entered, the father has to participate in the program regularly for sixteen weeks. The attraction to him is that he avoids jail and he need not pay up as long as he is in the program, although his arrearages continue to build. The program originally planned to put clients in unpaid work assignments. The idea was that if they did not produce earnings to pay support, they could at least work off the welfare that the government was paying their families. But in practice relatively few men have gone into such jobs; the majority have gone into job search, education, or training.

In cases in which the case manager does give the client an unpaid work assignment, a work supervisor monitors him daily at the work site. If problems arise, the supervisor helps the client solve them. But if the problems persist, the case manager takes the client back to court where jail is an option. The case managers act as drill sergeants to drive home that the program is obligatory. Normally the clients revolve through several placement iterations before they take the program seriously. The program seems to work, not because it is particularly punitive, but because it is inexorable. It is an obligation that the men cannot escape.

An early pilot of the program in Fond du Lac was bare-bones, oriented mainly to unpaid work and enforcement. A more service-oriented version emerged in Racine County. This program is contracted to Goodwill Industries where the case manager, in addition to the regular program, offers clients life skills classes and other services. These classes include how to search for a job, assessment tests, basic education classes, a traditional job placement service, and a nontraditional group-oriented job search club. The hallmark of the program is its parental responsibility class in which clients "deal with their feelings about the custodial parent and their children. At one point in the program, clients must write their own obituaries as they would be written by their children."[45] According to Gerry Hamilton, the director, this exercise is very moving. "I have seen very hardened individuals just break down. This helps noncustodial fathers understand why contact with their children is so important." He adds that the Racine strategy is to create "a father-friendly environment because we want people to feel comfortable."[46]

Originally program practitioners referred fathers to a fatherhood development curriculum, but now that 20 percent of the enrollees are female noncustodial parents, the curriculum has been expanded. "This component includes a great deal of parent-child interaction that reinforces parent-child bonds," Hamilton says. Another component is a peer support group to discuss particularly personal issues as well as an informal mediation service for the fathers and mothers.

An early nonexperimental state assessment compared the child support payment records of clients six months before entering the program and six months after. It found that Racine increased the number of parents paying support by 83 percent and support payments by 237 percent, whereas the figures in Fond du Lac were 61 and 37 percent (table 4-3). "Perhaps some of this difference," the report commented, "may be due to the enhanced services (additional motivational classes and support groups) that are offered in Racine County, although currently this is conjecture."[47] Racine is now considered a model for other counties, but it is expensive, even considering the amount of collections, and few counties are able to afford the same breath of services.

Overall, what does Children First achieve? A recent statewide assessment found that after six months clients in the program more than doubled the number of their child support payments. The average monthly payment also doubled, and the proportion of participants making any payment rose

Table 4-3. Children First Program Results in Racine and Fond du Lac Counties, Wisconsin, 1994

	Child support collected			*Number of parents paying*		
County	*Before enrollment*	*After enrollment*	*Percent change*	*Before enrollment*	*After enrollment*	*Percent change*
Racine	107.11	360.89	237	29 of 72	53 of 72	83
Fond du Lac	206.43	332.50	61	30 of 55	41 of 55	37

Source: Wisconsin Division of Economic Support, Madison.

from 40 to 71 percent. Twelve months after entering, all these apparent effects had faded only slightly, suggesting that the program had a lasting effect. The share of clients saying they were employed rose from 27 percent at program entry to 79 percent at completion.[48]

But none of these effects proves the program has been the cause. Such effects might arise without a program as men who have been down on their luck return to work. Fortunately, an experimental evaluation of Children First is under way in Racine. It compares clients in the program to an equivalent control group and thus cancels out this rebound effect. According to preliminary results, after they entered Children First clients sharply increased the amount of their child support payments, but not much more than controls. The increase in the number of payments made actually favored controls. This might be because the controls got ordinary child support enforcement treatment, and in Racine even the regular system is strongly insistent.[49] But the difference in employment very much favored Children First. The number of clients who had jobs rose by 167 percent between their entry into the program and case closure. For controls employment fell.[50]

Children First introduced a paternalist child support regime that had the virtue of distinguishing between the able and poor nonpayers and improving compliance for both. Its smoke-out effects makes fathers who have earnings pay, while its paternalistic service structure helps genuinely poor fathers move toward employment and family building.

The Young Unwed Fathers Project

The Young Unwed Father's Project ran between 1991 and 1993 in six cities, including Racine.[51] Although the project began after Children First, it pioneered the peer group intervention and parent curriculum that the Children First program uses in Racine. Goodwill Industries is also the YUFP contractor for the Racine site of the YUFP and kept those YUFP components after the demonstration ended. The YUFP demonstration assigned young, unwed fathers to case managers whose job was to help them become responsible fathers and pay their child support. This program pioneered the responsible fatherhood learning component later added to Children First and Parent's Fair Share.

Practitioners have believed that the program's major discovery was that a well-structured peer support program coupled with the right curriculum could have an extraordinary effect on young fathers. It motivated many to have frequent contact with their children, which in turn seemed to motivate them to more responsible behavior. However, the young fathers also exposed themselves to risk by participating. Once they agreed to establish paternity or pay support, their low incomes sometimes made it impossible for them to maintain payments, and they quickly built up large arrears.

This problem was accentuated by the program's major weakness: it lacked stable, reliable ties to government-sponsored employment training and to the CSE system. In contrast with Children First, it was not sponsored by a government agency. Thus it could not help the clients negotiate waivers of their obligations so as to facilitate participation. The urgency of payment and the pressure from CSE agents forced most participants to leave the program's skills training and education courses and go to work sooner than planned, usually in low-skill, low-paying jobs. This kept them from gaining skills and credentials that they might have used to obtain better-paying jobs with benefits and career potential.[52]

Unless they could negotiate waivers that permitted clients to manage their arrears, some case managers believed they had done their charges more harm than good by exposing them to the child support enforcement system. They needed more authority to negotiate arrears and payment schedules and thus help low-income fathers manage the risks of compliance.

Parent's Fair Share

Achieving a better interface with CSE and employment training agencies was a major goal of Parent's Fair Share, the largest child support demonstration now running. PFS was designed by the Manpower Demonstration Research Corporation (MDRC) to help unemployed nonresident parents of AFDC children secure jobs, pay child support, and be more involved with their children. The program was also intended to mediate conflicts between parents. It was authorized by the 1988 Family Support Act to demonstrate how the act's JOBS component could also provide services to unemployed noncustodial parents. The program has run at nine locations since 1992. In a preliminary assessment, MDRC found the program to be well implemented and is now conducting an experimental evaluation.[53]

Parents' Fair Share has four components. It offers conventional education and training services to participants, arranges enhanced child support enforcement with child support authorities, organizes peer support groups among participants, and, like the Young Unwed Fathers Project, offers mediation services to help participants work out conflicts with custodial parents.

Enhanced child support and employment training make PFS like Children First and unlike YUFP. The program is mandatory and involves enforcement. Clients have been referred to it by the authorities, and they must participate on pain of returning to the regular child support system. But while they participate, they get something back: their monthly child support orders are lowered to $50 or less.

Just as important, the programs have built ties with child support agencies to improve support enforcement in other ways. The goal is to make enforcement more insistent, in the sense that more effort is devoted to fathers with low incomes, but also more flexible, in that support obligations are adjusted more quickly up or down depending on a father's circumstances. This minimizes the risk a father takes by participating in PFS and acknowledging his obligations. Although establishing paternity was not formally part of the program, it has urged local CSE agencies to devote more attention to this.

Thus the program embraces enforcement. It is serious about the payment obligation. Like Children First, it tends to expose unreported sources of income. About a third of clients, according to MDRC, admit to employment once they are involved in the program. Furthermore, in two sites 14 percent of clients made purge payments.[54]

Because PFS is authorized under the 1988 Family Support Act to test its JOBS provisions for noncustodial parents, fathers participating in it can receive employment training and the related services paid for by JOBS programs. These services could not be guaranteed to participants in YUFP. As a result, once PFS participants acknowledge their child support obligations, they can receive the benefits needed to meet them. By contrast, once YUFP participants acknowledged their child support debts, there were not guaranteed services to meet those obligations.

In addition, the service components of PFS are more notable. Like YUFP the program has had trouble developing longer-term training activities because its clients are under pressure to move into jobs quickly. But peer support groups have been a conspicuous success. The rationale behind them is that noncustodial parents are more likely to pay support if they learn through interaction that other men are in the same boat. The groups offer their members understanding and encouragement, but also confront them as needed about their responsibilities. Finally, the program encourages fathers to be involved in the lives of their children. Facilitators are supposed to follow a curriculum emphasizing subjects such as a father's responsibilities and how to maintain relationships, but in practice they often do not.

Hard-nosed attitudes prevail in child support enforcement. CSE agencies tend to dismiss noncustodial fathers' excuses about nonpayment, believing they can pay much more than they do, while the men typically find the enforcement system impersonal and unyielding. But perhaps for this reason the support groups in PFS have struck a chord. The men value the chance to form new attachments and air their feelings about CSE and their own predicament. Participation has run high, with only about 10 percent of clients failing to join the groups at some stage. The attitudes of group members seem to improve; whether behavior has is less clear. MDRC has concluded that peer support is the most successful component, indeed the core of the program, and the engine that has driven the men's involvement in other activities.[55]

Participation in PFS has been high generally. Two-thirds of the men referred to the program have participated within four months, a higher rate than reported in MDRC's evaluations of welfare employment programs, which mainly serve welfare mothers (see chapter 2).[56] The response confirms the need to do more for noncustodial fathers, who are an underserved group. Greater receptivity to their needs, even if it is limited, does make it easier for them to respond to society's demands.

Unmet Needs

The paternalist regime so far exists only in the form of experimental programs like these. To introduce it widely would make serious demands on social agencies, which would have to mount even more complex programs than CSE. But even if this were achieved, the paternalist model would have some inherent limitations. It meets the needs of noncustodial parents better than mere enforcement does and draws some response from them. But it does not reach to the heart of their vulnerability.

The main problem of the poor nonpayers is their inability to secure a good job and often to work steadily at any job. Their lives are obsessed with a quest for earnings, a problem that undermines their position with their partners, other associates, and the child support system. If they could work and earn good wages, they could probably strengthen their family relationships and society would be off their backs.[57] But they cannot accept the low-wage, menial jobs open to them because these seem below their skills and experience as they rate them. And they have difficulty learning better skills in school or training programs, which generally are not successful with male clients. It is a box from which many fail to escape. Some find work in the underground economy because there are few alternatives in their communities.[58] Others work in illegal activities because, although they are dangerous, these activities are respected among their peers.[59]

At least in the short term, the only way many of these men can progress is to accept the low-wage jobs available to them but to work more steadily at them. That means lowering the wage they will accept to take a job—what economists call their reservation wage. If they work steadily, CSE will find them and garnish their wages, which will lower their take-home pay still more. Only if they endure for several years can they hope to build up the work history that may eventually enable some of them to get a good job. Only if they risk becoming a poor payer, in other words, can they one day become able payers.[60]

The chief merit of the paternalist regime is that it provides some of the nonmonetary support the men need to go through that tunnel. It is notable that in the Children First evaluations discussed earlier, the clients earned slightly *lower* wages after entering the program than they did before.[61] One might call this a failure, but it may actually suggest success. The clients may be lowering the wages they will accept so they can come to terms with the labor market as it is and get on with their lives. Perhaps the program helps them do this by providing nonmonetary rewards.

It is clear from the support group discussions that one of the strongest pulls in the nonpayers' lives is toward their families. They yearn to be able once more to spend time with their children and, perhaps, their partners. The usual inference in child support discussions is that the men need money to relate to the family. In peer group sessions men are confronted with how their own behavior hurts their children, and this motivates them to change.[62] But the reverse is also true: attention and support from the family can motivate employment.

Now a new problem emerges, perhaps the innermost one in child support: relationships. The more the noncustodial parents have faced their problems through the paternalist programs, the more they have returned to work and put their lives together and the more they aspired to reestablish contact with their children. But many single mothers want their partners out of their lives. In YUFP the father's urge to act responsibly toward his children set him on a collision course with the children's mother, which threatened the couple's ability to resolve conflicts and manage crises. In Parents' Fair Share, group discussions have revealed the depth of hostility and distrust dividing the men from their former partners.[63] The program offers mediation services to resolve such conflicts, but few fathers take an interest in them, in part because few of the custodial parents agree to participate.[64] The mothers have little incentive to interact with the fathers as long as they can draw secure support from welfare.

This suggests that in the end the only real solution of the child support problem is rebuilding the family. Only then do a mother and her children get secure support (and probably a higher income than welfare offers), and only then does a father get the emotional support that he needs to work steadily. But this is a reality that the paternalist regime, complex as it is, tends to ignore. Although it attends to some of the father's needs, it still treats him as an individual separate from a family. It places him in a relationship, but it is a relationship with other noncustodial fathers bereft of their families, whereas what he really needs is to build, or rebuild, ties to his partner and children. Paternalism also still construes his problems mainly as economic, when they are just as much emotional.

The Fragile Family Regime

The idea of the fragile family has emerged from such reflections, just as the earlier regimes responded to the limitations of still earlier structures. In thinking through the next steps, Ronald Mincy suggests treating the nonresident parent and the resident parent as a single unit of intervention: a fragile family.[65]

This perspective takes for granted much of the achievement of the earlier regimes. It accepts the need for child support enforcement, and it imagines programs with a supervisory structure that offers many services to low-income noncustodial parents. Its contribution is its focus on the inner problems of the fragile family. That emphasis can emerge out of paternalist programs as well. Parent's Fair Share encourages its clients to construe their relationship to their children as involving more than paying support.

Still, paternalism, like the earlier regimes, takes meeting children's monetary needs as the primary concern. What counts is whether the father pays his support obligation. A family perspective, however, looks toward nonmonetary contributions as well, including nurturing. From a family perspective, a child support policy could well address male responsibility, pregnancy prevention, and parenting as well as paternity establishment and child support.

Four recent events encourage such a change of focus. First, the 1996 welfare reform law encourages the formation and maintenance of two-parent families. But although Congress provides specific goals and timetables to achieve three other purposes (providing temporary cash assistance, encouraging work, and reducing teenage pregnancies), the new law includes no specific strategies for encouraging two-parent families. Clearly Congress and practitioners need to give more thought to achieving this goal.

Second, the 1996 welfare reform law demands that localities place even greater emphasis on establishing paternity. Many communities will find it costly to achieve the 90 percent establishment rate among poor nonpayers. Even successful paternalist demonstrations were unable to increase rates dramatically among never-married mothers.

Third, responsible fatherhood practices are linked to improved well-being for poor children.[66] Thus an increasing number of family service practitioners believe that the nonmonetary child support goals demonstrated by Parent's Fair Share are valuable and should be emphasized in the support enforcement effort. Family life among the seriously poor has deteriorated so badly that mending it must become a priority as great as finding economic support for poor families.

Fourth, as enforcement efforts against poor nonpayers succeed, many of these men may become poor payers. How can their lives be made tolerable unless their family life improves? When poor nonpayers enter programs that help them make stronger attachments to their children and solve problems with the children's mothers, they are likely to become poor payers, but they are less likely to remain poor payers indefinitely. They are more likely to look for permanent work even at low wages and so at last build the work history they need to get ahead. In motivating that commitment, relationships must do for them what economic rewards initially cannot.

A child support program such as Children First is already contracted out to nongovernmental bodies in many places in Wisconsin. In the same manner, child support agencies that wish to pursue building families might ally with a relatively new entity: a community-based responsible fatherhood program (CBRFP). Such a program intervenes with low-income noncustodial fathers to establish paternity and teach responsible parenthood.

An example is the Baltimore chapter of Healthy Start, a national child welfare program. In the early 1990s Healthy Start asked what children from low-income, single-parent households needed. Practitioners involved in the program believed that the answer included providing the children with access to both parents as well as financial support from both.

In searching of mechanisms to bring nonresident fathers into the program, administrators borrowed several mechanisms from Parent's Fair Share. The Baltimore chapter created a local fathers' service group, the Baltimore Program's Men's Services Program, run by Joe Jones. They asked him to direct a local version of Parent's Fair Share. In this case the program had nothing to do with family court. Simply, it asked noncustodial fathers to have contact with their children's mothers, establish paternity as their contribution to their children's welfare, and take part in structured peer-support fatherhood programs and job training to pay child support. As in the earlier demonstrations, the effort increased fathers' contact with their children and yielded higher child support payments. But it also led to more responsible behavior, including paternity establishment and more collaborative efforts with the children's mothers.

To encourage the formation and maintenance of two-parent families, Congress could promote partnerships between child support enforcement agencies and CBRFPs. Child support agencies might subcontract some of their paternity establishment caseload—poor nonpayers—to responsible fatherhood programs such as Healthy Start. In exchange for helping CSE meet its goals for establishing paternity, the programs might be granted authority over poor payers, much as family courts in Wisconsin extended their authority to paternalist Children First case managers acting on their behalf. CSE agencies should also agree to structure child support awards so that they do not exceed a low-income father's means, at least initially. As his income rises, the amount of the award should rise. His in-kind contributions might also be counted.

Finally, because family-building efforts can lead to incidents of domestic violence, family building, like Parent's Fair Share, explicitly seeks to help unwed parents manage tensions and collaborate on behalf of their children. Toward this end Baltimore's Healthy Start and Children First are developing service models called team parenting. However, CBRFPs might be required to avoid cases in which the mother is younger than age fifteen. Recent studies suggest that in 80 percent of cases involving such young mothers a family member or other sexual abuse issues are involved.

Another community-based program, the Paternal Involvement Project Demonstration begun in the Chicago area, also provided case managers to nonresident fathers to involve them more in the lives of their children. Between 1992 and 1996 three community groups enrolled 679 poor fathers of AFDC children.[67] This was not, strictly speaking, a paternalist effort because there was no enforcement component. The program did not interact with its clients primarily to secure child support on behalf of Title IV (D) agencies. Its goals were to get the fathers emotionally and financially involved with their children. It helped them find jobs and job training services, and it provided the same type of parent, social, and counseling case services as the demonstrations discussed earlier.

The demonstration reported that 52 percent of its participants found employment for at least six months at an average hourly wage of $6.75. The paternity establishment rate was 40 percent, and 80 percent of the men increased contact with their children. Twelve obtained legal custody of their children. As happened with Children First in Racine, the Paternal Involvement Project Demonstration's practitioners hoped that as nonresident fathers became more involved with their children and learned to resolve problems with their children's mothers, they would become team parents, forming fragile families. Possibly they would even marry and form traditional families.

As with the Children First assessment, of course, these apparent effects do not establish that the program has been a cause of the change. Conceivably, much of this improvement might have occurred without it. One challenge in family building is to undertake more definitive evaluations of programs than have occurred to date.

One difference between fragile families and the earlier regimes is that programs operate more as advocates for their clients. The earlier programs were oriented entirely to enforcing the social value of child support, however broadly they may have defined it. The essence of paternalism is that the values enforced are not themselves in question. If there is controversy, it is over the authority applied to achieve the values, which some see as coercive.

From a family perspective, however, tension can develop between the needs of struggling couples and established values, at least as they are embodied in existing social policies. The Paternal Involvement Project Demonstration takes the view that it must lobby for the reform of child support, welfare, public housing, and other local, state, and federal social service programs. In its view the closer poor parents come to forming fragile families, or even traditional families, the more these programs pose obstacles. As groups try to move poor nonresident fathers beyond simply paying child support and toward parental involvement and family formation, the more the new family may be denied housing or health coverage that are provided single-parent welfare families.

For the paternalism to be appropriate, there must be congruence between the needs of the client and the requirements of society. But organizations that advocate for fragile families must to some extent oppose government, at least until the systemic difficulties they see to family formation among the poor are alleviated. This may indicate that as poor citizens move toward functioning, the paternalist harmony of interests can no longer be assumed.

Conclusion

The development of child support enforcement marks a progression toward greater and greater institutional ambition. Each regime has added a new element to the enforcement structure. The self-administered system established the absent parent's basic obligation to support children. The CSE regime added administrative enforcement. To this the paternalist regime adds a supervisory structure to improve enforcement, but also directs more attention to the needs of fathers. Finally, the concept of the fragile family builds on all this to repair bonds within the poor family. Once the outside institutions are in place, the focus turns inward to the problems of private life.

We do not minimize the practical problems of authorizing or implementing any of these approaches. Child support has not recently been a subject of politic contention; left and right have agreed on ever tougher policies to secure support payments much more readily than they have on welfare reform. But division is bound to increase if, as seems likely, the newest and toughest standards lead to active hardship for the poorest fathers with little gain for their families.

To judge from the past, the administrative challenges are even more daunting. None of the regimes has overcome all its internal problems. The private regime lacked enforcement weight and the CSE regime, while tough in theory, has not yet solved the difficult tracking and oversight problems needed to obligate many nonpaying parents. Paternalist programs arose in part to meet those challenges, but are themselves complicated, requiring many more services and complex ties among agencies. The fragile family model is potentially the most demanding of all. Still in its early stages, it depends on inspired local leadership to develop.

The encouraging thing about the paternalist and fragile family regimes is that they transcend the debate on the roles of social structure and culture that has traditionally polarized discussions about poverty in America. Structuralists focus on the loss of jobs or racial exclusion as the main cause of poverty; culturalists focus on attitudes, behaviors, norms, and permissive government policy. In his best known work William J. Wilson made a brilliant effort to synthesize the two positions by seeing the cultural despair of the inner city as the product of economic restructuring.[68] Philip Moss and Christopher Tilly, among others, looked for policy options that bridge the divide.[69] Most recently, Wilson has restated his argument based on new research and advocates of family values have responded.[70]

Clearly, for youth and young adults ready and willing to work, opportunities should be provided. The critical problem has been what to do for young men who have formed a family without a commitment, rejected the workplace, and so forth. The poor nonpayers, whom the child support system grapples with, are a significant part of this group.

In recent policy debates, talk of tough love and coercive sanctions has dominated. The evidence says, however, that smart love—strengthening the bonds between fathers and children—may be better. From conversations among practitioners and tentative studies of pilot programs and demonstrations, the point emerges that for a marginalized man, contact with his children, an opportunity to reflect on his own fatherlessness, and nonadversarial relations with his children's mother are the greatest needs. Such contact can also ease the burden experienced by a mother rearing children alone. To achieve these results, the purpose of child support must go beyond enforcing payments to strengthening fragile families. These ties can also attach such a man to the labor force.

Such programs are still paternalist. To work, they require the enforcement of child support, backed up by the usual penalties. They still link new benefits with old responsibilities. However, the rationale for enforcement should not be statist. There is no virtue per se in weighing poor men down with public authority. Community groups are a vital part of the exercise, and we reject the idea that the state knows best. Indeed, the more families are rebuilt, the less formal authority is needed and the more antipoverty policy can move out from under the shadow of the state.

Notes

1. Major sources for the following discussion include Irwin Garfinkel, *Assuring Child Support: An Extension of Social Security* (Russell Sage Foundation, 1992); Office of Child Support Enforcement, "Nineteenth Annual Report to Congress for the Period Ending September 30, 1994," Department of Health and Human Services, 1996; and House Committee on Ways and Means, *1996 Green Book: Background Material and Data on Programs with the Jurisdiction of the Committee on Ways and Means* (Government Printing Office, 1996), pp. 529–623.

2. Robert G. Williams, "Establishing Paternity: Can States Meet the 90 Percent Welfare Reform Standard?" *Chicago Policy Review*, vol 1, no. 1, pp. 95–112.

3. Ronald B. Mincy, "Strengthening Fragile Families: A Proposed Strategy for the Ford Foundation Urban Poverty Program," Ford Foundation, New York, 1994.

4. Jeanne King, "Man Freed after Agreeing to $500,000 Child Support," *Philadelphia Inquirer*, December 8, 1995, p. A12.

5. Figures derived from House Committee on Ways and Means, *1996 Green Book*, pp. 577–80.

6. Elaine Sorenson, "The Benefits of Increased Child Support Enforcement," Welfare Reform Briefs 2, Urban Institute, Washington, April 1995.

7. These numbers are expressed as a range because they include estimates of private child support collections.

8. House Committee on Ways and Means, *1996 Green Book*, p. 583.

9. David T. Ellwood, "Welfare Reform As I Knew It," *American Prospect*, no. 26 (May-June 1996), pp. 22–29.

10. Office of Child Support Enforcement, "Nineteenth Annual Report to Congress," pp. 35, 40, 45.

11. House Committee on Ways and Means, *1996 Green Book*, pp. 595–97.

12. Office of Child Support Enforcement, "Nineteenth Annual Report to Congress," table 21.

13.Twenty years ago Aaron Wildavsky and Jeff Pressman first invited social scientists to pay more attention to the administration of policy, noting that implementation matters so much that if the interests, concerns, and engagement of implementers are not taken into account, the policy may fail. This contradicted the then prevalent view that implementation is pro forma and implementors are neutral. In the Wildavsky-Pressman paradigm, profits matter. That is, certain incentives to implementors help produce a successful policy. Paternalism assumes that profits are not enough. The client's perception of self-interest is also important to program success, and how an agent structures (or administers) a program affects how a client perceives self-interest.

14. Rebecca Maynard, ed., *Building Self-Sufficiency among Welfare-Dependent Teenage Parents: Lessons from the Teenage Parent Demonstration* (Princeton, N.J.: Mathematica Policy Research, 1993), p. xix.

15. Ronald B Mincy and Hillard Pouncy, "There Must Be Fifty Ways to Start a Family: Social Policy and the Fragile Families of Low-Income, Noncustodial Fathers," paper prepared for the conference Fatherhood Movement: A Call to Action, Minneapolis, October 1996.

16. "Executive Summary of the Paternal Involvement Demonstration Project," Chicago, 1996.

17. Elaine Sorenson and Mark Turner, "Barriers in Child Support Policy That Discourage Noncustodial Fathers' Involvement in the Lives of Their Children: A Literature Review," paper prepared for the System Barriers Roundtable, sponsored by the National Center on Fathers and Families, Philadelphia, Pa., May 29, 1996.

18. Mary Jo Bane and David Ellwood, *Welfare Realities: From Rhetoric to Reform* (Harvard University Press, 1994), chap. 2.

19. Ronald B. Mincy and Elaine Sorenson, "Deadbeats and Turnips in Child Support Reform," *Journal of Policy Analysis and Management* (forthcoming).

20. Elaine Sorenson, "A National Profile of Nonresident Fathers and Their Ability to Pay Child Suppport," *Journal of Marriage and the Family*, vol. 59 (November 1997).

21. Greg J. Duncan and Saul D. Hoffman, "A Reconsideration of the Economic Consequences of Marital Dissolution," *Demography,* vol. 22 (November 1985), pp. 485–97.

22. Mincy and Sorenson, "Deadbeats and Turnips," pp. 3–4.

23. Ibid.

24. We use *regime* as defined by Jay M. Shafritz, *The Dorsey Dictionary of American Government and Politics* (Chicago: Dorsey Press, 1988): "any generally accepted or customary procedures."

25. The following discussion relies on Garfinkel, *Assuring Child Support*, chap. 2.

26. Ibid., p. 30.

27. Bureau of the Census, *Statistical Abstract of the United States: 1981* (Department of Commerce, 1981), p. 65; and *Statistical Abstract of the United States: 1996*, p. 79.

28. Sara McLanahan and Gary Sandefur, *Growing Up with a Single Parent: What Hurts, What Helps* (Harvard University Press, 1994).

29. House Committee on Ways and Means, *1996 Green Book*, pp. 473, 533.

30. Ibid., p. 535.

31. Ibid., p. 538.

32. Ibid., pp. 580, 582.

33. Ibid., pp. 578, 580.

34. Maynard, *Building Self-Sufficiency*, pp. 22–23.

35. Dan Bloom and Kay Sherwood, *Matching Opportunities to Obligations: Lessons for Child Support Reform from the Parents' Fair Share Pilot Phase* (New York: Manpower Demonstration Research Corp, 1994), p. 3.

36. Lawrence M. Mead, "The New Paternalism in Action: Welfare Reform in Wisconsin," Wisconsin Policy Research Institute, Milwaukee, January 1995, p. 34.

37. Bloom and Sherwood, *Matching Opportunities to Obligations*, pp. 5–7.

38. This requirement can be calculated either as 90 percent of a state's entire past and present Title IV(D) caseloads (the Title IV(D) standard) or 90 percent of the state's previous number of nonmarital births (the universal standard).

39. Policy Studies, Inc., "Voluntary Paternity Acknowledge Program Results—Fact Sheet," Denver, 1997. See also Jane C. Venohr, Robert G. Williams, and Dawn E. Baxter, "Results from the Massachusetts Paternity Acknowledgement Program: Final Quarterly Report," Child Support Enforcement Division, Massachusetts Department of Revenue, September 1996; and Robert G. Williams and others, "Massachusetts Paternity Acknowledgement Program: Implementation Analysis and Program Results," Child Support Enforcement Division, Massachusetts Department of Revenue, May 1995.

40. Their compliance rate is less than 90 percent, but their rapid improvement satisfies alternative standards for rate of increase in yearly compliance.

41. Williams and others, "Massachusetts Paternity Acknowledgement Program," p. 52.

42. Children First, also known as the Community Work Experience Program for Noncustodial Parents (CWEP-NCP), was authorized by Wisconsin's 1987 Welfare Reform Act. The following discussion is based on State of Wisconsin, "Wisconsin Welfare Reform: The 'Children First' Program," June 1993; Sandra Cleveland, "Children First: Community Work Experience Program for Non-Custodial Parents," Wisconsin Department of Health and Social Services, May 1991; and Cleveland, "Process Evaluation of Wisconsin's Children First Program," Wisconsin Department of Health and Social Services, December 1995.

43. Clients enrolled in the program must have been ordered to pay child support by a court in a county where a Children First program exists. Criteria for consideration are that they work less than thirty-two hours a week in an unsubsidized job, their gross income is less than a specified multiple of the federal minimum hourly wage, they are not currently in a training program, they are able to work full time, and they do not have custody of their children.

44. State of Wisconsin, "Wisconsin Welfare Reform," p. 4.

45. Cleveland, "Children First," p. 8.

46. Interview with Gerry Hamilton, October, 26, 1996.

47. John A. Wagner, "The Children First Program: A Report to the Administrator," Wisconsin Department of Health and Social Services, 1993, pp. 5–8.

48. Cleveland, "Process Evaluation," pp. 22–27.

49. Joe Klein, "'Make the Daddies Pay,'" *Newsweek*, June 21, 1993, p. 33.

50. Sandra Cleveland, "Summary of 1994 Children First Data," Wisconsin Office of Strategic Finance, 1996, pp. 7–8.

51. The other sites were Annapolis, Md.; Cleveland, Ohio; Fresno, Calif.; Philadelphia, Pa.; and St. Petersburg, Fla.

52. Mary Achatz and Crystal A. MacAllum, "Young Unwed Fathers: Report from the Field," Public/Private Ventures, Philadelphia, 1994.

53. Bloom and Sherwood, *Matching Opportunities to Obligations*.

54. Fred Doolittle and Suzanne Lynn, "What Happens with Increased Enforce-

ment of the Child Support Obligations of Poor Men? A Ground-Level View from The Parents' Fair Share Demonstration," Manpower Demonstration Research Corp., New York, 1997.

55. Bloom and Sherwood, *Matching Opportunities to Obligations*, chap. 5.

56. Ibid., pp. 82–89.

57. Frank F. Furstenberg Jr., Kay E. Sherwood, and Mercer L. Sullivan, *Caring and Paying: What Fathers and Mothers Say about Child Support* (New York: Manpower Demonstration Research Corp., 1992); and Earl S. Johnson and Fred Doolittle, "Low-Income Parents and the Parents' Fair Share Demonstration," Manpower Demonstration Research Corp., New York, June 1996.

58.Katherine Newman, "Working Poor: Low Wage Employment in the Lives of Harlem Youth," in J. Graber, J. Brooks-Gunn, and A. Petersen, eds., *Transitions through Adolescence: Interpersonal Domains and Context* (Mahwah, N.J.: Erlbaum Associates, 1996), pp. 232–44.

59. Phillippe I. Bourgois, *In Search of Respect: Selling Crack in El Barrio* (Cambridge University Press, 1995); and Richard Majors and Janet Mancini Billson, *Cool Pose: The Dilemmas of Black Manhood in America* (Lexington, Mass.: Lexington Books, 1992).

60. Daniel R. Meyer, "Can Fathers Support Children Born outside of Marriage? Data on Fathers' Incomes over Time," in Daniel R. Meyer, ed., *Paternity Establishment: A Public Policy Conference*, vol. 2: *Studies of the Circumstance of Mothers and Fathers* (Madison, Wisc: Institute for Research on Poverty, 1992), pp. 223–61.

61. Cleveland, "Process Evaluation," p. 27; and Cleveland, "Summary of 1994 Children First Data," p. 8.

62. Bloom and Sherwood, *Matching Opportunities to Obligations*, pp. 109–10.

63. Furstenberg, Sherwood, and Sullivan, *Caring and Paying*.

64. Bloom and Sherwood, *Matching Opportunities to Obligations*, p.xxxvii.

65. Mincy, "Strengthening Fragile Families."

66. Sorenson and Turner, "Barriers in Child Support Policy."

67. Paternal Involvement Demonstration Project, "Statistical Summary of Direct Service Sites," Chicago, June 1996.

68. William Julius Wilson, *The Truly Disadvantaged: The Inner City, The Underclass, and Public Policy* (University of Chicago Press, 1987).

69. Philip Moss and Chris Tilly, "Why Black Men Are Doing Worse in the Labor Market: A Review of Supply-Side and Demand-Side Explanations," Social Science Research Council, New York, August 1991.

70. William Julius Wilson, *When Work Disappears: The World of the New Urban Poor* (Knopf, 1997); and David Blankenhorn, *Fatherless America: Confronting Our Most Urgent Social Problem* (Basic Books, 1995).

Five

Homeless Men in New York City: Toward Paternalism through Privatization

Thomas J. Main

New York City is the home of the nation's only unambiguous entitlement to shelter, or at least so thought the city's homeless policy community until very recently. In 1984 the "right to shelter" was the cornerstone of the city's homeless policy, and advocates for the homeless were already nostalgically "recalling the history of the successful fight to establish that right."[1] Indeed, something resembling such a right had been established by the consent decree that settled *Callahan* v. *Carey*. In 1992 a city judge wrote, "The current standard for entry into a shelter is simple—any family or individual who needs housing receives shelter."[2] Still today, through the Department of Homeless Services (DHS), New York City oversees the largest network of homeless shelters and services in the country. But the trend in city homeless policy, especially under the Guiliani administration, has for some years moved in an unmistakably paternalistic direction.

There has been a radical change in New York City's policy toward homeless men. It is strikingly illustrated by the story of the 8 East Third Street facility of the city's shelter system. I have studied New York City's shelter system for nearly fifteen years.[3] When I began my researches into homelessness in the early 1980s, 8 East Third Street, located in the heart of Manhattan's Bowery and serving as the citywide intake point for homeless single men, was a frightening place for anyone not inured to life on the streets. On my visits, there were always many ragged, unclean men loitering on the sidewalk for half a block on either side of the entrance. Even before entering, a strong unpleasant odor was very noticeable. Inside, scores of men waited in no apparent order to be seen by the "5 × 8 staff," who conducted a perfunctory interview that produced an index card with some basic information about the applicant. Security was not evident, and on one occasion I was unpleasantly approached by one of the men. Such security as there was focused on protecting the front office from break-ins. The *New York Times* remembered, "Chaos reigned as men checked in for meals and vouchers that purchased beds in nearby flophouses. Between meals, homeless men milled constantly on the street, dealing drugs and panhandling."[4]

A revisit to 8 East Third Street in the mid-1990s reveals an institution seemingly transformed as thoroughly as any pumpkin ever was by a fairy godmother. The building has been completely cleaned, repainted, and redecorated. The stale smell is gone, not to be found even in the facility's washrooms and kitchen. (To accomplish this it was necessary to tear up the sidewalk outside the building and lay new concrete.) The men themselves are clean and better clothed.

But as striking as the improved quality of life is the change in practices at the new 8 East Third Street. No clients are to be seen on the street. The men are issued laminated ID cards, and everybody wears them, visible for all to see. There is no pointless waiting or wandering. All the men one sees are either obviously doing something—attending a meeting, providing security, doing clerical or cleaning work—or seem to be on their way to do something. Nothing untoward was said or done to me during my visit. Indeed, when I entered one dormitory, a man who was also a sort of watchman got up from his desk, shook my hand, and bade me welcome. It turned out he thought I was a new client, who should be greeted in this fashion as standard operating procedure.

Besides the obviously improved levels of amenity and order, 8 East Third Street's program—the set of distinct services, procedures, and achievements that clients are expected to complete in some specific sequence—has also been revitalized. Fourteen years ago, as the intake point of the men's system the facility did not have a program beyond the interview with the 5 × 8 staff. A small infirmary that slept some dozen men was the only on-site service available. For everything else, including shelter and food, men were referred elsewhere in the system, or to commercial flophouses in the neighborhoods where the city paid for their stay.

Today 8 East Third Street no longer serves as a general intake point but as a program shelter to which men elsewhere are referred. Prospective clients must already be in the shelter system, suffer from substance abuse problems, and be willing to participate in the facility's highly structured six-month therapeutic program. Incoming clients sign a contract, specifying the cardinal rules they must obey, which include prohibitions on violence, substance abuse, and sexual activity. Clients also agree to shower daily, keep a neat appearance, and provide urine for drug testing on staff request.[5]

Once they are accepted, residents are assigned a case manager, with whom they work out a treatment plan that specifies attending at least three program meetings a week, perhaps including on-site GED classes or substance abuse meetings. As they complete their plan, they move through three stages, indicated by the color of a sticker they are given to wear on their identification. Compliance with the treatment plan is monitored by the case manager and enforced through various disciplinary actions. Residents are supposed to complete their plan in six months. If they do not, their stay may be extended for up to nine months. A resident who has not completed his program by then is referred out of the facility to another shelter with a less demanding or more appropriate program.

Thus the changes at 8 East Third are, first, an improved quality of life and degree of order and, second, the development of a strong, mandatory program. How typical are these changes of the development of New York City's shelter system in the past fifteen years? And more important for this book, what brought about these changes toward paternalism and what have the consequences been?

In researching this chapter during the spring of 1996, I interviewed representatives of the city's Department of Homeless Services and officials of the New York State Department of Social Services who were responsible for regulating the city system. I also talked with the director and chief shelter monitor of Coalition for the Homeless, the city's main advocacy organization, and the directors and various staff members of private, nonprofit shelters, including Project Renewal, the Doe Fund, and the Salvation Army. I visited facilities operated by all these organizations, giving special attention to 8 East Third Street and the Borden Avenue Veterans Shelter, which is operated by the Salvation Army.[6] I also reviewed recent court documents for *Callahan* v. *Carey* and other court cases that relate to the consent decree under which the city's shelters for individuals continue to operate. I examined city program material on the shelter system and the reports in the annual *Mayor's Management Report,* which includes figures for total numbers of men in the shelters. The available data however, did not include output indicators, such as out placement rates, and no evaluation has been done to assess the shelters' effects on their clients net of other influences.

My main impressions are that, first, during the past fifteen years the politics of policy on the city's homeless have metamorphosed from a rights-based struggle over services to administrative reorganization aimed at both better support and stricter governance of clients. Second, perhaps because of New York City's unique legal situation, implementing a more paternalistic regime in the homeless system has required greater privatization of the system. However, before I can discuss these developments I need to describe briefly how homelessness has been thought about and how this thought has influenced policy.

What We Thought We Knew about Homelessness

The two main schools of thought for understanding homelessness in America have been those of the functionalist sociologists and the structuralist accounts of recent researchers and advocates. Both approaches to the problem implied that what are here called paternalistic policies were likely to fail.

Functionalist sociologists, whose empirical work was done mostly among alcoholic skid row men, defined homelessness as a form of disaffiliation, a condition of extreme detachment from society. Earlier authors in this tradition suggested that homeless men might be cut off from any form of society at all, in which case they fit into the category of just barely human. As one author of this school wrote, the homeless are "about as different from *Homo sociologus* as it is possible to be while still remaining human."[7] Later authors backed away from this absolutism and emphasized that the homeless were disaffiliated merely from the mainstream society and its values of work, home, family, and self-reliance. By these accounts the homeless were well affiliated with the "deviant" societies of bottle gangs, skid row, hobos, and so forth.[8] The policy upshot of both schools' concepts was that the homeless should be accommodated in their lifestyle as much as possible because they were either irretrievably dissaffiliated or were already affiliated with a functional, if deviant, subculture. "Rehabilitative" therapies were rejected because they sought "to get the individual to change his behavior. . . . Such a view often leads to the persistence of forces which create human problems but lie outside the individual."[9]

In both its earlier and later elaborations, functionalist sociology left hanging the question of why homeless men were disaffiliated or affiliated with only deviant subcultures. Although earlier writers in this tradition suggested that some disabling condition had detached these men from society, later writers argued that this disability was merely apparent and that homelessness was more a matter of potentially functional men being oppressed by social forces such as police enforcement of vagrancy laws and the exploitive practices of missions and other skid row institutions.[10] But these explanations could not account for the apparent increase in homelessness during the late 1970s and early 1980s when police enforcement of vagrancy and public order laws had relaxed and there was no evidence that missions and skid row institutions were any more or less exploitive than they had ever been. At this point social research began to look for some new set of social forces to which homelessness could be attributed.

During the early 1980s researchers associated with the Coalition for the Homeless and Community Service Society in New York began to develop a purely structuralist account of homelessness. This view blamed the "new homelessness" not on personal problems but on cutbacks in social programs, deindustrialization, and housing shortages. Deinstitutionalization was recognized as another cause, but the high rates of mental illness and other disabilities among the homeless were held to be of secondary importance. As one analysis commented, "Again, the problem is not primarily one of personal inadequacy. . . . The decisive factor that transformed the wretchedly quartered deinstitutionalized into the wandering deranged was—and remains—the depletion of the low-income housing stock."[11]

Some structural analysts implied that the social forces that had increased homelessness were elaborate and global: "There are homeless people in the streets of New York because there are steel mills in South Korea."[12] By the early 1990s most academic researchers, while not denying the significance of disability and mental illness, settled on some mix of increasing poverty and decreasing units of affordable housing as the main trends that were driving people into the streets.[13] Frequently this literature analogizes homelessness to an impersonal machine or game: "homelessness is like a game of musical chairs. The more people playing the game, and the fewer the chairs, the more people left standing when the music stops."[14]

The structuralist interpretation of homelessness also implied that paternalistic programs aimed at changing lifestyles could not be a solution to homelessness because the attempt to enforce work, sobriety, and stability implied that a disordered life was a cause of homelessness. This connection the structuralist account denied. Homeless people might be disproportionately mentally ill, or substance addicted, but these traits were not the cause of their homelessness. Rather, less affordable housing and more poverty were. As one structural account commented, "in a hypothetical world where there were no alcoholics, no drug addicts, no mentally ill, no deinstitutionalization movement, no personal or social pathologies at all, there would *still* be a formidable homeless problem, simply because there is not enough low-income housing to accommodate the poverty population."[15]

In this view the alcoholic, mentally ill, or addicted should of course be offered treatment for their condition, but as a matter of decency and entitlement. There was no point in conditioning or regulating access to housing and other vital services on the basis of an achievement of behavioral norms that had no immediate relevance to the homeless man's plight.

Structural accounts of homelessness also had what might be called an antibureaucratic aspect. Paternalism requires an administrative structure that can link enforcement of behavioral norms with provision of services. For homeless men, that usually means a shelter of some sort. But strucutralist analysts denied that expanding or strengthening shelter systems could be a solution to homelessness. They might admit that shelters were the only feasible response in the short term, but if lack of affordable housing was the real cause of the problem, the real solution could only be government intervention to produce more affordable housing or reduce poverty or both. The solution, in short, was a reinvigorated welfare state. According to Dennis Culhane, who has done pathbreaking research on the dynamics of the homeless population, "the ability of shelters to serve as homeless management agencies is constrained by the structural causes of the homeless problem. . . . The fate of the shelter system is therefore tied to the functioning of the social welfare system and will be more determined by its policies than the policies that govern the behavior of shelter clients and providers."[16]

The structuralist account of homelessness, which until recently was the dominant analysis in academic circles, struck at both sides of the paternalistic contract. The dysfunctional behaviors of homeless men called for treatment but were not the primary causes of their homelessness. Requirements that they mend their ways could therefore not be part of a reasonable quid pro quo for services. And the main administrative forum for delivering services and enforcing behavioral norms—the shelters—are only a stopgap response to a crisis. The real answer was in a larger reform of society.

However, recent research and, more importantly, policy developments have cast doubt on the structuralist account. Evidence that a low-income housing squeeze in the late 1970s pitched otherwise functional men into the streets and shelters is not strong. Some increase in the number of poor households per affordable rental unit occurred in big cities during the late 1970s and early 1980s, but it was probably only about one-fourth as much as structuralist analysts had claimed.[17] In general, housing market trends have not developed as the structuralist analysis requires. For example, vacancy rates in affordable rentals have not dropped as one would assume they would during a low-income housing squeeze.[18] Attempts to explain homeless rates with structural economic and social variables have not been very successful.[19] So if ultimate causes are unclear, policy must after all focus on the immediate cause of homelessness, which is usually the disordered life of the homeless.

Nor has policy developed as structuralists have advised. As they feared, shelter systems built up in response to the homeless crisis of the 1980s remain the backbone of most cities' homeless policy, and the hoped-for revival of income and housing entitlement programs has not materialized. Cities have been finding that shelters and related services can be managed well or poorly. But to manage them well requires turning away from a purely entitlement-based system to a more paternalistically oriented one. And nowhere has this policy pendulum swung more dramatically than in New York City.

The Development of Homeless Policy in New York City

New York City's contemporary homeless policy may be said to have begun with the signing of the *Callahan* v. *Carey* consent decree in 1981. *Callahan* was a quintessential example of policy entrepreneurship through judicial means. The case was brought under New York state law against the state and city governments by Robert Hayes, a legal aid attorney and later council for the Coalition for the Homeless. Before the decree the city would provide shelter for perhaps one hundred men and turn others away when that capacity was reached. Hayes argued that a provision of the state constitution required the state and the city to provide shelter to whatever homeless man requested it.

The court never ruled on whether there was a state constitutional right to shelter. The case led to a consent decree between the city and state and the representatives of the homeless, the key provision of which was that any applicant was to be provided shelter if the man met the need standard to qualify for the home relief program established in New York State or if the man by reason of physical, mental, or social dysfunction is in need of temporary shelter.[20]

The decree also set detailed quality standards that city shelters had to meet. For example, the proper ratio of showers and toilets to clients was established, and when the city asked to have this ratio changed, a fierce legal battle ensued in which Hayes and the Coalition for the Homeless eventually persuaded the court to deny the request. In 1982 the right to shelter secured for men under the *Callahan* decree was extended to women in *Eldredge* v. *Koch*. And in *Lamboy* v. *Gross* and *McCain* v. *Koch* advocates "established a judicially enforceable right to immediate provision of appropriate emergency shelter to homeless families and their children."[21] Throughout the 1980s city homeless policy was driven by the pressure of the Coalition for the Homeless and other advocates to have every provision of the decree implemented generously and the city's resistance to that pressure on the ground that it was doing everything it could. Suggestions that clients ought to "give something back" in the form of required work in return for shelter services came to little. Policy continued to focus on expanding the supply of emergency shelter to which clients were entitled through various court rulings.[22]

During the Dinkins administration, policy emphasized expanding the entitlement, at least for homeless families, from emergency shelter to permanent shelter. During the spring and summer of 1990 the administration began relocating hundreds of homeless families in shelters and "welfare hotels" directly into refurbished, city-owned permanent apartments. Entries into the family shelter system increased from about 530 families a month in April to 650 in July.[23] The absolute increase was small, but it strained the city's supply of family shelters and welfare hotels. Before long, the administration was forced to rethink its policy. It established the New York City Commission on the Homeless, chaired by Andrew Cuomo, to do exactly that.

The Cuomo Commission's report, *The Way Home: A New Direction in*

Social Policy, released in February 1992, marked the beginning of the city's turn away from a purely entitlement-based policy and toward something recognizable as paternalism. One of the report's primary recommendations was to limit access to shelters by implementing eligibility determinations. The thought was that because resources were limited, "government should not, and cannot, be expected to provide housing to everyone who asks for it."[24] Therefore applicants should be required to make some sort of demonstration of need.

The commission might have stopped there, but perhaps because there was doubt as to whether eligibility determinations really would limit shelter entries, it went further and emphasized that the system could expect of applicants not only a demonstration of need but reciprocity. "The emergency shelter system must incorporate a balance of rights and responsibilities. A social contract and a mutuality of obligation must exist between those receiving help and society-at-large."[25] Such talk did not sit well with the more liberal factions of the Dinkins administration, but by this point it was too divided to take much action on any of the commission's recommendations.

Rudolf Giuliani, elected mayor in 1993, had no such compunction. The new administration's plan, "Reforming New York City's System of Homeless Services," explicitly embraced the Cuomo report and the concept of mutual obligation. Thus a primary reform objective of DHS under Commissioner Joan Malin was "mutual responsibility":

> Eligibility rules ensure that those most in need of assistance and services have access to them. . . . Mutual responsibility will be established through an agreement known as an independent living plan, signed by both the provider and recipient, which indicates the homeless persons' acceptance of the responsibility to participate in programs provided to assist them in resolving their crises and in moving toward independent living.[26]

However, the Giuliani administration soon discovered problems.

Paternalism through Eligibility Blocked

In the wake of the *Callahan* consent decree, no process for determining eligibility for the shelters had been developed because the language of the decree seemed to establish eligibility criteria so broad that any shelter applicant was likely to meet them. The mechanism through which the new mayor planned to enforce mutual responsibility was to "implement a comprehensive eligibility determination process and ensure that scarce resources will be available to those most in need."[27] The administration reasoned that however poor an applicant might be, there was still at least a formal question of whether he qualified for home relief or was physically, mentally, or socially dysfunctional. And if upon investigation applicants turned out to meet these criteria, was it not reasonable that they be "expected to cooperate with staff and not-for-profit providers to identify the resources to which they may be entitled, and the assistance and services they need"? If so, and given that the consent decree reserved the right of the state to promulgate regulations for the shelters, couldn't this expectation be expressed in a written and signed "independent living plan," as DHS's reform plan called for? The Giuliani administration asked Governor George Pataki to have the New York State Department of Social Services promulgate the regulations necessary to establish eligibility determinations and the independent living plans.[28]

Unfortunately, to date the city has not persuaded the courts of the validity of this approach. Shortly after the new state regulations were promulgated on an emergency basis, New York State Supreme Court Justice Helen G. Freedman temporarily barred the city from implementing them as far as homeless families were concerned.[29] The Coalition for the Homeless similarly requested of Judge Stanley L. Sklar, who oversaw the implementation of the *Callahan* decree, to declare the state regulations null and void. CFTH argued that the decree "established minimal eligibility criteria for the purpose of avoiding the disqualification of needy individuals from assistance who were unable to navigate bureaucratic requirements. It is just such requirements that the emergency regulations seek to impose on Plaintiffs now."[30] So far Judge Sklar has made no ruling on the permissibility of eligibility requirements and independent living plans under *Callahan*. The city has agreed not to implement the regulations and to notify the court should it decide to do so. While all parties await Justice Freeman's decision regarding families, the city is developing an implementation strategy that will pass muster under *Callahan*.

Paternalism through Privatization

If overt paternalism in city-run shelters is stalled in court, the city has found another strategy to achieve the same end: privatization. Before the late 1980s, contracting out for shelter provision had not been a major city policy. Both Manhattan Borough President David Dinkins and the City Council criticized what they believed was the city's underuse of nonprofits as shelter providers.[31] Perhaps in response to these criticisms, in its 1987 final report Mayor Koch's Advisory Task Force on the Homeless signaled a change in direction by recommending the city "increase participation by nonprofit service providers and other private sector groups in developing and operating temporary housing."[32] Despite his earlier support for the direction, however, when Dinkins became mayor in 1989 no dramatic privatizations took place, partly because other policy developments, especially the crisis in homeless families, distracted his attention.

When the Cuomo Commission reported, it also recommended that the city "not-for-profitize" the shelter system. The city should "refer individuals in need of service out of the shelters and into appropriate, existing not-for-profit residential service programs."[33] Although this recommendation really only restated Dinkins's earlier support for nonprofits, the commission's suggestion that the increased supply of apartments available to shelter families had caused the surge in new entries divided the administration and prevented action.[34]

In one of the debates of the 1993 mayoral campaign, Giuliani made a point of Dinkins's tardiness in embracing the Cuomo Commission report.[35] When Giuliani became mayor, he picked Joan Malin as commissioner of the new Department of Homeless Services. In May 1994 Malin's plan for reforming New York City's system of homeless services made the development of "small, community-based programs, provided by not-for-profits," one of its ten primary objectives. "The not-for-profit community has been at the forefront of identifying and providing for the needs of homeless people. An even greater reliance will be placed on it to deliver these services."[36]

Another virtue of privatization was economy. *The Way Home* denounced as absurd the $18,000 a year it estimated the shelter system spent for each homeless single person. It estimated that construction of shelters by nonprofits and for-profits would reduce future construction costs by 15 percent. The report argued further that nonprofit shelters would be more effective at enrolling clients in medicaid, JTPA, and other programs for which the city received federal reimbursements, thus saving an additional 15 percent.[37] When the Giuliani administration began to accelerate privatization, it claimed that some savings were realized. DHS's expenditures for the first quarter of fiscal year 1995 were $15.2 million less than what had been anticipated, and this Giuliani attributed to cost savings from contracting out.[38] How real these supposed savings were is questionable.

Privatization and the Exercise of Authority

What is clear is that privatization advanced under the Giuliani administration as never before. The improvements at 8 East Third Street may be attributed to it. Before 1991 the shelter was operated by the city. Since then the city has contracted with the private nonprofit Project Renewal (formerly the Manhattan Bowery Project) to operate the facility. It is now officially referred to as the Third Street Program, as if to stress the new emphasis on requiring clients to move through a process.

The percentage of occupied shelter beds for single homeless men offered by private nonprofits under contract to the city has grown dramatically during the 1990s (table 5-1). At the same time, the number of homeless men served by the shelters has decreased. This might be due to the new shelter policies or to some other force such as an improving economy. No evaluation has been done that could separate these factors.

Besides the possible cost savings and the decrease in the census numbers, privatization of the shelters made possible the development of a more

Table 5-1. Occupied Beds for Homeless Men Offered by Public, Private Nonprofit, and Other Providers, New York City, 1988–96

Dollars unless otherwise specified

	1988	*1989*	*1990*	*1991*	*1992*	*1993*	*1994*	*1995*	*1996*
City-run	73.1	82.1	78.8	77.4	70.0	67.2	63.0	59.5	45.7
Nonprofit	16.7	15.0	18.5	22.6	30.0	32.8	37.0	40.5	54.3
Profit	10.1	2.9	2.7	. . .	. . .	. . .	. . .	. . .	. . .
Total men	8,122	7,681	6,956	6,110	5,212	4,859	5,002	5,790	5,865
Average daily census	8,462	8,326	7,400	6,913	6,043	5,406	5,231	5,083	5,623

Sources: New York City, Department of Homeless Services, "Shelter Bed Statistics: Report No. 1"; New York City, *Mayor's Management Report*; and Interviews with James Dolan and Charles Elioseff of New York State Department of Social Services. Total occupancy and percentages are based on census of men's shelters on December 31 of each year, except for 1995 and 1996, which are based on the census of December 25 and 26 respectively. Some percentages do not add to 100 due to rounding.

paternalistic system. Whereas the courts did not allow the city to levy requirements on clients in city-run shelters, they have allowed it in the nonprofit-run facilities to which public shelters refer clients. Thus the *Callahan* decree so far effectively means the city must provide *some* shelter to every applicant and that such shelter be of a specified *quality*. But the decree had nothing to say on where or how shelter is to be provided. When the issue came up as to whether the Borden Avenue Veterans Shelter, a Salvation Army shelter under contract to the city, could require its residents to undergo drug testing, the city successfully argued that it could.

> The Salvation Army, if it were a state actor, would not be violating shelter residents' due process rights by refusing to allow them to stay at BAVS since there is no right to stay in a shelter of one's choice and since the City will provide alternate shelter to residents who do not wish to subscribe to the BAVS program. . . . The consent decree in *Callahan* wherein New York City agreed to minimum standards for homeless men's shelters does not effect this issue.[39]

Under privatization the shelter system developed two tracks. Clients who request shelter from the city without requirements can get it in such city-run general shelters as the Thirtieth Street Shelter at Bellevue Hospital, which, besides serving as the intake point to the single men's system, is a general population shelter for some 520 residents. Another city-run general shelter is the upstate Camp LaGuardia Shelter with approximately 1,000 clients. These facilities offer little in the way of services and programs. They do not enjoy the best reputation, but they are subject to the quality and access specifications of the *Callahan* decree, and in providing them the city fulfills its legal responsibilities.

To get better programs and services, shelter residents have to volunteer to enter the so-called program shelters, those that offer a set of services aimed at the needs of some particular type of client. Most program shelters are run by private nonprofits. This is so not because public shelters are incapable of offering programs; for example, the Greenpoint Shelter with its program for substance abusers is city-run. But since the state will only approve and subsidize those private shelters that offer some specific program, desirable programs tend to be in the private rather than the public shelters.

And the private shelters have the power to enforce rules that the city lacks. Because clients have no right to a particular shelter, private shelters may require and enforce participation in their program as long as noncompliant clients are free to return to a general shelter. The two-track system gives clients a degree of choice that is not available in an all-city-run system. It also makes possible an exercise of authority that is less drastic, but perhaps more effective, than the impermissible denial of city shelters. Indeed, the provision of choice and the existence of a useable sanction go hand-in-hand. It is because clients make a voluntary choice to go to a certain program shelter that the shelters can reasonably expect clients to adhere to their program. For what sense does it make to volunteer for a program of which one wants no part?

A Private, Nonprofit Shelter and Its Program

To get a sense of how the private nonprofits operate, it is useful to look at one of the oldest of these shelters, the Borden Avenue Veterans Residence (BAVR or, less commonly, BAVS). This shelter illustrates how the system has taken advantage of its de facto two-tier structure to become more paternalistic. It is also one of the best documented shelters because of the work of anthropologist Janice M. Hirota.[40] BAVR's program material makes clear its authoritative philosophy:

> To create an atmosphere where staff and veterans know how to proceed, BAVR has developed a two-part contract that "obligates" the new arrival to a social service plan that will lead to "mutual goals" agreed to by the man and the administrators of the residence.
>
> Part A of the contract is the price and ticket of admission. The man must be a veteran, and he must come from one of the more than twenty shelters in the city's system. The A Contract outlines the rules and regulations the veteran will be living by at BAVR. It leads to the signing of the B Contract. The B Contract calls for the man to "establish and comply" with a service program tailored to his individual needs.
>
> If the man fails to comply or breaks the rules after admission, the Borden Avenue Residence has the authority through the contract to put him out. Other shelters in the city, not nonprofit agencies, have a hard time imposing that kind of discipline. Because of the contract, BAVR stands as a beacon that guides its residents toward the ultimate goal of independent living, dignity, and self-confidence through job placement and work.[41]

It should not be thought, however, that the threat of dismissal from the program shelter and the fear of returning to a general shelter are the sole or primary means by which the two-tier system exerts authority. These concerns are real, but cannot regularly serve as the main source of discipline. Many clients, despite their having chosen to apply to BAVR, see their signing of the contract as involuntary or as an empty prerequisite. Indeed, a past director of the shelter has acknowledged that the contracts are primarily management tools rather than sources of realistic sanctions.[42] The force of the contract comes not so much from formal sanctions as the tie it helps establish between the client and the institution. Thus Hirota writes, "The contract system is emblematic of what is, from a social service point of view, the ideal relationship between worker and resident. Within such a system a client's problems are recognized and resolved by worker and resident working together in an individualized relationship of mutual respect and reciprocal accountability."[43]

Thus the contract represents written recognition by the client that he has certain problems (often some form of disability, but always at least the need to search for permanent shelter). It therefore establishes a basis for social service staff to periodically review the client's efforts to deal with those problems. In this way they may prompt him to fulfill the program.

The BAVR program is clearly paternalistic. It assumes that clients have some kind of "problem." They need help to "do the right thing" about it, and such help will be "good for" them. These assumptions are expressed more or less subtly. Al Peck, former director of BAVR and now director of homeless services for the New York City Salvation Army expresses them bluntly.

> Many of the veterans suffer from multiple dysfunctions. Most prominently, drug and alcohol addictions, exacerbated by post traumatic stress disorder (PTSD) and other mental illnesses, with resulting physical health problems. These must be treated before a veteran can make a successful transition to independent living. "We can find them jobs and a place to live, but if they don't address their real problems, its only a matter of time before they lose the job and end up back on the streets, or in some other shelter," said a social worker in the early days of the shelter. Since jobs were not the only answer, a system was set up to encourage those veterans who wished to change their lives from homelessness to be contributing members of the community.[44]

But clients do not face only clear-cut disabilities. Many display a set of behavioral and attitudinal stances that Hirota termed *drift,* which "means a basic lack of self-direction. . . . Drift seems extensive among BAVR residents; in particular, it marks their approaches to important personal decisions, including whether to stay or leave the shelter, what to do all day, and how to handle money."[45] Whether in fact most BAVR residents, or shelter clients generally, tend to drift is a question, and Hirota herself acknowledges that this trait, "tends not to be captured in the available statistics." The BAVR program, however, clearly assumes that left to themselves, clients will tend to drift, and that therefore "structures and programs [must] help clients make choices that will break the pattern of drift and thus encourage them to take control of their own lives."[46] The key aspect of the BAVR that Hirota identifies as encouraging clients to take control of their own lives is the nine-month review.

This process follows up on the A and B contracts clients signed earlier. After 270 days in the shelter (consecutive or not) the client and his caseworker meet with a review board consisting of the director of the shelter, the supervisor of social services, the head housemaster, and sometimes representatives from other shelter services. The caseworker has prepared a file on the client that includes a brief evaluative summary, an updated confidential medical report, the amount in the client's savings account, and a status report from the shelter employment programs. The board reviews the client's activities for the past months and his present and future plans, including his plans for leaving. The client makes a statement and the staff asks questions, which typically focus on substance abuse problems, emotional issues, and the search for permanent shelter. Out of this discussion the board generally makes specific service recommendations that are then drawn up in the form of a new B contract, which is scheduled for review in 30 to 90 days.

The review reinforces the shelter's paternalistic regime. First, reviews are a low-key method of enforcing the obligations clients enter into in their A and B contracts. This is not so much because clients might fail to "pass" the review and end up being sanctioned (most reviews end with the redrafting of the contracts), but because reviews provide the shelter administration and staff with an opportunity to concentrate their informal authority. The highest representatives of the shelter administration—the shelter director and the director of social services—take part in drawing up a new contract, which "puts teeth into whatever recommendations are made." Further, a review presents the client with a unified voice from the shelter administration and staff, and thus "limits chances for the client to play any end against the middle." Finally, without threatening to immediately eject a client, the review reasserts the temporary nature of shelter stays and thus focuses a client's attention on the need to search for a permanent situation.[47]

The other program shelters of the city system display the same directive orientation as BAVR. Project Renewal employs the referral-contract-program-monitoring model, as does the Ready, Willing, and Able shelter operated by the Doe Fund in Brooklyn. In general the trend toward privatization has made possible the development of a paternalistic shelter regime that could not have been achieved through other means.

Of course, a crucial question is whether the turn toward paternalism has made for a better shelter system. Given the paucity of publicly available data on such matters as shelter conditions and outplacement rates, the question is difficult to answer. One can only say that the conditions at some shelters have dramatically improved and that the caseload has decreased. But policy developments in New York City do bear on another key question: Is a paternalistic shelter regime achievable without inhumane consequences?

Advocates say that the answer is no. In his ethnography of women in Washington, D.C., shelters, Elliot Liebow makes the case that directive shelter programs are likely to invade personal liberty. He describes a shelter where "the staff saw themselves as professionals whose job it was to change the women, to help them out of homelessness." He argues that

> inevitably, this determination to force people to behave differently (for their own good) created many opportunities for conflict, most of them generated by pressure from the top to bring about change and counterpressure from the women on the bottom. This ideology of forced change required an authoritarianism that the staff, by training, experience, or personal need, were all too ready to deliver.[48]

Staff authority to enforce behavioral standards with sanctions necessarily undermined the clients' pursuit of their own interests. "The power of staff, nakedly exposed in the threat or reality of suspension or eviction, is more than enough to prevent most of the women from defending themselves and their interests as they see them and feel them."[49]

Generalizing from ethnographic studies is always hazardous, and Liebow's findings may hold true for the women's shelters he studied. But to judge from Hirota's work and my own observations, the men's program shelters of New York do not seem to have degenerated into authoritarianism. The clients at least acquiesce to change when they volunteer for a program shelter. The threat of eviction is softened—but not vitiated—by the fact that eviction will be not to the streets but to a general shelter. The contract structure provides another standard beyond what the clients currently see and feel for judging their self-interest. In short, New York City's program shelters seem to have found an organization that permits but also limits external authority.

The idea that external expectations violate self-interest presumes that individuals always know their own interest and never change. In fact, everyone's decisions are reviewed by other people, and all of us must harmonize the many expressions of self interest we make in the course of our lives. Family, friends, coworkers, and social institutions generally provide formal and informal sanctions when our current expression of self-interest is dramatically inconsistent with previous ones. For a given individual to rely relatively heavily on external structures does not necessarily constitute a capitulation to authoritarianism. This is especially true for the clients of New York City's shelters for men. They must answer the question that I saw on a poster in the office of a shelter worker who had been homeless once himself: "Your Way of Life Does Not Work. If It Does Work, What Are You Doing Here?" And shelter administrators must answer a corollary to this question: "What may we ask of our clients so that their lives do work?" In its new, more paternalistic configuration, New York City's shelter system is doing a better job of answering these questions than it did in the past.

Notes

1. Dan Salerno, Kim Hopper, and Ellen Baxter "Hardship in the Heartland: Homelessness in Eight U. S. Cities," New York: Community Service Society, June 1984, p. 30.

2. Abraham G. Gerges, "Moving Away from the Fringes on Homelessness," *New York Law Journal* (January 24, 1992), p. 2.

3. See Thomas J. Main, "Hard Lessons on Homelessness: The Education of David Dinkins," *City Journal*, vol. 3 (Summer 1993), pp. 30–39; Main, "The Homeless Families of New York," *Public Interest*, no. 85 (Fall 1986), pp. 3–21; and Main, "The Homeless of New York," *Public Interest*, no. 72 (Summer 1983), pp. 3–28.

4. David C. Anderson, "A Good Neighbor Shelter: No Longer a Horror on East Third Street," *New York Times*, December 11, 1991, p. A26. I first described the 8 East

Third Street Shelter in "The Homeless of New York." Now that I have seen the level of quality that can be expected of such an institution, I believe my earlier account was too accepting of 8 East Third Street's shortcomings.

5. Project Renewal, Eight East Third Street,"Orientation Manual," New York, undated.

6. Unfortunately, DHS did not grant my requests to visit city-operated shelters.

7. Theodore Caplow, "The Sociologist and the Homeless Man," in Howard M. Bahr, ed., *Disaffiliated Man: Essays and Bibliography on Skid Row, Vagrancy, and Outsiders* (University of Toronto Press, 1970), p. 6.

8. See Samuel E. Wallace, *Skid Row as a Way of Life* (Totowa, N.J.: Bedminster Press, 1965); and James P. Spradley, *You Owe Yourself a Drunk: An Ethnography of Urban Nomads* (Little, Brown, 1970).

9. Spradley, *You Owe Yourself a Drunk*, pp. 5–6.

10. See William McSheehy, *Skid Row* (Cambridge, Mass.: Schenkman, 1979), p. 106; and James F. Rooney, "Organizational Success through Program Failure: Skid Row Rescue Missions," *Social Forces*, vol. 58 (March 1980), pp. 904–24.

11. Kim Hopper and Jill Hamberg, *The Making of America's Homelessness: From Skid Row to the New Poor, 1945–1984* (New York: Community Service Society, 1984), p. 60.

12. Michael Harrington, *The New American Poverty* (Holt, Rinehart, and Winston, 1984).

13. Peter H. Rossi, *Down and Out in America: The Origins of Homelessness* (University of Chicago Press, 1989), pp. 181–82, 190; Karin Ringheim, *At Risk of Homelessness: The Roles of Income and Rent* (Praeger, 1990), p. 35; and Martha R. Burt, *Over the Edge: The Growth of Homelessness in the 1980s* (Washington: Urban Institute Press, 1992), pp. 6, 226.

14. Kay Young McChesney, "Family Homelessness: A Systemic Problem," *Journal of Social Issues*, vol. 46 (Winter 1990), p. 195.

15. James D. Wright, *Address Unknown: The Homeless in America* (Aldine de Gruyter, 1989), p. 50.

16. Dennis P. Culhane, "The Quandaries of Shelter Reform: An Appraisal of Efforts to 'Manage' Homelessness," *Social Service Review*, vol. 66 (September, 1992), p. 438–39. See also McChesney, "Family Homelessness," p. 195.

17. See Thomas J. Main, "Analyzing Evidence for the Structural Theory of Homelessness," *Journal of Urban Affairs*, vol. 18, no. 4 (1996), pp. 449–57.

18. See, Christopher Jencks, *The Homeless* (Harvard University Press, 1994), p. 83; and Dirk W. Early, "The Role of Subsidized Housing in Reducing Homelessness: An Empirical Investigation Using Micro-Data," paper prepared for Confronting an American Disgrace: The Systemic Causes of Homelssness, a conference sponsored by the School of Public and Environmental Affairs, Indiana University, South Bend, September 1966.

19. See Burt, *Over the Edge*, for the most sophisticated effort to construct a structural model of homelessness. In most of the models presented there, housing and income variables turn out to be weak explainers of variations in homeless rates across cities.

20. *Callahan et al.* v. *Carey et al.*, Supreme Court of the State of New York, County of New York, Index no. 42582/79 Final Judgment by Consent, August 26, 1981.

21. Mayor's Office on Homelessness and SRO Housing, "Revised and Updated Plan for Housing and Assisting Homeless Single Adults and Families," New York, March 1993, p. 3.

22. Main, "Homeless of New York," p. 27.

23. Main, "Hard Lessons on Homelessness."

24. New York City Commission on the Homeless, *The Way Home: A New Direction in Social Policy* (February 1992), p. 81.

25. Ibid., p. 15.

26. Department of Homeless Services, "Reforming New York City's System of Homeless Services," New York, May 1994, pp. 1, 6–7.

27. Ibid., p. 4.

28. Kevin Sack, "Pataki Proposes to Deny Shelter to Homeless Who Break Rules: Shifting the Balance to Personal Responsibility," *New York Times*, April 15, 1995, p. A1. Also see New York State Department of Social Services, notice for proposed rule making for the enactment of 18 NYCRR 352.35, November 7, 1995.

29. Shawn G. Kennedy, "Judge Blocks a Bid to Deny Emergency Shelter," *New York Times*, November 17, 1995, p. B2.

30. *Callahan et al.* v. *Carey et al.*, "Memorandum in Support of Plaintiffs' Motion to Declare State 'Emergency' Regulations Null and Void," p. 8.

31. President of the Borough of Manhattan, "A Shelter Is Not a Home: Report of the Manhattan Borough President's Task Force on Housing for Homeless Families," New York, March 1987, pp. 121–22; and City Council of the City of New York, "Report of the Select Committee on the Homeless," November 24, 1986, p. 78.

32. Mayor's Advisory Task Force on the Homeless, "Toward a Comprehensive Policy on Homelessness," New York, 1987, p. 59.

33. New York City Commission on the Homeless, *The Way Home*, p. 32.

34. Ibid., p. 73.

35. Celia W. Dugger, "Giuliani Calls Dinkins Indecisive on Housing and Homeless," *New York Times,* August 5, 1993, p. B1.

36. Department of Homeless Services, "Reforming New York City's System of Homeless Services," New York, May 1994, p. 6.

37. New York City Commission on the Homeless, *The Way Home*, pp. 106–09, 115.

38. City of New York, *Mayor's Management Report*, March 2, 1995, p. 288.

39. City of New York Human Resources Administration, Office of Legal Affairs, "Drug Testing Program for Residents at Borden Avenue Veterans' Shelter," June 7, 1989.

40. Janice M. Hirota, "Life and Work in City Shelters: Homeless Residents and Organizational Dynamics at the Borden Avenue Veterans Residence," City of New York Human Resources Administration, May 1991.

41. Salvation Army, Borden Avenue Veterans Residence, "What is BAVR?" New York, undated, p. 2.

42. Hirota, "Life and Work in City Shelters," p. 16.

43. Ibid., p. 21.

44. Alfred Peck, Isaac Pimentel, and Gerald Saunders, "Yesterday's Heroes, Today's Homeless: Strategies to Address African-American Veterans' Homelessness," Veterans Braintrust, Congressional Black Caucus, undated, pp. 2–3.

45. Hirota, "Life and Work in City Shelters," p. 41.

46. Ibid., p. iv.

47. Ibid., p. 60.

48. Elliot Liebow, *Tell Them Who I Am: The Lives of Homeless Women* (Free Press, 1993), p. 123.

49. Ibid., p. 132.

Six

Coerced Abstinence: A Neopaternalist Drug Policy Initiative

Mark A. R. Kleiman

Criminal law treats drunkenness in bizarre and inconsistent ways: as an aggravation to a charge of reckless driving, but potentially a mitigation to a charge of assault. That inconsistency illustrates some of the conceptual and practical difficulties of adapting essentially liberal institutions to situations that do not conform to the axioms of liberal thought. In particular, liberalism finds it hard to deal with the behavior, and to serve the needs, of those who do not conform to the axioms of individually self-interested rationality.

Intoxicated persons are more in need of paternalist care than healthy adults are assumed to be; it is as if intoxication temporarily transformed adults back into children while leaving them with the physical and social capacities and the legal independence of adults. Liberal institutions are ill fitted to deal with this fact. Addiction challenges the assumption of self-command and the institutions built around it in different but no less profound ways.

It should, then, come as no surprise that otherwise liberal societies and polities restrict the distribution and consumption of intoxicating and poten-

---

Will Brownsberger, David Boyum, and Lesley Friedman read the manuscript in various stages and made helpful comments. Jamil Jaffer provided able research assistance.

tially addictive chemicals in ways that go beyond the simple protection of third parties. The liberal regime assumes that healthy adults are capable of taking care of themselves and that they are willing, under appropriate inducements, to respect the interests of others. When those assumptions diverge sharply from reality, action should reflect different assumptions. One argument for paternalist intervention into intoxication is to avoid the need that would otherwise arise to build paternalism into other policies to provide protection for and from intoxicated persons.

But the proposition that paternalist intervention is justified does not entail the proposition that it will be done well. Indeed, one would expect that a liberal society trying to act paternalistically would, like a horse trying to swim, do so rather clumsily. Nor would that expectation be disappointed. Discourse and practice with respect to drug policy are confused and disjointed. Neither the nature of the divergences between actual behavior and the rational-actor model nor the problem of how to design policies to close that gap has been accurately grasped. The resulting policies have been both less effective and more expensive in money and in needless suffering than they might have been or ought to be.

Correctional policy faces an analogous problem. Crime—at least the varieties of crime that often lead to arrest and punishment—tends to attract those who are reckless and impulsive rather than those who fit the model of self-interested rationality. That simple observation has strong implications for efforts aimed at both deterrence and rehabilitation, but those implications have either not been drawn or not been acted on. Moreover, the obvious opposition of interest between offenders and everyone else has been allowed to conceal from the public consciousness the common interest in improving offenders' capacities for self-command.

But it is at the junction between drug abuse and criminality in the lives of drug-involved offenders where the failure of policy is greatest. The relatively small number of offenders who are frequent, high-dose users of cocaine, heroin, and methamphetamine account for such a large proportion both of crime and of the money spent on illicit drugs that getting a handle on their behavior is indispensible to the task of getting a handle on street crime and the drug markets. Yet current policies for dealing with them ignore everything we know both about addiction and about deterrence.

This chapter is about how to get paternalism right in managing drug-involved offenders. It will develop the following propositions:

—The assumption that healthy adults are capable of acting rationally in their own interests matches reality only imperfectly.

—The divergences between actual and normatively rational behavior are greater than usual with respect to the use of intoxicating and potentially addictive chemicals.

—Those divergences are greater among the population of frequently arrested offenders than in the population at large.

—The overlap between the offender population and the population of heavy users of expensive drugs is very wide.

—The 3 million or so persons who are both heavy users of expensive drugs and involved with the criminal justice system account for large proportions of criminal offenses and consumption of expensive drugs.

—Continued use of expensive drugs among offenders is linked with continued high rates of criminal activity.

—Illicit street markets cause enormous social damage. Reducing demand in those markets would reduce that damage.

—For the reckless and impulsive, deferred and low-probability threats of severe punishment are less effective than immediate and high-probability threats of mild punishment.

—Current practices for dealing with offenders rely too much on severity at the sacrifice of certainty and immediacy.

—The probation and parole systems are the key to managing the population of drug-using offenders. Abstinence from drug use ought to be made a condition of continued liberty, and that condition ought to be enforced with frequent drug tests and predictable sanctions.

—The benefits of mounting such a program would far outstrip its costs and the benefits of any other program using comparable resources that could be initiated against drugs and crime.

—The administrative and political barriers to instituting this kind of program are formidable but not insurmountable.

The Phenomenology and Politics of the Drug Problem

Taking drugs can create problems for those who engage in it and for those around them. It can damage health; lead to irresponsible, reckless, criminal, or violent behavior; and create the self-sustaining misery of addiction.

Drug control measures create problems of their own. Any severe regulation will generate attempts at evasion. If those attempts are not punished, the regulation becomes no more than a suggestion. If they are punished, the punishments themselves create suffering, and violence may be added to evasion as lawbreakers struggle to avoid capture. In either case the existence of markets not governed by law may lead to intramarket violence, with predictable endangerment of nonparticipants. In addition, the higher prices created by regulation (of which prohibition is the extreme) can generate robbery, theft, prostitution, and other crimes to pay for expensive habits.

Weighing these problems as they appear under contemporary U.S. conditions, one sees the two licit drugs, alcohol and nicotine, accounting for much more of the damage than one would guess from reading political discussions of the drug problem. Between them they are responsible for 500,000 deaths a year (400,000 for nicotine, 100,000 for alcohol).[1] No comparable calculation—taking into account chronic health damage as well as acute overdose—has been done for the illicit drugs, but even a full tally would not come close to these enormous figures. Cigarette smoking is the dominant drug-related source of health damage; alcohol dominates the problems of intoxicated bad behavior and addiction. The illicit drugs come up far behind.

Still, the damage associated with illicit drugs and their control is impressive enough:

—several million dependent users;[2]

—an illegal industry generating tens of billions of dollars in revenue;[3]

—recent cocaine or heroin use by nearly half of all those arrested for serious crimes in big cities;[4]

—hundreds of thousands of people, many of them very young, regularly committing felony drug-selling offenses;[5]

—enormous (though not well-measured) amounts of violence associated with drug transactions, or at least with weapons obtained for use in and with the proceeds of drug selling;

—neighborhood disruption caused by the disorder and violence of open illicit markets;

—$30 billion to $35 billion, out of a total national enforcement budget of $110 billion, spent on enforcing drug laws;[6]

—350,000 persons behind bars for drug sales or possession[7] out of a total national prison-plus-jail population of 1.4 million;[8]

—injection drug use a strong second to sex in the transmission of HIV.[9]

All this damage is highly concentrated in poor urban neighborhoods with primarily ethnic-minority populations. (Two-thirds of those admitted to state prisons for drug offenses are African American.)[10]

Cocaine and heroin (and in some places methamphetamine) are the illicit drugs most closely associated both with crime by users and the violence and disorder surrounding drug dealing. Persons dependent on cocaine and heroin dominate the publicly supported treatment systems. Yet gauging the drug problem in the United States by a content analysis of the political debate, one might easily conclude that marijuana use among teenagers was the primary problem. Making marijuana control the centerpiece of national drug policy is rarely advocated in so many words, but the focus is implicit in the use of survey data on the prevalence of illicit drug use, especially among teenagers, as the primary measure of the extent of the drug problem. Because marijuana is by far the most widely used of the illicit drugs, focusing on the total number of users of any illicit drug means in practice focusing on marijuana.

This disconnection between phenomenon and discourse is no accident. The politics of the drug problem is dominated by the fears of middle-class parents that their children will fall victim to drugs (not, for this purpose, defined to include alcohol, the most widely abused intoxicant among teenagers as well as adults). The illicit drug most widely used among teenagers is marijuana, and it is therefore marijuana that parents fear. Their fear is not to be mocked. At its worst in 1978, when more than one high school senior in ten reported using marijuana twenty or more times a month, the situation was not a tolerable one for these students, or for those trying to raise them, teach them, or learn with them.[11] Despite the absence of a marked physical withdrawal syndrome, persistent heavy use of cannabis can be a hard habit to shake, and although it rarely produces the concentrated misery of heroin or cocaine addiction or of alcoholism, it is more than bad enough to worry about.

For a variety of pharmacological and sociological reasons, however, marijuana forms only a small part of the crime-violence-disorder-prison drug problem. That problem centers on cocaine, heroin, and methamphetamine, and it is to that problem that this chapter addresses itself.

The Conceptual Basis of Paternalism

All paternalist interventions rest on one primary insight: that there are large and systematic divergences between the actual behavior of some human beings, or of human beings generally under some circumstances, and the canons of rationally self-interested action as microeconomists understand them.

The assumption that healthy adults are always or almost always capable stewards of their own well-being, or at least will achieve better results on their own than could be produced by any practicable system of outside interference, is basic to American social and political thought. Those who are called conservative tend to embrace it with special vigor in the economic realm, while those who are called liberal tend to insist on it more particularly as it applies to expression, sexual conduct, and family structure.[12]

Wherever applied, the assumption that individuals have sufficient wit and self-command to control their own actions in their own interests has powerful implications, in particular that freedom and facilitation are the sole means of helping individuals, leaving no role for authoritative restriction except protecting them from one another. If given a choice among options, a rationally self-interested person is capable of choosing the best. Adding options will at worst leave the person's well-being unchanged—this will be the case when none of the new options is as good as the one that would have been selected from the shorter list—and will improve well-being whenever one of the new options is chosen instead. By the same token, subtracting options will at best leave well-being (what the economists call welfare) unchanged, and any change will be for the worse. Replacing any option with one more preferable, for example by reducing the cost associated with some benefit, in effect expands the range of choice and thus, on the rationalist assumption, can only do good. Replacing an option with one less preferable, for example by increasing cost, can only do harm.

This is the argument that underlies John Stuart Mill's case for perfect liberty as applied to "self-regarding actions": if it is the nature of human beings to make good choices for themselves, there is no gain to be had in regulating their actions except where those actions affect others.[13] Forbidding someone to do something he would like to do, or imposing a cost on doing so, cannot make the person better off. It should only, in this argument, be engaged in when it can make someone else better off to an extent that more than compensates both for the loss to the person restricted and the social overhead costs of making and enforcing such restrictions.

One familiar challenge to Mill lies in the definition of the domain of self-regarding actions. Families, governments, charities, and insurance companies all tend to spread risk by calling on those with greater resources and fewer needs to help those with fewer resources and greater needs. Within that web of risk and resource sharing, a wide range of choices that Mill would think of as self-regarding, such as the decision to get up in the morning and go to work, come to have important effects on the well-being of others.

Fashion effects—instances in which people desire not to satisfy their own tastes but to be in step with conventional behavior—similarly narrow the range of activities that can properly be viewed as purely self-regarding. If we all wear shoes that hurt our feet when we walk, or fail to wear helmets to protect our heads when we bicycle, because doing otherwise would be unfashionable rather than because we like bunions or concussions, then requiring everyone to wear sensible shoes or helmets can improve everyone's well-being.

The paternalist challenge cuts even deeper. If I am not a perfectly rational actor as regards my own interests—if, for example, I have a tendency to procrastinate or to eat too much fat—increasing my range of options by offering me beef Wellington as an alternative to boiled tofu or a good mystery to read as an alternative to writing this chapter may make me worse off by inducing me to make a choice not in my best interest. Recognizing temptation as an important feature of life will radically expand the number of possibly useful policies.

One can, imperfectly, divide the sources of less-than-rational action into two categories: cognitive and behavioral. Cognitively, when rationality demands calculation, someone who gets the calculation wrong may act in ways not conducive to his goals, whether in a paper-and-pencil exercise or in life. But even a completely correct cognitive picture of the relationship between actions and results is not, by itself, enough to ensure rational behavior. There may also be gaps between what a person cognitively understands as rational behavior and the way that person actually behaves. Thomas Schelling has called these gaps "failures of self-command."[14] Aristotle called the problem *akrasia* (literally "weakness," but usually translated as "weakness of will").[15]

Casual empiricism and results from the psychology and behavioral-economics laboratories alike suggest that subtlety, delay, and uncertainty are all potential sources of divergence between rational-actor models and actual performance. If some commodity or service that I consume affects me in ways that are not obvious, my behavior toward it may not take into account all of the costs it imposes. Even if I am aware cognitively of subtle effects, they may not have much effect on my behavioral responses: an activity with obvious pleasures and hidden costs may be overindulged in even by a subject who at the cognitive level "knows better."[16]

Similarly, if the benefits of some activity arrive right away and the costs are delayed, there may be a mismatch between actual behavior and the behavior that a rational actor would choose, with present costs and benefits getting excessive weight compared to delayed ones.[17]

Consider offering a six-year-old the choice between a candy bar today and two candy bars a week from now. Then consider offering that same child the choice between a candy bar six months from now and two candy bars six months plus one week from now. In each case the choice is the same: he can wait a week to get two candy bars rather than one. If the choice and the opportunity to have a candy bar right now is immediate, the child is likely to take the smaller, quicker reward in preference to the larger, slower one. If the choice must be made now but the result is deferred, the child, no longer dazzled by the prospect of immediate gratification, is likely to prefer to wait. This preference reversal cannot be accounted for by the standard economic theory of rationally discounting future benefits.

Learning to have the capacity to defer gratification will improve the child's prospects in life. Assisting in the development of that capacity is a crucial element of the parental function. The problem of impatience and temporal myopia is, of course, not confined to children. Consider how your diet would change if you were to make all decisions about what to eat a day in advance, or how much effort you waste due to procrastination.

Behavior in the presence of risk presents a different set of problems. A rational person in the economic sense ought to be somewhat risk averse, that is, unwilling to accept a gamble with an equal chance of winning or losing the same sum if the sum is large compared with the person's total income or wealth. That follows from the capacity to budget. Because a rational person will spend money or other resources on the most pressing needs first, each additional dollar spent should deliver less and less additional satisfaction (the technical phrase is *declining marginal utility of income*). Applied statistical decision theory provides a complete normative account of rational behavior under uncertainty.[18]

But actual behavior in the presence of risk turns out to match more closely an inconsistent set of axioms known as *prospect theory*. Prospect-theoretic behavior is risk averse in gains but risk loving in losses; an even chance at doubling a gain of $100 will be rejected, but a chance to play double or nothing with a $100 loss will be accepted. In effect, prospect-theoretic behavior pays more attention to the frequency of gain or loss than to the magnitude of what is gained or lost. This can lead to inconsistent choices depending on how the issue is verbally framed.[19]

Learning to pay attention to hidden costs and benefits, to delay gratification, and to avoid unwise gambles are all important parts of growing up. The capacity to act well in such circumstances is not innate, and no one acquires the appropriate skills easily or perfectly. Classically, they are reckoned among the virtues. The capacity to endure present pain or danger when endurance is called for is named *courage*. The capacity to resist the lure of pleasure when accompanied by subtle costs is called *temperance*. The capacity to reckon with risk is part of *prudence*. The capacity to assimilate delayed costs or benefits into current actions is called *foresight*. Prudence and foresight together make up *wisdom*. (The fourth classical virtue after courage, temperance, and wisdom, *justice*, takes us beyond rational self-interest to consider the interests of others.)[20]

In wealthy societies, divergences from individual rationality in the economic sense will tend to be more frequent and severe among the poor than among the nonpoor, with causal arrows pointing both ways. In one direction the conditions of mass poverty amid affluence are not conducive to developing or maintaining prudence, foresight, or temperance. In particular, the lack of predictability in the relationship between actions and results tends to be highly demoralizing. (See Orwell's description of the impact of temporary poverty on the behavior of an Eton graduate in *Down and Out in Paris and London*.)[21] In the other causal direction, imprudence, improvidence, and intemperance all have poverty among their possible consequences. As a result, paternalism will have special importance in policies relating to the poor.

But given the deep roots of departures from rationality, it would be a mistake to assume that the appropriate reach of paternalism extended only to recipients of public income-support payments. There are many examples of such deviations, and of opportunities for interventions to improve well-being, among the nonpoor as well.

To be sure, identifying a behavioral divergence from individual rationality is not sufficient to establish the desirabiliy of a paternalist policy. Public decisionmaking is fallible, perhaps more fallible than private decisionmaking. If I am a bad steward of my own welfare, how good a steward am I, or the officials I help elect, likely to be of another's? Moreover, actually putting paternalist policies into practice involves restricting choice and imposing costs, which remain in general welfare-reducing actions. To all this must be added the costs of administration, the costs of punishing violators of paternalistally imposed rules, and the damage done by the rule-evasion behavior of those who find their desires thwarted for (assertedly) their own good. To fully justify paternalist intervention, it will be necessary to find instances in which the divergence of actual behavior from individual self-interest is large and systematic and the costs of intervention are smaller than the gains.

One should also ask of any paternalist intervention whether it tends to ameliorate or exacerbate the deficits in self-command that give rise to the need for such intervention in the first place. Improving someone's short-term well-being at the expense of his future capacity for self-management will usually be a bad bargain. This resembles the more familiar problem of whether formal social controls tend on balance to reinforce or displace informal social controls.

A likely place to look for instances in which paternalist interventions will be worth their costs is at points where behavior that is likely to be harmful to personal welfare intersects with behavior that is likely to damage others. Criminal activity is one such intersection; the excessive consumption of intoxicating and addictive chemicals (licit or illicit) is another. Picking out these areas of behavior for special scrutiny need not rest on the assumption that all criminal behavior or all drug taking is either irrational or socially damaging. It requires only that irrationality and external harm are more densely concentrated around crime and drug taking than around, say, home repair and bowling.

Where drug taking and criminal activity meet, in the drug consumption of those nominally under supervision by one or another element of the criminal justice system, the case for some sort of paternalist intervention seems especially strong. For a combination of conceptual and organizational reasons, the United States has developed policies toward drug taking by offenders that diverge dramatically from a sensible paternalist prescription. Although the laws nominally require abstinence from illicit drugs on the part of persons under criminal justice supervision, that requirement is enforced with infrequent tests and sporadic but occasionally severe sanctions. Such an enforcement strategy implicitly assumes the capacity of its subjects to make rationally self-interested choices about their drug taking when faced with small and temporally rather distant probabilities of large unwanted consequences.

A sensibly paternalist alternative would recognize that those whose drug habits have brought them into trouble with the law are less likely than average to be able to adjust well under such randomized severity. Higher probability—ideally the virtual certainty—of small penalties and perhaps the promise of small rewards for continued good conduct will be more effective in shaping behavior. The combination of high probability and low severity will also generate less total punishment, to the benefit of the user-offenders and the rest of the community alike.

The potential gains from an effective paternalist intervention to decrease the use of illicit drugs by persons on probation or parole are large compared with the returns available from investing comparable resources elsewhere in the criminal justice system or elsewhere in the effort to control drug abuse. Such a program would therefore repay the substantial investment in rethinking policy and building organizational capacity required to make it a reality.

Drug Taking as a Special Case

If the most appropriate targets of paternalist interventions are areas of conduct in which there are large and systematic divergences between actual behavior and rationally self-interested behavior, and in which those divergences damage not only the decisionmakers but others, it should not be surprising that drugs have been singled out from among other commodities and activities as the focus of special rules. Taking drugs challenges the axioms of the rational-actor model in two ways: intoxication, which involves failures of self-command once under the influence, and addiction, which involves failures of self-command over drug taking itself. Neither form of failure is inevitable, but both are more or less characteristic of many consumers of almost any pleasurably psychoactive drug.

Some, but by no means all, drug-induced states cause some, but by no means all, of those subject to them to act with less regard for consequences than they would act if sober. This liberation from the chains of calculated behavior may be one of the desired effects of taking a drug, as is frequently the case with alcohol. The fact that intoxication is a socially recognized phenomenon provides a layer of insulation between intoxicated behavior and personal reputation and thus an additional source of behavioral freedom. However, unless special care is taken about times, places, and circumstances, the results of intoxicated behavior may cause profound regret, not only for the intoxicated person but also for those around him. This effect of drug taking has been referred to as *behavioral toxicity*. Its nature and extent vary profoundly from drug to drug, from user to user, and from circumstance to circumstance in ways only imperfectly understood.

The ordinary mechanisms of social control, formal and informal, on which any open society must rely depend on the foresight and caution of those subject to that control: depend, that is, on their acting more or less according to the canons of rational self-interest. By making people less rational, intoxication makes them less controllable, reducing their capacity to respond to the promises and threats embodied in the institutions of social control. (This effect helps explain why laws against drunk driving are so hard to enforce: the very drunkenness that creates the prohibition on driving reduces the deterrability of the potential violator.)

Addiction, like intoxication, represents a departure from the self-interested self-command ascribed to healthy adults by standard economic theory. Although Gary Becker and Kevin Murphy have shown that a rational person might choose to consume a dependency-inducing drug and might become dependent on it, their account of "rational addiction" bears only a limited resemblance to addiction as it is actually encountered.[22] There are descriptions of long-term heroin users deliberately going through withdrawal in order to run themselves back down the curve of dependency so they can have the pleasure of running back up again.[23] But the typical account of a relapse with alcohol or cocaine is of a greatly feared and bitterly regretted failure of self-command, not of a voluntary, still less a rational, choice.

Thus the use of intoxicating and potentially addictive chemicals is a logical target of policies designed to protect people from themselves, and in fact drug taking has long been the subject of paternalist intervention. Restrictions on the availability of psychoactive substances, justified in part by the damage they do to those who (to all appearances voluntarily) use them, have been around in one form or another for many years, although the substances that attract concern have varied over time. Mill's *On Liberty*, the first comprehensive attack on paternalism, was written primarily in response to the enactment in the State of Maine of a statute prohibiting alcohol consumption, which in retrospect appears as the laboratory-scale version of the Volstead Act.

Paternalism and its Discontents: Drug Laws as an Example

The existence of commodities and behaviors that challenge both theoretically and practically the model of rational self-control in the service of individual self-interest poses a problem of policy design. What is needed is a politically and organizationally sustainable array of laws, institutions, and programs that protect actual and potential consumers of such commodities from the harm they would otherwise do themselves, improve (or at least not further impair) their capacity to regulate their own behavior in the future, and protect others from the collateral damage. All this must be done at acceptable cost and with tolerable levels of unwanted side effects. The problem thus stated is a formidable one, but by definition it must have some best solution or set of equally good solutions in any given social context. That is not, however, the face the drug problem presents to the political process, and the actuality of drug policy demonstrates the dangers of paternalist interventions.

First, paternalist policies can be expensive, because restricting powerful impulses will create powerful incentives for evasion. People convicted of drug offenses (not drug-related offenses such as theft by users or violence among dealers, but violations of the laws against manufacture, sale, and possession) now fill a quarter of America's prison cells.[24] This has two classes of undesirable effects: one on prisoners, the other on crime rates.

Imprisonment creates enormous suffering for those imprisoned and their intimates and enormous social dislocation in the neighborhoods from which they are mostly drawn. Although the canons of rational behavior as economists understand them would suggest that drug dealers as a class must come out ahead as a result of the drug laws (else rational persons would not enter the game), there is reason to suspect that dealing is often an irrational choice and that the net effect of the flashy, risky illicit jobs created by the dealing system is to reduce the well-being of those attracted to them.[25]

Retail drug dealing is precisely the sort of activity that produces less than rational behavior because the deferred and uncertain nature of the punishments for drug dealing weakens their effects on behavior when compared with the immediate and certain rewards. Only a stubborn insistence that all voluntary behavior must be the rational product of some set of preferences would generate the often heard assertion that retail crack dealing is a rational choice for young residents of poor urban neighborhoods. The cumulative probabilities of death, serious injury, addiction, and imprisonment are absurdly disproportionate to actual money received from dealing.[26] Moreover, if dealers were rational, they would have responded to the vastly increased severity of enforcement in the past decade by cutting back sharply on their willingness to supply drug-dealing labor at the old, rather modest, wages, thus forcing wages (and therefore prices) higher to compensate for the increased risk. The failure of dealing wages to rise, as evidenced by the failure of retail margins in the crack trade to increase, is therefore inconsistent with economic rationality on the part of the (predominantly youthful) retail dealers.[27]

The extensive use of prison cells to punish dealers also reduces the supply of cells available for crimes against persons and property. While many imprisoned drug dealers also commit nondrug crimes, on average they do so at lower rates than those imprisoned for nondrug offenses. Thus crime victims also pay part of the cost of drug-related incarceration.

Second, paternalist interventions sometimes increase the damage they were designed to limit. In general, whatever forbidden behavior is not prevented will become more individually and socially damaging than it would have been if permitted. The very high prices in illicit drug markets tend to impoverish users and create incentives for them to commit property crimes or engage in prostitution or sell drugs to maintain their habits. In addition, an illicit drug is likely to be more toxic, dose for dose, because it is made to less exacting standards, unpredictably adulterated, and of uncertain potency: going blind from bathtub gin came and went with Prohibition.

Third, vice laws create black markets. The illicit drug trade is marked by violence and corruption largely absent from the package-goods trade, and the money to be made from illicit dealing both attracts adolescents, especially from poor urban neighborhoods, into criminal activity and away from school or licit work and gives them motive and means to acquire highly lethal weapons.

Finally, paternalist restrictions can create hostility between public authorities and the very people the law was intended to protect. The refusal of drug users to be protected from drugs and their participation in the system of lawbreaking that is the illicit market convert them into public enemies. Messages from drug prevention campaigns sometimes reinforce that identification. Instead of trying to protect users from their own folly, the public aim becomes to damage them as a punishment and a warning to others. This effect undercuts paternalism at its foundations by eating away at the benevolent intentions that are supposed to undergird and justify the coercive interventions.

So, for example, the anonymous testing services that used to give buyers of illicit drugs some protection against adulteration or mislabeling have been regulated out of business lest the reduced risk encourage drug use. Similarly, providing sterile needles to heroin users is opposed on the grounds that it would condone and encourage injection drug use. As a result, the avoidable risks of poisoning and infection are added to the fundamental risks of using various mind-altering drugs.[28] Despite its modest capacity to produce lasting cures (defined popularly and politically in terms of immediate and total abstinence), drug treatment is clearly cost-justified by its contribution to crime and disease prevention while the treatment is going on and thereafter. But it remains politically unpopular and badly underfunded because it appears to be a measure of assistance to those who willfully damage themselves and others.

In this atmosphere of hostility the potentially valuable role of arrest and legal pressure in moving people away from addiction is perverted by making possession for personal use a crime punishable by prison. In California, for example, punching someone in the face or throwing a rock through a window is a misdemeanor, while possession—not sale, merely possession—of $5 worth of cocaine is not only a felony but a "serious felony" and thus a potential "third strike" subjecting the offender to a mandatory twenty-five years to life in prison. (Drug possession, specifically possession of marijuana, accounts for more third strike sentences in California than all other crimes combined.)

Insofar as one technique of paternalist intervention is preventive education, the efforts of prevention campaigns can inadvertently cripple research and policy debate. To shape the behavior of schoolchildren, prevention programs tend to simplify, overdramatize, and sometimes frankly falsify the facts about drugs, drug taking, and drug users. Such accounts enter the journalistic and political pool of accepted ideas and become part of the basis on which legislators and officials make laws and policies. Critics of current policies are urged to censor themselves for fear of damaging the prevention effort. Once that point is reached, the political logic of regulating vice can easily lead to the most extreme and perverse policies, such as the suppression of research into the therapeutic uses of banned drugs, that no one can oppose without risking the label of *legalizer*. Thus paternalist policies can immunize themselves from effective criticism and thereby partly escape democratic control.

Against the background assumption that healthy adults are by nature good stewards of their own well-being, the problem of drug addiction seems almost inexplicable. It is tempting to treat either the drugs or the addicts or both as qualitatively special cases. The alternative would be to acknowledge that all humans deviate, more or less, from full rationality, that all commodities are more or less potential objects of abuse, and that society needs to fit policies to persons and circumstances. It is much more comfortable to assume instead that drugs are discontinuously different from everything else and to forget everything else we know in making policies toward them.

Correctly understanding the theoretical underpinnings of paternalist interventions will allow us to understand and justify the regulation, and even the prohibition, of commodities and activities that are sources of harmless pleasure to some, or even most, of those who engage in them. This then allows us to acknowledge that the practice of taking mood-altering chemicals is not evil per se but merely risky in a specific fashion, and that our policies ought to be designed to manage those risks, whether by reducing the risk of any given incident or use career or by reducing the number of such incidents or careers. This is not a less value-driven approach to policy than the one underlying the quest for a "drug-free America," but it might well be less divisive and more capable of adapting itself to actual circumstances.

Offenders as a Special Case

For both practical and principled reasons, paternalist interventions are easier to justify when applied to those convicted of breaking the laws than when applied to ordinary adults. Paternalist policies can be thought of as *social prostheses* (the phrase is Steven Hyman's) for persons deficient in providence, prudence, and temperance. Those deficiencies are more common among convicted lawbreakers, and especially among recidivists, than they are in the general population, if only because most lawbreaking has immediate and high-probability benefits accompanied by larger, but deferred and lower-probability, costs.[29] "The wages of sin," it has been said, "are usually below the legal minimum." Therefore the average prisoner, parolee, or probationer will be less capable of minding his own business successfully than the average ordinary citizen.

Moreover, because repeat offenders impose costs on their victims and on those who incur expense or forgo opportunity in order to avoid victimization, their failures of self-command constitute a social rather than a merely personal problem. The public costs of paternalist intervention are easily justified if it has as one of its side effects reduced criminal activity and therefore reduced need for imprisonment.

At the level of principle, limiting the choices of those who have transgressed against the rights of others seems much less in conflict with the norms of liberal society than limiting the choices of those who have not done so. Advocates of paternalist interventions cannot deny that such policies limit (at least prima facie and in the short run) the freedom of those subjected to them, and that inevitably some of those whose freedom is limited will wind up worse off as a result of the intervention. (This is emphatically true if one uses the values of the subjects rather than those of the policymakers as the basis for evaluating "better off" and "worse off.") That puts a heavy onus of moral justification on the advocates of any given paternalist policy.

But some loss of liberty is incident to virtually any punishment, and loss of liberty seems to be an apposite response to the abuse of liberty that constitutes the original offense. The long-term interest of the offender in becoming a better steward of his own well-being coincides with the common interest of the offender and his neighbors in returning him to compliance with the laws, even against the offender's immediate preferences and will. All these reasons suggest that punishment should be shaped, to the extent possible technically within the bounds set by proportionality, to serve those paternalist and mixed-paternalist goals: should be shaped, that is, to the end of rehabilitation.

Drug-Involved Offenders

The two special cases I have discussed unite when drug use by convicted offenders is considered. The special characteristics of drug taking suggest that there will be more call for paternalist intervention in that realm of behavior than in most others; the special characteristics of offenders make them especially appropriate targets for such interventions. Because all of these matters involve degree rather than kind and probabilities rather than certainties, it will not be the case that all drug taking by all offenders requires or repays paternalist intervention. But attention is naturally drawn to what might be done around offender drug taking for the benefit of offenders and the rest of us.

Much has been made of the contribution of drug taking, and especially of illicit drug taking, to criminality: perhaps too much. If, as I have argued, repeatedly committing crimes and losing control of one's drug taking reflect similar failures of self-command, it is not surprising that there is a more-than-random overlap between the population of chronic high-dose drug takers and the population of repeat offenders. Moreover, the artificially high prices created by prohibition and enforcement guarantee that, in poor neighborhoods, only those with illicit sources of income have the wherewithal to use substantial quantities of heroin and cocaine. Biographical evidence suggests that the arrow of causation points at least as much from criminal activity to hard drugs as it does from hard drugs to criminal activity: most heroin-using criminals started to steal before they started to use heroin. Thus the observation that 50 percent or more of felony arrestees in big cities test positive for cocaine does not imply that eliminating cocaine taking would eliminate 50 percent of the crimes, any more than the observation that many lawyer-lobbyists drive Mercedes-Benzes implies that outlawing the importation of luxury automobiles would reduce influence peddling.[30]

Nonetheless, it remains true that continued use of expensive drugs by those who pay for their habits from the proceeds of their crimes virtually guarantees continued criminal activity. Among offenders the use of expensive drugs predicts both high-rate offending and persistence in crime. Therefore any policy to deal with hard-core offenders needs to address their substance abuse problems. Moreover, offenders make an enormous financial contribution to the illicit drug-dealing industries, with all of their undesirable side effects: violence, disorder, corruption, enforcement expense, imprisonment, and the diversion of adolescents in poor urban neighborhoods away from school and licit work and toward drug dealing. The numbers are startling.

About four-fifths of the cocaine and heroin sold is consumed by heavy, rather than casual, users. The precise proportion depends, of course, on the definition of *heavy,* but all of the plausible definitions have to do with people who spend more than $10,000 a year on their chosen drugs; for cocaine, this group accounts for somewhere between one-fifth and one-quarter of all the current (in the past month) users.[31] This highly skewed distribution of consumption volumes accords with the general heuristic principle known as Pareto's Law, which holds that 80 percent of the volume of any activity is accounted for by 20 percent of the participants, and with what is known about the distribution of alcohol consumption. It is also supported by a comparison of consumption-based and enforcement-based estimates of cocaine volumes: a projection of cocaine users' reports on how much they consume accounts for only about 30 metric tons of cocaine a year, while enforcement data suggest total consumption of about 300 metric tons.[32] That gap implies the existence of an unmeasured hard core that accounts for the bulk of the consumption. In any case no plausible definition of *casual use,* multiplied by the survey-estimated number of users, could account for any substantial proportion of the $30 billion estimated annual cocaine market.[33]

Statistics from the Drug Use Forecasting (DUF) system, soon to be renamed the Arrestee Drug Abuse Monitoring (ADAM) system, suggest that the hidden population of heavy users consists mainly of frequent offenders.[34] Although not all of those who are arrested and who test positive for cocaine are heavy users, the short detection window (forty-eight to seventy-two hours) for the urine monitoring of cocaine use means that heavy users are likely to account for most of the positive tests after arrests. By one calculation, about 1.7 million different heavy cocaine users are arrested for felonies in the course of any given year, or about three-quarters of the estimated 2.2 million total heavy users.[35] When not in prison or jail, these user-offenders tend to be on probation or parole.

If heavy users account for 80 percent of the cocaine, and if three-quarters of them are in the criminal justice population, then 60 percent of the total cocaine is sold to persons under (nominal) criminal justice supervision. Therefore any short- to medium-term effort aimed at reducing demand for cocaine must focus on this group, on the principle that if you are going duck hunting, you have to go where the ducks are.

Current Policies for Dealing with Addict-Offenders

Neither current drug policies nor current correctional policies offer any real hope of substantially reducing drug consumption by user-offenders. The drug policy triad of prevention-enforcement-treatment is largely irrelevant to them.

First, prevention. Not only is it obviously futile to try to prevent what has already occurred, there is no evidence that either school-based or media-based drug prevention messages have much to say to those who are likely to develop into drug-involved offenders, as opposed to the middle-class kids whose parents' concerns dominate the political side of drug policy. (A focus on preventing drug *dealing,* using some mix of messages to change attitudes and other policies to shrink dealing opportunities, might be more relevant, but that idea is nowhere near the policy agenda.)[36]

Second, by making drugs more expensive and harder to obtain, enforcement can reduce both consumption by current users and the initiation rate. Compared with the hypothetical baselines of either legalization or zero enforcement, prohibition and enforcement have certainly been successful: cocaine on the illicit market costs twenty times the price of the licit pharmaceutical product, and much of the population has no easy access to the drug. But the capacity of more enforcement to drive prices higher or even to prevent continued price declines is very limited, as the explosion of drug law enforcement in the past fifteen years demonstrates. Of all users, the hard-core user-offenders are least likely to find themselves unable to acquire supplies.[37]

Third, a wide variety of treatments has been shown to be effective in reducing drug consumption and criminal activity while the treatment lasts, seemingly regardless of whether entry into treatment is voluntary or coerced.[38] But even if there were sufficient treatment slots in programs appropriate to the criminal justice population, and even if treatment providers were motivated to serve user-offenders rather than other less refractory clients, there would remain the problem of recruitment and retention. Although some user-offenders want to quit and even want to quit enough to go through the discomforts of the treatment process, many prefer, or act as if they preferred, cocaine or heroin, as long as they can get it.

In the abstract there is a good case for expanding treatment capacity, focusing treatment on the user-offender population whose continued drug use imposes such high costs and using the courts, prisons, and community corrections institutions to force them to enter, remain in, and comply with treatment. Adding drug treatment to incarceration makes sense, and good in-prison treatment with good follow-up after release has been shown to reduce recidivism by about one-fifth.[39] This more than pays for itself in budget terms alone.

But the unpopularity of user-offenders makes the funding problems difficult if not insoluble; the capacity and willingness of treatment providers to address the needs of this population remain unclear; and the administrative problems of enforcing treatment attendance and compliance through the criminal justice system are daunting. Starting from the current political situation and the current capacities and practices of the treatment system and the criminal justice system, it would be fatuous to expect expanded availability of treatment to generate large changes in overall drug demand in the next several years.

So much for the repertoire of standard drug policies.

Turning to corrections policies, one sees a picture not much brighter. The routine functioning of the courts and corrections system does very little to address the substance abuse of those assigned to it, and much of that little is wrong.

Nominally, those on probation or parole are required to abstain from illegal activity, including drug possession, as a condition of their continued liberty. Almost all states give probation and parole officials the authority to administer drug tests, and a positive test constitutes a violation of the terms of conditional release. Positive test results are thus grounds for sanctions, including revocation of conditional release status and thus incarceration or reincarceration for a period up to the original nominal sentence.

In practice, however, most parole and (especially) probation offices are underbudgeted and overwhelmed by their caseloads; a big-city probation officer may be "managing" 150 offenders at a time.[40] Funds for testing are scarce, and facilities for testing, including equipment and staff to observe the specimen collection, even more so. If the specimens are sent out for analysis, turnaround time is measured in days. As a result, even special intensive supervision efforts rarely test more than once a month, and routine probation tests much less frequently than that.[41] Thus a probationer on intensive supervision who uses cocaine or heroin has less than one chance in ten of being detected on any given occasion of use. (Ironically, marijuana use is detectable for up to a month, making it the most likely to be caught.)

The result is widespread drug use and therefore high rates of detection even with infrequent testing. That leaves the corrections system in a bind. In most states, probation and parole officers have no individual power to apply sanctions: they can only refer their wayward clients back to the parole board or the court with a recommendation that conditional release status be revoked and the offender incarcerated. For probationers, the revocation hearing is a full adversarial proceeding; parole revocation is often simpler and usually swifter, but in any case there is a substantial burden of paperwork. If the judge or parole board takes any action against the offender (by no means assured given the problems of crowding in prisions) it is likely to be severe: a few months behind bars is typical, and offenders have been sent back to finish multiyear sentences for a single positive marijuana test.

As a result, there are strong incentives, especially in the probation system, not to take every positive test back to the judge. Probationers may be counseled, warned, or referred to treatment providers several times before being (in the perhaps unintentionally graphic jargon term) "violated." It is hard to fault probation officers for attempting to jawbone their charges out of drug use rather than proceeding immediately to drastic measures. But the resulting system could hardly be more perverse in its effects.

An offender who has a strong craving for cocaine or heroin is put in a situation in which the probability of detection conditional on one use is rather small, and the probability of punishment conditional on detection, although larger, is still unknown and far less than certainty. For a hypothetical rational actor the cumulative probability of eventually going to, or back to, prison for a period of months would be an ample deterrent. The expected value of the punishment would be greater than the user would willingly risk for the pleasure of a single evening with his favorite drug, and the randomness of the punishment would increase its disutility for anyone appropriately risk averse. That is to say, the current system would be adequate, although still not optimal, to deter drug use by the sort of people who make and administer the laws.

Those who run afoul of the laws tend to behave differently. Crack-addicted burglars are much less likely to make careful comparisons between current benefits and anticipated future costs. Otherwise they would be neither addicted nor burglars, since neither frequent crack smoking nor burglary is an activity with positive expected utility on any reasonable estimate of values and probabilities. The key to fixing the situation is to adapt the penalty structure to the decisionmaking styles of the people whose behavior one is trying to influence. That means swift and certain, though relatively mild, punishment rather than randomized draconianism.

Diversion and Drug Courts

Drug diversion and drug courts are the two major categories of special programs that attempt to use the authority of the criminal justice system to reduce drug taking by offenders. Each is useful but limited in its effects.

Drug diversion involves offering a defendant the option of a deferred, suspended, or probationary sentence in lieu of possible incarceration on the condition of receiving treatment for drug abuse. Diversion programs vary enormously. Some are formal treatment plans administered under the system called TASC (an acronym that once stood for "treatment alternatives to street crime" but now represents "treatment alternatives for special clients"), a network of specialists who find treatment placements for court-referred clients, monitor their progress, and report to the court on treatment compliance. Others are as simple as a judge's demand for "thirty in thirty" (attendance at thirty twelve-step meetings in the next thirty days) from someone accused of public intoxication or drunk driving.

In drug courts the judge acts as the case manager rather than delegating the responsibility to a TASC provider. Defendants come in frequently to review their treatment compliance and results of drug tests and are praised or rebuked for good or bad conduct by the judge in open court. After a period of months the defendant is sentenced on the original offense, with the promise that the sentence will reflect his presentencing behavior.

Because they are built around the idea of treatment, many diversion programs and drug courts put as much emphasis on showing up for treatment sessions as they do on staying away from drug use. Moreover, most TASC programs and drug courts do not rely much on immediate sanctions to enforce compliance. Instead, they depend either on the threat of removal from the program and sentencing on the original charge (for diversion programs) or the fact that sentencing is still to come (for drug courts). Many judges in drug courts believe that praise or reproof from the bench, backed with the judge's reserve powers of incarceration, will serve as sufficiently potent and immediate rewards and punishments without resorting to more material actions. Doubtless, they are right with respect to some judges and some offenders.

What diversion programs and drug courts have in common is that participation is voluntary (defendants can, and some do, choose routine sentencing instead) and is restricted to defendants whom the court and the prosecution are prepared *not* to incarcerate if they will just clean up their acts. By their nature as alternatives to incarceration, the programs cannot apply to those whose crimes have been especially severe. That excludes most violent crimes, and the federal law providing funding for drug courts also specifies that defendants admitted to treatment have no prior convictions for violent offenses. Thus many of the most troublesome offenders, those whose drug consumption it would be most valuable to influence, are excluded from the beginning.

Moreover, budget constraints limit drug court and diversion populations; there is no mechanism by which the net cost savings they likely generate for the corrections system are recycled into program operations. Budgetary stringency reinforces the programs' limited scope and creates a strong incentive for limited duration as well.

Typically, supervision under such programs lasts for periods measured in months, compared with the years or decades of typical careers in addiction and crime. This is not only a budgetary matter; it also derives from the limited leverage prosecutors have over most of the offenders eligible for diversion or drug court processing. Offenders who refuse to enter these voluntary special programs and choose routine processing instead face relatively short prison or jail stays. In practice, some defendants prefer a short fixed period of incarceration to a longer period of supervision that may lead to incarceration if they backslide. The longer the period of supervision, the greater the temptation to just do the time and get it over with. Thus limited scope and limited duration put an upper bound on the potential impact of diversion and drug courts. Making a larger impact requires a more comprehensive approach.

Coerced Abstinence

To make a visible dent in the drug consumption of addict-offenders, America needs a system that will extend the kind of supervisory capacity represented by drug courts and diversion programs to a larger proportion of offenders for longer periods. The system would have to be simple enough to be operated successfully by ordinary judges and probation officers rather than enthusiasts, cheap enough to be possible within budgetary constraints, and sparing of scarce treatment and confinement capacity.

One option would be to substitute, to the maximum feasible extent, testing and automatic sanctions for treatment services and personal attention from a judge. Instead of coerced treatment, this approach might be called *coerced abstinence* because it focuses on reduced drug consumption rather than on the intermediate goals of treatment entry, retention, and compliance.

Here is how such a system might work:

—Probationers and parolees are screened for cocaine, heroin, or methamphetamine use, using drug tests and reviews of records.

—Those identified as users, either at the beginning of their terms or by random testing thereafter, are subject to twice weekly drug tests. They may choose any two days of the week and any times of day for the tests as long as the two chosen times are separated by at least seventy-two hours. In effect, there is no window for undetected use.

—Every positive test earns the offender a brief (perhaps two-day) period of incarceration. (The length of the sanction and whether and how sharply sanctions should increase with repeated violations is a question best determined by trial and error, and the best answer may vary from place to place.) Missed tests count as positive tests (perhaps the sanction should be somewhat greater to discourage absconding).

—The sanction is applied immediately, and no official has the authority to waive or modify it. (Perhaps employed users with no recent failures should be allowed to defer their confinement until the weekend to avoid the risk of losing their jobs.) The offender is entitled to a hearing only on the question of whether the test result is accurate; the penalty itself is fixed.

—After some long period (perhaps six months) of no missed or positive tests, or alternatively the achievement of some score on a point system, offenders are eligible for less frequent testing. Continued good conduct leads to removal to inactive status, with only random testing.

To operate successfully, such a program will require:

—the capacity to do tests at locations reasonably accessible to those being tested (since they have to appear twice a week);

—on-the-spot test results, both to shrink the time gap between misconduct and punishment and to reduce the administrative burden of notifying violators and bringing them back;

—the capacity for quick-turnaround (within hours) verification tests on demand;

—either authority to apply sanctions after an administrative hearing or the availability of an on-call judge who can hear a case immediately;

—confinement spaces that are available on demand to hold short-term detainees; and

—the capacity to quickly apprehend those who fail to show up for testing.

None of these requirements should be, in principle, impossible to fulfill; but having all of them together and reliably available may well lie beyond possibility in many jurisdictions unless extraordinary political force is brought to bear. Thus if elected officials do not make coerced abstinence one of their goals, the system is unlikely to become a reality.

"Coerced abstinence" would be an appropriate label for a wide variety of progams. Shaping any particular program will require the resolution of some major design issues. One important but tricky decision involves what drugs to test for, both at the initial screening and under continuing monitoring. There is a strong case for omitting marijuana, at least at the initial screening. Because marijuana residues remain detectable for long periods and the drug is widely used, any program that does not exclude it is likely to have a substantial proportion of clients who use marijuana only. The individual and social benefits from reducing marijuana demand among offenders do not approach the benefits from reducing cocaine, methamphetamine, and heroin use. But once an offender is identified as a cocaine, methamphetamine, or heroin user, it may be that continued marijuana use will prove to be a risk factor for backsliding because acquiring it requires contact with drug sellers and because marijuana intoxication reduces sensitivity to the consequences of actions, which makes deterring offenders from using other drugs more difficult. These concerns, then, suggest that initial screenings should exclude marijuana but that ongoing monitoring should include it.

An especially touchy question is whether alcohol should be included in the list of drugs forbidden and tested for. Alcohol's very short detection window means that only very recent use can be discovered. Its legal status reduces the surface justification for forbidding it to offenders, but its link to violence (and complementarity with cocaine) creates a strong argument for prohibiting its use anyway. Alcohol could be another candidate for exclusion from preliminary screening but inclusion in routine testing.

The case for an automatic, and therefore necessarily formulaic, sanctions structure is very strong. But such a structure must start out with relatively mild sanctions or the program will collapse of its own weight as its confinement capacity fills and it becomes unable to deliver the sanctions it threatens. There is no analytic answer to the questions of how to start out and how rapidly or how strongly to increase the severity of sanctions as violations are repeated. Policy must be determined empirically in each jurisdiction.

Just as important as the sanctions structure is the reward structure: that rewards shape behavior more powerfully than punishments do is well established. Of course, the political problems of rewarding lawbreakers for obeying the law are substantial, so the best compromise may be to use praise and reduced supervision as the primary forms of reward. Collecting a participation fee or fine at the beginning of the treatment that could then be returned in small increments for each clean test might also greatly reduce the failure rate.

After an offender complies with program regulations for some specified time, the need to further reward desired behavior and to allay budget pressures argues that supervision should be reduced. Specifying a program will involve deciding when and how quickly to phase down the testing schedule, the nature of the ongoing monitoring, and what to do with those who backslide under reduced supervision.

Another crucial set of practical issues involves how to apprehend absconders and what sort of confinement capacity to maintain for violators. Again, these issues are highly context dependent.

Some participants will prove unable or unwilling to reform under punitive pressure alone. For them, treatment is essential, if only to reduce the burden they put on confinement capacity. In addition, it is probably true that the availability of treatment, or perhaps even a requirement to accept treatment, would reduce violation rates. What sort of paid treatment to offer (and how to make use of the Twelve-Step programs), to whom it should be offered, and whether and under what circumstances it should be required, are all open questions on which research could usefully be done.

Benefits and Costs

The benefits and costs of coerced abstinence programs will depend on details of their implementation, local conditions, and the (as yet unknown) behavior of offenders assigned to them. High levels of compliance will translate into great benefits and modest costs, low levels into high costs and few benefits. Only experience, ideally in the form of well-designed experiments, will allow informed judgments about whether, where, and how to put the concept of coerced abstinence into practice. Still, it is possible to estimate some of the benefits and costs of such programs under specified assumptions about design and results. Those calculations support the idea that coerced abstinence deserves thorough trials.

The primary benefit would be reduced abuse of the drugs tested for (partly but not totally offset by the substitution of other drugs), due not only to the deterrent effect of the sanctions but also to the tourniquet effect of interfering with incipient relapses before they can turn into full-fledged runs of heavy use. In a District of Columbia Drug Court experiment, coercion outperformed (admittedly not very good) treatment.[42] This would suggest that successful coercion programs might match the two-thirds reduction in drug consumption typical of users under treatment. If that estimate is accurate, and if all the high-dose user-offenders were under testing and sanctions, and if they accounted for 60 percent of total hard-drug consumption, dealers' revenues would be reduced by 40 percent. No other feasible antidrug program offers hope of comparable market shrinkage.

Smaller markets would mean diminished access for potential new users, neighborhoods protected from the side effects of illicit markets (most notably violence), fewer adolescents and young adults diverted from school or legitimate work into dealing, less diversion of police effort into drug law enforcement, and less prison capacity diverted into holding convicted dealers. With a fourth of prison cells now occupied by persons serving sentences for drug dealing offenses,[43] shrinking that number by 40 percent would allow either a 10 percent cut in prison spending, for a savings of about $3.5 billion per year, or increased imprisonment (numbers of offenders or time served or both) for nondealing offenses.[44]

The direct benefits for offenders of reduced consumption are comparably diverse: improved health, improved social functioning (job, family, neighborhood), and reduced crime by the offenders subject to testing. This would lead to reduced imprisonment among a population whose members tend to cycle in and out of confinement. With drug-involved offenders committing about half of all felonies committed in big cities, these potential benefits are great, though it would not be reasonable to expect a shrinkage in crime proportionate to the shrinkage in drug use.[45] But if the reduction in overall offending were even half as large as the reduction in drug consumption, and if the sort of drug-involved offenders who would be subject to coerced abstinence account for 40 percent of the population behind bars for other than drug dealing offenses, that would be another 13 percent of total confinement capacity (costing about $4 billion a year) saved, giving states the option of cutting their prison budgets or increasing deterrence and incapacitation for nondrug offenses.

A reliably operating system of coerced abstinence as part of probation and parole could also be expected to change the confinement decisions of judges and parole boards. By making probation or parole more meaningful alternatives to incarceration, a system of coerced abstinence should lead to more use of such nonincarcerative sanctions in otherwise borderline cases. Instead of having to guess whether a drug-involved offender will go straight this time, the decisionmaker can allow the offender to select himself for conditional freedom or confinement by his drug taking behavior as revealed by urine tests.

Coerced abstinence could also be expected to have beneficial effects on the treatment system. Some of those now referred to treatment by the courts would show themselves, under the steady pressure of testing and sanctions and perhaps with the aid of a Twelve-Step fellowship or similar self-help group, capable of abstaining from drug use without treatment, thus freeing treatment slots for those who need them. Those in treatment would have increased incentive to succeed, with the pressure coming not from the therapist or the program but from an external force. Those not in treatment who found themselves incapable of complying on their own would have a strong incentive to find treatment; their repeated failure would bring their treatment need to the attention of the courts and community corrections authorities, while the cost of their continual short confinements would create a financial incentive for the local government to provide it.

The cost picture is somewhat simpler, although still speculative until there are some working models to study. The important elements of cost would be testing operations, probation or parole supervision, the capacity to enforce sanctions and make arrests, and treatment. A cost calculation will require both unit cost and volume estimates. For unit costs, one can assume the following:

—Community corrections officers at $60,000 a year, including fringe benefits, overhead, and supervision. Police officers at $100,000 a year, also inclusive.

—Testing at $5 for a five-drug screen. This is less than most agencies currently pay, but consistent with the current costs in the mass-production District of Columbia Pretrial Services Agency and reasonable given the testing volumes that would exist with a full-scale national program of coerced abstinence.

—Confinement costs of $50 a day, less than a typical jail but consistent with the reduced need for services and security for short-term confinement: roughly the cost of a mediocre motel room.

—Treatment at $5,000 a year, reflecting a blend of methadone substitution, outpatient drug-free counseling, and therapeutic communities for the most intractable (partly a design decision).

In terms of volume it can be assumed that:

—Ten percent of the tests will be positive or no-shows. (This should be realistic for early stages of the program but perhaps pessimistic once the reliability of the tests and sanctions has been established in the minds of participants.)

—The average sanction for a violation will be three days.

—Ten percent of active cases will be in mandated (paid) treatment, over and above those who would have been in treatment in the absence of the program. This is a guess and partly a design decision.

—One-quarter of the population that originally qualified for active testing will have complied to the point of being moved to some form of low-cost monitoring and will not have been moved back to active testing as a result of a violation. This is another guess and partly a design decision.

—One probation or parole officer can manage 50 active testing and sanctions cases.

—One police officer to chase absconders will be needed for each 250 active cases.

On these assumptions, total program costs for 1,000 probationers who originally qualified for testing and sanctions, with 750 on active testing at any one time, would be:

15 probation officers @ \$60,000 = \$0.9 million
3 police officers @ \$100,000 = \$0.3million
750 offenders × 104 tests a year = 78,000 tests @ \$10 = \$0.8 million
78,000 tests × 10 percent × 3 days = 23,400 days @ \$50 = \$1.2 million
750 offenders × 10 percent = 75 treatment slots @ \$5,000 = \$0.4 million
Total = \$3.6 million, or \$3,600 per offender per year.

This estimate represents one-eighth of the annual cost of a prison cell. The probation department's share (probation salaries plus testing costs) would be \$2,100 per offender, about twice the average annual cost of probation supervision.

Sources of Resistance

Anyone advocating a major change in the way part of the public's business is done must confront the public sector version of the old question, "If yer so durned smart, why ain't ye rich?" If this is such a good idea, why is it not being pursued? A variety of conceptual, organizational, and practical barriers stand in the way of developing testing and sanctions into a working piece of administrative machinery.

First, a program of testing and sanctions challenges current understanding of deterrence and addiction. It seems difficult to believe that small sanctions would prove effective deterrents to offenders so signally resistant to the threat of more serious punishment. This resembles the question posed about bottle-deposit laws in beverage industry TV spots: "If a $500 fine doesn't stop a litterbug, what is a 5 cent deposit going to do?" The answer, of course, was that the fine was largely notional, but the nickel would actually be collected.

To some, the concept of addiction as a disease involving loss of voluntary control over drug taking implies that threats cannot change addictive behavior. This idea is related to the empirically discredited but still powerful notion that addiction implies that changes in price have little impact on the quantity purchased (inelastic demand).[46] There is evidence from experiments with laboratory animals that addictive demand is sensitive both to price (in the form of effort required to obtain drugs) and the consequences of drug use.[47] Experiments with humans have shown that small but immediate rewards for nonuse of drugs can substantially improve treatment success among those trying to quit.[48]

Because even pathological behaviors can still be responsive to consequences, the disease model of addiction does not rule out the possibility that coerced abstinence can succeed. Nonetheless, the notion that addicts are sick and therefore unresponsive to incentives remains powerful and a strong source of resistance to proposals for testing and sanctions.

In ideological terms a system of testing and sanctions does not, at least at first blush, satisfy either the moralistic and punitive or the compassionate and therapeutic impulses that dominate political discourse about drug use, although it has something to offer each side. That, plus its conceptual complexity, makes it unattractive as a political campaign proposal, except in the masquerade of yet another get-tough-on-drugs program.

Alongside this lack of popular appeal is active unpopularity with an important interest group: treatment advocates. The primary form this resistance has taken has been an attempt to redefine testing-and-sanctions proposals of programs of coerced treatment or treatment needs assessment for the offender population. By no means do all treatment providers dislike coerced abstinence, but it tends to encounter resistance on three grounds. Ideologically, it seems to be in tension with the disease concept of addiction, which is central to treatment providers' self-understanding. In economic terms, coerced abstinence is one more competitor for scarce funds. (Curiously, proponents of drug courts, who might also have been expected to consider a system of testing and sanctions a competitor for funding, have instead been rather friendly toward the idea.) But at a deeper level, those with a strong commitment to drug treatment may reasonably regard testing and sanctions as an inferior substitute for treatment.

For some drug-involved offenders, removal of drug dependency would allow them to live much happier lives. But for many, drug habits are only a part, and not the largest part, of their problems. Drug treatment often involves addressing far more than drug problems, which is most evident in therapeutic communities with their holistic attempt to reshape character but is also reflected in the provision of job, family, and social service counseling by many outpatient drug treatment programs. From the viewpoint of those most concerned about persons with addictions, testing and sanctions threaten to provide much if not most of the benefits of treatment from the viewpoint of crime victims and government budgets while not providing the other services those suffering from addiction need.

Nor are the agencies that would be most effected by coerced abstinence, the ones that would have to do most of the work, necessarily its supporters. Probation departments, usually badly overworked and understaffed, have not in general been aggressive in seeking out new missions and responsibilities. Police are anything but eager to make warrant service a high priority, although shifts toward community policing and the policy of holding area commanders responsible for reducing rates of criminal activity may be changing that attitude. Corrections officials are not looking for new business, especially not for the short-stay clients whose processing takes so much effort.

Moreover, by contrast with alternatives such as mandatory sentencing that are virtually self-implementing once legislation is passed, the interagency coordination required to make a program of testing and sanctions a success will require enormous effort on the part of whoever takes on the entrepreneurial responsibility.

Finally, coerced abstinence suffers from two budget mismatches, one of timing and one of level of government. Even if such a program turns out to be cost neutral or better in the long run, it would involve significant immediate costs and make immediate demands on scarce confinement capacity. The long-term savings are likely to be dismissed as typical program-advocate pie in the sky. Similarly, it is a rare county executive or sheriff who is eager to spend the county's resources on testing and sanctions to save the governor money in the form of reduced prison spending.

Experience

No large jurisdiction has instituted testing and sanctions on the model described here as part of routine probation and parole supervision. Scattered judges have created such programs on their own initiative, and informal reports suggest good results, but there have been no published evaluations. In any case such pioneer efforts often turn out to rely too heavily on the charismatic characteristics of their founders to be easily replicable. There have been four systematic efforts.

Santa Cruz County, California, instituted aggressive testing of known heroin users on probation in the late 1980s, along with a focused crackdown on street-level dealing. The county reported a 22 percent reduction in burglaries the following year, when burglaries were slightly up in adjacent comparable counties, but there was no careful examination of the relationship, if any, between the testing and the burglary reduction.[49]

The Multnomah County (Portland), Oregon, Drug Testing and Evaluation Program looked like a testing-and-sanctions program at the outset but evolved into merely one more tool for the probation officer. In the end it had neither continuity of testing, predictability of sanctions, nor program integrity (in terms of which offenders were subject to it and which not). No firm conclusion could be drawn about its performance.[50]

Project Sentry in Lansing, Michigan, has provided mostly short-term testing for drug-involved offenders on probation or presentencing release (about one-third of them felons) during the past twenty-five years. In the 29,652 specimens collected in the fifteen months ended December 31, 1996, there were 3,061 positive tests (each drug tested for counted as one test). If each positive test represented a different specimen, the positive rate per specimen would have been just over 10 percent; double counting for multiple drugs detected from a single specimen would bring that figure down somewhat.[51]

The largest controlled trial has been the "sanctions track" of the District of Columbia Drug Court, where defendants randomly assigned to twice-a-week testing with immediate sanctions based on a formula have taken drugs less often than have those mandated to treatment or those assigned to routine drug court processing (with test results reviewed by a judge and considered at sentencing time). Because the drug court is not restricted to drug-defined offenses but includes drug-involved defendants facing a variety of charges, this result may have some application to the broader run of felony and misdemeanor offenders. But the fact that the drug court is a voluntary diversion program limits the inferences that can be drawn about the potential of testing and sanctions as an element of routine probation.[52]

The Breaking the Cycle program in Birmingham, Alabama, now getting under way with federal research funding, is intended to be a full-scale test combining testing and sanctions with treatment. Details of program implementation have yet to be announced, but an elaborate evaluation is planned and some results should be available sometime in 1998.

Experimental Approaches

Two sorts of experiments ought to be done to help define the feasibility and utility of programs based on testing and sanctions: one taking the offender as the unit of analysis, the other taking the jurisdiction. Given the variety of circumstances and possible program implementations, each type of experiment should probably be run in more than one location. A strong argument can be made for a shakedown period of program development before any formal evaluation starts. Too many promising innovations have run aground on the shoals of single, premature evaluations.

At the individual level, one would want to test the extent to which offenders subject to a well-implemented testing and sanctions program would modify their drug-taking behavior and the effect of those modifications on crime and social functioning. That same test would provide estimates of failure rates and thus of the demand for sanctions. At its simplest, an experiment would involve the random assignment of offenders to either business-as-usual processing or testing and sanctions. Introducing systematic variation within the testing-and-sanctions condition would complicate the experimental design, but it would help answer questions about the optimal sanctions structure and the appropriate role of formal treatment.

Jurisdiction-level experiments would be, in effect, pilot implementations, with results compared either to control jurisdictions or historical results. Either basis of comparison brings with it significant methodological problems, but there are two sets of questions that can be answered only at the jurisdictional level. How closely can the actual performance of courts, probation, police, corrections, and treatment organizations approach to the theoretical design of a testing and sanctions program? What effect would such a program have on the local drug markets? Here the quantities of interest would include the level of dealing activity, the extent of market-related disorder and violence, and the numbers of dealing-related arrests, convictions, and sentences.

Recent Developments

Proposals for coerced abstinence never gained any traction in the Bush administration; concerns about undue interference with the automony of the states proved overwhelming. The idea started to float in Clinton administration circles almost from the beginning of the first term, but they were sidetracked into the more treatment-oriented Breaking the Cycle experiment and never emerged into political prominence. During the run-up to the 1996 elections, however, coerced abstinence was adopted, first as an administration proposal and then as a law requiring every state to create a program of testing and sanctions for drug-involved offenders as a condition of receiving federal grants to build prisons.

At minimum, every state will now have to consider whether and how to make coerced abstinence based on testing and sanctions abstinence a part of the criminal justice process. Maryland has already announced a pilot program in Baltimore, and planning is also under way in Massachusetts.[53] The current approach to drug-involved offenders makes so little sense from any perspective that something has to replace it. Perhaps that something will turn out to be some version of coerced abstinence.

Notes

1. Willard G. Manning and others, "The Taxes of Sin: Do Smokers and Drinkers Pay Their Way?" *Journal of the American Medical Association*, vol. 261 (March 17, 1989), pp. 1604–09.

2. Office of Applied Studies, *Preliminary Estimates from the 1995 National Household Survey on Drug Abuse* (Rockville, Md: Substance Abuse and Mental Health Services Administration, Department of Health and Human Services, August 1996).

3. William Rhodes and others, *What America's Users Spend on Illegal Drugs, 1988–1993* (Washington: Office of National Drug Control Policy, Spring 1995).

4. Office of Justice Programs, *1996 Drug Use Forecasting Annual Report on Adult and Juvenile Arrestees* (Department of Justice, June 1997).

5. Peter Reuter, "Can We Make Prohibition Work Better? Assessing American Drug Policy," University of Maryland, February 11, 1997, p. 6.

6. Ibid., p. 2.

7. Ibid.

8. Bureau of Justice Statistics, *Sourcebook of Criminal Justice Statistics,1994* (Department of Justice, 1995), tables 6.11 and 6.24.

9. Centers for Disease Control and Prevention, *U.S. HIV and AIDS Cases Reported through June 1996*, vol. 8 (Atlanta: Department of Health and Human Services, 1996), table 3.

10. Reuter, "Can We Make Prohibition Work Better?" p. 5.

11. Lloyd D. Johnston and others, *National Survey Results on Drug Use from the Monitoring the Future Study, 1975–1995*, vol. 1: *Secondary School Students* (Rockville, Md: National Institute on Drug Abuse, Department of Health and Human Services), table 14.

12. Harvey C. Mansfield Jr., *The Spirit of Liberalism* (Harvard University Press, 1978), chap. 1.

13. John Stuart Mill, *On Liberty*, ed. David Spitz (Norton, 1975), p. 13.

14. Thomas C. Schelling, *Choice and Consequence* (Harvard University Press, 1984), pp. 83–87.

15. Aristotle, *Nicomachean Ethics*, VII, in J. L. Ackrill, ed. *Aristotle's Ethics* (London: Faber and Faber, 1973). See also Jon Elster, *Ulysses and the Sirens: Studies in Rationality and Irrationality* (Cambridge University Press, 1979), p. 52.

16. Richard J. Herrnstein, "On the Law of Effect," *Journal of the Experimental Analysis of Behavior*, vol. 13 (March 1970), pp. 243–266. See also Gene M. Heyman, "Resolving the Contradictions of Addiction," *Behavioral and Brain Sciences*, vol. 19 (December 1996), pp. 561–610.

17. George Ainslie and Nick Haslam, "Hyperbolic Discounting," in George Lowenstein and Jon Elster, eds., *Choice Over Time* (Russell Sage Foundation, 1992), pp. 57–92.

18. Howard Raiffa, *Decision Analysis: Introductory Lectures on Choices under Uncertainty* (Addison-Wesley, 1968).

19. Amos Tversky, "Contrasting Rational and Psychological Principles of Choice," in Richard J. Zeckhauser, Ralph L. Keeney, and James K. Sebenius, eds., *Wise Choices: Decisions, Games, and Negotiations* (Harvard Business School Press, 1996), pp. 7–8.

20. Or perhaps not. Plato's Socrates asserts that all unjust actions are contrary to self-interest, properly understood, because injustice damages the *psyche* (soul), and no benefit gained by injustice can be adequate to compensate for a damaged psyche. (See *Republic* I. 351d–354.)

21. George Orwell, *Down and Out in Paris and London* (London: Secker & Warburg, 1949).

22. Gary S. Becker and Kevin M. Murphy, "A Theory of Rational Addiction," *Journal of Political Economy*, vol. 96 (August 1984), pp. 675–700.

23. John Kaplan, *The Hardest Drug: Heroin and Public Policy* (University of Chicago Press, 1983).

24. Reuter, "Can We Make Prohibition Work Better? p. 2. See also Bureau of Justice Statistics, *Sourcebook of Criminal Justice Statistics,1994*, tables 6.11 and 6.24.

25. David Boyum, "Reflections on Economic Theory and Drug Enforcement," Ph.D. dissertation, Harvard University, 1992.

26. Peter Reuter, Robert MacCoun, and Patrick Murphy, *Money from Crime: A Study of the Economics of Drug Dealing in Washington, D.C.* (Santa Monica, Calif.: RAND, 1990).

27. Reuter, "Can We Make Prohibition Work Better?" p. 4.

28. Whether, to what extent, under what circumstances, and at what costs needle exchange programs would reduce the rates of infection, and how they compare with alternative approaches, remains an open question. See Mark A. R. Kleiman and Jenny W. Rudolph, "Assessing Needle Exchange and Distribution: The Limits of Benefit-Cost Analysis," working paper 04-03-94, Program in Criminal Justice Policy and Management, John F. Kennedy School of Government, Harvard University, 1994. But the political opposition to such programs runs far deeper than the empirical and operational issues.

29. On the commonness of the deficiencies, see James Q. Wilson and Richard J. Herrnstein, *Crime and Human Nature* (Simon and Schuster, 1985), pp. 194–98.

30. The 50 percent figure is from Office of Justice Programs, *1996 Drug Use Forecasting*.

31. Rhodes and others, *What America's Users Spend on Illegal Drugs*, table 3.

32. For the lower number see Office of Applied Studies, *Preliminary Estimates from the 1995 National Household Survey on Drug Abuse*. For the higher number see Reuter, "Can We Make Prohibition Work Better?" p. 3.

33. Rhodes and others, *What America's Users Spend on Illegal Drugs*, table 3.

34. Ibid., p. 10.

35. William Rhodes, "Synthetic Estimation Applied to the Prevalence of Drug Use," *Journal of Drug Issues*, vol. 23 (Spring 1993), pp. 297–321.

36. Mark A. R. Kleiman, "Reducing the Prevalence of Cocaine and Heroin Dealing among Adolescents," *Valpariso University Law Review,* vol. 31 (Spring 1997), pp. 551–64.

37. Reuter, "Can We Make Prohibition Work Better?" pp. 4–5.

38. Carl G. Leukefeld and Frank M. Tims, *Compulsory Treatment of Drug Abuse: Research and Clinical Practice*, NIDA research mongraph 86 (Rockville, Md.: National Instiute on Drug Abuse, 1988).

39. Harry K, Wexler, Gregory P. Falkin, and Douglas Lipton, "Outcome Evaluation of a Prison Theraputic Community for Substance Abuse Treatment," *Criminal Justice and Behavior*, vol. 17 (March 1990), pp. 71–92.

40. Bureau of Justice Statistics, *Sourcebook of Criminal Justice Statistics,1994*, table 1.71.

41. Joan Petersilia and Susan Turner, "Intensive Probation and Parole," in Michael Tonry, ed., *Crime and Justice:A Review of Research*, vol. 17 (University of Chicago Press, 1993), pp. 281–335.

42. Adele Harrell and Shannon Cavanagh, "Preliminary Results from the Evaluation of the DC Superior Court Drug Intervention Program for Drug Felony Defendants," Urban Institute, Washington.

43. Reuter, "Can We Make Prohibition Work Better? p. 2. See also Bureau of Justice Statistics, *Sourcebook of Criminal Justice Statistics,1994*, tables 6.11 and 6.24.

44. For the savings figure see Bureau of Justice Statistics, *Sourcebook of Criminal Justice Statistics,1994*, table 1.3.

45. Office of Justice Programs, *1996 Drug Use Forecasting Annual Report.*

46. Jonathan P. Caulkins, "Estimating Elasticities of Demand for Cocaine and Heroin with DUF Data," Carnegie Mellon University.

47. Heyman, "Resolving the Contradictions of Addiction."

48. S. T. Higgins and others, "Incentives Improve Outcome in Outpatient Behavioral Treatment of Cocaine Dependence," *Archives of General Psychiatry*, vol. 51 (July 1994), pp. 568–76.

49. Botec Analysis Corp., "Program Evaluation: Santa Cruz Regional Street Drug Reduction Program," Cambridge, Mass., June 1990.

50. Adele Harrell, William Adams, and Caterina Gouvis, "Evaluation of the Impact of Systemwide Drug Testing in Multnomah County, Oregon," Urban Institute, Washington, April 1994.

51. J. J. Gallegher, "Project Sentry Final Program Report," Project Sentry, Lansing, Mich., 1996. See also "Project Sentry Quarterly Program Report: Summary," Project Sentry, Lansing, Mich., 1997.

52. Harrell and Cavanagh, *Preliminary Results.*

53. See Faye S. Taxman, *Task Force on Drug-Addicted Offenders* (Annapolis, Md.: Office of the Lieutenant Governor of Maryland, 1997).

Seven

Paternalism Goes to School

Chester E. Finn Jr.

Mediocre academic achievement has placed the nation at risk in the past two decades. Simply put, the average student emerging from the typical U.S. school does not possess sufficient skills and knowledge for his or her own or society's good. For disadvantaged young people the problem is graver still. Sixty-nine percent of black and 64 percent of Hispanic fourth graders could not read at even a basic level in 1994, compared with (a still lamentable) 29 percent of whites and 22 percent of Asian Americans. It is generally understood that children who cannot read satisfactorily by this point in their schooling are likely never to catch up.[1]

America has recognized this problem since at least 1983, when the National Commission on Excellence in Education sounded an alarm about "a nation at risk"; yet the many reforms undertaken since then have made little difference. The renewal schemes have been of almost every description, and there is evidence of movement on the surface of the school system; yet the waters beneath remain largely undisturbed. What actions might yield greater improvement in academic attainment?[2]

In pursuit of an answer, states and communities are trying more radical innovations, reforms that overturn long-cherished assumptions, ancient ground rules, and ingrained power relations within the education system. Important examples include school choice (even, in Milwaukee and Cleveland, vouchers to attend private schools), charter schools (independent public schools that escape red tape by promising better results), public schools managed by private companies, innovative school designs (such as those sponsored by the New American Schools Development Corporation), and complex efforts to impose standards and accountability on a system that has largely escaped such strictures in the past.[3]

Most of these innovations are rooted in the assumption that true change will come to American education, if at all, through market forces and grassroots initiatives rather than elaborately planned systemic or top-down changes. That is a gamble, of course, both because the market-style reforms have not been fully tested and because evidence indicates that many Americans are reasonably content with their own children's schools and see no great need to change (although they are quick to favor changes for the folks across town).[4]

The more radical the reform, of course, the more resistance it encounters, especially within the tradition-bound, ideologically becalmed, and interest-group-riddled school establishment. That is why today's market-style innovations are making slow headway: some 500 charter schools were in operation in 1996–97, for example, among 85,000 public schools.

I am a partisan of the bust-it-up or market-style strategy. I believe that it will yield results far beyond those that more limited reforms can produce. But there is something to be said for gradualism when undertaking changes that we cannot yet be certain will boost achievement. Far harder to explain is why we have not already installed throughout the land an approach to instructional improvement and school management that displays an uncommonly robust research base and a convincing track record, especially on behalf of disadvantaged children. It is also less disruptive of established governance systems and power relationships.

This chapter examines that approach: purposeful paternalism that deploys such classroom strategies as "direct instruction" and "mastery learning" to intensify young people's acquisition of basic skills and knowledge. This approach, commonly termed *behaviorism* by psychologists and *instructivism* by Diane Ravitch and me, is almost as controversial within the education profession as vouchers.[5] Of late, it is also resisted by many noneducators, especially those on the political right. It may do less violence to formal structures, but it is nearly as disruptive of cherished ideologies. Because it would, in this sense, break up a long-established and deeply embedded structure of beliefs, it has generally been ignored and spurned, despite its proven capacity to boost educational attainment, especially among disadvantaged young people.

Education and State Authority

Except for prison, school is the most paternalistic of our major social institutions. State law compels children's attendance during prescribed ages at institutions that government deems to be schools. Parents can be fined or jailed if their sons and daughters fail to turn up. While in school, young people are expected to follow various codes of behavior. Some of these resemble the norms of any civilized neighborhood—no drugs, guns, alcohol, violence—but others are additional burdens unique to school (and perhaps the military): not speaking unless called on, not being in the corridor without a pass, not going to the restroom without permission, taking no more than twelve minutes for recess and twenty-five for lunch. Many U.S. high schools have metal detectors at the doors and even more have guards in the hallways and bullet-proof glass in the windows. Students must come to some schools in uniforms. The message is clear: only approved forms of behavior will be tolerated.

Society uses its police powers to back up this paternalism, and there are occasional vivid examples of law enforcement activity meant to make young people comply. Charleston, South Carolina, Police Chief Reuben Greenberg and Houston Constable Victor Trevino are living examples of close cooperation between police authorities and schools to raise attendance.[6] Greenberg (who is black) has gained a national reputation for his commonsense strategies for keeping violence and drug dealers out of Charleston's housing projects and keeping youths in the city's schools. Trevino (who is Hispanic) deploys volunteer police in Houston's tough Sixth Precinct to visit the homes of truants, talk with their parents, remind them of the Texas compulsory school attendance law, and try in other ways to counter the powerful influence of gang culture in their neighborhoods. Such a home visit may help a young person resist peer pressure to cut school the next day. Not surprisingly, where this program is functioning, school attendance has risen dramatically.

Paternalism in attempting to ensure attendance takes other forms as well. It is not unusual to find on-site day care for the babies of high school students, an arrangement intended to woo young people into at least going through the motions of completing school despite their early parenthood. Wisconsin's Learnfare program reduces parents' welfare benefits if their minor children are not in school, thus linking two domains of social policy in paternalist union. Ohio's Learning, Earning and Parenting (LEAP) program tries to boost school attendance by increasing the welfare checks of pregnant and parenting teenagers if they attend regularly and by shrinking the checks of those who skip school. Evaluations by the Manpower Demonstration Research Corporation indicate that these incentives and disincentives have yielded modest success.[7]

Many communities are more passive about school attendance. Truant officers and special programs cost money, and some principals would happily be rid of the very kids who would as soon be rid of school. One rarely hears of parents actually going to jail because of their children's truancy. Yet few would dispute society's right to oblige young people to attend school. On the left fringe one can find the occasional anarchist and on the right edge a handful of libertarians who believe that education is a private matter that government should entirely forswear.[8] But the rest of us would be dumbfounded by any suggestion that compelling school attendance by the young is not a proper role for society and the state.

The Limits of Paternalism

Paternalism as commonly practiced in U.S. education has mostly to do with physical presence and discipline, not skills and knowledge. Society can mandate where one's body is but not what one's mind absorbs. The compulsory attendance law does not say that youngsters must learn anything.

It is not that society has not tried to prescribe curricular content and performance standards. People have long understood that the adult community has a right, even a duty, to satisfy itself that the young acquire certain skills, lore, and behaviors before taking their own places as adults. There are religious versions of this threshold requirement, such as confirmation and bar mitzvah, and there are secular: "we hire only high school graduates in this corporation"; "you may not drive a car in our state until you pass a prescribed test of knowledge and skills"; "you may not join the army unless you can read at a certain level." The expectations for actual learning may be low (driver's license tests) or exacting (board certification of neurosurgeons), but they are grounded in general acceptance of society's authority to protect itself from entry by people ignorant of its norms.

If, however, a person does not wish to learn, society's ability to compel him to do so is weak. It can deny him a license but it cannot force him to learn enough to obtain one. Learning is a voluntary act. No legislature or constable can make it happen. Saying someone must sit in a biology class for fifty minutes a day throughout a school year does not cause him to grasp the difference between a phylum and a species. Nor can he be prevented from learning other things that interest him more. Modern totalitarian societies tried hard to shape what their young people would learn, and they had some success within the schoolroom, but even they could not stanch the flow of outside information. And democratic societies have other traditions—freedom of speech, inquiry, belief—that are as powerful as the ancient norm empowering adults to prescribe what children should learn.

Besides the voluntariness of learning, four limits on state power in education need to be borne in mind. First, although one may be required to attend *some* school, if one does not like the norms of a *particular* school, one can usually choose a school with different rules. Three quarters of a century ago the Supreme Court, in *Pierce v. Society of Sisters,* established that a person can obey the state's compulsory school attendance law without attending state schools.[9] Today, 11 percent of primary and secondary school students attend private schools, and the spread of home schooling attests to the states' willingness to accommodate families for whom no conventional public or private school seems satisfactory. It also attests to the limited hold that compulsory attendance laws and school behavior codes have on the actions of children and parents. If one is clever, wealthy, or determined, one can find a private or public school whose priorities suit one's own. If one does not want to learn biology, one can seek out a school where that subject is an elective or is not taught at all. In extremis, one can create one's own school around the kitchen table.

These freedoms, and the constraints they place on state action, arise because in a democracy the principle of society's responsibility for education is in perpetual tension with individual rights and family prerogatives vis-à-vis rearing children. That is what the Supreme Court grappled with in *Pierce v. Society of Sisters* and what most of today's livelier education policy battles are about. People have different values and emphases with respect to their children's education, some of them strongly held, some out of religious belief. Education may be partly a public good, as the economists say, something that benefits the larger society by making it more productive and competitive, and is thus within the purview of government. But education is also a private good that liberates, enlightens, and enriches the individual receiving it. The proper rearing of children may be a legitimate interest of the entire village, according to Hillary Rodham Clinton, but it is fundamentally the responsibility of parents. Thus the Supreme Court's ruling in *Pierce* was that "the child is not the mere creature of the state" and that parents may select the school their child will attend. That right remains intact; today's big argument is the extent to which the state will provide and underwrite the choices.

The government's power in education is also limited because there is dogged political resistance to overreaching by the state—even more so when Washington gets involved—with respect to educational content and curriculum. The current backlash against outcomes-based education has multiple origins, but it has been so powerful that it has caused many elected officials to shy away from efforts to specify and enforce the acquisition of skills and knowledge, even the three R's, notwithstanding survey evidence that most parents want schools to ensure that pupils learn these basics.[10] In fields such as history, literature, and art, all government mandates—even voluntary standards—have become politically risky, and few people would suggest that education policymakers have any business involving themselves with values, attitudes, and behaviors. Such cherished educationist goals as "higher-order cognitive skills" may be acceptable for individual schools to impart, especially if families are free to choose their schools, but when the state tries to universalize them, it is seen as treading on people's freedom. (This is not an entirely irrational reaction. For those who inhabit a faith-bound world, the prospect of government officials compelling their children to reason critically and think independently—or else no diploma and perhaps no job—verges on sacrilege, as well as constituting an unreasonable intrusion into family matters.)

State power is limited in another way because Americans are a pragmatic people, less awed by lofty state objectives and elaborate written standards than by marketplace signals. The real world tells young people that they can get promoted to the next grade, even get a high school diploma, mainly by sitting long enough in a building called school (and perhaps passing a low-level test of basic skills). If it looked as though understanding the origins and outcomes of World War I were truly a prerequisite for college entry or gainful employment, many more people would muster the rudiments of such an understanding. (Never mind that many would acquire it from a cram course, Cliffs Notes, or video cassette, and that it would not stay with them much longer than last week's allowance.)

The fact is, however, that in the United States there is no universal reward for learning anything in particular, nor any universal punishment for not doing so. Anyone can attend some college no matter how badly he did in high school, indeed no matter whether he even graduated. Federal grants and loans flow to those without diplomas as well as those who do spectacularly on the advanced placement examinations. Rare is the employer who checks a high school transcript for evidence of academic attainment, and rarer still one who rewards such attainment with higher pay. Thus the absence of real stakes associated with academic achievement and the limited capacity of teachers and parents to convince young people that how they do in school will make a big difference in their later lives.[11]

The ultimate limit on state power is that young Americans do not spend much of their lives in school anyway. The influence of school is dwarfed by home, peer group, neighborhood, and television. A dutiful U.S. youngster who begins kindergarten at the age of five and has perfect attendance through high school will, upon reaching his eighteenth birthday, have spent 9 percent of his hours on earth in school. (After sleep is taken into consideration, these proportions resolve to 15 percent in school.) It is possible to learn a lot during that time, and some do, but if society's capacity to compel learning through schooling is the focus, we have to be constantly aware that school affects just a thin slice of a person's sentient being.

The Failure of the Economic Model

Faced with such limitations, one may reasonably ask what leverage remains for policymakers keen to strengthen student achievement. By the 1960s, long before *A Nation at Risk,* a consensus was emerging that student achievement was too low, especially for disadvantaged and minority young people. Thus their prospects for success in life were dim. Thus Uncle Sam ought to take action. Or so went the reasoning in Washington. It was the era of Head Start, Title I (the federal government's largest effort to provide compensatory education to disadvantaged young people), school desegregation, *The Other America* (Michael Harrington's influential discussion of the plight of the underclass),and the War on Poverty. The country still labored under the illusion that its middle class was in sound educational shape and the main challenge was to help poor and minority children get up to speed.

How to do that? The Great Society's answer was a massive federal effort to introduce new programs and direct additional resources into the nation's schools in the name of equalizing educational opportunity, especially for low-income and minority students. These were soon joined by the disabled, children with limited English proficiency, and other "special populations," what people outside the Beltway sometimes refer to as "victim groups." At the same time, the federal government set out to boost school resources and education services in the sublime belief that such actions would yield more acceptable student academic achievement. The reform initiatives hinged on an economic model of education: the more the nation invests in the enterprise, the richer the harvest it will reap. Indeed, thirty years later that remains the underlying assumption of most federal education programs.[12]

But experience has proven that assumption mainly false. One may be able to justify these programs (and the many similar state, local, and private efforts they spawned) on grounds of simple justice, reparations, or social peace. But one cannot find much evidence that they lastingly boost pupil absorption of academic skills and knowledge. Study after study of Head Start has shown that its effects on cognitive achievement dissipate within a few years. Study after study of the Chapter I program has similarly shown it to have little effect.[13] Nor can anyone take much comfort from the experience of school districts that muster their own resources from state and local funds. Newark, Hartford, the District of Columbia, and other cities, amply supplied as they are with at-risk students, are nearing $10,000 per pupil in annual outlays, more than half again as much as the national average. Yet their results remain woeful. Kansas City, obliged by a federal judge to pump billions of extra dollars into its inner-city schools, has posh facilities and esoteric programs to show for the money but little by way of improved achievement. No matter how many books the social critic Jonathan Kozol publishes with the aim of making Americans feel guilty that some schools are well equipped while others have leaky roofs, evidence simply does not support the contention that changing the allocation of financial resources will significantly alter student learning.[14]

The Quest for School Effectiveness

The central premise of the Great Society's education programs, in other words, rests on quicksand. And as events played out, this understanding began to dawn even as the Great Society reached its apogee. A year after the Elementary and Secondary Education Act was signed into law, James S. Coleman stunned the education world with his massive report, *Equality of Educational Opportunity.*[15] This study found no reliable relationship between the resources that go into schools and the learning that comes out. It suggested that what schools spend and do accounts for little of the difference in their results, thus apparently obliterating economic notions of an education production function. Instead, Coleman's results indicated, what accounts for most of the difference in student achievement are elements over which schools have scant control, factors such as family background and peer group.

Although this conclusion was not well recognized at first, the Coleman report marked a watershed in American education. The premier dilemma of contemporary education policy, after all, is how to get the average child to emerge from the average school with a great deal more skill and knowledge than is typically the case. As long as the school production function was believed to link inputs to outputs, one took for granted that adjusting school resources would reliably change results. In the wake of Coleman, however, Americans came to understand that augmenting school resources and services does not predictably translate into stronger pupil achievement. The main reason there is now more concern with educational effectiveness than with simple service delivery is because we can no longer assume a firm bond between them.

Coleman's findings thus seemed at first to throw cold water on the idea of effective schools and instructional practices. (If "schools do not make a difference," why spend time looking for meaningful differences between them?) As time passed, however, Americans came to see that these findings actually gave an important boost to the search for such schools and practices. As long as a simple production function was assumed, there had not been much reason to scrutinize the subtler, noneconomic ways schools differ, for example in curriculum, instructional method, and institutional ethos. After 1966, however, analysts faced a whole new challenge.

Coleman, after all, never said that schools produced identical results, nor did out-of-school variables account for all the differences in their results. Yet neither did conventional inputs. This raised a profound question: could some substantial portion of the wide gap visible in educational attainment be traced to school and classroom practices?

About the same time, another intellectual breakthrough lent further gravity to the analysis of school practices. Survey research such as Coleman's is inevitably confined to measures of what significant numbers of existing institutions are already doing. This tends to limit the universe of possibilities to present realities. But John B. Carroll offered a new insight: schools historically have held key production elements such as teaching time and student classroom time constant while accepting widely disparate results. They might instead produce more equal outcomes, Carroll suggested, by purposely varying those production elements. One could set standards for all, then devote extra resources and effort to some schools, if necessary, to achieve them for all.[16]

Spurred by these challenges, scholars made new efforts to understand what school practices worked best, particularly with poor and minority youngsters. One pioneer in such research—"effective schools" research as it came to be known—was England's Michael Rutter.[17] Another was America's Ronald Edmonds.[18] Each studied schools as production units. If student learning is the product, and some units produce more than others even though their raw materials are similar, something in the production process must add differing amounts of value.

Subsequent studies of educational productivity are prominently associated with scholars such as economist Eric Hanushek, psychologist Herbert J. Walberg, and former Stanford education dean Marshall Smith. Coleman did his share of this research, too, particularly by examining private schools to determine why their students' achievement is superior to that of public school pupils.[19] Of course that line of inquiry stirred new controversy. America's public school establishment has always been nervous about anything, even the most sophisticated analyses, suggesting that private schools might be better.

Yet there was more to effective schools research than measuring public-private differences. The research of Rutter and Edmonds, for example, was confined to public schools and focused on disadvantaged youth. So was Marshall Smith's.[20] Yet their essential findings were as similar as they were straightforward and commonsensical. It turns out that effective elementary schools—most scholars avoided the organizationally more complex high schools—typically display

—a clear sense of institutional mission that is shared by principal and teachers;

—high expectations for all students;

—well-developed team spirit on the part of those working in the school;

—a safe and orderly environment; and

—adroit leadership of the instructional process, typically by a principal who views his role more as educational executive than building manager.

As for *classroom* practices, other research examined instructional strategies and found some more effective than others, especially for disadvantaged children. Variously called "explicit teaching," "mastery learning," "direct instruction," and "precision teaching," these methods had much in common. Here is Walberg's summary of the research into two of the strategies.

> *Direct teaching.* Many studies show that direct teaching can be effective in promoting student learning. . . . Six phased functions of direct teaching work well:
>
> 1) daily review, homework check, and if necessary, re-teaching;
> 2) rapid presentation of new content and skills in small steps;
> 3) guided student practice with close teacher monitoring;
> 4) corrective feedback and instructional reinforcement;
> 5) independent practice in seatwork and homework with a high (more than 90 percent) success rate; and
> 6) weekly and monthly reviews. . . .
>
> *Mastery learning.* More than 50 studies show that careful sequencing, monitoring, and control of the learning process raises the learning rate. Pre-testing helps determine what should be studied. . . . Ensuring that students achieve mastery of initial steps in the sequence helps ensure that they will make satisfactory progress in subsequent, more advanced steps. Frequent assessment of progress informs teachers and students when additional time and corrective remedies are needed.[21]

Any fair-minded analyst of research into effective schools and productive teaching strategies (including those associated with such eminent practitioners as Marva Collins and Jaime Escalante) will be struck by the powerful role of—choose your word—instructivism, behaviorism, or paternalism. Success in strengthening student achievement generally accompanies the active use of goals, standards, expectations, assessments, and feedback, the persistent redoing of what is not yet done well and, perhaps especially, accountability for results. As the psychologist J. E. Stone has commented, the most effective instructional programs feature a "brief list of powerful and teacher-alterable classroom interventions, most of which are supported by experimental evidence. High expectations for effort and achievement is one, the use of incentives is another. In general, [these] methodologies are structured and teacher directed; they aim to instill preconceived academic and intellectual outcomes; and most of them employ practice, feedback, and incentives."[22]

Oversimplified, an effective teacher (or school) is precise about what students must learn, communicates these expectations clearly, focuses effort on the production of the desired results (and does not get distracted by other matters), has precise measures of performance, provides frequent feedback on progress, rewards success, does not accept failure, and persists until the goal is attained.

How do such programs actually function? Here is a sketch of Success for All, a well-regarded program developed by Robert Slavin and associates at Johns Hopkins University to impart basic reading skills to disadvantaged primary students.

> Our basic approach . . . begins with two essential principles: prevention and immediate, intensive intervention. . . . When learning problems do appear, corrective interventions must be immediate, intensive, and minimally disruptive to students' progress in the regular program. . . . Instead of letting students fall further and further behind . . . Success for All gives them whatever help they need to keep up in the basic skills as soon as they need it. . . . The reading program itself has been designed to take full advantage of having 90 minutes of direct instruction. The program emphasizes the development of basic language skills and sound- and letter-recognition skills in kindergarten. . . . Every eight weeks, reading teachers assess students' progress. . . . The results . . . are used to determine who is to receive tutoring, to suggest adaptations in students' programs, and to identify students who need other types of assistance.[23]

The Establishment Fights Back

The most important thing to know about these proven and empirically tested instructional strategies is that they are little used in American schools. That is because the educational philosophy that underlies them conflicts with the "child-centered" or "developmentalist" philosophy that has ruled the education profession throughout this century.

Do not be misled by conferences at which governors and corporate chieftans renew their vows of faith in education standards, assessments, and accountability—the key elements of programs such as mastery learning. Those are the earnest views of important people who spend their days outside the schools. Their instincts are sound, their motives honorable, and their prescriptions would make for significant improvement. Within the education system itself, however, such views collide with the regnant belief structure, which is rooted in developmentalism, the celebration of differences, ceaseless augmentation of resources, affinity for the status quo, and careful avoidance of accountability for results.

One can see self-interest in this bundle of attitudes, to be sure. As long as there are no clear standards or high-stakes assessments, instructors are not apt to be held responsible for the academic achievement of their students. Thus they are not likely to lose their jobs or be penalized for failing to produce desired results. (Nor will anyone be pulled from the crowd for special accolades and bonuses in recognition of superior performance. The culture of American schools does not welcome pioneers or rate-breakers.) Moreover, as long as voters, taxpayers, and elected officials have no means of judging schools by their results, one can continue persuading them that whatever may be less than perfect in U.S. education today can easily be set right by the application of more money, the delivery of additional services, smaller classes, extra classroom aides, more free periods for teacher planning, and so on.[24]

Yet self-interest is only the beginning. Undergirding the profession's divergent view of schooling is the educational philosophy known as "progressivism." The education historian Diane Ravitch described it as generally emphasizing

> active learning through experience rather than passive learning through systematic instruction; cooperative planning of classroom activities by teachers and pupils; cooperation among pupils on group projects rather than competition for grades; and the merging of traditional academic subjects into functional problem areas related to family life, community problems, or student interests. Progressive teachers rejected drill and memorization as teaching methods; the teaching of traditional subject matter unrelated to functional, "real-life" problems; traditional policies of promotion and failure; reliance on textbooks; and evaluation of the school program by tests of subject matter mastery.[25]

Today one might add the following observations to a description of progressivism in American education: the child learns best when he learns what interests him, at his own pace and in his own way; children differ in learning styles, even in the nature of their intellects, and these differences must guide their instruction; true learning means constructing one's own meaning from the information at hand, not parroting somebody else's notion of what is important; learning how to learn is more important than any specific knowledge; because each child is unique and requires self-esteem, uniform standards and competition are harmful; invidious tracking of students by ability or achievement should give way to individual assessments; objective tests of basic skills and knowledge should be replaced by "authentic" or "performance" assessments gathered into portfolios; diversity and tolerance mean not making judgments about individuals or groups (or political and economic systems); and the purpose of education has more to do with making society equal than maximizing anyone's skill or knowledge.

Educational progressivism, in sum, is the opposite of what psychologists call *behaviorism* and policymakers *paternalism:* the purposeful manipulation of behavior toward desired ends through the application of tangible incentives, rewards, and punishments. That is why educators have long scorned behaviorism—consider the calumny heaped on B. F. Skinner—and instructional strategies that tend toward it. With roots that run back to the turn of the century, progressive educators believe that school must be bent to the child's contours rather than the child to the school's. Such child-centered education is commonly contrasted with and preferred to standards-based education. Indeed, a recent article in one of today's most influential education journals, *Phi Delta Kappan,* refers to "the monster of standards in the classroom."[26] And J. E. Stone writes, "In essence, developmentalism leads to schools in which attendance is compulsory but study is not. Students are expected to make an effort only if they feel interested and enthused. Study is expected to be more like fun than work. If students waste time and educational opportunity because they find schoolwork boring, their behavior is not merely tolerated, it is understood and excused as the product of insufficiently stimulating instruction."[27]

Today's educators are willing to be paternalist only in a few nonacademic areas such as "service learning" (requiring students to engage in community service), racial desegregation (obliging students to attend a distant school to produce desired ethnic ratios), and appreciation of individual and cultural differences (such as by mainstreaming disabled children in regular classrooms and spending every February on black history). It seems that the profession can tolerate paternalism in schools only as long as it serves political goals. This is no more defensible—or helpful to children's acquisition of the three R's—than the insistence of some people that the schools drum into their pupils certain attitudes toward sex, families, nuclear weapons, or the environment.

Progressivism and Educational Effectiveness

Despite heightened concern about school standards, progressivism rides as high within the education profession today as in the 1960s and 1970s. Indeed, the profession's animus toward paternalist or behaviorist strategies has deepened, partly in reaction to the excellence-and-standards movement, partly in emulation of trends toward relativism and expressionism in the academic and artistic communities. All this reflects the general loosening of traditional authority and erosion of social norms that the country underwent in the 1960s and 1970s and from which it has not recovered.

Educators prefer to define their task as teaching critical thinking and complex reasoning because this allows them to deemphasize the accumulation of basic skills and knowledge, which is hard work for both teachers and pupils. Yet basic skills and knowledge are what disadvantaged youngsters, in particular, most acutely lack (and middle-class children are somewhat more apt to acquire outside school). Research and experience show that skills of a higher order, which children also need, can only emerge when a sturdy foundation has first been laid through purposive instruction that follows an orderly plan and insists on demonstrable results. Many educators, however, have persuaded themselves that the skills they admire will emerge only if students direct their own education and teachers act mainly as facilitators. Instructional strategies that are especially powerful in imparting skills to disadvantaged youngsters therefore get rejected because they are considered teacher dominated, preoccupied with basic skills, vaguely robotic, illiberal, and authoritarian.[28]

It is not that today's educators are oblivious to two decades of research into school and classroom effectiveness. It is that, for ideological reasons, they have drawn from that research only the parts they agreed with. They omit the behaviorist-paternalist part that their reigning philosophy rejects and focus instead on the softer and more welcome implications of the same research: those having to do with decentralization and deregulation, empowerment and site management, cooperative learning and team building. The "principal as instructional leader," for example, can be interpreted as anything from friendly advisor to dictator. The need for "clear objectives" is as easily applied to the quest for self-esteem as to multiplication tables. Feedback on progress can be derived from "authentic assessment" as well as from standardized tests. And the call for "high expectations" for students can be translated with far less effort into the sappy mantra that "all children can learn" than into precise skill and knowledge targets tailored to each child's current performance level.

Effective schools research, in other words, was heeded by educators, but only the jam on its surface, not the chewy bread beneath. That is why, for example, the findings of the huge, federally sponsored Follow Through experiment were all but ignored.[29] It was most unusual to build an experimental design into such a program: a post–Head Start early childhood intervention meant to boost the school readiness and success of disadvantaged youth and to deploy various instructional methods to see which worked best. But this was in fact done and the scientific results were clear. The most effective methods for boosting the academic skills of poor children were those such as "direct instruction" with strong behavioral elements: explicit goals, purposeful teaching strategies, constant assessment, and patient reteaching. Yet the methods that endured in Follow Through (and most of U.S. early childhood education) were instead the softer, constructivist, child-centered methods dear to the heart of the education profession. The results of a billion dollar controlled experiment in rival education methods were essentially discarded. As Cathy L. Watkins has observed, "The educational problems of this country are unlikely to be fully solved until it is recognized that how well students learn is more a function of how they are taught than any other factor."[30]

Although the Follow Through experiment took place in the early 1980s, the situation in education has basically not changed. Behaviorist teaching strategies still collide with the philosophy of developmentalism. Their successful implementation takes much hard work and disrupts established interests and practices. The strategies invite unwelcome accountability to outside policymakers and parents interested in test scores and other hard evidence of attainment. Unless well disguised, therefore, such strategies are largely confined to individual schools and educators that dare to be different.

Observe, for example, the late John Saxon's long battle with the National Council of Teachers of Mathematics over whether children must accumulate "math facts" and reliable arithmetic skills before they can tackle complex problem solving. Saxon insisted on this in defiance of the mathematics profession's now-conventional wisdom that problem solving is all that really matters and one can always use a calculator for those irksome long divisions. Observe, too, the criticism directed at E. D. Hirsch by many U.S. educators for daring to outline a specific body of knowledge that constitutes cultural literacy and at Diane Ravitch and me for suggesting in *What Do Our 17-Year-Olds Know?* that high school students lack important information about U.S. history and literature. Observe, too, that Jaime Escalante, sometimes described as the greatest teacher in America and the hero of the film *Stand and Deliver,* believed he had to leave Los Angeles's Garfield High School because his colleagues there were more disposed to resent than to emulate his successful and deeply behaviorist methods.

Outside Reformers and New Foes

It was mainly outside the profession that attitudes toward education changed dramatically after the nation was declared educationally at risk in the early 1980s. Economic angst resulting from America's flagging international competitiveness directed more attention to worrisome signs of decay in the schoolroom. The growing involvement of influential governors, legislators, and business leaders in shaping education policy meant that the profession's child-centered ideology finally had a serious competitor. These outsiders said that schools must become more productive and efficacious places that give greater value for money and, above all, produce better academic results.

These new reformers came to realize in the mid-1980s that added school expenditures and other input and services reform schemes were not paying off, so they took steps to refocus education on standards and results. Thus arose standards-based or "outcomes-based education" (OBE), as it is often known. The idea gave rise to the national goals adopted by President Bush and the governors in 1989–90 and now enshrined in the federal Goals 2000 program. Standards-based reformers typically seek to align the goals, performance benchmarks, curriculum, teacher training, tests, and accountability mechanisms of an entire jurisdiction to an agreed-upon set of desired standards.

Standards-based education has been much argued over at the national level, but most of the action has been among the states, where one legislature, governor, or state board of education after another has decreed that precise standards must be set and then met and that schools and their staffs will be judged by their effectiveness in producing the desired results. Variants of that policy are now law in many states, and standards were the main topic of discussion at the second gubernatorial education summit in March 1996.

But the summit did not go far enough. Despite its attention to standards for education content, it neglected the student performance standards that actually begin to answer the question "how good is good enough?" It practically ignored the tests that monitor the extent of progress toward meeting such standards. It had little to say about consequences, the real-world side of educational accountability, namely the rewards and punishments that might lead to palpable changes in student (and staff) behavior. And of course it was silent on methods of instruction.

In concept, standards-based education at the policy level has much in common with behaviorism in the classroom. It starts with the straightforward observation that there are really only two ways to gauge educational efficacy: in relation to school inputs (dollars spent, hours devoted, courses taken, and the ratio of teachers to pupils) or to learning outcomes (knowledge of historical events, ability to write a grammatical paragraph, capacity to perform mathematical operations). If one's concern is with inadequate outcomes and if one cannot take for granted that changed inputs will translate into stronger results, one had better construct a policy framework around the results one seeks. Just as teachers should set out to instruct their pupils in what they want them to learn, policymakers should endeavor to shape the education system around the outcomes that they want it to yield.

So far, so good. But the devil, as always, lurks in the details. Unfortunately, the responsibility for detailing a state's or community's new standards has often been handed to educators with radically different goals. Rather than itemizing the skills and knowledge that well-educated children should be able to demonstrate in core academic subjects, the outcomes that were actually listed had more to do with social attitudes, ideological positions, and interpersonal relations. The standards, in short, came straight from the progressive or developmentalist sourcebook and seldom dwelt on mastery of the three R's. Sometimes this was the product of committees and task forces created to write goals or specify outcomes for a particular jurisdiction; sometimes it was the reward for hiring itinerant vendors of prepackaged outcomes-based curricula that were heavy on the "transformational"—social justice, individual liberation, radical reform—role of schooling and light on core skills, fundamental knowledge, and civic culture.

This development was bound to alarm many parents, particularly when such dubious outcomes were mandated for every school and child in the state. Families that find their neighborhood school teaching their children behaviors or beliefs that they deem abhorrent, even heretical, can be expected to become forceful, possibly even hysterical, in trying to rectify the situation. The result, ignited by angry Pennsylvania parents but rapidly spreading throughout the country, has been a conflagration of protest against outcomes-based education in general as well as each state's own wrongheaded outcomes in particular. The backlash rests on an unlikely alliance between progressive educators opposed to accountability and fundamentalist parents who fear that state-imposed standards will undermine traditional values and weaken their ability to shape their daughters and sons.

Matters only worsened when, in the aftermath of the 1989 Charlottesville, Virginia, education summit, the federal government invited a number of professional groups to draft national standards for their particular subjects. The history standards that surfaced in 1995 and the English–language arts standards that emerged a year later were widely ridiculed for their softness, vagueness, and left-leaning political content and deepened the OBE protesters' fears and outrage.[31] And President Clinton's Goals 2000 program, with its controversial provisions for federal supervision of state standards, "opportunity to learn" (that is, input) standards, and a National Education Standards and Improvement Council (NESIC) that critics compared to a national school board, made matters worse.

OBE has become as big a red flag for today's policymakers as behaviorism, its classroom cousin, is for today's education professionals. The fracas has crippled any serious approach to standards-based reform at the national level and weakened it at the state level. As a result, the doctrine of local control has been reinvigorated, even though education's rule by unchecked (and often uninformed) local boards and superintendents is precisely what brought U.S. achievement to its present weakened condition.

Where We Disagree

Nothing much is going to change, at least on a massive scale, until and unless the United States develops a clearer consensus on what is wrong and what needs to be done differently, a consensus that unites policy leaders, parents, and educators in something akin to common purpose. Today Americans lack such agreement at any level of the education enterprise, particularly when it comes to academic standards and the steps needed for most children to attain them.[32]

Most parents believe in high standards, but mainly in the acquisition of basic skills. They would like schools to do a better job of imparting skills and knowledge, and they are receptive, at least in concept, to drastic changes in the education system's operating assumptions and ground rules. They say they would welcome national exams for promotion and graduation. A majority favors market-style schemes for encouraging schools to differ from one another and families to choose among them.

Parents are even more concerned that schools be safe, orderly, and disciplined places. This certainly suggests they would welcome behaviorist practices in school, as long as these are directed toward ends such as eradicating violence and drugs from classrooms and corridors. But they are mistrustful of higher-order skills and of other people setting standards for their children in subjects outside the basic academic core. And they are weary and dubious of what they see as faddish schemes by educators to introduce "authentic assessments," "cooperative learning," and "problem solving" in lieu of multiplication tables; "whole language" rather than phonics in reading class; "invented" spelling in writing class; and so on. It is the kind of standards educators push that has helped discredit the idea of standards.

Teachers claim to favor high standards, too, but not nearly as strongly as parents and not as strongly as they favor their more progressive reforms. In this regard, Public Agenda's John Immerwahr and Jean Johnson summarized some troubling data for the 1996 gubernatorial education summit,

> even though large numbers of teachers voice support for higher standards, they do not generally see *low* standards—or youngsters finishing school without the basics—as widespread or urgent problems. Perhaps since teachers are generally satisfied with public schools' performance in teaching academic skills, their support for standards is less vigorous than the public's. . . .
>
> While a majority of the public . . . believes the schools are not placing enough emphasis on the basics, most teachers . . . believe they do. Almost half . . . of the public, and 65 percent of community leaders, believe that "a high school diploma is no guarantee that the typical student has learned

> the basics." Only three in ten teachers . . . share that belief. A majority of the public . . . thinks kids are not taught enough math, science and computers; most teachers . . . think they are. . . .
>
> Possibly more worrisome to those backing high-level, rigorous academic standards is teachers' tepid response to the value of advanced learning and study. . . . Only 21 percent of teachers think that an excellent academic education is the most important determinant of career success.[33]

Yet alternatives to progressivism are making inroads even among educators. There is already a widening acceptance of half-disguised behaviorist programs such as Success for All. Highly structured tutoring programs such as those of Sylvan Learning Systems are not only popular with tuition-paying parents but also with more and more urban school systems that are now contracting with this private company to provide federally funded remediation services to their pupils. The curricular and instructional practices of E. D. Hirsch's Core Knowledge Foundation are attracting more principals and teachers—in 200 schools to date. Such cherished icons of progressivism as whole-language reading instruction are under challenge along a widening front, including a powerful backlash in California.[34] A few more universities, weary of providing remedial instruction to young people who did not learn basic skills in high school, are beginning to demand something akin to mastery as a condition of entry. At the 1996 education summit, employers pledged to weigh job seekers' school records when hiring and states' commitments to high education standards when deciding where to locate their next plant. Even the federal Title I program, after its latest reauthorization (and three decades of failure), is now more explicitly shaped around academic standards and accountability than ever before.

Also encouraging is the admission by a few prominent practitioners long associated with the progressive philosophy that this approach does not work very well, particularly for disadvantaged and minority pupils. Barbara Sizemore, for example, is a former District of Columbia school superintendent once famous for abolishing standardized testing and savaging the "racist white power structure" in Congress who now serves as dean of the School of Education at DePaul University. Here is how a recent profile in *Education Week* describes her current views and their reception.

> What African-American children who live in poverty need most, she insists, is a highly structured school with firm discipline that is focused on teaching them to take and pass standardized tests. . . .

> Chicago reformers, most of them liberals devoted to improving the education of minority children, are horrified at Sizemore's focus on testing. With its aim of sorting and labeling children—and its cramped view of what is worth knowing—standardized testing is widely disparaged.
>
> Yet, Sizemore's views are shared by many African-American educators and parents who fear that abolishing standardized testing would disenfranchise their children just as they are making gains. And more than a few black teachers and principals are, like Sizemore, wary of the progressive pedagogy that accompanies the contemporary reform agenda.[35]

Nor is Sizemore alone. The same issue of *Education Week* also profiled Louisiana's Lisa Delpit, a MacArthur Foundation "genius award" winner and black educator whose recent book, *Other People's Children,* sent tremors through the structures of educational progressivism with its tough critique of progressivism's failure to meet the educational needs of disadvantaged youngsters.

> What a lot of the newer educational ideas have in common is a deemphasis on the rote aspects of schooling—the phonics drills and the sentence diagramming, for example—in favor of promoting critical thinking in children. . . .
>
> But Delpit says the trouble is that poor, minority children do not come to school with the same basic academic skills and familiarity with standard English that white, middle-class children bring with them.
>
> It's not that standard English is a better way to talk, to Delpit's way of thinking. . . . But it is a passport to a better future. . . . It's what poor, minority children need to know to prosper in a society dominated by the rhythms, grammar, and conventions of white, middle-class life.
>
> Black teachers intuitively know that, Delpit says. "Progressive white teachers seem to say to their black students, 'Let me help you find your voice. I promise not to criticize one note as you search for your own song,'" she writes in the first of her essays. "But the black teachers say, 'I've heard your song loud and clear. Now, I want you to harmonize with the rest of the world.'
>
> "If minority people are to effect the change that will allow them to truly progress, we must insist on 'skills' within the context of creative thinking," she adds.[36]

The Sizemores and Delpits remain a tiny, if vocal, minority among practicing educators. Yet their instinctual and experience-based view of the kind of education that best meets the needs of disadvantaged youngsters has gained a solid research foundation in E. D. Hirsch's acclaimed recent book, *The Schools We Need and Why We Don't Have Them.* In marked contrast to the reception accorded *Cultural Literacy* a decade ago, this book and its author are being respectfully received even in colleges of education. Yet their message amounts to a powerful indictment of "romantic progressivism" in the classroom, particularly its baneful effect on disadvantaged youngsters. As Hirsch writes,

> The Romantic idea that learning is natural, and that the motivation for academic achievement comes from within, is an illusion that forms one of the greatest barriers to social justice imaginable, since poor and disadvantaged students must be motivated to work even harder than advantaged students in order to achieve equality of educational opportunity. It was Antonio Gramsci, that wise spokesman for the disadvantaged and disenfranchised, who wrote that the gravest disservice to social justice entailed by Romantic theories of education is the delusion that educational achievement comes as naturally as leaves to a tree, without extrinsic motivation, discipline, toil, or sweat.[37]

Although such views remain heresies in many precincts of the education profession, they accord with the commonsense views of much of the American public and with those of business leaders and a growing number of elected officials. For example, they pervaded both President Clinton's 1997 State of the Union address and Michigan Republican Governor John Engler's 1997 State of the State address, each of which stressed high standards, tests, and personal and institutional accountability for results. In time they could make a substantial impact, particularly if the education monopoly keeps cracking, the ground rules keep loosening, and the chances to experiment with bold reforms keep proliferating.

The Prospect

Without wider consensus about what is important for children to learn and schools to do, the prospects for the renewal of the education system are not bright. Instead Americans will increasingly put reform eggs in two baskets. One will contain the kinds of changes (on-site management, staff development, higher salaries, smaller classes, developmentalist curricula, additional services) beloved by education producers: teachers, principals, professors of education, and school board associations. The other basket will hold the kinds of reforms (education vouchers, charter schools, privatization of schools, and out-of-school supplements obtained from commercial suppliers) favored by parents, employers, and other education consumers.

Left to follow their own reform instincts, most producers will avoid paternalistic schools and behaviorist instructional strategies. The closest many educators will tiptoe is to the concept of full-service schools that offer health and social services to children and families under the school roof. These are paternalistic in the sense that they go well beyond academics but not in the sense that they set clear standards for academic achievement and press students to meet those standards.

Parents, employers, and other consumers are a different story. Although nearly all parents would run screaming from schools that *call* themselves paternalistic, in practice paternalism seems to be what many want: institutions with explicit standards for skills, knowledge, and behavior, and with the gumption to hold both teachers and pupils accountable for achieving those norms. Certainly these are the guiding organizational precepts of many of the popular new charter schools as well as many of the private schools that more parents would choose for their daughters and sons if they could afford it.[38] Paternalism also seems to be what employers and governors intend when they talk of schools so obsessed with the successful transmission of the three R's that they can "guarantee" the quality of their graduates. Insofar as the consumers favor what they would term "disciplined" and "traditional" schools that emphasize "basic skills" and have clear norms and standards, paternalism in practice has a brighter future in their hands than in those of the education profession.

I do not claim that highly structured, paternalistic schools appeal to all education consumers. A significant proportion of charter and private schools embrace the tenets of developmentalism and progressivism. Indeed, when one asks why families chose the school they did for their child, liberal parents often explain that the previous school was too rigid and insensitive to individual differences. From conservative parents one frequently gets a more complex message, a lament that the "other school" was too relaxed with respect to discipline and values yet too pushy with respect to attitudes and private matters like sex education.

The movement toward embracing pluralism and decentralization portends a messy and uneven fragmentation of our once monolithic education system, but it is the likeliest direction for the next decade or so and preferable to the status quo. It remains possible, of course, that pluralism and decentralization will be joined—or overtaken—by the more centralized, standards-based, reform strategies favored by some governors, President Clinton, many business leaders, and thoughtful observers such as E. D. Hirsch and the late Albert Shanker. Although standards-based reform is far harder to bring about and thus less likely to happen, it has the virtue of coherence. And what it coheres around is the same view of education that many of the "decentralized" reformers are already living by: the view that children learn best when adults are clear about what they must learn and organize schools in ways that ensure that they learn it.

Notes

1. National Center for Education Statistics, *NAEP 1994 Reading Report Card for the Nation and the States* (Department of Education, 1996), table 3.3.

2. Academic achievement is my primary concern, an emphasis shared by many contemporary education reformers, especially elected officials and business leaders. But we must not fail to notice the pressures on schools to also solve such problems as drug abuse, AIDS, adolescent pregnancy, violence, racism, and environmental degradation. These added mandates illustrate people's limitless faith in the efficacy of education and their willingness to reallot scarce time and resources from the 3 R's to matters that other institutions have bungled or avoided.

3. Chester E. Finn Jr. and Diane Ravitch, *Education Reform 1995–96* (Indianapolis: Hudson Institute, 1996), pp. 23–39.

4. Stanley M. Elam, Lowell C. Rose, and Alec M. Gallup, "The 26th Annual *Phi Delta Kappa*/Gallup Poll of the Public's Attitudes toward the Public Schools," *Phi Delta Kappan* (September 1994), p. 41; Stanley M. Elam and Lowell C. Rose, "The 27th Annual Phi Delta Kappa/Gallup Poll of the Public's Attitudes toward the Public Schools," *Phi Delta Kappan*, vol. 76 (September 1995), pp. 41–56; and Steve Farkas and Jean Johnson, *Given the Circumstances: Teachers Talk about Public Education Today* (New York: Public Agenda, 1996).

That these market-style reforms are being implemented without having been thoroughly researched is not the fault of their proponents, nor is it a reason to resist them. The education establishment is known to fend off bold reforms that threaten it by asserting that nothing should even be tried until it has been proven—and then blocking its being tested. The result is that education rarely lends itself to experimental research.

5. For an explanation of instructivism and how it differs from progressivism-constructivism, see Finn and Ravitch, *Education Reform 1995–96,* p. 47.

6. See Lamar Alexander, *We Know What to Do: A Political Maverick Talks with America* (Morrow, 1995), p. 81. See also Gregg Vanourek, Scott W. Hamilton, and Chester E. Finn Jr., *Is There Life after Big Government? The Potential of Civil Society* (Indianapolis: Hudson Institute, 1996), p. 32.

7. David Long and others, *LEAP: Three-Year Impacts of Ohio's Welfare Initiative to Improve School Attendance among Teenage Parents* (New York: Manpower Demonstration Research Corp., April 1996). See also Dan Bloom and others, *LEAP: Implementing a Welfare Initiative to Improve School Attendance among Teenage Parents* (New York: Manpower Demonstration Research Corp., 1991); and David Long, Robert G. Wood, and Hilary Kopp, *LEAP: The Educational Effects of LEAP and Enhanced Services in Cleveland* (New York: Manpower Demonstration Research Corp., 1994).

8. The Separation of School and State Alliance in Fresno, California, is a good example.

9. *Pierce v. Society of Sisters,* 268 U.S. 510 (1925).

10. Jean Johnson and others, *Assignment Incomplete: The Unfinished Business of Education Reform* (New York: Public Agenda, 1995), p. 18.

11. The only significant exception pertains to the handful of young people headed for America's few dozen truly selective colleges and universities. Particularly insightful analyses of the need to tie school achievement to real world incentives can be found in the work of Cornell economist John H. Bishop. See, for example,"Signaling, Incentives, and School Organization in France, the Netherlands, Britain, and the United States," in Eric A. Hanushek and Dale W. Jorgenson, eds., *Improving America's Schools: The Role of Incentives* (Washington: National Academy Press, 1996), pp. 111–145. See also Bishop, "The Effect of National Standards and Curriculum-Based Exams on Achievement," working paper 96-22, Cornell University, January 1997.

12. Chester E. Finn Jr., "Towards Excellence in Education," *Public Interest*, no. 120 (Summer 1995), pp. 41–54.

13. Office of Policy and Planning, *Reinventing Chapter 1: The Current Chapter 1 Program and New Directions* (Department of Education 1993), pp. 48, 71, 72, 82.

14. Jonathan Kozol, *Savage Inequalities: Children in America's Schools* (Crown Publishers, 1991). This topic remains somewhat controversial among economists, of course, but I believe it is well handled in Eric A. Hanushek and others, *Making Schools Work: Improving Performance and Controlling Costs* (Brookings, 1994); and Gary Burtless, ed., *Does Money Matter? The Effect of School Resources on Student Achievement and Adult Success* (Brookings, 1996).

15. James S. Coleman, *Equality of Educational Opportunity: Summary Report* (Office of Education, Department of Health, Education, and Welfare, 1966).

16. William G. Spady, "Outcome Based Education," in James H. Block, Susan T. Everson, and Thomas R. Guskey, eds., *School Improvement Programs: A Handbook for Educational Leaders* (Scholastic, 1995), pp. 387–88.

17. Michael Rutter and others, *Fifteen Thousand Hours: Secondary Schools and Their Effects on Children* (Harvard University Press, 1979).

18. Ronald R. Edmonds, *An Overview of School Improvement Programs* (Michigan State University, 1983).

19. James S. Coleman, Thomas Hoffer, and Sally Kilgore, *Public and Private*

Schools (Department of Education, National Center for Education Statistics, November 1981).

20. Marshall S. Smith and Stewart C. Purkey, "Effective Schools—A Review," *Elementary School Journal*, vol. 83 (March 1983), pp. 427–52.

21. Herbert J. Walberg, "Generic Practices," in Gordon Cawelti, ed., *Handbook of Research on Improving Student Achievement* (Arlington, Va: Educational Research Service, 1995), pp. 12, 16.

22. J. E. Stone, "Developmentalism: An Obscure But Pervasive Restriction on Educational Improvement," *Education Policy Analysis Archives*, vol. 4, no. 8, http://olam.ed.asu.edu/epaa/v4n8.html, April 21, 1996.

23. Robert E. Slavin and others, "Whenever and Wherever We Choose: The Replication of 'Success for All,'" *Phi Delta Kappan*, vol. 75 (April 1994), pp. 640–42. For other discussions see Nancy A. Madden and others, "Success for All: Longitudinal Effects of a Restructuring Program for Inner-City Elementary Schools," *American Educational Research Journal,* vol. 30 (Spring 1993), pp. 123-48; Barbara Wasik and Robert E. Slavin, "Preventing Early Reading Failure with One-to-One Tutoring: A Review of Five Programs," *Reading Research Quarterly*, vol. 28 (April-June 1993), pp. 179–200; and John J. Pikulski, "Preventing Reading Failure: A Review of Five Effective Programs," *Reading Teacher,* vol. 48 (September 1994), pp. 30–39.

24. The meager means by which we have been able to make such judgments in the past are weaker today in light of the College Board's decision to "recenter" the scores on its SAT tests.

25. Diane Ravitch, *The Schools We Deserve: Reflections on the Educational Crises of Our Times* (Basic Books, 1985), pp. 81–82.

26. Kathe Jervis and Joseph McDonald, "Standards: The Philosophical Monster in the Classroom," *Phi Delta Kappan*, vol. 77 (April 1996), p. 569.

27. Stone, "Developmentalism."

28. Douglas Carnine and others, "Direct Instruction to Accelerate Cognitive Growth," in Block, Everson, and Guskey, eds., *School Improvement Programs,* pp. 129–30, 151.

29. For a longer and angrier discussion of this response, see Siegfried Engelmann, *War against the Schools' Academic Child Abuse* (Portland, Ore.: Halcyon House, 1992).

30. Cathy L. Watkins, "Project Follow Through: A Story of the Identification and Neglect of Effective Instruction," *Youth Policy,* vol. 10 (July-August 1988), pp. 7–11.

31. For additional information, see Bruno V. Manno, "Outcome-Based Education: Miracle Cure or Plague?" briefing paper 165, Hudson Institute, Indianapolis, June 1994.

32. Farkas and Johnson, *Given the Circumstances*; and John Immerwahr and Jean Johnson, *America's Views on Standards: An Assessment by Public Agenda* (New York: Public Agenda, 1996).

33. Immerwahr and Johnson, *America's Views on Standards,* pp. 26–28.

34. Former California state school superintendent Bill Honig, during whose tenure the state plunged with disastrous results into whole-language methods in the primary grades, went back to review the research evidence on reading instruction and has produced a superb summary of what is known about how best to teach this most basic of skills. Bill Honig, *Teaching Our Children to Read: The Role of Skills in a Comprehensive Reading Program* (Thousand Oaks, Calif.: Corwin Press, 1996).

35. Ann Bradley and Debra Viadero, "Unconventional Wisdom: Two Distinguished African-American Educators Dissent from the Progressive Ideology of Contemporary School Reform," *Education Week,* March 13, 1996, p. 36.

36. Ibid., p. 40.

37. E. D. Hirsch Jr., *The Schools We Need and Why We Don't Have Them* (Doubleday, 1996), p. 214.

38. Johnson and others, *Assignment Incomplete*, p. 11.

Eight

Implementing a Paternalist Welfare-to-Work Program

Eugene Bardach

Between putting laws on the books and achieving any useful result lies implementation, a process that includes bureaucracies, budgets, contracts, procedures, legislative watchdogs, performance measurements, and other such visible entities. It also involves bargaining, exhorting, experimenting, communicating, and learning. Although the literature describing and explaining the failures of public sector implementation is diffuse, it teaches, among many other things, that the odds of a policy or program successfully surviving implementation tend to drop

—the more unrelated or conflicting goals are piled on it;

—the more agencies are needed to contribute to it;

—the more subtle the underlying psychological, social, or economic design;

—the more it depends on a high level of administrative talent and motivation; and

—the more it depends on investments that pay off only after the next relevant election.

Passages in this chapter are reproduced, with permission, from Eugene Bardach, *Improving the Productivity of JOBS Programs* (New York: Manpower Demonstration Research Corp., 1993).

Many paternalist policies and programs discussed in this book are afflicted by just these troublesome conditions.

Troublesome does not mean impossible, of course. Alongside the implementation literature sits a more optimistic literature on public management.[1] Within the limits set by budgets and local job markets, which are hard to predict and hard to generalize about, a great deal can be done. Before turning to the particulars, though, let me describe the moral dimensions of paternalist programming that make implementing such programs especially challenging.

Varieties of Paternalism

One of the chief vulnerabilities of paternalist policies is their contested moral status. This is not simply a philosopher's problem. A well-functioning paternalist program must be grounded in a coherent moral theory. Such a theory must work at many levels. It must help motivate the people who become a program's clients. It must give the staff the moral authority and self-confidence to deliver the mix of support and pressure that are successful with clients. It must suggest principles to top administrators for organizing their agencies and managing in such a way that their staffs may have the freedom and the resources to do their jobs effectively. Finally, it must motivate elected officials to make at least the basic required financial and managerial investments in the service delivery system. An incoherent or misguided moral theory will not only fail at all these tasks but will also provoke cynicism and quiet sabotage.

In a family, paternalism means substituting a wise and benevolent parent's prescriptions for a child's welfare for the child's own prescriptions. In a liberal democracy, such an attitude is at odds with the officially sanctioned presumption that the state and the government are always and ever the servants of the citizens. This presumption can be weakened or extinguished if the citizen in question is harming others by his or her acts and if these others have a legitimate claim on the society's protection, for example as taxpayers not wishing to subsidize the follies of others or citizens desiring protection from criminals. But once the state decides to exercise legitimate paternalistic control over a citizen or client, two difficult questions come to the fore. First, even though the paternalism I discuss here respects both the welfare of the client and that of society, at the margin there will sometimes be a trade-off between the two. When this occurs, which way should policy tilt? Second, in a pluralistic society that tolerates a variety of legitimate normative systems, which of these should be embodied in the government's conceptions both of social welfare and of the welfare of the client?

The answers will largely depend on the types of clients in the program and the methods used to treat them. These answers will, in turn, imply better and worse implementation strategies. Although I recognize that real-world programs are hybrids and that the clients the programs manage are diverse, I nevertheless suggest in table 8-1 some appropriate implementation strategies.

The example in the first column of clients who are socially very troublesome presumes that there is strong and self-protective social disapproval of their behavior. The moral as well as practical dimension of the implementation problem is to differentiate the types of citizens who fit this category from those who present a lesser social threat. In regard to abusers of illegal drugs, chapter 6 in effect argues that one can accomplish this differentia-

Table 8-1. Varieties of Paternalist Policies and Approaches to Implementing Them, with Reference to Other Chapters in this Book

	Strong concern for society	*Strong concern for client*
Strong normative consensus	Segregated clientele and prescriptive, hierarchical, centralized administration (Heavy, troublesome drug abusers—Kleiman; child support—Mincy and Pouncy)	Service mission and sanction structure defined centrally, but detailed execution left to localities (Welfare-to-work—Mead)
Limited normative consensus	Public facilities with lowest-common-denominator normative structure; private facilities with varied normative structures (Homeless men—Main)	Service mission and sanction structure defined publicly, but life-style issues often better handled by private agencies (Pregnant teenagers—Maynard)

tion by targeting those heavy abusers who also happen to be convicted felons.

The bottom of the second column presents an example of clients for whom there is great concern and toward whom a variety of social attitudes are considered legitimate. The moral ambiguities of how to treat such people are resolved by heavy reliance on private nonprofit agencies. The consensual public stake is in taxpayer protection.[2] Thus rules must be clear and rigorous about the conditions under which benefits are to be granted.

The clients in the lower left cell resemble those in the lower right except that some aspect of their conduct is more disturbing to society. Lack of normative consensus implies that in publicly managed facilities close supervision and tight controls keep order but do not invest much in trying to socialize the clients.

In the upper right cell the proportion of clients who require paternalistic treatment at all is probably smaller than in the other cells. It would be morally wrong and impractical to treat all clients the same. And it is not necessary to do so. Various means of assessment can be used to sort them into different forms of treatment. In addition, the programs to aid these clients can be designed to let their conduct in the program dictate the sorting as well. In moving people from welfare to work, for instance, clients' different abilities and desires to cooperate in the program make a difference in how they should be treated. Because they are not as troubling to society as homeless men or fathers who do not pay child support, errors in the sorting process are more easily tolerated. And because there is relatively solid consensus on underlying norms, more errors are tolerated than would be allowed for pregnant teenagers, for example.

It is the relative abundance of potential error in treating clients in the upper left cell that makes it a particularly good case for analysis of implementation. Managing drug abusers has more to teach about implementing paternalist social policy in general than does working with any of the other groups shown in the table.

I discuss problems and solutions in welfare-to-work implementation in four stages. First, I consider "persuasive paternalism," the sort of paternalist staff-client relationship that relies on some mixture of counseling, moral suasion, and instruction to increase welfare recipients' efforts to join or rejoin the labor force and become productive jobholders. Second, I consider managerial strategies for facilitating and encouraging such staff-client relationships. Third, I fold into the idea of persuasive paternalism an element of coercion.[3] This element is present because current policy, as embodied in the 1996 Personal Responsibility and Work Opportunity Reconciliation Act (the Welfare Reform Act), enshrines at its center the idea of workfare, the requirement that welfare recipients do some sort of work in exchange for their receiving cash and in-kind assistance. Finally, I take up the problem of motivating appropriate managerial and policy-level investments. Before turning to substance, however, I will describe briefly the empirical basis for my analysis and recommendations.

Empirical Bases

The most important statistical study linking staff pressure on aid recipients to whether the recipients found jobs is the the Manpower Demonstration Research Corporation's (MDRC) controlled experiment study of California's GAIN program, the state's version of the national JOBS program authorized by the 1988 Family Support Act. JOBS was folded into a larger block grant by the 1996 welfare reform act. To help clients overcome barriers to employment, the program provided career and vocational counseling, basic education, life skills education, training in specific occupations, training in how to search for a job, and extended eligibility for medicaid and child care assistance to recipients of aid to families with dependent children. The MDRC study found that the outstanding performer among the six California counties studied was Riverside.[4] Compared to a control group, Riverside AFDC recipients assigned (randomly) to participate in the JOBS program were able to boost their earnings 49 percent, and Riverside's welfare costs fell 15 percent. In fact, the Riverside results were the most impressive ever obtained in two dozen or more studies of welfare-to-work programs over more than a decade. Speculating about what made Riverside so successful, the MDRC researchers said it was the county's attempt "to communicate a strong 'message' to all registrants (even those in education and training activities), at all stages of the program, that employment was central, that it should be sought expeditiously, and that opportunities to obtain low-paying jobs should not be turned down."[5] In a separate MDRC study, I characterized the philosophy underlying the Riverside emphasis on jobs as one of high expectations, and in the rest of this chapter I use *high expectations* almost interchangeably with *paternalist*.[6]

Although Riverside was one clear embodiment of a high-expectations program, there are other specimens of it as well, along with evidence that it can produce results: Lawrence Mead's studies in Wisconsin and his 1986 study of twenty-two Work Incentive Program (WIN) offices in New York and LaDonna Pavetti and Amy-Ellen Duke's study of Utah's SPED demonstration program in the Kearns office (near Salt Lake City) of the state social services agency.[7] Mead's findings are also supported in a broader Urban Institute study of the WIN program, which surveyed nine states and 214 local programs within them.[8]

The main purpose of this chapter is to illuminate the interplay of a high-expectations program philosophy and managerial practice. Not all instances of this interplay represent full-blown welfare-to-work programs. Some are simply parts of programs—a caseworker or two, for example, who attempt to create a high-expectations environment for their own caseloads. Other instances, such as the Riverside program, represent much more systematic efforts to create such an environment.

From the point of view of an empirical researcher, programs such as the one at Riverside, where the leaders self-consciously attempted to make every program detail reflect a high-expectations program philosophy, are unfortunately rare.[9] I did, however, visit the program twice over a two-year period and interviewed twenty-five to thirty people at all levels of the organization. I have also interviewed extensively in Oregon, over a three-year period, at both the state and local levels, where program managers have made self-sufficiency the animating concept behind their overall strategy, which is in many ways similar to Riverside's high-expectations strategy. Like Riverside's, Oregon's efforts have been unusual. Jan Hagen and Irene Lurie's study of JOBS implementation in ten states showed Oregon to be the only one among them that chose to "signal the importance of focusing on promoting client economic self-sufficiency."[10] During the past five years I have also visited welfare-to-work programs in four other California counties and in Oklahoma, Michigan, and Colorado.[11]

Program philosophy is of course a subjective matter, a matter of intentions and beliefs. How does one discover what it is and how it influences program administration? At the level of the individual caseworker or manager, one listens carefully to people's rhetoric, engages them in conversation about how their beliefs do or do not affect their actions, and asks peers or other observers about the validity of what one has been told. This is not necessarily the most reliable way to answer the question, but it can be a fast and low-cost way. And it can produce much richer information than administering questionnaires to much larger numbers of staff. Therefore, this is what I did.

It is somewhat more difficult, and less reliable, to judge whether and how administrative agencies, as opposed to individual staff members, embodied program philosophy in their practices. In Riverside nearly all the caseworkers, supervisors, and administrators I interviewed in the county social services department proudly and self-consciously articulated the same core ideas; and the agency leadership emphatically asserted that it was attempting to create an organization that would carry out these ideas. Organizational practices such as supervision, personnel evaluation, recruitment, training, and intraorganizational communication did in fact change over time. It was not too difficult, therefore, to infer that the emerging practices often did in fact reflect philosophical intention, although, of course, it is never easy to disentangle the skein of causal threads. Other cases of philosophy putatively affecting program decisions were much less clear-cut than in Riverside, and the causal analysis correspondingly more complicated.

Paternalism with Persuasion

Most welfare recipients in some sense want to work. Most do not like the below-poverty-level grants that AFDC pays in virtually all states. And most do not much like the idea of depending on the dole. But wanting to work does not necessarily ensure that a welfare recipient will actually try to work. For the jobs available to this population, wages will almost certainly be low and benefit packages, if provided at all, might lack medical coverage as good as that provided by medicaid. Children will have to be left with a relative or child care provider, whose care may not always be regarded as acceptable, and provider arrangements often prove unstable. For many people transportation will be a problem, as will meeting and interacting on the job with relative strangers. Overcoming these and other barriers requires a strong desire to work. A well-designed and well-run welfare-to-work program will recognize the centrality of motivation and will make use of whatever means of motivation are available.

The five-year lifetime welfare cap imposed by the 1996 welfare reform bill and the two-year time limit for welfare recipients to find work aim to increase work motivation through threats. But it remains to be seen whether these threats survive the next three to five years unmodified, whether administrative problems and perhaps legal strategies do not subvert them, and whether welfare recipients come to believe in them enough to alter behavior. But it would still be desirable to have welfare recipients who are able move into the labor force at a faster rate. Eliminating the major financial disincentives, especially loss of health insurance, involved in moving from welfare to work is, in general, the most important motivational tool available. But there is also the moral dimension. In its simplest (and, as we shall see, rather unhelpful) form, it turns up as an asserted moral obligation to the society for the welfare recipient to make an effort to seek work.

At the level of the state welfare agency and the street level of the local welfare office, where the gritty details of implementing this national consensus get worked out, the abstractions about recipients' obligations and rights become encrusted with all the complications that arise when abstractions are applied to individual lives and circumstances and when principles run into bureaucratic imperatives and government budget constraints.[12] In particular, it is at the level of the individual recipient and her family that recipients and welfare administrators alike need to consider obligations to society in relation to sometimes competing obligations to children, other family members, lovers and former husbands, and so on.

How welfare recipients resolve these moral issues, using what might be called moral reasoning for lack of a better term, has an effect on their work aspirations. Moral reasoning also makes a difference for program staff. Whether staff members make the effort to work at a high level depends in part on how much they believe in the moral rightness of what they are doing, which in turn depends on how much they believe in the moral rightness of what they are asking welfare recipients to do. Program staff members, for instance, are not very likely to pressure recipients to conform to norms valued by potential employers and coworkers unless the staff believe these norms are reasonable and that they have a right to apply such pressures. Such pressures touch on such delicate and personal matters as recipients' personal and career aspirations, habits of dress and speech (for example, urging recipients to use standard English rather than black English), attitudes toward child care arrangements, and the use and abuse of alcohol and drugs.

Recipients' Aspirations

Because nothing motivates people so much as their own goals, even in the most paternalist of programs effective case managers respect those goals as much as possible, as long as the goals involve moving the recipient toward eventual employment.

"How will you spend your first paycheck?" is a standard question used by line workers to motivate clients. Even if the answer is "Take the children to Disneyland," which might seem unrealistic to the line worker, the client's capacity for invention is nevertheless respected and encouraged: maybe she will take the bus, stay with relatives, or get additional money for the trip from other family members.[13]

Respecting clients' goals does not, however, imply accepting their choice of means. Many caseworkers I interviewed thought it was their responsibility to discourage enrollment in training programs for which a client showed no aptitude. They also felt obliged to steer clients away from training for a market that was already saturated, such as cosmetology in some localities. Such advice posed a particular moral and political dilemma in communities where private occupational training schools were marketing their services in ways that JOBS staff believed misled clients about the opportunities available.

Of course, client goals nearly always include financial betterment and often a career.[14] However, it may be difficult for an aid recipient at the beginning of JOBS participation to envision the details of such a career. Depending on the JOBS program philosophy, clients might not even have been encouraged to try. In Riverside, in contrast, the message to clients was that any job is a good job, because any job is a stepping stone to some other job. According to this theory, it is easier to look for a better job and lay the foundations for a career while employed than while unemployed and on welfare. Prospective employers can see evidence of work discipline and will be able to evaluate references from someone who knows the applicant as an employee. It may also be easier for a client to select a career once she is in a job because one gets a better view of one's own abilities and the options and challenges presented by the real world.

A manager in the San Francisco GAIN program expressed a similar view: the first job will not be perfect, but it will provide encouragement to stay in the labor force, keep on looking, and learn the norms of the working world. For many welfare recipients, moving into the world of work represents a first step in a sometimes difficult psychological transition, so it might be acceptable if the first, perhaps part-time, job were to be supplemented by welfare payments.

Self-Respect

For some people the distance between stepping stones may be great, and in the meantime nonfinancial goals are important. The Job Club workshops in Oklahoma used a job-readiness workbook, *The Choice Is Yours,* that listed seven reasons for working that are not related simply to improving one's financial status:

—meet other people and make new friends;
—set a good example for my children;
—don't like being dependent on others for money;
—gives me something worthwhile to do with my life;
—feel better about myself when I have a job;
—people expect me to work;
—will make me feel like I belong. I want to be someone.[15]

The common theme in these reasons is that a job improves self-respect even if it does not pay enough to make a person economically self-sufficient.

Self-Confidence

But self-respect and employment are involved in something of a catch-22: if a job can bring self-respect, it sometimes takes self-respect or its near relation, self-confidence, to get a job in the first place. Many welfare recipients do not have the required minimum. Program staff members consistently say that "a large minority" to "a substantial majority" of AFDC recipients lack self-confidence. They also describe this as being a significant barrier to job acquisition and retention as well as to success in an educational or training program. Many speak of the high incidence of physical and sexual abuse, psychological codependency, and the complete absence of any source of "positive strokes" in clients' lives, except perhaps from their children.

In many cases, long-term welfare dependency has also created or aggravated the problem.[16] At Northeastern Oklahoma University A & M more than 200 Older Wiser Learning Students (OWLS) were enrolled in a program to earn a GED or an associate of arts degree. Most of them are JOBS participants. The program director said of them,

> When those people walk up to the registrar's window and they get one answer that's not caring and not nurturing, they will walk away. . . . [They

> may have] dropped out in the ninth or tenth grade . . . got pregnant . . . [think] that they're no good and that all these things that they've heard and that they've told themselves [are true]. . . . They are their number one worst enemy. . . . About 20 percent have "the look" [of bad teeth, sagging posture, unkempt clothing, home haircut].[17]

Paradoxically, the demands of a well-run high-expectations program can be very supportive of such troubled people. When the expectations come from a sympathetic source, they can be interpreted as evidence that the outside world believes in one's abilities. Within limits, the higher the expectations, the greater the perceived affirmation. For this dynamic to work, however, it would appear that the source of expectations must be genuinely and unmistakably sympathetic. A Riverside Job Club facilitator described her and her coworkers' attitudes:

> There's no one judging anyone here. . . . We are never judgmental. . . . We could all be in a situation where we'd need some assistance. . . . We sit down with people and say, "Let's dispel all the barriers, that's what we're here for." You don't have to be mean to someone for them to do the job. You flatter somebody: "Did you change your hair? I love the way you look. . . . Oh, look how your shoulders go back." We've seen changes in hard-core folks. They come back and say "I never thought I could do it."

But for many aid recipients the psychological barriers on the road to self-respect, never mind a job, are much larger than can be overcome by a change of clothing or posture. Toby Herr and her colleagues at Project Match, who have worked with hundreds of welfare recipients, describe a journey that may take years. For "the most disadvantaged welfare recipients" it is "a long and difficult process, not a discrete event. . . . While on the surface leaving welfare appears to be a matter of helping people enroll in education and training programs or find jobs, at a more basic level it is about personal growth and change."[18] She advocates an "incremental ladder," perhaps stretched out over several years, that may include, in its earlier stages, work-preparation activities such as volunteer work in the client's children's school. In its middle stages it may include retention counseling for recipients having trouble staying in their job. Its most advanced stages may include placement services for those who leave a job, voluntarily or involuntarily, and need to find another.

Reciprocity and Responsibility

Behind the "welfare reform" thinking of at least the past decade is an implicit belief that welfare recipients have made a social contract: they get financial assistance while they are down and out; but the taxpaying public requires them, by way of reciprocity, to make various prescribed efforts to get back to work as soon as possible.[19] In practice, however, this was not the idea communicated to clients even in the high-expectations programs I observed.[20]

One reason is that some line workers do not believe in the validity of the social contract concept. Conservatives accuse these workers of being bleeding hearts, and the conservatives' skepticism is partly responsible for the emerging consensus on mandatory workfare. But even those line workers who believe in welfare recipients' obligations to society and whose efforts to motivate them are strongly rooted in these beliefs do not usually talk to their clients in terms of a quid pro quo, of welfare exchanged for effort to find a job or otherwise participate in the program. Instead, they emphasize the self-respect to be gained by becoming a fuller member of society. The differences between the the emphasis on a social contract and on fuller membership are subtle but important.

First, the idea of membership in society is more identity affirming than the idea of fulfilling a contract with taxpayers. Emil Durkheim might have said that the idea of membership betokens organic solidarity but fulfilling a contract implies no more than mechanical solidarity. Second, in a society as respectful of individualism as our own, full membership implies, somewhat paradoxically, that social approval and a sense of self-respect hinge to a great extent on the successful achievement of autonomy, of taking control of one's life, which includes taking control of appearance, children, relationships, and so on. Getting a job is therefore only part of a much larger idea of membership in society that is distilled as learning to assume personal responsibility.

Viewed in this light, responsibility is not just an obligation, it is also liberation from a life of passivity and disorganization. For some people the liberation entails helping counsel other welfare recipients to follow the same path. Sometimes this idea has had a dimension, too, of enhancing the dignity and improving the security of women and ethnic minorities. Thus, taken as a whole, because of its connections to self-interest broadly construed, the fuller-membership–self-respect concept and its derivative, learning to assume personal responsibility, are potentially far more motivating to clients than is the idea of a social contract, so it should not be surprising that line workers should choose to deemphasize the social contract.

Not all clients understand the concept of responsibility, however. A caseworker in Riverside commented that responsibility was "taught in childhood but forgotten or lost or maybe never learned. . . . A lot of clients have come from dysfunctional backgrounds where responsibility was never something they addressed or had to address." For some clients, then, it is not enough to furnish the opportunity to take greater responsibility for their lives; something like an appreciation of responsibility must be taught too.

One way to do so was to use the JOBS program setting. Another caseworker in Riverside summarized her message as, "What I'm going to do for you is to teach you a better way of life, how to handle things better, to like yourself better, [but] you've got to show up every day and try your hardest."Another in the same program explained how he tries to structure professional relations with the client around mutual expectations. "I'll tell them, 'I'll go the whole way with you, but don't lie to me. . . . I'll tell you right up front what we expect.' Whenever I do a Job Club, I tell them, 'Look, I'm going to do this much [gestures with finger and thumb apart]; but this, the majority, has to come from you.'" A Riverside Job Club facilitator described her work with a group of alcoholics: "They drank at lunch and they were happy as clams in the afternoons. Once I realized it, I asked, 'If I were your employee and came in tanked like this, what would you do?' 'Well, I wouldn't put up with it,' they say. So, I lost three and retained ten, and those ten got employed."[21]

Coaching

Overcoming the common barriers to employment faced by many welfare recipients—inconvenient or inaccessible child care, unreliable or time-consuming transportation, jealous or threatened boyfriends—is another opportunity for them to learn to take responsibility. The best line workers, said the Riverside GAIN director of staff development and training, were not rescuers but pragmatic counselors. They had "a real commonsense approach to life [with] very realistic views of the people they're dealing with. . . .They shoot from the hip, but in a positive way, and work for problem solving as opposed to pointing fingers or making excuses." Another worker in Riverside said, "Yes, they do face these barriers, and they can be hard. I am sympathetic, but I do not propose solutions. At least not right away. I say, 'Yes, you are right, that's a real problem, I can see that. How do you think you might solve it?'"

The temptations are great, however, for caseworkers to substitute their own wisdom and sophistication for the client's. First, the worker will often have genuinely useful ideas and will be inclined out of natural sympathy to share them. Second, accelerating the client's movement toward employment or toward education or training goals is consistent with line workers' most literal conception of their job responsibilities. Finally, clients with lots of unsolved problems are often clients who take up a lot of caseworkers' time and energy, resources that are badly needed simply to manage large caseloads and serve other deserving clients.

But allowing such a substitution would be paternalism of the most inappropriate sort. "Coaching" rather than rescuing, lecturing, or even teaching may be the right spirit in which to offer advice. As important as protecting the client's opportunities to practice self-reliance, the coaching image also helps line staff cope with ambivalence about their paternalist role. If they are indeed helping a client discover a "better way of life," as the Riverside counselor put it, their presumption of the moral authority to define such a life can be justified only if their own good will, efforts, and competence measure up to a very high standard of personal, professional, and bureaucratic responsibility. The standard image of a coach, in high school basketball for example, to act benevolently with respect to her charges at the same time that she is ordering a player to stay on the bench for coming late to practice could be a useful source of legitimation.

Of course, jobseeking is not basketball, and it is not always clear in the context of welfare dependence and finding jobs whose standards ought to be applied or what they ought to be. What, for example, should be the approach on sexual behavior that might disrupt the job search or might lead to an unwanted pregnancy? Job search and job retention might also be affected, albeit indirectly, by the welfare recipient's standards of child care, child-rearing practices, and relationships with family members. Is it the government's right to tell a free human being that she should dress more conservatively to make herself more appealing to potential employers? Obviously, many such matters can instigate trouble. This is not the place to discuss them all. A well-run high-expectations program does not need to have a particular set of answers nor a complete set of answers for every contingency. What it does need is the self-confidence at every level, and particularly at the line level, to engage openly with clients whose desires and conduct put such matters on the table.

Some Management Strategies

If welfare-to-work programs consisted largely of coachlike case managers emphasizing the value of jobs and work and if labor markets offered a reasonable supply of entry-level jobs, it would be easy to imagine running effective and humane programs.[22] In the real world, however, matters stand otherwise. After decades of treating welfare recipients as little more than sources of eligibility information of doubtful reliability, the culture of welfare offices is more often that of low rather than high expectations. In the 1970s, federal regulations separated eligibility determination for aid recipients from the delivery of services. The unintended result was to make the bulk of assistance workers into overworked clerks with high caseloads and a fear of approving claimants whom federal auditors might later disqualify. The claimants came to think of the welfare office as a heartless, impersonal bureaucracy; and the "eligibility technicians" (ETs) came to think of welfare recipients as little more than faceless applicants, a fair number of whom were bent upon hiding income or assets. Many ETs also came to think of recipients as irredeemably apathetic. These mutual stereotypes were inevitable, of course, given the limited and highly structured interactions that the system permitted. Moreover, the physical surroundings of the typical welfare office—drab, uncomfortable, crowded, and unkempt—represented just one more symbol, to all the parties, of what the character of the aid recipient was supposed to be.

When welfare acquired work requirements, "services" again became part of most welfare agencies. That change began in the late 1960s but intensified with the creation of the JOBS program in 1988. However, the JOBS units have typically been segregated organizationally from the ET units. In some cases the JOBS unit has had to make special efforts to persuade or remind ET workers to help sign up volunteers for the JOBS program.

Segregating the JOBS unit had some benefits. The workers might be able to establish their own organizational culture and methods. The GAIN program in Riverside, for instance, set up shop in completely new and tastefully appointed quarters. An extra expense, said the director of the welfare agency, but well worth it: "You treat them like kings and queens and they will act like it." The director also insisted that staff dress for office work. "I didn't want them coming out in jeans and plaid shirts. . . . I wanted it to look like a class act employment place. I wanted a message to [the clients] that we did all this because we think you are important."[23] In addition, he wanted a message sent about how important, committed, and competent the staff would be: "I wanted a different perception in the eyes of the recipient. This was not going to be a welfare-as-usual program. I wanted them to think, 'This is a powerful group of people who can help me.'" And the relevant group of people in Riverside included the clerical staff, who took to the idea of welcoming GAIN with warmth and respect and along with the caseworkers and job developers contributed to the pool of job leads created by the office as a whole.

Riverside, unlike many other JOBS programs, did not select its case managers by seniority or by reference to scores on written tests. Nor did it treat the GAIN program as a place for burned-out caseworkers escaping from children's protective services. It announced that GAIN would become a central function in the Riverside Social Services Department, that applicants would be recruited externally as well as internally, and that paper qualifications and credentials did not count but the ability to motivate GAIN participants to get a job did. As part of its screening, Riverside had applicants simulate selling a used car.

In further support of the job placement mission, caseworkers were obliged to accept quarterly placement goals and have their performance measured against them. The number of placements expected was initially set relatively low. But as caseworkers showed they could meet and exceed them, the number was slowly increased.[24] Although there was initially some resistance, the staff eventually accepted the idea, and many enthusiastically participated in the competition that arose among units, some of it encouraged by top management. An additional attraction for many staff members was that, with a system of outcome-based accountability in place, managers were prepared to allow them to be as creative as they liked in achieving the prescribed goals.[25]

Creativity

Creativity is especially important in job developers, the specialists who have sometimes been employed in JOBS offices to find job leads for clients. They must not only find leads in volume but they must also help match jobs with particular welfare clients, sell potential employers on the virtues of welfare recipients as employees, worry about job retention for the sake of the welfare agency and its clients, and worry about poor on-the-job performance for the sake of the employer. I know of no studies evaluating the cost effectiveness of this strategy, but Riverside managers support it strongly. As a matter of contemporary management theory, however, allowing the job developer "the full business experience" of producing a complete service—to the client, employer, and case manager—should be more motivating than simply having him or her put job possibilities into a pool.[26] If a welfare-to-work program invests in such specialists, therefore, they should probably not be assigned to produce jobs for a general pool but should be teamed with particular case managers whose working styles and caseloads they come to know. This proposition is supported by an Urban Institute study of more and less effective WIN programs in the late 1970s.[27]

Creativity has taken a particularly interesting turn in a demonstration program in Oregon to help clients retain jobs. A discretionary fund available to case managers can be used for such standard expenses as gas and uniforms, but it has occasionally also been used to pay for haircuts, auto insurance, and rent.[28] A discretionary fund of this kind makes very good sense. Unfortunately, it is easily perceived as government coddling of welfare recipients. Worse yet, even small instances of perceived, never mind actual, abuse by clients or staff could damn such a fund and those connected with it.

Another controversial activity in which staff creativity can make a difference is intake. In Oregon, where recipient self-sufficiency has been the goal of the state welfare department since the earliest days of JOBS, the endlessly detailed eligibility determination form and interview have been reduced to a streamlined and highly pragmatic set of procedures designed to elicit what problems applicants are having in making ends meet, what sort of help it might take to tide them over, and for how long. The intake workers are also permitted to act expeditiously to offer practical assistance as well as counseling. Although this sort of discretion in the hands of punitive or highly distrustful intake interviewers could end up depriving claimants of support to which they are legally and morally entitled, the welfare watchdog groups in Oregon have generally approved the shift in policy.

In Utah the SPED staff, seeking to involve the community in moving welfare recipients into work, held a kick-off event and planned a major media campaign. The community responded in various ways. For example, an investment bank organized thirty volunteers who provided help with budgeting to clients who needed it. After six months or so, welfare advocacy groups gave up battling SPED's high-expectations program and instead became its stauch supporters.[29]

The Most Disadvantaged

Aid recipients who are not living in a depressed or discriminatory labor market, who are reasonably literate and numerate, who have acquired workplace skills through previous employment, and who are psychologically and physically fit will probably be able to find jobs and leave the welfare rolls within a year or two at most. But a sizable minority will have to struggle up the rungs of Toby Herr's incremental ladder, falling or stepping off occasionally for a period on welfare before returning to the ladder. As welfare departments succeed in shortening stays on welfare for those ready to accept a job and discouraging others who are job-ready from even applying for aid, those least ready will loom ever larger as the core managerial problem.[30] Managerial systems must be designed with unusual care to deal with such people.

Those on the incremental ladder do not readily fit the standard bureaucratic categories. Are they on or off welfare while in a possibly temporary job? Herr and her associates studied a federally funded postemployment services demonstration program in Oregon in 1994–95 and observed that the system usually restarted a client in the welfare system every time he or she wanted to move back onto the rolls for a brief period. The person had to wait weeks for an appointment to reapply for benefits, then was obliged to go through the steps of job search at the branch office, career counseling, Job Club, and so on, before the person's supposed case-manager retention worker learned that he or she was not working.[31] In theory it is not hard to fix problems like this—and Oregon did so—by means of better information systems, more customized procedures, and better communications among the various units. Actually fixing such problems, however, requires discarding the vestiges of a low-expectations, paper-shuffling, bureaucratic culture and adopting a commitment to producing real results.

Contracting Out

Given the many constraints on public bureaucracies, it may be very difficult to reinvent welfare agencies as engines of client self-sufficiency.

In many instances it may be preferable not to try, but instead to contract the work out to organizations such as Maximus, Curtis and Associates, America Works, or community-based employment and training organizations.[32] In any event, the threat of possible competition from such quarters ought to motivate the existing welfare agency staff to work harder at reinvention. In Wisconsin, although JOBS was run in most counties by the welfare department, in areas where the state did not trust the local welfare department, it was contracted out.[33] The need to cope with the workfare requirements of the 1996 welfare reform act, furthermore, should motivate the search for new possibilities even more intensely.

Paternalism with Pressure: Workfare, Participation, and Sanctions

The moral stance of the welfare organization would be difficult enough to develop if the only issues requiring moral reasoning concerned the proper relationship between the welfare recipient and the labor force—for example, the extent to which a recipient should be willing to accept a second-choice child care arrangement as the price of taking a job. But matters are further complicated by the fact that the welfare staff members exercise state power. Within certain broad legislative guidelines, they can threaten to cut recipients from the rolls or reduce their grants.

Under the JOBS program, one grounds for grant reduction was failure to participate in assigned program activities.[34] In the GAIN program 14 percent of participants claimed to have had their AFDC grants reduced because of failure to participate, although the true rate of sanctioning was probably 5 to 10 percent.[35] Some 18 percent of participants were threatened with sanctions, however, in their first eleven months after orientation. Yet 63 percent of 2,100 welfare recipients sampled said that it was "fair" or "very fair" to require participation and to reduce AFDC grants if the requirement was not met.

Under the provisions of the 1996 welfare reform act, states will be obliged to have nearly all recipients who have been on the rolls more than two years perform some sort of work activity in exchange for their benefits. And there will be strong financial incentives to keep a relatively high percentage of all recipients (25 percent in 1998 and rising to 50 percent in 2002 and thereafter) in such activities. The states will not generally be permitted to use federal funds to assist recipients who refuse to participate in work activities.[36] For the purposes of the act, work activity is to mean mostly work per se, but may also include work-preparation activities such as job training and, for up to 20 percent of the caseload, vocational education.

"Work" is in some sense more demanding than the participation required of JOBS participants.[37] But earlier experience with workfare (mandatory "work experience" placements in public and nonprofit agencies) participants in seven states in the mid-1980s found that most liked their jobs, felt valued by fellow employees, believed they had learned something new on the job, and believed that the assignments would help them get "a decent-paying job" later. Seventy percent said they were very or somewhat satisfied that their welfare grants were tied to a job, and 71 percent agreed that "I feel better about receiving welfare now that I am working for it." Almost all the interviewees knew that participation in the workfare program was mandatory for them.[38]

Workfare does in some sense improve social equity. It does this by treating welfare recipients in the same way that the working poor—or for that matter, almost everybody else in the society—are treated: they all have to work for their incomes. Joel Handler and Yeheskel Hasenfeld, two students of welfare administration, have questioned the validity of this argument by pointing out that mandatory work "runs counter to the basic tenet of the capitalist market economy that work is a private commodity to be exchanged freely in the marketplace."[39] However, welfare grants are not made by the capitalist market economy but by what is in effect the government social insurance economy. In this light a recipient's obligation to work while receiving welfare can be construed as a copayment required of the insured in tandem with the benefits paid out by the insurer (government). Like any insurance copayment, it is intended to deter moral hazard and reduce inappropriate claims.[40]

Copayments that are set too high can overdeter, of course, discouraging legitimate applicants from pressing their claims. In the case of workfare the work assignments could be demeaning or disgusting or excessively strenuous. They could also be sterile, the sort of make-work assignments that would produce no output of real value and would symbolically undermine the whole idea of work effort as a source of self-respect. These were not problems in the relatively small-scale and short-term workfare programs studied by the Manpower Demonstration Research Corporation in the mid-1980s.[41] But they will almost certainly present problems for welfare agency managers that have to operate workfare on the scale mandated by the 1996 welfare reform act.

Some Management Strategies

Extrapolating from experience in small-scale and short-term programs, it is reasonable to assume that the welfare agency's demand for workfare placements will exceed the supply of slots where useful work can be accomplished, the work is not degrading, the supervisory costs to the host agency do not exceed the value of the work to the agency (and, indirectly, to the public), and the presence of workfare-connected personnel does not provoke a serious backlash from employees and their unions. As one state administrator said, "I am having trouble getting counties to develop placements for a small number of AFDC-U cases. I cannot imagine what I would do to get them to place thousands of cases."[42] If indeed the demand for workfare slots is to be met at all, the welfare agency will have to decide which placement characteristics are really the most important to it. More significantly, it will want to hire workfare placement specialists who can cajole and pressure cooperating agencies into making more and better placement slots available.

The workfare placement specialist should also want to improve working relations between the host agencies and the welfare department. Especially, the hosts must report to the welfare agency promptly and regularly on participant attendance. One workfare specialist in Oregon told me that in agencies hosting a large number of his charges he arranged for one of the welfare recipients to act as an informal crew chief, for example supervising a workfare crew assigned to improve a ball field. In some instances the crew chief would also be responsible for taking attendance and reporting problems with crew members to the workfare specialist, like a trusty in prisons. Equally, if the host agency were causing untoward problems for the workfare participants, the crew chief would also report this to the workfare specialist.

In a high-expectations program, it is important that the welfare agency do all it can to respect participant preferences for one sort of assignment over another and, as in Oregon, act as an advocate for the participant when advocacy is called for. The more difficult part of managing participants, though, is dealing with noncooperation. Experience with this problem in the context of obliging JOBS registrants to meet their participation requirements may be instructive.

The first point is that the purpose of threatened sanctions, as a Riverside manager explained, "is not to punish but to shape behavior." This means that the way threats are delivered may be as important as their content. Great variation is possible, anything from "You'd better show up tomorrow or you'll find your grant reduced $150!" to "Remember, participation is expected, and any reduction in your grant for nonparticipation will take three months to be restored, so why don't you do yourself and me a favor and shape up?" Line staff must learn how to match the style of the threat to the person and situation. In the Utah SPED program the most noncooperative clients simply accepted the grant reduction and never contacted either their eligibility worker or their self-sufficiency worker. Home visits were made to all such individuals by a specialized worker, who was able to turn around the behavior of one-third to one-half of these people.[43]

Even when a sanction has been applied, it should not always be considered the execution of a threat. A Riverside GAIN manager observed to me that "the people who get sanctioned are not really less motivated to be cooperative than anyone else, they're just more preoccupied with their own difficulties."[44] Applying a sanction on such people is just part of a process of defining structure and expectations. It is done more with an eye to shaping future conduct than to punishing past failure.

The second, and more important, lesson from the JOBS experience is to treat mandatory workfare participation as a medium through which to exert a more diffuse pressure on clients to shape up their lives, make something out of their participation, and look for paying work outside the welfare system. Existence of the mandate furnishes an opportunity for contact with clients. "Contact! . . . Once a week, twice a week, there's no such thing as too often," said one Riverside supervisor; "it reminds them that you *care* and that you're *watching*." In addition, it is an opportunity to reinforce for recipients the necessity of autonomy and personal responsibility. In Utah, failure of SPED clients to participate in self-sufficiency activities entails a $100 a month grant reduction analogous to the sanction in the JOBS program, but the staff do not call it a sanction or view it that way. "Rather, they view it as a consequence that is attached to a choice a recipient makes. . . . The cash assistance available to a recipient who chooses not to participate in self-sufficiency activities is $100 less than the cash assistance available to a person who chooses to participate."[45]

The Risk of Underinvestment

Clearly, it is a big job to reinvent the welfare system as a jobs system. The states and local welfare offices will have to make enormous investments of money, policy design creativity, and managerial self-renewal.

In some respects the political circumstances could not be more propitious. The 1996 welfare reform bill essentially tells welfare recipients "Work or else!" In effect it gives state welfare agencies an analogous message: "Get those people to work, or else!" The federal government gives each state a block grant for use as temporary assistance for needy families, sets a standard for some minimum percentage of the recipients required to be participating in work activities, and subtracts block grant dollars to the extent that a state fails to reach its standard.[46]

The welfare act increases federal pressure on the states to move aid recipients into the work force in a more subtle way as well. Within broad limits, a state gets to keep any block grant dollars that it saves when it moves someone off the rolls into unsubsidized or partly subsidized employment. All else equal, the more effective a state's work placement efforts, the more it can profit financially. This was true under the pre-1996 system as well but to a lesser extent because the state would save only that portion of a recipient's aid check that was paid for by the state rather than by federal matching funds. Now, the state captures the entire savings.

Of course, the state can also realize a financial benefit by reducing aid levels and simply dumping recipients from the rolls, thereby gaining immediate savings and also avoiding the hassle and expense of running workfare activities, which ranged from $700 to $2,100 per participant in the relatively unintensive and mainly small-scale programs reviewed by MDRC.[47] This strategy might save the state money in the short run, although not necessarily in the long run, but it would impose costs on the erstwhile aid recipients and on the charitable organizations (and some local governments) that might choose to fill the vacuum of support. Political liberals and others who are concerned that the welfare rolls not be reduced in such an uncaring way now have a stronger incentive than ever to look for creative strategies to get aid recipients back into the labor force and into jobs. As Michael Wiseman has observed, if welfare recipients fail to meet their obligations to strive for self-sufficiency, they will pay; and if the state and local welfare managers fail to deliver adequate services that the recipients need to meet their obligations, the recipients will also pay.[48]

One such strategy will certainly be to make assistance payments into a form of income-matched cash supplementation so as to encourage recipient work effort.[49] Optimists could even hope that states would get very creative with this strategy and develop a welfare policy that functions as a full-fledged policy of family-income supports for the working, workfare, and nonworking poor all in one, as appears to be happening in Oregon and Wisconsin.[50] This would entail solving many challenging problems of policy design and program management.[51]

The new-era welfare agency will need to give its staff the freedom to motivate and assist clients in creative ways, the latitude to devise a strategy of progressive discipline, and the flexibility to move clients in an out of various work-welfare combinations. Because it needs to learn from experience, it will also need to consult staff members and clients continually about what is or is not working and adapt current practices in the hopes of getting better results. Fulfilling these needs will entail investing in efficient useable information systems, in physical surroundings that show respect for clients, and in training staff not just in how to follow the rules of the system but also how to motivate client effort, use discretion, and work cooperatively across agency boundaries. Fulfilling these needs will also require self-conscious attention to the organizational principles of the welfare agency itself. Hierarchy and procedural controls will have to yield in some unknown degree to flexibility and pragmatism.[52]

Change on this scale requires leadership, and the crucial leadership must come from the managers who stand at the intersection between the operating system and the political environment outside the system. In many places this will be the local welfare-to-work program director. In the WIN program, for instance, it proved possible to run an effective program at the local level within a state's employment services agency even if the agency leadership was indifferent to the program, as it often was.[53] In Riverside the force behind change was the director of the county welfare department, who decided to make welfare-to-work a priority. This was one of the most important ways in which he was able to boost the department's political standing among the county supervisors.[54] In the Massachusetts Employment and Training (ET Choices) program, which virtually pioneered a high-expectations approach in this country, leadership came from state headquarters, particularly from the director and deputy director of the program.[55] But the Massachusetts welfare system is administered by the state, and the state is small enough to permit the headquarters staff to establish reasonably direct connections with the field should they wish.[56]

What is involved in leadership? Fortunately, the answer is not too complicated. It requires articulating the goal of achieving client self-sufficiency through paid work, setting and constantly revising challenging numerical targets, persuading staff that the goals are worthwhile, and persuading others within the organization and outside it that success is possible. I have already discussed the first three points sufficiently; I turn now to the fourth.

Public managers and lower-level staff may be forgiven if they do not often believe that success in government human service programs is possible. Frequently they are right. As helpers of last resort, government agencies serve hard-to-serve individuals whom families, voluntary organizations, and the market have already proved unable or unwilling to help. Budgets for productive services are inadequate—often grossly inadequate—even though at the same time money is wasted on unproductive activities that serve special bureaucratic or professional interests or clientele groups. Incentives toward high performance are weak, while the constraints on removing incompetents and sluggards are strong. Like many welfare-to-work clients themselves, agency staffs often live under a cloud of low expectations.[57]

Who is to lead the charge against these low expectations? Who is to trumpet the simple and true idea that with the right sort of coordinated efforts and a moderate amount of determination, this target can be achieved? People near the top, of course. But one should not be misled by the high visibility of those leaders who also happen to be at the top of the managerial hierarchy. Leadership is not a personal trait, nor is it necessarily the exclusive property of officially defined organizational positions. Leadership is at its core an assortment of tasks that help groups or organizations achieve collective goals.[58] Although it is often useful to have strong personalities and top hierarchical positions take on these tasks, it is not absolutely necessary. Certainly it is not necessary for these tasks to be performed by a single individual called the leader. In fact, given the natural suspicions evoked in our democratic and egalitarian political culture by anyone looking very much like the leader, it is often best to have leadership responsibilities distributed widely and for those undertaking them to deny that these are really leadership activities at all.[59] And in some sense they are not. For their essence is to illuminate the humanistic and pragmatic logic behind a high-expectations welfare-to-work program, explain what that entails in the way of administrative structure and operations, and pass the word that others are getting behind the idea. This is the sort of nonleadership leadership that makes perfect sense even in bureaucratic cultures that are very suspicious of their nominal leaders.

Notes

1. Very roughly speaking the literature on bureaucracy and implementation has focused more on the problems of implementation than on the solutions. The so-called public management literature has looked more at solutions than problems. For the more problem-centered view, see James Q. Wilson, *Bureaucracy: What Government Agencies Do and Why They Do It* (Basic Books, 1989); and Laurence E. Lynn Jr., *Public Management as Art, Science, and Profession* (Chatham, N.J.: Chatham House, 1996). For the more solution-centered view, see Michael Barzelay, *Breaking through Bureaucracy: A New Vision for Managing in Government* (University of California Press, 1992); and Mark H. Moore, *Creating Public Value: Strategic Management in Government* (Harvard University Press, 1995). My own early work on implementation, *The Implementation Game: What Happens after a Bill Becomes a Law* (MIT Press, 1977), infuses the problem-focused analysis in this chapter. On the challenges entailed in taking a more solution-centered stance, see my "The Problem of 'Best Practice' Research: Comment on Laurence E. Lynn Jr., 'Public Mangement Research: The Triumph of Art over Science,'" *Journal of Policy Analysis and Management,* vol. 13 (Spring 1994), pp. 260–68.

2. The extent of consensus will vary. Toward teenage pregnancies there is probably a strong consensus against children having children but less consensus on the appropriate level of sexual activity for older teenagers. For the nondangerous mentally ill, there is probably very little consensus on how much tolerance should be accorded minor deviance, provided it is not practiced by large numbers of people congregating in comparatively small public spaces.

3. George Lakoff analogizes the parent and the government in *Moral Politics: What Conservatives Know That Liberals Don't* (University of Chicago Press, 1996), as do the authors in this book. But his focus is mainly on conflicts of punitiveness and nurturance, which do not directly concern the present authors, to all of whom, I believe, punitiveness would appear undesirable unless strongly justified by a larger social good.

4. James Riccio, Daniel Friedlander, and Stephen Freedman, *GAIN: Benefits, Costs, and Three-Year Impacts of a Welfare-to-Work Program* (New York: Manpower Demonstration Research Corp., 1994).

5. Ibid., p. xxv.

6. Eugene Bardach, *Improving the Productivity of JOBS Programs* (New York: Manpower Demonstration Research Corp., 1993).

7. Lawrence M. Mead, "The New Paternalism in Action: Welfare Reform in Wisconsin," Milwaukee, Wisconsin Policy Research Institute, 1995; and Mead, "The Decline of Welfare in Wisconsin," Milwaukee, Wisconsin Policy Research Institute, March 1996; and Mead, "Expectations and Welfare Work: WIN in New York State," *Polity*, vol. 18 (Winter 1985), pp. 224–52.

The SPED program routed all applicants for aid to a "self-sufficiency worker" before determining eligibility for AFDC. It eliminated all exemptions from the JOBS program and expanded the definition of self-sufficiency activities to include options such as mental health counseling, substance abuse treatment, and parenting classes. It also aspired to a 100 percent participation rate, and came very close to achieving it (more than 90 percent). See LaDonna A. Pavetti and Amy-Ellen Duke, *Increasing Participation in Work and Work-Related Activities: Lessons from Five State Welfare Reform Demonstration Projects,* 2 vols. (Washington: Urban Institute, 1995), especially the Utah case study in volume 2. After thirty months, an experimental design evaluation showed that SPED clients were leaving the rolls at a much higher rate than the controls and that grant expenditures were being reduced as well. LaDonna A. Pavetti, ". . . And Employment for All: Lessons from Utah's Single Parent Employment Demonstration Project," paper prepared for the 1995 annual Research Conference of the Association for Public Policy Analysis and Management.

8. See John J. Mitchell, Mark Lincoln Chadwin, and Demetra Smith Nightingale, *Implementing Welfare-Employment Programs: An Institutional Analysis of the Work Incentive (WIN) Program* (Washington: Urban Institute, 1979). Mark Lincoln Chadwin, John J. Mitchell, and Demetra Smith Nightingale, "Reforming Welfare: Lessons from the WIN Experience," *Public Administration Review,* vol. 41 (May-June 1981), pp. 372–80, summarizes the Urban Institute report. WIN was a precursor to the JOBS program that flourished on a relatively small scale from 1967 through the mid-1980s.

9. Some studies of welfare-to-work program administration exist, but there is not enough qualitative richness in most of them to indicate how program philosophy was articulated, justified, and embodied in the details of program administration. There are some exceptions, however. See the studies by Toby Herr and her colleagues at Project Match in Chicago: Toby Herr, Robert Halpern, and Aimee Conrad, *Changing What Counts: Rethinking the Journey Out of Welfare* (Chicago: Project Match, Erikson Institute, 1991); Toby Herr, Robert Halpern, and Ria Majeske, *Bridging the Worlds of Head Start and Welfare-to-Work: Building a Two-Generation Self-sufficiency Program from the Ground Up* (Chicago: Project Match, Erikson Institute, 1993); Toby Herr, Robert Halpern, and Suzanne L. Wagner, *Something Old, Something New: A Case Study of the Post-Employment Services Demonstration in Oregon* (Chicago: Project Match, Erikson Institute, 1995); and Toby Herr and others, *Understanding Case Management in a Welfare-to-Work Program: The Project Match Experience* (Chicago: Project Match, Erikson Institute, 1995)

Lawrence M. Mead writes about New York and Wisconsin in "New Paternalism in Action," "Expectations and Welfare Work: WIN in New York State," and "Expectations and Welfare Work: WIN in New York City," *Policy Studies Review,* vol. 2 (May 1983), pp. 650–62.

Robert D. Behn writes on Massachusetts in *Leadership Counts: Lessons for Public Managers from the Massachusetts Welfare, Training, and Employment Program* (Harvard University Press, 1991). Useful too is Riccio, Friedlander, and Freedman, *GAIN*; and Mitchell, Chadwin, and Nightingale, *Implementing Welfare-Employment Programs.* Richard Nathan writes on five states implementing the JOBS program in *Turning Promises into Performance: The Management Challenge of Implementing Workfare* (Columbia University Press, 1993). See also Jan L. Hagen and Irene Lurie, *Implementing JOBS: Progress and Promise* (Albany, N.Y.: Rockefeller Institute of Government, 1994). In *Increasing Participation*, Pavetti and Duke study demonstration programs in five states. The Utah SPED case study in volume 2 of Pavetti and Duke is an especially subtle and comprehensive account of transforming a traditional check-writing welfare agency into one that supports employment and self-sufficiency.

10. Hagen and Lurie, *Implementing JOBS,* p. xxiv.

11. Some visits I made in connection with a project for MDRC on JOBS implementation (see Bardach, *Improving Productivity).* Most of the material I reference here on the Riverside program also appears in my Manpower Demonstration Research Corporation monograph. Other visits were made in the course of writing a book on interagency collaboration under the auspices of the State and Local Government Innovations program at Harvard's Kennedy School of Government, funded by the Ford Foundation.

12. On the term *street level* see Michael Lipsky, *Street-Level Bureaucracy: Dilemmas of the Individual in Public Services* (Russell Sage Foundation, 1980). The rights side of the debate has been muted in recent years. At issue, however, would be procedural due process in denying or withdrawing benefits.

13. I picked up this example from Greg Newton, a Boston-based trainer who offers workshops in how to run a high-expectations program.

14. This presents a problem for both clients and JOBS line workers in high-benefit states, inasmuch as leaving welfare for work at a minimum-wage job without health benefits or child care is not necessarily a road to financial betterment in the short run. Riccio, Freedman, and Friedlander, *GAIN,* pp. 188–91, computed take-home pay for a variety of welfare and work combinations (for example, part-time and full-time work) and concluded that "the monetary incentives to work, particularly to work full time, were very mixed." Their calculations did not even take into account the prospects of losing medicaid eligibility once a person is off welfare for a year.

15. This book, along with videotapes, was prepared by Paul E. Walker, Oklahoma state director of the JOBS program, along with Richard A. Fuchs, for use in the state and for wider commercial distribution. It is one of perhaps more than a half a dozen such training packages.

16. Unemployment and frustration in previous efforts at job search can also aggravate the problem.

17. The other 80 percent, however, were virtually indistinguishable from the rest of the student body.

18. Herr, Halpern, and Conrad, *Changing What Counts,* p. 3. Judith M. Gueron, "A Research Context for Welfare Reform," *Journal of Policy Analysis and Management,* vol. 15 (Fall 1996), p. 555, estimates that less than 25 percent of welfare recipients cannot work or could work only with special support.

19. This, at least, is the most current version of the social contract. An earlier and softer conception was the one Michigan imposed, by that name, in 1992: work could include such activities as volunteering in church, caring for an ill or disabled child or adult, or participating in a prenatal activity. Pavetti and Duke, *Increasing Participation,* vol. 1, p. 20.

20. Buttressing my own observations is a ten-state study of 943 JOBS line workers in which 16 percent said they emphasized client obligations during eligibility interviews while 62 percent said they emphasized opportunities. Many of these workers acted in opposition to their own agencies' officially prescribed emphases, inasmuch as 26 percent said that their agencies preferred an emphasis on obligations. Jan L. Hagen and Ling Wang, "Implementing JOBS: The Functions of Frontline Workers," *Social Service Review,* vol. 68 (September 1994), p. 373.

21. She continued, "the three have come through [the Job Club component of the

program] twice since then, and two of those succeeded. And the last, well, maybe it wasn't the right time for that person." See also the MDRC monograph on the Riverside program.

22. The assumption about receptive labor markets will certainly not always be met. Katherine Newman and Chauncy Lennon, *Finding Work in the Inner City: How Hard Is It Now? How Hard Will It Be for AFDC Recipients?* (Russell Sage Foundation, 1995); and William Julius Wilson, *When Work Disappears: The World of the New Urban Poor* (Knopf, 1996). Ethnic and racial discrimination as well as general economic circumstances could work strongly against recipients in certain areas.

23. In the Utah SPED office, a volunteer professional designer worked over the waiting room. Chairs were rearranged so that the room would not always feel the same to participants. Signs were changed. Forms were changed so that they used the word *employment* wherever possible.

24. Mitchell, Chadwin, and Nightingale, pp. 147–49, found a correlation of WIN success with performance measurements, based on office units rather than individuals, when challenging goals were set. On goal setting generally see Henry P. Sims Jr. and Peter Lorenzi, *The New Leadership Paradigm: Social Learning and Cognition in Organizations* (Newbury Park, Calif.: Sage, 1992) for an excellent overview. See also Paul J. Champagne and R. Bruce McAfee, *Motivating Strategies for Performance and Productivity: A Guide to Human Resource Development* (Quorum Books, 1989); Dov Eden, "Pygmalion, Goal Setting, and Expectancy: Compatible Ways to Boost Productivity," *Academy of Management Review,* vol. 13 (October 1988), pp. 639–52; Valerie Englander and Fred Englander, "Workfare in New Jersey: A Five-Year Assessment," *Policy Studies Review,* vol. 5 (August 1985), pp. 33–41; Lee W. Frederiksen and Richard P. Johnson, "Organizational Behavior Management," in Michel Hersen, Richard M. Eisler, and Peter M. Miller, eds., *Progress in Behavior Modification,* vol. 12 (Academic Press 1981), pp. 67–118; and Edwin A. Locke, Gary P. Latham, and Miriam Erez, "The Determinants of Goal Commitment," *Academy of Management Review,* vol. 13 (January 1988), pp. 23–39.

25. The virtues of "loose-tight coupling," with top management setting goals and line workers being given discretion as to means, are developed in Behn, *Leadership*, and Mitchell, Chadwin, and Nightingale, *Implementing Welfare-Employment Programs.*

26. Edward E. Lawler III, *The Ultimate Advantage: Creating the High-Involvement Organization* (San Francisco: Jossey-Bass, 1992), p. 63.

27. Mitchell, Chadwin, and Nightingale, *Implementing Welfare-Employment Programs.*

28. Herr, Halpern, and Wagner, *Something Old, Something New*, pp. 23–24.

29. Pavetti and Duke, *Increasing Participation*, vol. 2, pp. 134–35.

30. This dynamic was very apparent in the Utah SPED progam. Pavetti and Duke, *Increasing Participation*, esp. vol. 2, pp. 116–54.

31. Herr, Halpern, and Wagner, *Something Old, Something New.*

32. Lyn A. Hogan, *Work First: A Progressive Strategy to Replace Welfare With a Competitive Employment System* (Washington: Democratic Leadership Council, 1996).

33. Lawrence Mead brought this to my attention.

34. The basic definition of participation was accepting an assignment for at least twenty hours a week and showing up at least 75 percent of the time.

35. Riccio, Freedman, and Friedlander, *GAIN*, pp. 59–61.

36. An exception is made for recipients with children younger than age six who cannot find acceptable child care. Federal funds may also not be used for individuals who refuse to cooperate in child-support enforcement or who do not assign certain support rights to the state. Mothers younger than eighteen will also be required to live in adult-supervised settings.

37. However, the 1996 welfare reform act does count as work some of the vocational and basic educational training that satisfied the participation requirements of the JOBS program. It also counts participation in community service activities as work.

38. Thomas Brock, David Butler, and David Long, *Unpaid Work Experience for Welfare Recipients: Findings and Lessons from MDRC Research* (New York: Manpower Demonstration Research, 1993); and Gregory Hoerz and Karla Hanson, *A Survey of Participants and Worksite Supervisors in the New York City Work Experience Program* (Manpower Demonstration Research Corp., 1986), p. 28.

39. Joel F. Handler and Yeheskel Hasenfeld, *The Moral Construction of Poverty: Welfare Reform in America* (Newbury Park, Calif.: Sage, 1991), p. 39.

40. For evidence of workfare's effect in reducing welfare rolls, see: C. Nielsen Brasher, "Workfare in Ohio: Political and Socioeconomic Climate and Program Impact," *Policy Studies Journal,* vol. 22, no. 3 (1994), pp. 514–27; Englander and Englander, "Workfare in New Jersey, pp. 33–41; Bradley R. Schiller and C. Nielsen Brasher, "Workfare in the 1980s: Successes and Limits," *Policy Studies Review,* vol. 9 (Summer 1990), pp. 665–80; and Mead, "Decline of Welfare." Whether workfare produces its effects by means of countering moral hazard or in some other fashion, however, is not established by these studies. Studies by the Manpower Demonstration Research Corp. in Illinois, San Diego, and West Virginia showed very small or statistically insignificant effects of workfare programs on reducing welfare payment or receipts within the experimental groups. Thomas Brock, David Butler and David Long, *Unpaid Work Experience for Welfare Recipients.*

41. Brock, Butler, and Long, *Unpaid Work Experience*; and Judith M. Gueron and Edward Pauly, *From Welfare to Work* (Russell Sage Foundation, 1991), p. 166.

42. Brock, Butler, and Long, *Unpaid Work Experience*, p. 66.

43. Pavetti and Duke, *Increasing Participation*, vol. 2, p. 131.

44. In addition, this manager said, they may be testing limits to see how little they need to cooperate before staff will start pushing back. Mitchell, Chadwin, and Nightingale in *Implementing Welfare-Employment Programs,* their study of 241 WIN programs, found that higher-performing programs were more apt to counsel uncooperative clients as opposed to routinely imposing sanctions.

45. Pavetti and Duke, *Increasing Participation*, vol. 2, p. 130.

46. The law provides that a state can reduce its required standard from year to year by reducing the number of families in its caseload.

47. Brock, Butler, and Long, *Unpaid Work Experience*, p. 4.

48. Michael Wiseman, "State Strategies for Welfare Reform: The Wisconsin Story," *Journal of Policy Analysis and Management,* vol. 15 (Fall 1996), p. 537.

49. An interesting and partly successful effort to do something like this has been New York State's Child Assistance program. It also involves an effort to enforce child support. An important lesson of an early evaluation of the program was that local-level

management made the difference between success and failure. William L. Hamilton and others, *The New York State Child Assistance Program: Program Impacts, Costs, and Benefits* (New York: Abt Associates, 1993), pp. 150–52.

50. On Wisconsin see Wiseman, "State Strategies."

51. Michael Bangser, James Healy, and Robert Ivry, *Welfare Grant Diversion: Lessons and Prospects* (New York: Manpower Demonstration Research Corp., 1986).

52. Fulfilling client's needs might entail smaller caseloads than many state welfare agencies are used to. However, an MDRC experiment in Riverside that doubled the size of the staff showed no improvement relative to the normal ratio of staff to clients. Riccio, Friedlander, and Freedman, *GAIN*, pp. 161–62, 230–34.

53. Mitchell, Chadwin, and Nightingale, *Implementing Welfare-Employment Programs,* p. 109.

54. For more on the political environment and personal choices of welfare directors, see Laurence E. Lynn Jr., "Managing the Social Safety Net: The Job of Social Welfare Executive," in. E. C. Hargrove and J. C. Glidewell, eds., *Impossible Jobs in Public Management* (University Press of Kansas, 1990), pp. 133–51.

55. Behn, *Leadership Counts.*

56. Even though Oregon is a much larger state, its leadership also came from the state agency director and deputy director. The magnitude of change in Oregon was vast, however, and stretched over many years. It encompassed substantial devolution of power to county-level administrators and new collaborative service delivery relationships at both the local and state levels with the community college system, the state employment services agency, and the Job Training Partnership Act program.

57. See, for instance, Evelyn Z Brodkin's account of how the Illinois Department of Public Aid was implementing the JOBS program in Chicago between 1991 and 1993; "Inside the Welfare Contract: Discretion and Accountability in State Welfare Administration," *Social Service Review*, vol. 71, no. 1 (1997), pp. 1–33.

58. Ronald A. Heifetz, *Leadership without Easy Answers* (Harvard University Press, 1994).

59. In America public opinion can also be a "leader." As Lawrence Mead commented in a personal communication to me, "somehow the political process takes a certain direction, and operators at all levels get the message. Then leadership can occur spontaneously at all levels, low as well as high, without anyone appearing to be in charge. This clearly has occurred in welfare reform in Wisconsin. The idea of enforcing work has taken hold as if by an invisible hand."

Nine

Poverty and Paternalism: A Psychiatric Viewpoint

George E. Vaillant

In trying to address the ways that paternalism might help people out of poverty and the underclass, I wish to introduce two metaphors. I wish to suggest drug addiction as a metaphor for reversible poverty and employee assistance programs (EAPs) as a metaphor for effective paternalistic government.

I want to use addiction as a metaphor to discuss poverty for two reasons. The first is to underscore that my conception of paternalism comes from the medical model. Thus, the economic model of an externally, socially caused state of poverty is replaced by the medical model of a disordered individual. In my metaphor I also replace the model of an often patronizing and judgmental, sometimes totalitarian paternalistic governmental overlord with the medical model of an *altruistic paternalistic servant* epitomized by the physician. Public servants and economists look at groups structurally to obtain the greatest good for the greatest number. Physicians, like EAPs, put the welfare of the individual above that of the group.

In saying this I do not mean the individual is entirely responsible for poverty. Individualism and structuralism work reciprocally. I accept that

This work was supported by research grants KO5-MH00364 and MH42248 from the National Institute of Mental Health. The chapter owes much to the extensive editorial suggestions of Lawrence M. Mead and William N. Brownsberger.

poverty has many causes besides dysfunctional upbringing, drug abuse, and mental illness. Economic depression, teenage mothers with children, and racial and gender discrimination are also major causes of poverty that need to be combated by structural change. The solutions offered in this chapter will do nothing to alleviate teenage pregnancy, racial prejudice, migration of jobs to the suburbs, or sexism. In the arguments that follow, all of the persons were middle-aged men who came of age during the economic boom period from 1940 to 1970. Thus I am addressing only one facet of the problem of poverty, the role of the individual.

The medical model usually means treating the individual, not society, but at the same time, the medical model fails if it blames the victim. The medical focus is not on the percentage of the population that is in poverty. Rather, it is on the person who is in poverty: why, for how long has he or she been that way, and what differences have contrasting forms of intervention made on that individual. To oversimplify, sociologists and economists often see troubles as coming from without and pay attention to group process and structure. Physicians see troubles coming from within and focus attention on individual process. Unlike economists, physicians try to treat each person differently. Differential diagnosis is important.

The second reason that I use addiction to discuss poverty is that poverty, although it is not an addiction, is often both caused by drug addiction and causes drug addiction. To the extent that addiction is the cause of poverty, to cure it is often to cure the poverty. In addition, because regular employment provides a competing, potentially reinforcing activity, it is not only one of our most potent antidotes to poverty but also to addiction.[1]

Poverty has as many negative connotations as paternalism. To many people poverty connotes sloth or victimization or incurable membership in the underclass. But by equating poverty with addiction, I hope to show that it is due neither to sin nor victimization. Nor is it without cure. Rather, addiction is a disease, a self-detrimental illness in which the afflicted individual, although not exactly responsible for causing the illness, must be the author of recovery. Like addiction, the joblessness of welfare recipients is a self-detrimental illness that is susceptible to cure.

However, the medical model fails to the extent that physicians can suggest but not coerce. Because the medical model is inherently voluntary, in the face of addiction it fails. It cannot adequately confront self-destructive behavior. Medicine is not sufficiently paternalistic. Unlike the government official, a physician often feels powerless in the face of smoking or drunk driving. Economists and government officials may view drunk drivers and their automobile accidents as inevitable, but they appreciate that government-mandated breathalyzers, higher alcohol taxes, safer highways and air bags will save lives.

Employee assistance programs are a metaphor for paternalism that extends the medical model. EAPs are union-management partnerships that use the threat of job loss to coerce employees with problems to submit to clinical treatment and supervision for their own good. Fundamental to EAPs is the principle that "we will protect your job but only if you behave in ways that will help to overcome your dependency on drugs."[2] Historically, EAPs evolved out of the programs that began in the 1940s, especially in the automobile industry, to combat alcoholism. In the 1970s, through the Association of Labor-Management Administrators and Consultants on Alcoholism, the programs broadened to include emotional and marital problems. The Drug Free Work Place Act of 1988 encouraged still further expansion. At present, 90 percent of the *Fortune* 1,000 companies have EAPs.[3]

Paternalism has two unpalatable connotations: authoritarian judgmental behavior and patronizing-infantalizing behavior. Paternalism threatens to disempower the individual and underscores why so many responsible people—epitomized by John Stuart Mill—have mistrusted paternalistic government. However, paternalism, as it is addressed in this volume, is meant to empower the individual. Therefore, I offer the metaphor of a caring EAP that strives to help an employee recover from alcoholism.

Paternalistic corporations discovered the value of an EAP as a structure within which union members could be coerced to act in their own best interest. Unions discovered the value of the EAP as a structure by which members could be helped, not disempowered. One of the definitions of a good EAP is that it always works *for* the individual. EAPs use coercive paternalistic power to help workers engage in supervised behaviors that help themselves. In addition, under optimal circumstances EAPs provide support and coaching to supervisors.

On the one hand, EAPs, unlike physicians, often have the power to coerce; on the other hand, EAPs, unlike many governmental policies, are accepted by the individual. For example, an EAP can have the authority to monitor an employee's urine if addiction has interfered with his work and to mandate that the employee attend Alcoholics Anonymous if he is to retain his job.[4]

Responsibity for Addiction and Poverty

It is easy to shift responsibility for detrimental human behavior from one scapegoat to another. Thus in the realm of welfare, society goes from emphasizing one verse of *West Side Story*'s memorable song, "Gee, Officer Krupke," to focusing on the next. The welfare candidate is lazy or deserving or bad or victimized. In the first decades of the twentieth century, American society regarded both alcohol and drug addiction as self-indulgent sins to be eradicated. All that was needed was to legislate morality.[5] In 1914 the Harrison Act was passed to abolish narcotics abuse and in 1919 the Volstead Act to abolish alcohol abuse. These laws failed to achieve either goal, and in the 1920s the scapegoats changed. Addiction was not a sin; it was imposed on the innocent by the evil Mafia and irresponsible doctors. In the 1940s blame was shifted from society to the drug itself. It was the special pharmacological properties of heroin that were dangerous. Addiction was a disease that detoxification could cure. Detoxification, too, was also a failure: as Mark Twain observed with regard to smoking, stopping was so easy he had done it twenty times. The parallels with attitudes toward welfare should be obvious.

More recently still it has become clear that neither the Mob nor the addicting properties of drugs nor sinful human nature is the main cause of heroin addiction in the United States. Instead, it has become popular to shift responsibility for both addiction and poverty back to society. So on the one hand society allocates more funds for clinics and welfare and on the other allocates more funds for prisons and enforcement of the narcotics laws. But reassigning blame solves nothing. Rates of poverty and addiction continue to climb, each catalyzing the other.

Empirically, in combating addiction, EAPs, parole, and Alcoholics Anonymous have enjoyed the greatest success.[6] EAPs, parole, and AA all avoid blame. Ideally, they do not blame the individual for causing the condition but assign him the responsibility for curing it. They work *with* the addict, not *on* him. They paradoxically support individual autonomy by infringing on the right to indulge in self-detrimental behavior. They all require that addicts experience the consequences of their behavior but do so in a way that permits them to change.

By analogy, then, assigning blame for poverty will not help. Neither arbitrary withdrawal of welfare nor granting welfare without asking for reciprocity will change behavior. Sociologists and economists who perceive poverty as a product of a dysfunctional economy or even of dysfunctional families miss the point. Certainly, they do not wish to blame the victim, but to ignore the individual is to imagine that poverty is caused by external, rational reasons. To ignore individual responsibility for poverty is to ignore unconscious irrational motivation. Such motivation goes by many different names: conditioned behavior, self-punitive expression of anger, bad genes, poor self-esteem and self-efficacy, maladaptive ego mechanisms of defense, undersocialization, or penance to assuage a guilty conscience. Often the unconscious irrational motivation is due, at least in part, directly to alcohol or drug dependency, sometimes from hopelessness that any other alternative is possible.

Poverty as a Disease

One reason for examining poverty via the psychological-medical model is because in rich nations poverty in white men without children *is* almost indistinguishable from mental illness, broadly defined. By this I mean that the disposable weekly income of single welfare recipients in the southeast Bronx would allow them a solid bourgeois status in most third world countries. Their weekly income would represent an adequate stipend for many mentally healthy, drug-free graduate students living cooperatively. Joblessness is toxic for reasons other than not having enough money.

In a thirty-year follow-up of 456 tenement-dwelling, undereducated adolescent white males with immigrant parents and limited intelligence, I found poverty and mental illness, broadly defined, to be almost indistinguishable.[7] Variables reflecting individual psychopathology were more predictive of poverty than being raised in a dysfunctional family or a family supported by welfare. To be specific, if for a family the poverty line was drawn at $7,000 (in 1978 dollars) a year, then at age forty-seven, 52 of these 456 inner-city men fell below the poverty line (table 9-1). Of these men only 3 (7 percent) were not psychiatrically ill. Twenty-four of the 52 were alcohol dependent; 25 manifested schizophrenia or disabling personality disorder or were mentally retarded (IQ less than 80). If instead I focused on the 34 of the 456 who, before age forty-seven, had been unemployed for ten years or more, 17 were alcohol dependent and 14 suffered disabling personality disorder. Again, only 3 men remained chronically unemployed without significant drug addiction or psychiatric "disease."

Table 9-1. Adult Economic Dysfunction Differences between Men Who Were Mentally Ill and Socially Disadvantaged

	Alcoholic	*Mentally ill*	*Well*
52 of 456 men below poverty line	24	25	3
34 of 456 men chronically unemployed	17	14	3

	Unemployed ten or more years	*Below poverty line*	*Well*
41 of 456 men from dysfunctional families	4	8	21

Source: unpublished data.

However, there is an important difference between poverty due to alcohol dependence or personality disorders and poverty due to schizophrenia or mental retardation. Bad habits, however severe, are often reversible; severe schizophrenia and mental retardation are often not. Welfare policy requires individual differential diagnosis, not just structural solutions. The problem is that inability to work is like a learning disability during the school years. Sometimes remediation and the combating of hopelessness incurred by earlier deprivation is possible, in which case intervention alleviates distress and acting out. In similar fashion, poverty caused by addiction and delinquency is remediable and will alleviate alienation. Sometimes, as is the case for some individuals with Down's Syndrome and some schizophrenics, intensive intervention increases distress, and a reduction in social demands is most effective. When to require and facilitate work and when to grant welfare ungrudgingly is a critical distinction.

If poverty is often a result of mental illness, employment reflects health. The foes of social Calvinism may overlook the fact that work can reflect competence, social utility, and self-esteem. A history of working is one of the most powerful predictors of recovery from schizophrenia, from drug addiction, from delinquency, and from alcoholism.[8] Robert Sampson and John Laub, especially, have shown the power of reestablishing social bonds, of which a stable job is a prime component, to heal extremely socially alienated adolescents.[9]

In contrast to mentally ill and alcoholic men, the economic fate of the inner city men in my study whose social disadvantage lay in their adolescent environment and not in themselves was very different. Forty-one of the 456 men had been raised in multiproblem, welfare-dependent families defined by ten or more markers such as mother mentally retarded, father alcoholic, separated from both parents for six months or more, or known to nine or more social agencies. By age forty-seven, only 8 (20 percent) of these socially disadvantaged 41 men still fell below the poverty line; only 4 had been unemployed for ten years or more.

In short, poverty can be viewed within the framework of the medical model, with one important caveat. Some conditions, such as appendicitis and broken legs, require treatment by someone else. Some, such as gingivitis and diabetes, must be treated by rational motivation and disciplined self-care. Some diseases, however, like truancy and suicidal behavior, alcoholism and most poverty, are irrational. Although the disorders can be cured only by self-care, that care must be coerced because the irrational self does not view such self-detrimental behavior as a disease. Society must evolve the same paternalistic controls over drug abuse and reversible poverty that it has evolved for truancy and suicide.

Caring and Coercion Must Be Integrated

Just as law can provide structure to society without destroying freedom of choice, so without threatening genuine individual freedom, the law can sometimes provide structure for individuals. Compulsory education and hospitalization for suicidal intent are cases in point. In such instances the American Civil Liberties Union trusts society to be caring. But what right, many ask, has society to interfere with an individual's choice to use drugs or to choose not to work? How can one distinguish between unconscious self-destructive behavior and mere violation of middle-class morality?

The answer is twofold. First, poverty, like truancy and suicide, is often a result of an individual's having too little structure, and coercive treatment is better than benign neglect. To forbid truancy in elementary school, for example, is a far cry from denying individuals free choice with regard to college or church attendance. But psychiatric commitment laws and truancy laws and union-blessed EAP sanctions have been decided democratically. A few voluntary paternalistic approaches to unemployment and addiction already exist. For the severely disadvantaged, in the days before the voluntary military, "the army made a man out of me" was more than an advertising slogan. Models for democratically determined smoke-free workplaces are facilitating smoking cessation.

But is being made to work really like compulsory school attendance? The term *task completion* is apt to bring to mind middle-class morality, toilet training, and the imagery of "doing one's duty." We forget that sometimes task completion can serve as a sensitive indicator of ego function.[10] Work plays a central role in an individual's life, and work has as much to do with health as it does with middle-class conformity.

Governments, in contrast to *good* families and *ordinary* coaches and EAPs, are usually unable to integrate care and punishment. They are unable to integrate voluntary and coercive strategies. Unlike a good coach, society does not know how *simultaneously* to reward (offer welfare) and to coerce (enforce good behavior by sanctions). Too often drunks and truants, both in need of integrated care and discipline, are sent off *either* to jails or to clinics. EAPs, unlike either jails or mental health workers, have the power to coerce their clients into behavior change in a community setting.

Coaches and EAPs offer both carrots and sticks. In contrast, many caretakers and social workers (liberals) in our communities are at war with the stick-wielding disciplinarians and police (conservatives). This is true for both addiction and poverty. On the one hand, liberals often insist that a juvenile's criminal addict's record be sealed when he reaches his eighteenth birthday. This makes it impossible for judges to make intelligent sentencing decisions until the youth has the time to reestablish an adult criminal track record, when it is usually too late. This is as foolish as denying a professional football coach information about a young rookie's college athletic accomplishments or denying a doctor an adult diabetic's adolescent medical record.

On the other hand, the Federal Bureau of Investigation, anxious only to punish, will release its records to any cooperative police department to facilitate the arrest and punishment of individuals. The FBI will not release the same records to social scientists who wish to test programs of prevention and determine the paths out of addiction. Similarly, mandatory sentences such as "three strikes and you are out" throw away the power of parole—arguably the strongest therapeutic tool that criminal justice possesses.[11]

Successful paternalistic treatments of social disability, whether it is the parenting of adolescents, an EAP for addicted physicians, or coaching an inner-city basketball team, requires combining care and coercion through continuous *external* (paternalistic) supervision. Discipline in EAPs is tough, but it is fairly administered and highly predictable. Employees' continued employment depends on their compliance with recommended treatment regimens. In contrast, the discipline in a medical clinic is nonexistent. The most caring family physician or psychotherapist is powerless over a patient's fatal cigarette habit. The discipline in jails is powerful but too often unpredictable and punitive. Jails lack the element of care and choice essential to individual reform.

Paternalism versus Medical Treatment of Heroin Addiction

Economists and social policymakers appeal to what is rational in human behavior, but poverty and addiction will not be stamped out by appeal to reason. Paternalistic interventions in both drug abuse and poverty demand that society focus on irrationalities common to self-destructive people and not just on the rational characteristics of external economic and legislative conditions.

For example, the consumption of drugs that are used socially (that is, rationally) are highly price sensitive; but consumption of drugs that are used addictively are more price insensitive.[12] After the 1914 Harrison Act outlawed over-the-counter sale of narcotics in America, more than 100,000 middle-aged hypochondriacal but rational women gave up dependence on opiates.[13] But the passage of the Harrison Act probably did not significantly affect the prevalence of hitherto legal heroin dependence among miserable, delinquent, unemployed young men.[14]

Evidence for the Efficacy of Paternalism in the Treatment of Addiction: Two Examples

Study of the natural history of New York City heroin addicts expands the argument. I shall offer two examples. The first is a composite graph of the employment careers of fifty consecutive New York City heroin abusers of above average intelligence admitted to the U.S. Public Health Service in Lexington, Kentucky, in 1952 (figure 9-1). They were selected for special study because they were born between 1920 and 1924. Largely derived from their social security records, the graph shows the proportion of these

Figure 9-1. Employment History of New York City Heroin Abusers Admitted to U.S. Public Health Service in Lexington, Kentucky, 1952

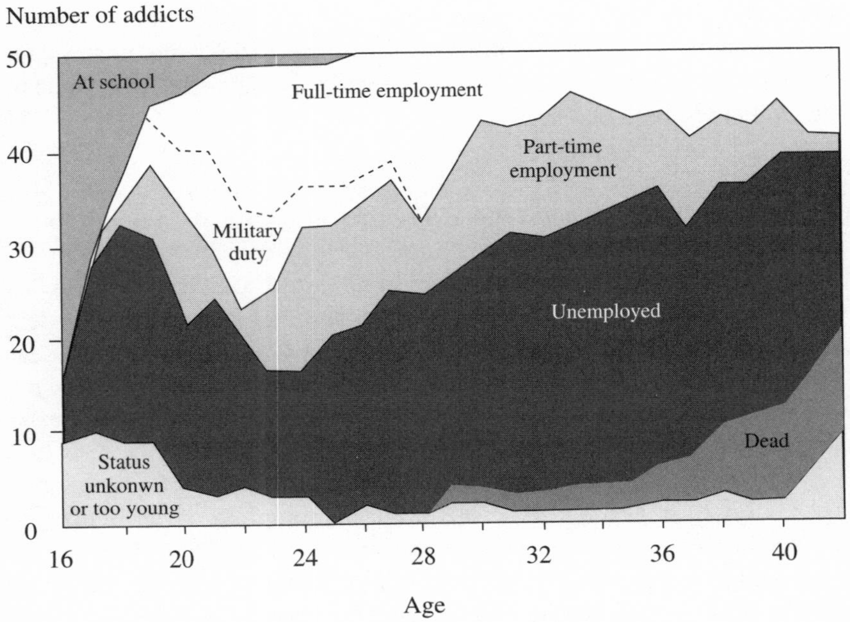

addicts that were employed at any given age. Military duty was ascertained from other sources.

The figure reflects the special conditions existing during World War II when the men first entered the work force. Restrictions on world trade meant that from 1940 to 1945 heroin addiction in New York City was impossible, and a booming war economy led to full employment even for minority groups. However, even during the special wartime conditions more than half the men were jobless or working part time. The average age of first addiction was not until twenty-five, after the war had ended, at which time, of course, their unemployment became worse.[15] But their inability to work was clearly already apparent during the war years.

In short, the figure shows that even premorbidly heroin addicts had difficulty working. By the age of forty, the average addict among those studied had spent only 20 percent of his adult life actively addicted, but he had spent 80 percent of the same period unemployed. Yet he was neither stupid nor schizophrenic. Thus one point of the figure is to illustrate that future heroin addicts, even when intelligent, able bodied without major mental illness, and drug free, have difficulty remaining employed. The figure supports the medical model. For these men inability to work had more to do with individual deficits (situational depression, personality disorder, and undersocialization by dysfunctional families) than with structured deficits (addiction, bigotry, or economic conditions).

The figure also illustrates that before age forty a significant proportion of the time the men were employed was within the paternalistic setting of the military. Not illustrated is the fact that some of these same men, unable to find work even during the favorable conditions of World War II, found regular employment after age forty when work was made a condition of their parole from state penitentiaries. Thus employment was again due to wise but voluntary coercion. They could work or remain in jail.

Coercion, however, works only when it has meaning to the individual. Making heroin illegal seems meaningless to depressed, undersocialized adolescents. Until 1960, opiates were in fact among the best antidepressants on the market. However, making people join the army during a "just" war or insisting on work to maintain parole from a state penitentiary has meaning. Similarly, society can pass enforceable laws against suicide and truancy because they seem meaningful. But to many, individual laws against particular religious observances or the sale of alcohol make no sense and become unenforceable.

The fact that abstinence from heroin is strengthened by compulsory supervision is at variance with our intuitively derived knowledge of adults' recovery from emotional difficulty. Meaningful maturational change is difficult to impose on someone from without, for most people agree that motivation is important in determining response to psychiatric treatment. It is never enough to tell someone not to bite his nails or to stop being shy. Addicts make it only too clear that they resent authoritarian approaches.

Suppose, however, that society ceases to think of drug addiction (and, perhaps, unemployment) as choice, as a more or less conscious seeking of emotional solace or an exquisite self-indulgence. If instead we conceive of drug addiction and unemployment as a whole constellation of conditioned, unconscious behaviors, the relative success of parole over conventional psychiatric intervention begins to make sense. Addicts need structured change in behavior, not insight and advice. Like a melancholic rescued by police from a building ledge, once order is restored to his or her life, an addict becomes less self-destructive.

Evidence suggests that narcotic addicts experience the best chance of recovery when certain conditions are met: first, when they remain in a community setting where they are required to work; second, when they receive compulsory supervision to deter relapse; third, when they are permitted some substitute for drugs, preferably human rather than chemical; fourth, when the *abuse,* not the *use* of the drug, is made illegal; and fifth, when the coercion is compatible with the addict's own value system, that is, when it is seen as fair.[16] This is the case, for example, when physicians are compelled by their medical societies to submit to urine testing, or when union members are compelled to attend AA by their EAP.[17] In such instances the results were very much superior to those reported from purely voluntary programs.

Let me illustrate this bold generalization with a second example. The example comes from the therapeutic vicissitudes of one hundred consecutively admitted inner-city New York heroin addicts over an eighteen-year period.[18] (Most of these men were too young to have been included in the group of older addicts during World War II.) Fifty of these addicts were white; fifty were African American. Among the two groups 30 percent were Hispanic. In 1952 at the time of their first admission to the Public Health Service Hospital in Lexington, 82 percent had been addicted to heroin for at least twelve months and 75 percent had been motivated to seek treatment voluntarily. The other 25 percent had gone to Lexington under the coercion of New York City courts. Within a year after discharge from the hospital, almost all the addicts had relapsed to the chronic use of heroin. Willpower and sympathetic medical treatment were not enough.

However, in 1964, twelve years later, forty-nine of these addicts were abstinent from drugs and in the community; thirty had achieved stable abstinences that averaged almost eight years, and half were regularly employed. In 1972, twenty years after admission, only one-third of the surviving men were still addicted. What sticks and what carrots led to this eventual high rate of "cure?"

In the 1950s both New York City and the federal government offered facilities for the voluntary, confidential withdrawal from drugs in medical settings. The one hundred addicts whose experience is reflected in table 9-2 had been particularly fortunate. First, they were all admitted to the hospital

Table 9-2. Efficacy of Five Modes of Treatment in Facilitating Drug Abstinences of a Year or More

	1952–64		*1965–70*	
Mode	*Treatment exposures*[a]	*Percent followed by abstinence*	*Treatment exposures*[a]	*Percent followed by abstinence*
Voluntary hospitalization	270	4	91	2
Short imprisonment (less than 9 months)	279	4	84	3
Long imprisonment (greater than 9 months)	46	13	4	25
Prison and parole	30	67	4	100
Methadone maintenance	. . .	. . .	15	67

a. Over a period of eighteen years 90 percent of the one hundred addicts encountered several treatment exposures.

at Lexington, which offered five months of free hospitalization and a modest amount of free psychiatric treatment, especially to motivated patients. In addition, for three years after discharge, a social service agency tried to contact them at regular intervals. Nevertheless, at the end of twelve years, ninety-seven of the one hundred had relapsed, and as a group they had been voluntarily withdrawn from drugs in a medical or psychiatric setting 270 times. The carrot of humane, voluntary treatment of drug addiction had proven worthless.

From 1950 to 1960, state and federal law enforcement agencies were also responding to a wave of concern generated by the publicized rise in postwar narcotic addiction among urban youth. The sale or possession of narcotics met with stiff penalties. Between 1952 and 1964 the one hundred underclass addicts in this study were also treated harshly as criminals. They were sent to jail for one to eight months on a total of 279 occasions. Again, 96 percent of the sentences failed to deter relapse to addiction even for a year. In other words only 4 percent of short imprisonments or short hospitalizations were followed by abstinence from narcotics for a year or more. On fifty occasions during the eighteen-year follow-up period the one hundred addicts were imprisoned for nine months to three years without significant parole. Even with such prolonged institutionalization 87 percent still relapsed within a year. Used in isolation neither the carrot of the medical model nor the stick of criminal justice had proved effective.

The treatment of alcohol abuse is no different. Voluntary methods and willpower are little help. Legalizing alcohol (a solution often advocated for heroin) by repealing the Volstead Act in 1932 doubled both the number of alcoholics and their death rate from cirrhosis.[19] During the 1980s providing alcoholics with insurance-paid fourteen- to twenty-eight-day hospitalization for alcohol abuse did little to alter the natural course of alcoholic dependence. Nor does it help just to punish alcohol abuse. Mandating Antabuse (a drug that causes even one drink to result in severe physical discomfort) treatment is ineffective after a year because of noncompliance. Like mandated prison sentences for heroin abuse or refusing welfare to the poor, Antabuse offers the afflicted nothing to replace what society has taken away. The moral is that if welfare is taken from the poor, they must be offered meaningful jobs, not just vocational training.

Fortunately for the one hundred addicts whose experience I have discussed, there were two other kinds of paternalism: parole and methadone maintenance. Both were coercive and both were caring. They took away what was self-destructive and offered in return a relatively caring substitute.

On thirty-four occasions during the eighteen years of follow-up the addicts received at least nine months of imprisonment followed by at least a year of parole. By definition, such severe sentences were given to the most "undeserving" addicts. But community abstinences of a year or more resulted from twenty-four such experiences, and in at least eleven cases, once parole was terminated the addicts continued to maintain their employment. Work is gratifying once one gets used to it. This therapeutic effect of parole was unintentional. The law had intended to punish these men severely, either for repeated felonies or large sales of narcotics. Their parole was a function only of the length of their sentence. Their recovery was unexpected.

Ten other addicts from our study whose remission is not reflected in table 9-2 remained abstinent for a year or more following compulsory supervision without long imprisonment. Five were under conventional court parole or probation, one under the supervision of his county medical society, and two under the supervision of fundamentalist religious groups. Two more patients were abstinent while in the army. Parenthetically, in about half the cases, if addicts manage to enlist in the army, they get dishonorable discharges, a seemingly terrible failure rate. But looked at differently, if induction into the army is viewed as a treatment for addiction, the result, an abstinence rate of about 50 percent with steady employment for two or four years, borders on the miraculous.

Table 9-3. Percentage of Heroin Addicts Who Achieved Parole, by Factor, 1954–66

Factors	*Addicts with parole (n = 26)*	*Addicts without parole (n = 74)*
Graduated from high school	12	22
Served in the military	54	43
Four or more years of employment before hospitalization	23	19
No opiates before age twenty-one	46	38
First addicted less than three years before hospitalization	73	57
No permanent loss of a parent before age six	77	70
No parent-child cultural disparity[a]	42	36

a. Disparity means that addicts' parents grew up in a foreign country or in the rural south, and the addict grew up in New York City.

In interpreting the success of the compulsory supervision of addicts, it is important to bear five points in mind. First, in terms of their clinical and criminal histories, the thirty-four addicts whose experience is reflected in table 9-2 who received parole did not comprise a prognostically more favorable group. They were not better educated, less criminal or addicted, or blessed with better premorbid work histories than addicts who did not receive parole. Rather, table 9-3 contrasts addicts with and without parole for the seven premorbid variables most associated with good outcome. Using the chi square test with Yates correction, I found no statistically significant differences between the two groups for any of the variables.[20]

Second, age may have been one factor that aided the success of parole. By the time that these addicts received sentences of sufficient severity to merit parole, they were about thirty years old. (Age figures were unavailable to include in table 9-3, but they differed little between addicts with and without parole.) Evidence from a number of sources indicates that parole is less effective among younger parolees.[21]

Third, before receiving parole these men had all received other forms of treatment and had relapsed. Eighty percent had relapsed after hospitalization and 55 percent after short imprisonment. In effect, they had served as their own controls. Fourth, and more important, after the crutch of parole was removed, the abstinent addicts did not relapse more rapidly than did other addicts who achieved a year of abstinence voluntarily. In other words, for abstinence to be maintained it does not have to be voluntary nor does the paternalistic parole have to be maintained indefinitely. For many people employment, like downhill skiing, is gratifying only after one gets used to it.

Fifth, successful parole, unlike Antabuse, did not demand that the addict abandon one habit without providing him with an alternative. Parole provided a fairly rigidly defined schedule of behaviors that competed with the one the addict formerly pursued. To get parole, the addict had to earn it. To keep parole, the addict not only had to avoid certain associates, but he had to maintain both stable employment and contact with a helpful, powerful authority figure. Each week he had to show his pay stub to his parole officer. Reliable community supervision was precisely the paternalism that the addicts had never received in the past. Even in addicts with the poorest previous work histories, the correlation between parole and employment was dramatic.

It has been said that 50 percent of success in work is just getting started. What one does affects how one feels just as much as how one feels affects what one does. There is need, then, to integrate the psychodynamic techniques that alleviate the learning disabilities of emotionally disturbed children and the coercive techniques used to combat suicide into the offices of welfare workers. Caring and coercion must be combined. And it must also be remembered that vocational training in preparation for work is less important than training in an actual job. This is why the army is probably more successful with the underclass than vocational rehabilitation or prison workshops.

The question that must be asked at this point is why the paternalism of parole was better than the paternalism of involuntary hospitalization or mandatory prison sentences. First, the parole jobs were real, not make-work as with hospital vocational rehabilitation or producing license plates in prison. As Robert Sampson and John Laub note in their groundbreaking work, *Crime in the Making,* the therapeutic element of the prison-parole combination appeared to rest with parole, not the institutionalization. Prolonged compulsory community supervision reforms; mandatory jail sentences do not.[22]

Second, coercion (whether via the army or via parole) was chosen by the addict; this is in contrast to some civil commitment programs. The distinction is important. This element of choice is also integral to the success of employee assistance programs. If an employer or a police chief says that a person must be supervised because he uses drugs, the addict may find the fiat unreasonable. If an employer says a person has to be supervised because of poor work performance, or the judge trades him the rigors of parole in return for a shortened sentence for a bank robbery or to keep a medical license, the addict will see the coercion as reasonable. Coercion must have meaning to the individual.

Third, coercion must have teeth. Urine testing for physicians is useless if producing the urine specimen is unsupervised. Truancy laws are only as good as the perseverance of the truant officer. The last point suggests why parole officers, not caseworkers, should provide this compulsory supervision. The biggest difference between parole officers and physicians or social workers is not that the officers seem to care less but that they have the power to care more. In addition, a police officer will pursue a parole violator more readily if the officer is exacting payment of a debt to society than if he is trying to enforce civil commitment. In fact, prolonged parole is offered only to those society wishes to punish, not help. Society sometimes forgets that acutely suicidal patients must be taken to hospitals against their will by police officers, not by nurses or doctors who are untrained in coercion.

Another cogent reason parole is more effective than psychiatric and social service intervention is that the intervention can never occupy more than a few hours of an addict's week. A parole-mandated job lasts forty hours. Under the incentive of parole, the minority, former addicts or former felons living in inner-city neighborhoods with high rates of unemployment, did not seem to encounter insuperable difficulty in finding and maintaining regular employment.

Admittedly, the 1950s and early 1960s were different from the 1990s. In the 1950s many of the addicts were shooting very diluted heroin. In the 1990s the street heroin is much purer and also cheaper. In addition, urban unemployment and violent crime rates are higher today, and most parolees are returning to more disordered neighborhoods. Finally, the criminal justice system is much more overextended, and it has also been weakened by the dominant antirehabilitation philosophy of the 1980s. The quality and intensity of supervision and services in prison and in the community has deteriorated by all accounts. But that does not mean that it has to stay that way.

Methadone Maintenance

Methadone maintenance was not developed as a treatment for heroin addiction until 1964. Thus it was only during the second follow-up period

(1964–70) that fifteen of the forty still chronically addicted men received the treatment. Under methadone maintenance ten were heroin free for at least eighteen months and for an average of three years; five of the men were also working. Indeed, methadone maintenance programs are perhaps the most effective method society has for inducing abstinence from heroin in unselected populations.[23]

At first glance, methadone maintenance would appear an example of a paternalism that is too permissive. Thus, when first introduced, the treatment (helping the addict remain addicted) was counterintuitive to many. Yet like the good coach, methadone provides both carrot and stick. Like parole's compulsory employment, the treatment takes advantage of the fact that the best way to stop a bad habit is not to forbid it out of hand but to provide a less noxious, yet still gratifying, substitute. Methadone fully satisfies the pharmacologic addiction and partly satisfies the addict's need for narcotics. But at the same time, it blocks the high of heroin; and like an EAP or parole, it coerces the addict to remain closely tied to a treatment facility.

Civil Commitment

In the United States there have been two major efforts to evaluate the effects of coercion in reducing drug abuse and facilitating subsequent employment: the 1961 California Civil Addict program (CAP) and the 1966 New York Narcotic Control Commission (NACC).[24] These programs and similar less comprehensive efforts are reviewed in more detail elsewhere.[25] Similar programs have been instituted with great success for physicians.[26]

Initiated in 1960 by the state of California, the CAP provided involuntary commitment for narcotic addicts (without other criminal charges) followed by prolonged parole for both civil and criminal commitments. In-patient treatment was conducted in a center at Corona run by the California Department of Corrections. The guards were armed, and to escape past the barbed wire fences was a felony. After release from the institutional phase, which was rather inflexible, the addict had to undergo compulsory supervision of from one to seven years, depending on his commitment. This supervision was by a parole officer with a caseload of approximately thirty-three people. During the supervision the addict was expected to work regularly and to undergo frequent urine testing. If he violated the terms of the parole, he could, on the recommendation of his parole board, be reinstitutionalized. After three years of successful community adjustment, addicts were released from their commitment.

In contrast to other programs the CAP enjoyed a low caseload per parole officer, compulsory urine testing, and the capacity for rapid response if the individual returned to narcotics. Employment was neither mandatory nor assessed. Compared to matched controls (a total of 292) for whom the time spent using was 50 percent, after two years of supervision the time spent in the community using heroin by 289 men in the treatment group fell to 22 percent.[27] Ten years later and three years after termination of supervision, the controls spent 27 percent of the time and the treatment group 17 percent using narcotics. Close community supervision and objective narcotics testing appeared to be the most important factors.[28]

In contrast, the New York Narcotic Control Commission, costing more than $300 million and offering compulsory supervision to 4,000 addicts, was a failure. It serves as a model of how not to conduct such a program. The NACC did not employ urine testing to determine relapse. In addition, caseworkers had much higher caseloads than their counterparts in California and lacked the power to arrest. Thus, abscondence rates were twelve times higher than for men on parole for criminal offenses.

Both the CAP and the NACC have been criticized for producing sustained community abstinence in only about 20 percent of first admissions, lower figures than parole produced in the Lexington study.[29] The former chief of research at Corona called the results of the program disappointing.[30] Only a third of first admissions remained abstinent from narcotics for a year after discharge; only one-fifth remained abstinent and without criminal convictions for three years. Thirteen months of institutionalization is a steep human price to pay for these results. However, the Corona results were still ten times better than those obtained by imprisonment or therapy alone.[31]

There are various explanations why these deliberate programs seemed less successful than the serendipitous results noted in table 9-2. First, the Lexington study described only a small sample, so it could have been more successful by chance alone. Second and more likely, the shorter follow-up of civil commitment programs may have understated their long-range effectiveness. For example, men who absconded from the CAP and NACC program for reasons other than relapse or who succeeded after a second admission are still scored as relapses. In contrast, in my twenty-year follow-up I counted all the eventual successes. Third, the addicts in my study who received parole were considerably older than the average addict in the civil commitment programs, and age increases the effectiveness of community supervision. Fourth, the parole for criminal offenses in the Lexington addicts was more thorough and better enforced than the supervision provided by civil commitment programs for the CAP and NACC addicts. Fifth, an addict who feels oppressed by his parole officer can turn to other "good" agencies for help. Civil commitment can act to make all "helping" agencies appear oppressive. Finally, there may have been adverse selection of the clients in CAP. Physicians and judges confuse the dimension *voluntary-involuntary* with *therapeutic-punitive*. Thus California physicians were reluctant to commit addicts with good prognoses to the CAP because they could not believe paternalism was therapeutic.[32]

Self-Help Groups

In the United States one group of paternalistic programs for addiction has focused exclusively on the person and virtually ignored the drug. These programs involve former addicts helping current addicts to abstain in a quasi-religious communal environment. Phoenix House and Narcotics Anonymous are the best known examples. A review of the results from these programs shows that they have been roughly as successful as either prolonged compulsory supervision or most methadone maintenance programs.[33] Like methadone maintenance, these voluntary programs depend for their success on a backdrop of laws forbidding the use of narcotics. Addicts often seek admission to self-help programs under direct compulsion by the courts. Also, the programs borrow heavily from psychodynamic concepts, especially the concept that people use drugs for unconscious self-detrimental purposes as well as for kicks and the alleviation of anxiety. On one hand the individual, not society, is held responsible for recovery. On the other the paternalistic self-help group agrees to share responsibility for facilitating recovery.

Thus these programs resemble the Marine Corps more than they do parole or methadone maintenance. Acceptance into them is to be considered a privilege, not a right nor a retribution. Like the Marine Corps they ask the individual to respect a power greater than themselves. Neither sympathy nor moral judgment is provided. To remain in the program requires a twenty-four-hour-a-day commitment and involvement. Unlike residence in a jail or hospital, getting into a self-help residential program is hard and getting out is easy. The addict in an institution run by former addicts is continuously confronted by his obligations to the tangible community of former addicts in which he lives. No job is too menial. But the people who invite him to scrub floors have credibility: first, that they are not doctors and policemen; second, that they once scrubbed those floors themselves. The motto in AA is "Identify, Don't Compare" because sobriety, like jogging and achieving regular employment, rarely seems fun until one finds companions with whom to identify. In other words, the poor must realize that the people who are successfully recovering are similar to them. In the marines all drill sergeants began their careers as privates, and dyslexics are often the best teachers of the learning disabled. Those who themselves have escaped from welfare may make the best administrators of compulsory work programs for the poor.

Self-help groups do not demand that the addict give up drugs and obtain nothing in return. The very close-knit, quasi-familial, quasi-religious community offers in real coinage what the addict had been previously seeking in pharmacological counterfeit. In their solidarity the Marine Corps, or Hell's Angels, or Phoenix House resemble each other.

As any former smoker knows, the best defense against relapse is reaction formation. By this I mean the tendency of former smokers to turn black into white. They now gag at ashtrays and lecture their friends who still smoke on the dangers of lung cancer. Whenever someone lights a cigarette across the room, the former smoker with reaction formation thinks, "Am I glad I don't have that nasty habit!" Similarly, the unshakable morality of the Phoenix House resident, the gung-ho discipline of the marine drill sergeant, and the staunch conservative's Calvinist work ethic depends on both reaction formation and identification.

Finally, self-help programs deal directly with the addict's irrationality. The addict must talk, and talk honestly, about himself and why he does things. His defense of pleading social alienation or seductive pushers is directly challenged. His unemployment cannot be blamed on economic depression and racial bigotry, only on personal depression and low self-esteem. Nobody in a Phoenix House cares what the addict did; he must confront himself with why. Stock replies—"curiosity," "kicks," "bad associates"—will not do. Addicts are not permitted to persist in denying either patently self-defeating behavior or depression. In AA, alcoholics are not permitted "poor me's" and "resentments." Such a self-help model for welfare mothers deserves study.

The Treatment of Addiction and the Treatment of Poverty

All the programs—EAPs, parole, civil commitment, methadone maintenance, self-help halfway houses—depend on close supervision (paternalism), but supervision in the community and at the hands of caring yet powerful and unsentimental human beings. Such programs demand regular compulsory employment but in a setting of the individual's choosing. Indeed choice and change "one day at a time" are crucial. All these programs depend on a backdrop of the arbitrary loss of personal freedom if, and only if, self-destructive behavior is maintained. To be effective, successful parole programs and successful coercive work programs are all labor intensive and expensive. But they are all less costly than the alternatives: welfare, chronic unemployment, and imprisonment.

Each method is far from perfect, but each is more effective and less expensive than unsupervised welfare or jails. Self-help programs are useful only to those few addicts who seek them out and can accept quasi-religious group membership as a substitute for narcotics. Imprisonment with adequate parole is widely applicable but does not always provide a substitute for addiction and requires both conviction for felony and prolonged suspension of personal liberty. The Marine Corps is good for addicts, but addicts are bad for the Marine Corps. The perfect cure is not in sight. But all these examples lead to sustained employment for a group of formerly unemployable social misfits.

Again, a caveat is necessary. Coercion will solve the work problems of the undersocialized but not of schizophrenics. Similarly, equal employment opportunities and child care, not coercion, are needed to solve poverty induced by racial bigotry and teenage pregnancy. Jobs must be moved back into the inner cities from the beltways. Intelligent, differential diagnosis must always be part of any proposed coercive solution.

But can society respond toward poverty in the same way that it does toward truancy, suicide, and narcotics addiction without seriously violating the individual's civil liberties? I have no concrete answers, but I can offer three suggestions.

First, legislative answers to difficult social problems evolve; they rarely emerge by fiat. Melancholics were once burned as witches by the clergy, hung as self-murderers by the judges, and bled to death by high-minded physicians before a balance between law, medicine, and self-determination was reached. In principle, new legislation regarding welfare poverty must be designed to confront self-detrimental behavior, not to punish hedonism. Whether or not prolonged welfare is made illegal, the act of using it self-destructively should be illegal. In practice, truancy, heroin addiction, and welfare dependence are not fun, but the laws designed to combat them must by design make the alternative of coerced employment rewarding. The Marine Corps is a more caring and esteem-building environment than much inner-city street life, but that is because the Marine Corps gives as much as it takes. In contrast, truancy may be more rewarding for a dyslexic than mandated attendance in a classroom without empathic understanding or shame-free special education. An addict can understand the high morale of elite marines; a dyslexic may be bewildered by a dispirited, underfunded inner-city school. The difference between the two is expense, structure, care, and pride.

Second, solutions must permit choices, albeit difficult ones. The marines and Phoenix House are often offered as alternatives to jail. To mitigate the potentially totalitarian dangers of paternalism, the model of the EAP is instructive. How the UAW and CIO got paternalistic management to work *for* them rather than *on* them is the lesson still to be learned by paternalistic social agencies such as the Indian Service. Coercive coaches should always be servants, not masters, to their athletes; and if welfare recipients are going to be coerced, they must in some way ratify the leaders that coerce them.

My third suggestion is that government agencies and social policy-makers must remember that poverty is a disorder of individuals as well as of structures. Small longitudinal study designs following subjects for decades will often be as instructive and as valid as the huge cross-sectional samples favored by economists and sociologists. For example, over twenty years the rate of poverty in a community may stay the same, but important lessons are to be learned from those who have recovered and from those who have taken their place. Such longitudinal research means intelligent, planned, and confidential use of public records. The longitudinally gathered records of the FBI, IRS, and Social Security Administration should be harnessed to the public good rather than employed only for punishment and tax collection. In my study of Lexington drug addicts I could never have identified the importance of parole to employment, nor the impotence of prisons and hospitals, had I not by great good luck, not public policy, gained access to FBI, Social Security, and public treatment records. Privacy is often raised as an objection, but when overseeing medical research hospital human subjects committees have learned to protect the privacy of far more sensitive clinical information than criminal records and quarterly social security statements.

The intent of this chapter should be clear. I am suggesting that John Stuart Mill was too restrictive when he said, "The only purpose for which power can rightly be exercised over any member of a civilized community, against his will, is to prevent harm to others." I am suggesting that power may be used to prevent such unintentional self-destructive behavior as drug abuse and truancy. Personal motivation or sticks or carrots alone will never cure poverty; these three factors must be integrated. Previous legislative policies toward suicide and truancy and current EAP policies toward alcoholism in the workplace offer possible models for an enlightened paternalistic response to poverty.

Notes

1. Warren K. Bickel and Richard J. DeGrandpre, "Price and Alternatives: Suggestions for Drug Policy from Psychology," *International Journal of Drug Policy,* vol. 6 (1995), pp. 93–105.

2. James T. Wrich, *The Employee Assistance Program* (Center City, Minn.: Hazelden, 1980).

3. Dale A. Masi, *Evaluating Your Employee Assistance and Managed Behavioral Care Program* (Troy, Mich.: Performance Resource Press, 1994).

4. Diana C. Walsh and others, "A Randomized Trial of Treatment Options for Alcohol-Abusing Workers," *New England Journal of Medicine*, vol. 325 (September 12, 1991), 775–82.

5. Charles E. Terry and Mildred Pellens, *The Opium Problem* (Montclair, N.J.: Paterson Smith, 1970).

6. On EAPs, see Walsh and others, "Randomized Trial," pp. 775–82. On parole, see George E. Vaillant, "What Can Long-Term Follow-Up Teach Us about Relapse and Prevention of Relapse in Addiction?" *British Journal of Addiction*, vol. 83 (1988), pp. 1147–57. On AA see George E. Vaillant, *The Natural History of Alcoholism, Revisited* (Harvard University Press, 1995).

7. Vaillant, *Natural History of Alcoholism*; and George E. Vaillant and Caroline O. Vaillant, "Natural History of Male Psychological Health, X: Work as a Predictor of Positive Mental Health," *American Journal of Psychiatry,* vol. 138 (November 1981), pp. 1433–40.

8. For schizophrenia see Joseph H. Stephens, "Long-Term Prognosis and Follow-Up in Schizophrenia," *Schizophrenia Bulletin,* vol. 4 (1978), pp. 25–47. For drug addiction see George E. Vaillant, "A 12 Year Follow-up of New York Narcotic Addicts: IV. Some Characteristics and Determinants of Abstinence," *American Journal of Psychiatry,* vol. 123 (November 1966), pp. 573–84. For delinquency see Sheldon Glueck and Eleanor Glueck, *Criminal Careers in Retrospect* (New York: Commonwealth Fund, 1943). And for alcoholism see Raymond M. Costello, "Alcoholism Treatment and Evaluation: In Search of Methods," *International Journal of the Addictions*, vol. 10 (1975), pp. 251–75.

9. Robert J. Sampson and John H. Laub, *Crime in the Making: Pathways and Turning Points through Life* (Harvard University Press, 1993).

10. Vaillant and Vaillant, "Work as a Predictor of Positive Mental Health," pp. 1433–40.

11. Sampson and Laub, *Crime in the Making.*

12. Vaillant, *Natural History of Alcoholism.*

13. Terry and Pellens, *Opium Problem.*

14. Perry M. Lichtenstein, "Narcotic Addiction," *New York Medical Journal*, vol. 100 (November 1914), pp. 962–66.

15. George E. Vaillant, "A 12-Year Follow-up of New York Narcotic Addicts: II. The Natural History of a Chronic Disease," *New England Medical Journal,* vol. 275 (December 8, 1966), pp. 1282–88.

16. Vaillant, "12-Year Follow-Up, IV," pp. 573–84.

17. G. Douglas Talbott, "Reducing Relapse in Health Providers and Professionals," *Psychiatric Annals*, vol. 25 (November 1995), pp. 669–72; and Walsh and others, "Randomized Trial of Treatment Options," pp. 775–82.

18. George E. Vaillant, "A 12-Year Follow-Up of New York Narcotic Addicts: I. The Relation of Treatment to Outcome," *American Journal of Psychiatry,* vol. 122 (January 1966), pp. 727–37; and Vaillant, "What Can Long-Term Follow-Up Teach Us?" pp. 1147–57.

19. Vaillant, *Natural History of Alcoholism.*

20. Vaillant, "12-Year Follow-Up, IV," pp. 573–84.

21. Harold Alksne, Ray E. Trussel, and Jack Elinson, "A Follow-Up Study of Treated Adolescent Narcotic Users," Columbia University School of Public Health and Administrative Medicine, 1959; and William H. McGlothlin, M. Douglas Anglin, and Bruce D. Wilson, "A Follow-Up of Admissions to the California Civil Addict Program," *American Journal of Drug and Alcohol Abuse,* vol. 4, no. 2 (1977), pp. 179–99.

22. Sampson and Laub, *Crime in the Making.*

23. Vincent P. Dole, Marie E. Nyswander, and Alan Warner, "Successful Treatment of 750 Criminal Addicts," *Journal of the American Medical Association,* vol. 206 (December 16, 1968), pp. 2710–11.

24. On the CAP see M. Douglas Anglin, "Efficacy of Civil Commitment in Treating Narcotics Addiction," *Journal of Drug Issues,* vol. 18 (Fall 1988), pp. 527–45; John C. Kramer and Richard A. Bass, "Institutionalization Patterns among Civilly Committed Addicts," *Journal of the American Medical Association,* vol. 208 (June 23, 1969) pp. 2297–2301; and McGlothlin, Anglin, and Wilson, "A Follow-Up of Admissions to the California Civil Addict Program," pp. 179–99. For the NACC see James A. Inciardi,

The War on Drugs: Heroin, Cocaine, Crime and Public Policy (Palo Alto, Calif.: Mayfield, 1986).

25. Carl G. Leukefeld and Frank M. Tims, eds., *Compulsory Treatment of Drug Abuse: Research and Clinical Practice,* NIDA research monograph 86 (Department of Health and Human Services, 1988).

26. Louis E. Jones, "How 92% Beat the Dope Habit," *Bulletin of the Los Angeles County Medical Association*, vol. 88 (April 3, 1958), pp. 19, 37–40; and Talbott, "Reducing Relapse in Health Providers and Professionals," pp. 669–72.

27. Dean R. Gerstein, "The Effectiveness of Drug Treatment," in Charles P. O'Brien and Jerome H. Jaffe, eds., *Addictive States* (Raven Press, 1992), pp. 253–82.

28. Anglin, "Efficacy of Civil Commitment," pp. 527–45.

29. Edward M. Brecher and the editors of *Consumer Reports, Licit and Illicit Drugs: The Consumers Union Report on Narcotics, Stimulants, Depressors, Inhalants, Hallucinogens, and Marijuana—Including Caffeine, Nicotine, and Alcohol* (Little, Brown, 1972), pp. 70–71; and Richard Stephens and Emily Cottrell, "A Follow-Up Study of 200 Narcotics Addicts Committed for Treatment under the Narcotic Addict Rehabilitation Act (NARA), *British Journal of Addiction*, vol. 67 (1972), pp. 45–53.

30. Kramer and Bass, "Institutionalization Patterns," pp. 2297–2301.

31. Alksne, Trussel, and Elinson, "Follow-Up Study of Treated Adolescent Narcotic Users"; and Henrietta J. Duvall, Benjamin Z. Locke, and Leon Brill, "Follow-Up Study of Narcotic Drug Addicts Five Years after Hospitalization," *Public Health Report,* vol. 78 (March 1963), pp. 185–93.

32. Gerstein, "Effectiveness of Drug Treatment."

33. Ibid.

Ten

Psychological Factors in Poverty

Miles F. Shore

During the 1960s public attitudes celebrated diversity and the inclusion of persons with different life styles into the mainstream of American life. Embraced in this welcome were low-income people who became the targets of President Lyndon Johnson's War on Poverty. The aim at the time was to alleviate the burden of poverty on those who were poor. Today the overriding goal is to relieve the burden of welfare on taxpayers and to solve what is widely viewed as the moral dilemma of poverty. As public concern has moved from the condition of poverty to the cost and the moral status of poverty, attention has been directed to welfare dependency. The psychological question that excites considerable interest is the motivation, or lack of motivation, that leads to long-term dependence on public assistance.

After a long absence, paternalism is back as a social policy option for dealing with poverty and welfare dependency. With paternalism comes a new emphasis on the psychology of welfare recipients: the assumption is that they can respond to a set of expectations accompanied by consequences. This is in contrast to one of the traditional assumptions in social policy that welfare recipients are victims with few options.

Since at least the fourteenth century the distinction between "valiant beggars" and "impotent poor" has oriented views on the psychology of poverty and public dependency. Much of the current turmoil about welfare divides the recipients into those considered entitled to help because they are not responsible for their situation and those not entitled to help because they seem to be at fault.[1]

Two enduring theories of the causes of poverty and public dependency reflect this dichotomy. The earliest theory in American social thought was that poverty results from some personal failing: intemperance, improvidence, indolence. Of these, the greatest by far was thought to be intemperance. The other theory, which emerged somewhat later, was that the poor were helpless victims of flaws in the economic or social system. Beginning in the first quarter of the nineteenth century, pamphleteers and writers concerned with pauperism began to discuss low wages, unemployment, fluctuations in the economy, and the unequal distribution of property as responsible for the growth of public dependency.[2]

Neither theory could easily accommodate psychological factors portrayed objectively, free of moral judgment. For theorists who blamed social conditions or the economy, psychological explanations of poverty seemed to demean or blame the victim. For those who asserted that poverty was the result of bad behavior, psychological concepts appeared to excuse irresponsibility. What was true in the early history of social policy remains largely true today. However presented, the idea of "host factors" in the psychological makeup of individuals who are poor and publicly dependent is offensive to some group of ideological theorists.

In addition, both theories assume that those who are poor and dependent on welfare are homogeneous psychologically, possessed of only one psychological makeup and one set of motivations. Consequently, it is supposed that one psychological remedy will change their behavior. This chapter contends instead that it is possible—indeed essential—to differentiate persons on welfare into subgroups with different psychological characteristics and needs, different psychological strengths and vulnerabilities, so as to identify and recommend different psychological interventions.

Major advances in research in the social and biological sciences have led to a better understanding of human personality and behavior and an erosion of the once-rigid boundaries between nature and nurture. It is now generally accepted that genetically determined predispositions can be altered by experience. It is equally clear that there are genetic influences on many of the personality traits and capabilities that have customarily been assigned to environmental influences.[3] Behavioral scientists no longer believe that psychological development is frozen at five or eighteen or any other age. Rather, emotional and cognitive learning and change are lifelong processes. Finally, there have been striking advances in the treatment of mental disorders that might be useful to psychologically vulnerable individuals whose disturbed behavior is a factor in their poverty and welfare dependency. It is thus possible to reopen the matter of the influence of psychological factors in poverty and welfare dependency with some expectation that moralistic and political disputes will not, as in the past, cut off inquiry.

Paternalism or any other social policy must inevitably make certain assumptions about the behavior of welfare recipients in response to paternalistic measures. An inquiry into psychological aspects serves to complicate the picture by stratifying the population of persons who are in poverty and publicly dependent. The purpose is not to equate a single psychological factor or mental disorder with either poverty or welfare dependency, for these are not diagnoses but conditions of life that have come about through a variety of circumstances. Rather, it is to broaden the view of these circumstances to include psychological factors that may be remediable by means that have not customarily been considered in discussions of what to do about poverty.

Poverty and Mental Illnesses

Providers of human services have long been aware of the association between major mental illnesses (schizophrenia, anxiety disorders, severe depression, manic depressive disorder, substance abuse, severe character disorders) and poverty. The causal relationships underlying this association are far more complex than simply that poverty causes mental illness or vice versa. The stresses occasioned by poverty and its associated features—physical and sexual abuse, homelessness, physical illness—clearly can cause depression and anxiety and can precipitate mental disorders in those predisposed to such conditions. Conversely, most major mental disorders interfere with the capacity to function socially and vocationally. Persons who are disabled by schizophrenia, bipolar disorder, social phobia, or severe character pathology suffer inevitably a painful mixture of poverty and social dependency. Thus the most likely model of causation is a reciprocal one in which mental disorders and poverty are mutually reinforcing.

The first formal psychiatric epidemiologic study was done in Massachusetts in 1854 by Dr. Edward Jarvis, and it included consideration of poverty as an impairment. Jarvis set out to identify every "insane" person in the state. In his report to the Massachusetts legislature he described four categories of impaired individuals: "idiots," "insane," "demented," and "paupers." He found that the pauper class had sixty-four times as many insane individuals as did the class of "independent" citizens.[4] In the 1930s in the next population study of mental disorders, Robert Faris and H. Warren Dunham found a disproportionate concentration of schizophrenia in lower socioeconomic status groups in Chicago, a finding that was replicated by Augustus Hollingshead and Frederick Redlich in the 1950s in New Haven.[5]

There have been three large epidemiological studies in recent times. Using structured interviews, the Midtown Manhattan Study in the 1960s included 1,660 people in New York City. Its findings confirmed those of the earlier studies; lower socioeconomic status was highly correlated with mental illness. The study rated interviewees on functioning and found that 31 percent of the group with the lowest socioeconomic status fell in the two most impaired categories, while only 6 percent of those in the highest SES had the same level of impairment. The study also analyzed the response to stress by people of different socioeconomic levels. Holding the number of stresses constant, they found that those in the lowest SES tended to respond with psychotic reactions characterized by profound distortions of reality, such as hallucinations, delusions, or paralyzing depression, which cause significant functional impairment. These symptoms generally are thought to have a strongly biological base. Individuals of the highest SES were found to respond with neurotic reactions reflecting psychological conflicts—anxiety, mild depression, phobias, or compulsions—that created distress but interfered with functioning much less dramatically. Investigators inferred that there was a "host" factor of vulnerability to psychosis, perhaps biological in origin, that was related to low SES.[6]

In 1979–82 the National Institute of Mental Health conducted the epidemiological catchment area (ECA) study that surveyed five U.S. cities using structured interviews of 20,000 adults. It found that the odds of individuals in the lowest SES group having any mental disorder, as defined by their criteria, were 2.59 times the odds for individuals in the highest SES group, controlling for age, gender, race or ethnicity, and marital status. Some 21.6 percent of persons in the lowest SES group reported some disorder in the previous thirty days compared with 11 percent in the highest SES group. And 10.1 percent in the lowest SES group reported that they had experienced a serious mental disorder in the previous thirty days compared with

6.1 percent in the highest group. These serious disorders included schizophrenia, affective disorder, manic episode, major depressive disorder, and antisocial personality disorder. Severe cognitive impairment was present in 5.1 percent of those in the lowest SES group but less than 1 percent in any of the higher SES categories. In the study severe cognitive impairment was defined as a score of 17 or less on the Mini-Mental State Examination, a psychological test that measures cognitive functioning.[7]

Such low scores have been shown in dementia, mental retardation, and other severe mental disorders that affect cognitive functioning. Because the rate of severe cognitive impairment rose sharply with advancing age, some of this finding was related to the oversampling of elderly in the populations studied. From the Mini-Mental State Examination data it could not be determined whether the extra burden of cognitive impairment of those in the lowest SES group caused downward socioeconomic drift or whether the impairment might be due to the conditions of life in poverty: subtle brain damage from exposure to occupational hazards, poor nutrition, neonatal trauma, and subclinical strokes.[8]

Reanalysis of the ECA data by Andrew Leon and Myrna Weissman found that lifetime rates of affective disorders in interviewees receiving either AFDC or disability assistance were twice those of interviewees not receiving financial assistance. Seven percent of those with no diagnosable mental illness and 9 percent of those with no affective disorder received financial assistance, while about 15 percent with an affective disorder received financial assistance.[9] Again, the direction of causation between being on financial assistance and suffering from a mental disorder could not be precisely ascertained.

Most recently, Ronald Kessler and colleagues reported the findings of the National Comorbidity Study (NCS), in which a research interview schedule was administered to 8,098 people between the ages of 15 and 54 in the contiguous forty-eight states, selected as a national sample of the population.[10] Using interview techniques that allowed subjects time for reflection and recall of events, researchers determined that twelve-month and lifetime prevalence of fourteen disorders were substantially higher than in earlier studies that relied on rapid responses to questions. The most common disorders were major depression (17 percent lifetime) and alcohol dependence (14 percent lifetime). The next most common were social and simple phobias (13 percent and 11 percent lifetime).

The most striking new finding was the importance of comorbidity (the presence of more than one disorder at the same time in any individual respondent). Although 52 percent of respondents never had any disorders as defined by this study, 14 percent had three or more. Fully 89 percent of ten severe disorders, including active mania, schizophrenic psychoses, and other disorders requiring hospitalization or marked by severe role impairment, afflicted the 14 percent of the population that reported three or more psychiatric disorders. Thus the major burden of mental illnesses is concentrated in the one-sixth of the population that reported more than three disorders occurring at the same time. In the lowest income range (less than $19,999) the lifetime odds of suffering three or more disorders is 2.46 times higher than in the highest income group ($70,000 or more) and substantially higher than in either of the two middle groups. This concentration of mental disorders in a small group poses the paradox that the population is both healthier and sicker than had been understood heretofore.

Table 10-1 translates odds ratios for thirty-day prevalence (that is, reporting the occurrence of any anxiety disorder, any mood disorder, alcohol disorder, or any disorder sometime in the previous thirty days) into per-

Table 10-1. National Comorbidity Study Thirty-Day Prevalence of Behavioral Disorders, 1993

	Any anxiety disorder [a]		*Any mood disorder* [b]		*Alcohol disorder*		*Any disorder*	
Family income	*Percent*	*s.e.* [c]	*Percent*	*s.e.* [c]	*Percent*	*s.e.* [c]	*Percent*	*s.e.* [c]
Below poverty level	18.8	2.4	8.6	1.8	6.6	1.0	27.0	3.0
Low (1–2 times poverty level)	13.7	1.3	6.4	0.9	6.2	0.8	20.4	1.6
Medium (2–4 times poverty level)	11.1	1.2	5.3	0.8	3.8	0.5	16.1	1.4
High (greater than 4 times poverty level)	9.4	0.8	4.3	0.6	4.0	0.5	14.2	1.1

Source: Ronald C. Kessler, Harvard Medical School, 1996.

a. Includes panic disorder, agoraphobia, social phobia, simple phobia, and generalized anxiety disorder.

b. Includes major depressive episode, manic episode, and dysthymia.

c. Standard error.

centages of the population by poverty level.

In addition to discovering this striking concentration of major psychopathology in the lowest SES group, Kessler and his colleagues also determined that only 10–20 percent of persons with mental disorders receive treatment in the mental health or substance abuse services sectors, a finding with vast implications for remediation.

Susan Ettner and her colleagues reviewed a substantial number of studies that document the considerable ill effects of mental illness on work performance, participation in the labor force, and yearly income, depending additionally on age, sex, and type of disorder. Their analysis of the NCS data found that psychiatric disorder was associated with a reduction in income among women and a reduced probability of employment among men, which led to a substantial total social cost. The most prevalent conditions for women were major depression, simple phobia, and social phobia (fear of situations in which the person is exposed to possible scrutiny by others). Men suffered from major depression, alcohol dependence, and social phobia. Schizophrenia, drug dependence, mania (extreme elevated, expansive, or irritable mood, often with psychotic features), and agoraphobia (fear of being in places or situations from which escape might be difficult) had the greatest economic impact on women. Schizophrenia, mania, drug dependence, and generalized anxiety had the greatest effect on men. The authors concluded that the high rates of mental disorders among low-income people would limit the success of mandatory work programs if these disorders were not treated.[11]

These studies have established that a significant number of people who are poor and receive financial assistance suffer from identifiable mental illnesses. The National Comorbidity Study data confirm and add detail to earlier studies showing that mental disorders, and misfortunes such as physical illness, divorce, and auto accidents, cluster in a relatively small sector of the population. The data also demonstrate that mental illnesses constitute a formidable barrier to economic success because many of their manifestations interfere directly with successful work performance. For example, profoundly depressed persons are apathetic, sleep poorly and are chronically fatigued, have numerous physical complaints, are irritable and uncooperative, and lack initiative and drive. Persons with schizophrenia are distracted by hallucinations and delusions, tend to be mistrustful and suspicious of other persons, and resent supervision. Those more seriously affected lack initiative and direction, are unkempt, and their thinking and behavior are disorganized. People in the manic phase of manic depressive (bipolar) disorder are grandiose, unreliable, hostile to others, unrealistic in their expectations, emotionally labile, and at times unpredictably aggressive.

Again, the causal relationships are reciprocal. The symptoms of major mental illnesses not only interfere seriously with vocational success but also with social relationships. Marriages break up; family members may be blamed by patients and may wear out as caretakers. The result for the patients is social isolation, loneliness, vocational failure, and an unsteady descent into poverty. These vocational and social failures and a disorganized life in turn act as potent stresses that can precipitate mental illnesses and worsen the symptoms after the illness is established.

Because poverty and mental illness are so tightly connected, the question of which causes the other is essentially irrelevant to intervention with a given person. Most sophisticated treatment of serious mental illness also aims to relieve poverty and its associated hardships: bad housing, disorganized lives, and vocational and social failure. Equally, intervention with poverty should include the identification and treatment of associated mental disorders. The fact that only 10–20 percent of persons with mental disorders receive treatment in the mental health or substance abuse services sectors presents an undeniable opportunity for aggressive intervention. Because most mental disorders are eminently treatable, intervention may do much to reduce poverty and social dependency in those people who are on welfare and are afflicted with mental disorders.

Such interventions with primary mental disorders may have significant secondary benefits. Kessler and his colleagues have used the National Comorbidity Study data to examine what they term the "social consequences" of psychiatric disorders. In a series of reports they have investigated the effects of early-onset psychiatric disorders—those occurring in adolescents—on educational attainment, teenage childbearing, marriage, and marital stability. They compared patterns of educational attainment among respondents who had no history of any assessed disorder before terminating their education and those who had one or more disorders. The disorders studied were anxiety disorders, mood disorders, substance abuse, and conduct disorder. The measures of educational attainment were failure to complete high school among eighth grade graduates, failure to enter college among high school graduates, and failure to complete college among college entrants. Their summary findings, projected to the U.S. population, were that 3.53 million more people in the age range of the NCS study (176.9

million persons age 15–54 in 1990) would have completed high school, and 4.29 million more would have graduated from college were it not for these disorders. They noted the effect of this reduction in educational capital on work force training, limitation of functioning in civic life, and increased demands on welfare entitlements.[12]

They also estimated that more than 2.5 million women and 2.1 million men in the NCS age range became teenage parents because of early-onset psychiatric disorders. And they found evidence of an increase in the proportion of teenage childbearing in recent age cohorts. Again, the societal costs were noted.[13] Finally, they compared marriage and divorce rates of people with and without prior disorders. Mental disorders led to an increase in teenage marriages, a decrease in later first marriages, and an increase in divorce. They estimated the effects to be 50 million lost years of marriage among men and 100 million lost years of marriage among women.[14]

Overall, these studies provide a view of the mechanism connecting psychiatric disorders with poverty. They suggest that vigorous treatment of early-onset primary mental disorders in particular may help to interrupt the cycle of bad decisions leading to social failure that connects mental disorders and poverty.

Other Psychological Factors and Poverty

In addition to serious mental disorders, a host of other psychological factors can interfere with functioning and contribute to poverty. These fall in the category of personality traits, "enduring patterns of perceiving, relating to, and thinking about the environment and oneself that are exhibited in a wide range of social and personal contexts."[15] These patterns are of sufficient severity, inflexibility, and deviation from the expectations of the individual's culture that they lead to impairment in social, occupational, or other significant areas of functioning. The patterns cannot in most cases be defined as clinical illnesses because they involve behavior, which may be gratifying, rather than symptoms, which are distressing. However if the patterns are exaggerated or rigidified, they may cause enough problems to be classified in the official psychiatric terminology as character disorders of varying degrees of severity. The generally accepted classification scheme, the *Diagnostic and Statistical Manual of Mental Disorders,* includes a number of such collections of traits under the heading "Personality Disorder."[16]

Personality disorders are grouped in three clusters. The first includes the paranoid, schizoid, and schizotypal personalities. Paranoid persons appear odd and eccentric, mistrustful and suspicious, bear grudges, and are sensitive to slights. Schizoid persons are detached from social relationships, emotionally flat, and prefer solitary activities. To the schizoid detachment from relationships, schizotypal individuals add ideas that they have special powers to foretell events, read others' thoughts, or magically control others.

The second cluster consists of the antisocial, borderline, histrionic, and narcissistic personality disorders. The antisocial type, also referred to as psychopathic, is marked by disregard for the rights of others, leading to deceit, manipulation, and criminal behavior unrestrained by empathy or guilt. Borderline personality disorder is defined as "a pervasive pattern of instability of interpersonal relationships, self-image, and affects, and marked impulsivity beginning by early adulthood and is present in a variety of contexts."[17] Persons of the histrionic personality type exhibit excessive emotionality and attention-seeking behavior; they are suggestible, flamboyant, and avoid intimacy through superficially seductive behavior. The narcissistic personality type is self-centered, grandiose, driven by the need for admiration, and generally unaware of the needs of others while being extremely vulnerable to criticism or lack of approval.

The third cluster includes avoidant, dependent, and obsessive-compulsive personalities. Avoidant personalities exhibit pervasive shyness, social inhibition, feelings of inadequacy, and hypersensitivity to criticism that may seriously impair vocational performance and social relationships. Dependent personalities seek relationships in which they are taken care of, leading to submissive, clinging behavior; fears of separation; passivity in social relationships; and lack of initiative at work. Obsessive-compulsive persons are preoccupied with orderliness, impossibly high standards, and mental and interpersonal control at the expense of flexibility, openness, and efficiency. Paralyzed by perfection, these people may be seriously impaired at work and function far below their potential.

Although the nature of the component traits of personality disorders and the inflexibility that defines them as pathological conditions are prima facie evidence of the economic disadvantage they can inflict on people, there are no specific studies of their relationship to poverty. However, during the late 1960s Vernon Allen reviewed the available studies on psychological correlates of poverty.[18] The review covered a number of specific personality traits—not full-blown personality disorders—that had been alleged to distinguish persons in poverty from more affluent members of society.

Allen first considered the assertion that persons in poverty had a short time perspective and were anchored in the present, a view later put forward by Edward Banfield.[19] Allen found few empirical studies that addressed this hypothesis, and those that did were methodologically flawed or their results failed to support the contention. Similarly, there was little evidence of difficulty in delaying gratification that could not be explained by subcultural or individual factors not tied specifically to poverty. He did find that in most studies, lower-class people were much less likely to demonstrate the need for achievement, but cautioned that the correlations might be reduced significantly if there were controls for IQ. Studies of response to incentives such as money, praise, or other rewards were flawed by problems in defining incentives and also because potent incentives for some groups or individuals were not responded to the same way by others. Studies of self-esteem were methodologically flawed and inconsistent in that some lower-income children had higher self-esteem than their more affluent counterparts of the same age.

A number of studies examined the extent to which low-income people expected that rewards would come from their own efforts (internal locus of control) versus the expectation that rewards were the result of external forces such as luck, chance, fate, or powerful persons (external locus of control.) These expectations were associated with a cluster of personality constructs: active-passive orientation, alienation, anomie, and powerlessness. In most of the studies, people with lower SES showed strong feelings of external control and anomie.[20] These findings have been contradicted by later work using longitudinal data sets, fueling considerable controversy.[21] They are, however, consistent with recent work on cognitive style and learned helplessness that will be discussed later.

The Psychology of Welfare Dependency

Various studies have explored the psychology of the dependent personality. In a major review Robert Bornstein noted that in recent years psychological research has focused on the function of cognitive processes in the genesis of dependency, a focus that has replaced psychoanalytic and social learning theories.[22] Psychoanalytic theories postulated that dependency resulted from a failure of psychological development to progress beyond the stage of infantile dependency on the mother; such failure, or "fixation," was attributed to experiences either of excessive frustration or overgratification in the oral stage of development. Social learning theorists emphasized that in providing biological and psychological gratification (the primary reinforcers) to the child, the mother becomes a "secondary reinforcer" associated with pleasurable experiences. Thus dependency is regarded as a learned phenomenon whose intensity is determined by the nature of the learning situation.[23]

Cognitive theories assert that dependency results from how people think about their experiences. Seeing oneself as powerless to change or influence events is now believed to be crucial to the development of dependent relationships. Empirical studies of dependency find that women tend to be more dependent than men; that suggestibility and yielding to others is characteristic of dependent individuals; that dependency is linked to underachievement, alcohol abuse, and smoking; and that dependency and depression are significantly linked both in clinical (diagnosable) and nonclinical populations. Bornstein noted that cognitive processes, the individual's view of his or her experience, can be responsible, whether dependency is considered the cause of depression or its consequence.

From his review Bornstein distilled what he called the "core motivation" of dependent people, which is to behave in ways that will maximize the chance of obtaining and maintaining supportive relationships with others. This formulation makes it possible to understand the widely varying behaviors of dependent people, some of whom seek supportive relationships by abject passivity, while others can be extremely aggressive in pursuing them.

In an article on poverty and motivation, Thomas Kane reviewed theories of motivation.[24] Expectancy theory, that taking action depends on the desirability of a goal and the expectation that the goal can be attained by one's actions, was applied to poverty by Gerald and Patricia Gurin.[25] In this formulation, not looking for work reflects the expectation that the search will not be successful, ("I really want a job, but why try if there is no hope of getting one?") rather than lack of motivation to work ("Why should I work? It's a lot easier to be on welfare").

Kane's emphasis was on studies of locus of control and learned helplessness. He noted that poverty is precipitated by loss of income and the restriction of options and described two phases of response to uncontrollable circumstances. The first is *reactance,* aggressive attempts to regain control and mastery of the environment based on prior expectations of control and on the duration of the loss of control. In the second phase, if the attempts to regain control are not successful and lack of control persists, a conviction of helplessness erodes further attempts to regain control. Repeated experiences of loss of control lead to a state of *learned helplessness* that interferes with the ability to seek and make use of opportunities to exercise control. Eventually, this becomes a persistent motivational deficit and is associated with resignation and depression.[26]

Although Kane used the term *depression*, he likely referred to dysthymic disorder, defined in modern psychiatric nomenclature as a "depressed mood for most of the day, for more days than not, as indicated either by subjective account or observation by others, for at least two years." Dysthymic disorder is associated with poor appetite or overeating, insomnia, low energy or fatigue, low self-esteem, irritability, poor concentration, and feelings of hopelessness. Although similar to major depression in some respects, it is different in that major depression consists of one or more discrete episodes that can be distinguished from the person's usual functioning, whereas dysthymic disorder is typically so persistent that it is regarded as the person's usual state of functioning.[27] In the Epidemiological Catchment Area data 3.6 percent of respondents in the lowest SES group suffered from dysthymic disorder, as compared with 2.9 percent of respondents in the highest group.[28]

Kane reviewed evidence from other studies of poverty that support the idea that lack of control and learned helplessness are important factors in poverty. Using these studies and the material on motivation, he proposed interventions that would counteract learned helplessness by improving options for the exercise of choice and control and creating opportunities for successful outcomes of individual actions.

Kane's paper is important in summarizing studies on motivation and applying them to the study of poverty. The limitation of his work is that he and the studies he cited do not differentiate among individuals in terms of their mental illnesses, personality disorders, cognitive styles, or paths to learned helplessness. For instance, the route to helplessness for a person with schizophrenia will be very different from that of a person with a major depressive disorder. And both of these will be different from that of people with a cognitive style that predisposes them to learned helplessness. Different sources of helplessness demand different remedies. Further, in proposing that expanded options will counteract learned helplessness, Kane underestimates the fact that such helplessness reflects tenacious habits built up by the learning process that are defined and identified as helplessness by their imperviousness to new experience.

Martin Seligman has approached this question of individual variation by studying cognitive style. His launching point was the following observation: experiments were conducted in which human beings were subjected to a loud noise and given the task of turning it off by manipulating a panel of buttons. One group could turn it off by pushing the correct pattern of buttons; a second group could not turn it off no matter what pattern they tried; a third group was subjected to no noise. In the second phase of the experiment people in the three groups were taken to another room with a box into which they were instructed to put their hands. If their hands went to one side there was an annoying whooshing sound; moving the hand to the other side stopped the noise. The subjects in the first phase of the experiment who had been unable to turn off the noise would put their hands in the box but not move, whereas the other two groups of subjects quickly extinguished the sound by moving their hands. This was interpreted as a demonstration that in humans, helplessness could be learned, corroborating earlier findings in laboratory animals. Two-thirds of the human subjects exhibited this helpless reaction. But one-third of the subjects, exposed to the same experimental frustration, moved their hands to stop the second sound. They did not give up and become helpless; instead, they seemed highly resistant, even impervious, to helplessness. This observation led to a series of experiments that resulted in Seligman's theory of *explanatory style.*[29]

Seligman identified three crucial dimensions of explanatory style: permanence, pervasiveness, and personalization.[30] These dimensions divide people into two groups: pessimists, who respond to adversity by giving up and adopting a helpless stance, and optimists, who resist helplessness and keep trying despite frustration. Pessimists explain bad events as permanent and thus unchangeable, universal and not specific to the immediate situation. Bad events are also personalized; pessimists ascribe misfortune to their own faults or failings. Optimists take adversity as temporary, as reflecting features of the specific situation rather than universal causes, and as due to external factors, not to their own characteristics. Pessimists dismiss good fortune as temporary, specific to the particular setting or situation, and due to luck, the skill of others, or other forces outside themselves. Optimists believe that favorable events are due to the fact that things always turn out well, reflecting general good fortune rather than the specific situation. These events are the result of their own skills and abilities, not random or uncontrollable forces. Not surprisingly these explanatory styles are related to susceptibility to depression, although the diagnosis of depression relies on the length of time symptoms are present and the severity of disability, rather than simply the presence of a pessimistic style, which in most cases is best described as dysthymic disorder.

Seligman's theory has been operationalized in the Attributional Style Questionnaire, which he has used to predict the effects of cognitive style on success. Prospective studies of fledgling insurance salesmen demonstrated that optimism was associated with successful selling, while pessimism led to relative failure and a tendency eventually to select another career. Seligman asserted that children develop an explanatory style based on the way parents explain events, the extent to which they are criticized for their failures by their parents, and the reality of such losses as parental death and divorce.

He has also ventured into remediation of pessimism, using a variant of the cognitive therapy of depression developed by Aaron Beck.[31] Cognitive therapy is an organized form of psychotherapy that aims to change the negative thoughts accompanying depression into more positive ones. It is contrasted with insight-oriented psychoanalytic psychotherapy that aims to understand the underlying conflicts that lead to depression. Cognitive therapy uses five tactics: recognition of automatic thoughts that accompany profound depression; learning to dispute the thoughts by thinking of contrary evidence; assembling "reattributions," different explanations of events to dispute the thoughts; learning to distract oneself from them; and identifying and questioning the assumptions that underlie the thoughts. These are tactics that can be applied individually or in groups. They are usually applied in a time-limited format and emphasize self-generated activity to conquer depression. Outcome studies have shown cognitive therapy to be at least as good as and in some cases better than either insight therapy alone or antidepressant medication alone.[32]

Policy Implications

These studies have multifaceted implications for assessment and treatment.

Assessment

Studies suggest that at least 30 percent of people in poverty have had an identifiable mental disorder within the last twelve months. An unknown additional percentage would rate as pessimistic on Seligman's Attributional Style Questionnaire. Even pessimism is important in view of his findings that a variety of misfortunes accrue to people with a pessimistic style.[33] These considerations suggest that psychological assessment of welfare recipients would be a useful and inexpensive policy. The purpose of the assessment would be twofold: to identify treatable disorders and offer appropriate interventions and to use the information to tailor case management, vocational placement, and other social service interventions to the cognitive and emotional capabilities of the recipients. For example, those with demonstrably low IQs need approaches from caseworkers that are very different from those needed by persons with low-grade schizophrenia.

The epidemiological studies I have cited required elaborate interviewing techniques carried out on a large sample of the population. But screening instruments have long been used to identify specific conditions in individuals. This methodology is well established in screening for depression. These instruments have been applied in primary care settings, industry, and voluntary efforts with large populations such as National Depression Screening Day.[34] They could easily be adapted to the welfare casework setting.

Health screening of the general population has fallen into disrepute because the yield from measures such as annual physicals is so low. The reason for this is documented by Ronald Kessler's finding that 52 percent of the general population has never had any mental disorder. But screening of high-density populations such as those in lower SES groups is clearly worthwhile. In fact, the idea of comorbidity, and studies by Milton Mazer on Martha's Vineyard of "human predicaments," such as single-car auto accidents, marital separation and divorce, and minor crimes, confirm social service workers' experience with multiproblem families. Together, these considerations suggest that psychological assessment of persons in poverty and those on welfare will identify a sizable number with serious mental illnesses, character disorders, and disadvantageous personality traits and will yield rich rewards for coordinated, targeted interventions.[35]

Screening for mental disorders should focus on depression, anxiety disorders, drug and alcohol dependence, and schizophrenia because these are the most prevalent conditions, impose the heaviest economic burden of income loss and interference with productivity, and are most treatable. The appropriate screening instruments include the Brief Psychiatric Rating Scale for psychosis, the Beck Depression Inventory, the Beck Anxiety Inventory, and the Zung Self-Rating Depression Scale.[36] Substance and alcohol abuse disorders can be identified by any of several instruments: the Alcohol Use Disorders Identification Test, the Michigan Alcoholism Screening Test, and the Short Michigan Alcohol Screening Test.[37] Pessimism can be measured by Seligman's Attributional Style Questionnaire. Some of these screening instruments are self-administered; all of them are short, easy and inexpensive to administer, and their psychometric properties are well established. Screening could be included readily and economically in welfare intake procedures. In addition, there are specific, effective interventions for these disorders, with the possible exception of substance abuse. Treatment for substance abuse is more controversial because there are strongly held but conflicting beliefs about methods of treatment and because the clinical course is marked by cycles of improvement followed by relapse.

Treatment

The new methods of treating depression constitute one of the great advances in modern psychiatry. In the past thirty years several generations of antidepressant medications have become available to treat major and minor depressive disorders. The most recent of these are the serotonin uptake inhibitors, the earliest and best known of which is Prozac. Prozac has nearly achieved cult status because of its lack of side effects, ease of administration, and because in some patients it seems to alter attitudes to reality, improve morale, and strengthen resistance to discouragement and recurrent depression. Some of these patients report feeling like new persons in their improved outlook and ability to cope with difficulties.

There have also been advances in psychosocial methods for treating depression. Clinical trials have demonstrated the effectiveness of two forms of focused psychotherapy in treating depression, and in some studies their effectiveness is equal to that of antidepressant medication. Cognitive-behavioral therapy, described earlier, is one of these. The other, interpersonal therapy, is based on the clinical-epidemiological studies of Gerald Klerman and Myrna Weissman, which found that mental illnesses were precipitated by breakdowns in significant relationships.[38] Interpersonal therapists seek to understand why significant relationships have foundered and how the resulting depression is ruining relationships with the remaining important people in the person's life. Often combined with antidepressive medications, interpersonal psychotherapy is focused and short term, and it tends to deal with the here and now rather than with the past. Because it is structured, it can be taught to clinicians of varying backgrounds and educational levels.

The treatment of depression may have additional payoffs because the symptoms can take many forms: fatigue, physical complaints, apathy, indecisiveness, difficulty concentrating, and irritability.[39] Depression is frequently misdiagnosed as physical illness by primary care physicians, regarded as bad character or spitefulness by family members and friends, and considered laziness or low motivation by supervisors at work. The result is overuse of medical care, marital difficulties, child neglect and abuse, and low performance ratings in the workplace.[40] Because the symptoms affect so many areas of life, successful treatment of depression will have widespread secondary beneficial effects in the form of reduced medical costs, improved family relationships, and increased productivity at work.[41]

Depression is generally considered a major factor in the physical abuse of children. In addition, parents who are depressed create a home atmosphere in which children blame themselves, feeling that they have done something wrong or that the parents are angry with them. The psychoeducational interventions pioneered and studied by William Beardslee can be used to teach children that the affected parent is suffering from an illness that is unrelated to anything that the child might have done. Such interventions also teach children and parents how to establish healthier relationships while the depression is being treated.[42]

The treatment of anxiety disorders has benefited from a major reclassification of these conditions based on systematic studies of their phenomenology and their biological underpinnings, which establish that generalized anxiety, social phobia, and panic attacks are different conditions. It turns out that antidepressants are demonstrably effective in treating panic attacks. The treatment of generalized anxiety has been improved due to better versions of benzodiazepines. Obsessive-compulsive disorder has been differentiated in terms of its symptoms, its biological roots have been clarified, and new medications have been developed that are strikingly successful in some patients. In addition, the focused psychotherapies, particularly cognitive-behavioral and structured-behavior therapy, have been adapted to be effective in these conditions.[43]

The treatment of schizophrenia has also benefited from advances in psychopharmacology and psychosocial methods, although the causes remain mysterious. Schizophrenia in some individuals has a long course and is persistently disabling, but Clozapine, Risperidone, and other new medications are highly effective in some of the most intractable cases. Intensive case management and social and vocational rehabilitation programs have made a major difference in the quality of life of those who develop continuing disability.[44] Psychosocial methods include vocational rehabilitation and ways of integrating people with this disorder into at least partially productive activity. There is also a genre of psychoeducational techniques to teach methods of coping with the environment to those whose social and vocational skills are impaired by schizophrenia. These techniques include modifications of behavior therapy based on rewards and sanctions, and educational methods, such as grooming, making eye contact, understanding the work environment, and education in the motivations of others, targeted at specific behavioral deficits. Such techniques could be adapted to guide caseworkers in delivering social services to people with schizophrenia.

The treatment of personality disorders is sharply different from the treatment of mental illnesses. Mental illnesses are defined by symptoms, subjective evidence of disease observed by patients. These are generally uncomfortable and motivate patients to seek treatment. Personality disorders are defined by inflexible and maladaptive personality traits, behaviors of various kinds that are typically regarded as problematic by others, but not by the patients. Rather than causing the person direct discomfort, they are usually gratifying, at least in the short term. Typically the person with a character disorder is not uncomfortable, regards the traits as "the way I am" rather than as evidence of sickness, and blames everyone else for the consequences. The treatment of character disorders may not be effective until a person experiences sufficient pain and anxiety generated by the disturbed behavior. People may have to lose several jobs, have more than one marriage break up, or go to jail before they recognize that their behavior is the problem. For this reason the treatment of character disorders is perhaps the most promising area for paternalism because of its explicit reliance on the consequences of behavioral choices.

Paternalism and the Psychological Aspects of Poverty

Paternalism in social policy assumes that adults in poverty will respond to closer supervision and painful consequences of not following behavioral requirements. But if many in poverty suffer from mental disorders, is the assumption valid? Are mental disorders so deeply rooted in psychological and biological underpinnings that persons experiencing them cannot respond to environmental incentives? From the psychiatric viewpoint the two important questions are will paternalistic, involuntary interventions work, and can they be justified ethically and legally?

Paternalism has long been a feature of the treatment of mental illnesses and character disorders, and the most modern treatments seek to restore the capacity for choice when judgment and volition are altered. Restoring the capacity typically involves making choices available along with real consequences of choices based on altered judgment. Thus the presence of mental illnesses in the welfare-dependent population is no impediment to appropriately structured paternalistic interventions. However, it is important to note that the history of paternalistic treatments of mental disorders has been marked by swings from inhumane abuse to enlightened, methodologically sophisticated, and effective interventions, and a body of statutory and case law has been constructed to regulate coercive interventions and protect the civil rights of patients. It is also true that the most effective psychiatric treatment methods have always emphasized the importance of offering patients maximum opportunity for a collaborative approach to treatment, which minimizes coercion.

To be legally and ethically permissible, the assessment of mental disorders among poor people would require consent unless consent were made a condition of eligibility for financial aid or social services. If it were, simple procedures for screening for mental illness could be used as standard intake measures. As with general health screening, clients would be informed of the potential benefit to be derived from the identification of treatable disorders. As Alan Wertheimer notes in discussing coercive treatment of mental illnesses, the reaction of clients and the ethical constraints for caseworkers are intimately connected with the way the proposal is framed. Clients show much less resistance if the proposal for treatment is presented as an opportunity for personal benefit than if it is presented in coercive terms.[45]

Referral of welfare recipients for treatment and requiring participation in treatment are more complex. In general, voluntary participation in treatment conduces to successful outcomes. But it is also true, as George Vaillant makes clear in his chapter, that when people lack internal structure, outcomes are improved by the selective application of constraints. Since the discovery of antibiotics, health authorities no longer use quarantine as a method of controlling infectious disease, leaving psychiatry as virtually the only medical specialty that includes coerced, involuntary treatment in its therapeutic armamentarium, although it is permissible only under the authority of the court.

Involuntary treatment of psychiatric disorders is clinically indicated and legally permissible in only a few cases—the most seriously ill people whose illnesses pose a danger to themselves or others. Since the deinstitutionalization movement there have been experiments with outpatient commitment that require participation in treatment as a condition of residence outside institutions. More commonly, and at a less exigent level, the personal disorganization that is caused by mental illnesses is customarily the target of voluntary social rehabilitation programs provided in outpatient or community-based programs close to clients' home environments. These programs teach patients such basic social skills as dressing appropriately, picking up their rooms, shopping and cooking meals, and making eye contact with acquaintances and eventually with strangers. The experience with these programs, either voluntary or carried out under outpatient commitment, is particularly applicable to paternalistic approaches to persons on welfare. The rewards would be welfare "wages," and the expected behaviors could include cooperation with the treatment of mental disorders, substance abuse, and disruptive personality patterns, as well as progress in work programs. Based on the findings of studies of psychiatric rehabilitation programs, such measures, adapted to the welfare population, appear potentially to be effective.[46]

The task of the psychiatrist treating an involuntary or resistant patient is to establish a "therapeutic alliance" based on the assumption that patients, however disturbed, retain the desire to return to health and effective functioning. The therapeutic alliance is between the therapist and the part of the patient that desires to get well. With patients who are involuntarily committed, the therapist seeks to establish the alliance by emphasizing the reality that involuntary treatment is the judge's decision, although it is based on psychiatric evidence of the symptoms that led to hospitalization. The offer of an alliance goes something like this: "I understand that you want to get out of the hospital. The way to accomplish that is to participate in treatment, and I will assist you in that aim."

This stance is one that makes it possible for many patients to cooperate with treatment. It also reassures the treatment staff that their use of coercive methods has a therapeutic aim for the good of the patient. It is not unusual for persons who suffer from severe mental disorders to be grateful, after the fact, for treatment that is imposed in the acute psychotic state, despite their protests at the time. Some of these people, between episodes, fill out the equivalent of a living will requesting treatment during states of psychotic disorganization. For other patients, commitment and involuntary treatment generate intense resentment that continues for a long time.

The analogy with psychological screening for welfare recipiency is that the ultimate purpose of such screening is to identify mental conditions whose treatment will be in the best interest of the client, relieving distressing symptoms and improving the capacity to function socially and vocationally. Some people may resist the idea that they have a mental disorder or may refuse screening on other grounds. As long as the insistence on screening applies to all applicants for assistance, it is likely to be legally acceptable.

The role of paternalistic treatments is even more important with people who have personality disorders. One defining feature of personality disorders is that they consist of behaviors that may be gratifying and are typically explained away by the patients as the fault of others. These behaviors serve defensive functions protecting the individual from various forms of anxiety. Thus they are anchored by psychological forces that work against their being given up easily. Coercion, confrontation, and consequences help to create constructive anxiety, and these paternalistic measures may be the only way to generate constructive responses from patients and alter their behavior.

Conclusion

It is an unhappy task to complicate further what is already a complicated tangle of social, political, economic, and moral issues, but that is the lot of anyone who discusses the psychological features of people who live in poverty and depend on public assistance. Neither Bob Cratchit nor the Artful Dodger quite does justice to the complexity of the psychological characteristics of those on welfare. Like other citizens, persons on welfare have their psychological strengths and vulnerabilities. Many exhibit enormous resilience in the face of adversity, and it would be both unfair and inaccurate to believe that as a group people on welfare are either helplessly incompetent or totally capable of responding to opportunity or only capable of responding to harsh treatment.

In fact, a main aim of this chapter is to contend that the welfare population cannot be regarded as a single group. It must be differentiated along accepted lines of psychological classification. Such differentiation is especially important in view of the data that a significant portion of people in poverty suffer from definable mental illnesses and personality disorders that can be treated if they can be identified.

In view of the prevalence of such disorders within the ranks of those in poverty and on welfare, it is not surprising that previous programs of intervention have failed to the extent that they have presumed a single set of psychological characteristics associated with poverty and ignored the presence of the disorders.

As this volume attests, reacting to the failures of the past, new approaches are attempting to apply paternalistic methods to treat poverty and welfare dependency. It is clear that for the effective implementation of paternalistic strategies it is essential to identify these mental illnesses and personality disorders. Only after identifying them will it be possible to offer specific, effective interventions shaped by psychological sophistication about the assets and the limitations of the persons who will be the beneficiaries of what is done.

Notes

1. Stuart Alfred Queen, *Social Work in the Light of History* (Philadelphia and London: Lippincott, 1922), pp. 168–69.

2. Benjamin Joseph Klebaner, "Public Poor Relief in America, 1790–1860," Ph.D. dissertation, Columbia University, 1952, pp. 6, 15–18.

3. Robert Plomin and others, "The Genetic Basis of Complex Human Behaviors," *Science*, vol. 264 (June 17, 1994), pp. 1733–39.

4. Edward Jarvis, *Report on Insanity and Idiocy in Massachusetts by the Commission on Lunacy under Resolve of the Legislature of 1854*, Massachusetts House document 144 (1855).

5. Robert E. L Faris and H.Warren Dunham, *Mental Disorders in Urban Areas: An Ecological Study of Schizophrenia and Other Psychoses* (University of Chicago Press, 1939); and August B. Hollingshead and Fredrick C. Redlich, *Social Class and Mental Illness: A Community Study* (Wiley, 1958).

6. Leo Srole and others, *Mental Health in the Metropolis: The Midtown Manhattan Study* (McGraw-Hill, 1962).

7. Marshall F. Folstein and others, "Mini-Mental State: A Practical Method for Grading the Cognitive State of Patients for the Clinician," *Journal of Psychiatric Research*, vol. 12 (November 1975), pp. 189–98.

8. Darrel A. Regier and others, "One-Month Prevalence of Mental Disorders in the United States and Sociodemographic Characteristics: The Epidemiologic Catchment Area Study," *Acta Psychiatrica Scandinavica*, vol. 88 (July 1993), pp. 36–47.

9. Andrew C. Leon and Myrna M. Weissman, "Final Report: Analysis of NIMH's Existing Epidemiologic Catchment Area (ECA) Data on Depression and Other Affective Disorders in Welfare and Disabled Populations," National Institute of Mental Health, June 28, 1993.

10. Ronald C. Kessler and others, "Lifetime and 12-Month Prevalence of DSM-III-R Psychiatric Disorders in the United States," *Archives of General Psychiatry*, vol. 51 (January 1994), pp. 8–19.

11. Susan L. Ettner and others, "The Impact of Psychiatric Disorder on Labor Market Outcomes," Working Paper 5989 (Cambridge, Mass.: National Bureau of Economic Research, April 1997).

12. Ronald C. Kessler and others, "Social Consequences of Psychiatric Disorders, I: Educational Attainment," *American Journal of Psychiatry*, vol. 152 (July 1995), pp. 1026–32.

13. Ronald C. Kessler and others, "The Social Consequences of Psychiatric Disorders, II: Teenage Parenthood, *American Journal of Psychiatry* (forthcoming).

14. Ronald C. Kessler and others, "The Social Consequences of Psychiatric Disorders, III: Marriage and Marital Stability," April 1996.

15. American Psychiatric Association, *Diagnostic and Statistical Manual of Mental Disorders*, 4th ed. (Washington, 1994), p. 630.

16. Ibid., pp. 629–73.

17. Ibid., p. 650.

18. Vernon L. Allen, ed., *Psychological Factors in Poverty* (Chicago: Markham Publishing, 1970).

19. Edward C. Banfield, *The Unheavenly City Revisited: A Revision of the Unheavenly City* (Little, Brown, 1974).

20. Allen, *Psychological Factors*, pp. 242–66.

21. Mary Corcoran and others, "Myth and Reality: The Causes and Persistence of Poverty," *Journal of Policy Analysis and Management*, vol. 4 (Summer 1985), pp. 516–36.

22. Robert F. Bornstein, "The Dependent Personality: Developmental, Social and Clinical Perspectives," *Psychological Bulletin*, vol. 112 (July 1992), pp. 3–23.

23. Banfield, *Unheavenly City Revisited.*

24. Thomas J. Kane, "Giving Back Control: Long-Term Poverty and Motivation," *Social Service Review* (September 1987), pp. 405–19.

25. Gerald Gurin and Patricia Gurin, "Expectancy Theory in the Study of Poverty," *Journal of Social Issues*, vol. 26 (Spring 1970), pp. 83–104

26. Judy Garber and Martin E. P. Seligman, eds., *Human Helplessness: Theory and Applications* (Academic Press, 1980).

27. American Psychiatric Association, *Diagnostic and Statistical Manual*, 4th ed. p. 349.

28. Regier and others, "One-Month Prevalence," p. 38.

29. Martin E. P. Seligman, *Learned Optimism* (Knopf, 1991), p. 44.

30. Ibid., pp. 44–52.

31. Aaron T. Beck and others, *Cognitive Therapy of Depression* (Guilford Press, 1979).

32. Aaron T. Beck and A. John Rush, "Cognitive Therapy," in Harold I. Kaplan and Benjamin J. Sadock, eds., *Comprehensive Textbook of Psychiatry V*, vol. 2 (Baltimore: Williams & Wilkins, 1989), pp. 1541–50.

33. Seligman, *Learned Optimism*, pp. 93–185.

34. Shelly F. Greenfield and Miles F. Shore, "Prevention of Psychiatric Disorders," *Harvard Review of Psychiatry*, vol. 33 (September-October 1995), pp. 120–22.

35. Milton Mazer, "People in Predicament: A Study in Psychiatric and Psychosocial Epidemiology," *Social Psychiatry*, vol 9 (1974), pp. 85–90.

36. Lloyd I. Sederer and Barbara Dickey, eds., *Outcomes Assessment in Clinical Practice* (Baltimore: Williams and Wilkins, 1996).

37. M. L. Selzer, A. Vinokur, and L. van Rooijen, "A Self-Administered Short Michigan Alcoholism Screening Test (SMAST)," *Journal of Studies of Alcohol*, vol. 36 (January 1975), pp. 117–26; and K. L. Barry and M. F. Fleming, "Computerized Administration of Alcoholism Screening Tests in a Primary Care Setting," *Journal of the American Board of Family Practice*, vol. 3 (April-June 1990), pp. 93–98.

38. Gerald L. Klerman and others, *Interpersonal Psychotherapy of Depression* (Basic Books, 1984).

39. American Psychiatric Association, *Diagnostic and Statistical Manual,* 4th ed., pp. 344–45.

40. E. M. Kinard. "Mother and Teacher Assessments of Behavior Problems in Abused Children," *Journal of the American Academy of Child and Adolescent Psychiatry*, vol. 34 (August 1995), pp. 1043–53; and Gregory Simon and others, "Health Care Costs Associated with Depressive and Anxiety Disorders in Primary Care," *American Journal of Psychiatry*, vol. 152 (March 1995), pp. 352–57.

41. Ernst R. Berndt and others, "Workplace Performance and the Treatment of Chronic Depression," paper prepared for the 1996 annual meeting of the American Economic Association.

42. William R. Beardslee and Harriet L. MacMillan, "Psychosocial Preventive Intervention for Families with Parental Mood Disorder: Strategies for the Clinician," *Developmental and Behavioral Pediatrics,* vol. 14 (August 1993), pp. 271–76.

43. Kaplan and Sadock, eds., *Comprehensive Textbook of Psychiatry V*, vol. 1, pp. 952–1000.

44. Ibid., pp. 699–806.

45. Alan Wertheimer, "A Philosophical Examination of Coercion for Mental Health Issues," in Charles W. Lidz and Steven K. Hoge, eds., "Coercion in Mental Health Care," *Behavioral Sciences and the Law*, vol 11 (Summer 1993), pp. 239–58.

46. Dorothy D. Campo, "Approaches to Psychosocial Rehabilitation," *Harvard Review of Psychiatry*, vol. 4 (March-April 1997), pp. 328–33.

Eleven

Paternalism, Democracy, and Bureaucracy

James Q. Wilson

Paternalism seems to have democracy as its enemy and bureaucracy as its friend. Americans take umbrage at many ideas precisely because they appear paternalistic and lament bureaucratic rule because it seems to create the paternalism that democracy is designed to prevent. "Unless I hurt someone else, nobody can tell me what to do"; that phrase has probably passed the lips of virtually every American adult at one time or another, and it is a daily credo to some. When a bureaucratic agency tries to tell people what to do even when no one else is being hurt, the democratic argument is used against it.

Democracy and Rights

Democracy, narrowly defined, means allowing rulers to be chosen by the people in regular and free elections, and so defined would permit the state to do anything from providing minimal services to imposing stringent requirements. But democracy, broadly understood, is not simply a means of choosing leaders. In the West at least, and certainly in America, it is inextricably bound up with liberal political theory. The central idea of that theory is, as Michael Sandel has said, that the government "should be neutral toward the moral and religious views its citizens espouse."[1] Since people disagree about how to define the good life, government should not attempt to impose any requirement beyond those agreed to by voting and allowed by constitutionally protected individual rights. There is no Western democracy that does not to some degree guarantee that its citizens will have their self-regarding views—their political beliefs, religious convictions, and much of the way they live—removed from political debate.

If there is any philosopher whose writings would gather the support of most Americans, it is John Stuart Mill. In his essay, *On Liberty,* published in 1859, he wrote a sentence that now captures much of the American attitude toward government: "the only purpose for which power can be rightfully exercised over any member of a civilized community, against his will, is to prevent harm to others."[2] So deeply have we embraced this view, and so amenable to it are our independent judiciary and the constitutional protections they enforce, that we can describe the American regime as more preoccupied with the assertion and maintenance of rights than that of any other democracy in the world.

Democracy and Character

This is not the only way democracy might be practiced. It could be carried out under the view that every citizen has an obligation to participate in making society better. This view, which Sandel calls republican political theory, requires that adults join with others in ways more powerful than voting in order to deliberate about the common good. Democracy not only rests on a belief in equal rights, it aspires to a concept of equal obligations. But deliberating about the common good implies that that there is some way to reach an agreement about what is good, and that in turn implies that the citizens share some moral bond, one defined loosely as having a good character. The narrow definition of democracy suggests that what is good is simply the algebraic sum of individual preferences, each separately recorded by voting, with none having clear superiority over any other. The civic or republican theory of democracy suggests that what is good is in some sense knowable, and that the people most likely to know it are those with a good character.[3]

Americans also support this moral view of democracy. They worry deeply about the weakness of personal character to which they ascribe many of our most urgent contemporary problems. From the time of the Revolution to the present, we have expected each other to possess a certain character that is essential to living a decent life. People should be in control of their emotions, not erratically in the grip of the most extreme ones; they should be honest and not predatory; they should be studious in their classes, loyal to their spouses, helpful to their children, and supportive of the country; they should display a reasonable degree of sympathy for the plight of others and applaud those who make sacrifices to help victims caught against their will in a dangerous condition. These qualities are virtues, people think, because they are the right course of action, and they are the right course because some combination of human evolution, religious training, and daily experience convinces us that a decent life is impossible if people ignore these lessons.

And so beneath our procedural theory of democracy there is alive and well a deep regard for private virtue and a belief that public action, if it is to be effective, should enlist and support that virtue. Although the chapters in this volume are largely about paternalism toward poor or dependent people, America has long worried about paternalism for everyone, including the affluent and independent. In many states we want the rich as well as the poor to wear motorcycle helmets and to avoid drug abuse; we want to exclude pornography vendors from rich as well as poor residential neighborhoods; we are concerned about how the rich as well as the poor make use of bankruptcy laws. We often say that the government cannot legislate morality, and so we allow obscenity to be sold in book stores and on film, but we also believe that such stores should be away from schools or homes, that parents should control the films their children see, and that public spectacles should not include gross or offensive actions. We do not wish to see people walk nude down the streets or urinate in public, even though the nudity does not palpably harm anyone and human urine is no more offensive than that produced by dogs. Most Americans are deeply opposed to legalizing the sale of dangerous drugs even when both buyer and seller want to engage in the trade and the buyer thinks he harms no one but himself. Most people think it wrong for unmarried teenage girls to bear and raise children and be paid by the government to do so.

In short, Americans only half believe that government cannot legislate morality. Of late, the problems of American life have increasingly been bound up with questions of character. Once we thought that giving aid to the mothers of dependent children was a decent way to mitigate the effects of a husband's death or desertion; now we are more likely to think that welfare has produced a degree of dependency that contributes to the formation of bad character and its consequent social evils. Once we thought that the public schools were doing a good job of training our children; now we worry that too many such schools allow children to indulge in the excesses of adolescent culture. Once we thought that government deficits were always bad; then we persuaded ourselves that some deficits are helpful because they prevent recessions; now many people have returned to thinking that deficits are simply wrong.

Thus Americans have embraced liberal democratic philosophy while retaining a deep interest in promoting character and the virtuous life. We are democrats—up to a point. When democracy seems to support the weakening of character or to encourage the ambitions of those who lack it, we criticize our governmental practices. We are utilitarians—up to a point. We believe that public policies should produce the greatest good for the greatest number, but we also want many of these policies to have a moral basis deeper than the possibility that they will do the most good for the most people.

The point up to which democracy and utility are good is often defined by the advantages we think we notice in other cultures. Many Americans seem to like Singapore, with its puritanical culture enforced by laws that regulate its public's conduct and punish, often severely, its miscreants. Many Americans admire Japan, with its emphasis on shame and its consequent low crime rate. Neither Singapore nor Japan is the product of the Western Enlightenment even though each has done well in achieving the economic prosperity that the Enlightenment promised. In those countries, material success has not yet been acquired at the expense of radical individualism, an adversarial political culture, or a belief that each person should do his own thing.

Americans would like, I think, to retain all of the benefits of the Enlightenment—skeptical reason, religious freedom, and democratic rule—without paying a moral or cultural price for it. But of course we must pay. The best we can do is to reduce the price. And so we look for ways whereby public policy can support a certain kind of character formation, which is, politely, what we mean by paternalism, that will help the weak without threatening the competent.

The Politics of Character

The most consistent complaint of Americans is that the nation does not seem to foster good character. Most of us consider high rates of crime, drug abuse, teenage pregnancy, and welfare dependency as examples of that defect. Some of us believe that many of these problems are in large measure the result of the failures of society. Crime, drug abuse, and welfare dependency are produced by joblessness and discrimination, and teenage pregnancy, if it is bad at all, is the result of other social ills visiting themselves on young girls. The debate between the characterological and the sociological explanation of these matters is perhaps the most important domestic political argument that now exists.

Increasingly our political parties have come to reflect these differences. Conservatives (mostly Republicans) worry about character, liberals (mostly Democrats) worry about benefits. President Clinton promised to "end welfare as we know it," but there is a little chance that if Congress had remained under Democratic control it would have done what he said he wanted. The Democratic party, apart from Mr. Clinton, has become a utilitarian party. It assumes that a denial of opportunity or an absence of benefits explains most social problems and so is committed to widening opportunity and supplying benefits. Because there are many problems for which these strategies will in fact work, the Democratic view must always be taken seriously, especially since the evidence is not yet clear as to how far the government can build character even if it tries.

In trying to referee that debate, it is important to recall that many of the underlying issues might have been decided differently. A woman's right to an abortion is a much more contentious issue in this country than in Europe, and our welfare programs are less generous in some ways than those found abroad. Americans generally treat criminals, especially property offenders, more strictly than do many European nations.[4] And our drug policies are more harsh than what one finds in Switzerland, the Netherlands, or several other countries. Because of these differences, it would appear that democracy itself does not inevitably produce certain cultural problems. Democrats have, to some extent, a choice.

A central difference between American and European democracies is that here public opinion has a greater effect on public policy than it does abroad. The openness of the political system, the multiplicity of elective offices, and the fragmentation of political power have ensured that government officials will operate under more continuous and powerful public pressure than will the more distant elites who govern much of Europe. In those countries, decisions about crime, welfare, or the political integration of Europe may worry the public, but citizens there have little regular opportunity to affect these choices. In the United States, political elites, except for those in the courts, are more regularly in contact with opinion polls and interest groups. For example, capital punishment is much too popular here for politicians in most states to oppose it, whatever they may privately think. Similarly, the popular desire to end welfare dependency is too powerful for elected officials to resist.

In America, even the effort to take issues out of politics can make matters worse. Our independent judiciary, by attempting to decide some questions outside of politics, can make these matters even more powerfully political. The Supreme Court decision legalizing abortion changed the issue from a state-by-state debate into a popular obsession that has dominated electoral politics in many places. In much the same way, the control of welfare policy by liberal elites from the 1960s into the 1980s stimulated conservatives to make welfare reform into a crusade. From 1935 when AFDC was first enacted to 1996 when responsibility for overseeing welfare was returned to the states, welfare policy has been more influenced by the beliefs of professional and bureaucratic specialists than by the complaints of mass opinion. When the public would no longer tolerate elite policies, a massive change—the repeal of the federal AFDC legislation—became inevitable.

Can Policy Promote Character?

A democratic regime based on popular rule and the protection of rights is not very hospitable to finding out what character-shaping programs might work. We may all agree that a cultural problem exists, but the electoral system rewards, in the short run, candidates who promise to solve it by supplying benefits. And if rights are protected, people have ample opportunity to fend off any program, especially an untested one, that challenges them to improve themselves by work or self-denial. The idea of requiring able-bodied people to accept jobs as a way of ending their receipt of a welfare check has been around for decades, but only in recent years has it gained much acceptance.

The chapters in this volume give many examples of how hard it is to find a local welfare agency that will actually use its authority to replace welfare with work. A few have, and they become celebrated cases as much for their rarity as their success. Attempts to reduce teenage pregnancy have not yet enjoyed even this level of success. Wherever the problem is raised, the standard response has been to call for programs that will allow girls to understand their sexuality and make use of contraceptive devices. As Rebecca Maynard shows in her chapter, this rarely makes much difference. That is a far cry from simply calling promiscuity wrong and shaming people who practice it.

Bureaucratic agencies differ from democratic rule in that they will have their mission shaped more by agency culture or personnel selection than by the currents of public opinion. Their authority to rule will be based more on laws and court decisions than on customer satisfaction or practical success. Many welfare agencies have expected little from their clients except information on their eligibility. The bureaus will strive to verify that information in ways that frustrate the human relationship between employees and clients and will reward employees by simpler measures than any connected to changing a client's life. At one time welfare workers were supposed to supply services as well as cash to the poor, but in the late 1960s federal law was interpreted in ways that changed the workers from what some experts thought they were—intrusive, moralizing, and excessively therapeutic—into clerks that simply verified eligibility and requested checks. In the 1980s new federal laws have instructed welfare agencies to try to put recipients to work, but for this new orientation to work will again require a major and difficult change in agency culture.

And achieving any culture change must survive the countless challenges that will be mounted by clients in agency hearings and by poverty lawyers in court. Thomas Main has explained in his chapter how powerful these challenges have been in the lives of organizations supplying shelter for the homeless. In New York City there has been a dramatic increase in the proportion of homeless men cared for in private nonprofit shelters and a corresponding decrease in those managed in city shelters, in part because the private shelters are freer to impose a more paternalistic scheme on their clients. By paternalism Main means requiring of the applicants that they show a need for shelter life and of the inmates that they perform required work and obey shelter rules. Public shelters have been required by court orders to grant to virtually every applicant permission to enroll, while private ones can choose whom to admit and impose rules on those who are admitted.

In their chapters Eugene Bardach and Lawrence Mead provide excellent accounts of how the welfare programs in some counties try to get the women whom they support to be more active and constructive in getting training and finding a job. No court has barred what the Riverside, California, welfare office has tried to do. But no one is quite certain how bureaucratic selection rules and incentive systems could be modified to make Riverside commonplace. The greater barrier for other counties may be agency heads who lack the energy and commitment of the man who created the Riverside program.

The many efforts made to improve urban schools reveals just how difficult it can be to move an unresponsive bureaucracy. In his chapter, Chester Finn recounts the many failed attempts to make schools teach more by spending more money on them. He argues that that efforts to change a large public school system often make only sporadic progress until the system itself is changed by providing parents with a choice among schools, authorizing the creation of essentially unregulated (although publicly supported) charter schools, or allowing private firms to manage public schools.

Schooling virtually defines what paternalism means in a democratic society. For a long time children have been legally obliged to attend school because education, if it is acquired in school, makes them better citizens, better workers, and better voters. The requirement is paternalistic because young people will not know what they must learn until after they acquire the benefits of learning. To make schools work as they handle millions of children, many of them interested in very different activities, order must be established and learning standards enforced. Truancy, fighting, and drug abuse must be discouraged.

According to Finn, the central problem of America's schools is that we enforce attendance, spend money, and construct buildings, but we do not require learning. Our failure to do more than ensure participation (and in some schools we fail to do even that) is not the result of ignorance; there are many studies showing conclusively what kind of schooling produces learning. Our failure arises from ideological and philosophical resistance. What courts have done to homeless shelters, wrongheaded educational theorists and their trade-union allies have done to schooling. "Child-centered" theories of learning do not insist that skills be acquired, only that the child be "developed."

But at least in schools we are serious about requiring, somehow, that education occur. In welfare reform we have until recently chiefly cared only about paying out cash to the needy. In other social policies as well, programs have generally been passive efforts to subsidize lives without changing them.

Two propositions emerge rather clearly from the discussions in this volume. The first is that what some people believe is the defect of paternalism—telling people how to behave—is in fact its strength. We do better in changing people when we tell them how they are supposed to behave. This means insisting that pupils learn certain things (and not that their schools have more money), insisting that teenage girls avoid unwed pregnancy (and not that they only join programs that help them think about pregnancy), insisting that the homeless take responsibility for maintaining a decent group home (and not that they are simply invited to enter such a home), and insisting that able-bodied welfare recipients really work (and not simply that they be given advice on how to look for work). In short, these chapters make a case for the government enforcing *outcomes* instead of merely providing resources or offering opportunities.

The second lesson is that it may often be easier for some private organizations to do better than most government agencies at insisting on outcomes. Private homeless shelters in New York City do better at managing client behavior than do government-run ones. Private employers can require adequate work efforts in ways that help employees confront drug or alcohol abuse. Private companies may even do better at supplying welfare benefits than do government agencies. Such firms are lining up for a chance to try, but we as yet do not know how well they will operate. The effort to use private firms will always be opposed by some critics using the time-worn phrase that "profits must not be made on the backs of the poor." (Of course, every time poor people buy products from a firm, it is making a profit from the exchange.)

Private firms enjoy several benefits: Unlike government agencies (and unless they adminsiter public programs), they are not bound by the equal protection clause of the Constitution, and so they can make distinctions among the kinds of people they will help without having to treat all more or less alike. Businesses can hire and fire employees more easily than government can, and thereby enforce more easily a coherent organizational culture. Private groups can more easily adopt and act on a religious principle in managing their clients. And unlike government agencies, firms can be easily held accountable by the government for achieving certain outcomes. The government can regulate firms more easily than it can regulate itself.

But firms may also have a defect: they may find it easier to avoid helping the most difficult and intractable people. Dealing with that problem requires designing careful contracts in a competitive environment so as to avoid private-sector creaming of only the easiest cases.

The Uses of Paternalism

Paternalism works when paternal commands cannot be ignored. Lawrence Mead makes clear that successful welfare work programs make women feel that they *must* work. Paternalism without compulsion is simply advice. Parents both advise and command their children, but if the advice is heeded or the commands obeyed, it is because of the special relationship between parents and children. Recreating that special relationship in public policy is the core of the matter. Success can occur because a welfare worker constantly urges and guides a welfare recipient or because what the recipient wants will be lost if the commands are not obeyed.

Programs that require people to achieve certain goals often alter the motivation of those who already want to achieve the goals by supplying them with a command that overcomes self-doubt. Many welfare recipients want to work, but finding a job seems so difficult or risky that they often do not look very hard until they are told that they must do so. Drug-addicted criminals often want to be drug free, but the practical obstacles, the short-term love of a high, and the lure of party-loving friends makes becoming drug free impossible until they are told that they must do something. School children generally want an education, but many of them find it so easy to ignore boring studies and focus on adolescent pleasures that they do not seek what they say they want until they are told that they must.

In his chapter Miles Shore makes clear that paternalism may be especially effective with people who believe that their lives are determined by outside forces over which they have little control. Poor people are inordinately at risk for mental illnesses, and people with a single psychiatric disturbance are very likely to have many such disturbances. This problem—comorbidity—is especially concentrated among the poor. Many such people are highly dependent on others and easily become pessimistic when things do not go well. They have, in psychiatric language, an external locus of control. Because of this, they are likely to benefit from being told what to do and how to do it and encouraged to see that doing it will increase their own happiness.

Most of us are suspicious of being paternalistic toward adults because the special relationship that makes paternalism effective undermines our desire for autonomy and freedom. In thinking this way we reveal that we have different personalities than those portrayed by Shore. We are less dependent on the good will of others, are optimists about the future, find it easier to make long-term commitments, and have an internal locus of control. Our desire for autonomy leads us to insist on the same freedom for others, even people who have great difficulty in making use of it.

Autonomy versus Dependency

Striking a balance between autonomy and dependency is a central problem for a large, benefit-conferring, regulation-imposing state. In the past the balance was easily struck because the state expected little of its citizens and offered little in return. A century ago the state demanded only that we obey the criminal law, pay (modest) taxes, and support the regime in wartime. It neither gave much in the way of benefits nor imposed much in the way of regulations. But the modern welfare state now requires us to think seriously about the struggle between autonomy and dependency. When we do, we shall discover, I think, that it is not easy to insist on the kind of autonomy (and, occasionally, misery) we enjoyed when the state was minimal.

The modern state is inevitably intrusive, even coercive. The more we want from government, the more we are obliged to do what it expects of us in return. If anyone doubts this, consult the Internal Revenue Code. That document requires that we divulge our complete financial records and prepare immensely complex tax returns because the government wants our money. Other laws subject our business affairs to minutely detailed regulation, often in the same way that the state tries to educate our children—namely, with a heavy insistence on supplying government-required inputs rather than defining government-approved outputs.

Unless we were to return to a minimalist state—an unlikely event—paternalism is a permanent feature of the government's relationships with its citizens. One cannot, therefore, simply oppose paternalism because it abridges freedom; government already abridges it in countless ways. What is necessary is to ask under what circumstances, to what ends, and in what ways government should expand the extent to which it makes demands on its citizens.

The studies summarized in this volume generally answer that question by saying that paternalism needs to be revived and strengthened where it is already accepted (the schooling of children) and enlarged and extended for people—the homeless, criminals, drug addicts, deadbeat dads, unmarried teenage mothers, and single mothers claiming welfare benefits—who have by their behavior indicated that they do not display the minimal level of self-control expected of decent citizens.

Most citizens reading these accounts will probably agree that people living disorderly or dishonest lives need to have their lives managed in ways that will make them less disorderly or dishonest. By their actions such people have already made themselves subject to intensive state regulation; the only question is how that regulation should be managed. We clearly want criminals and drug addicts to stop what they are doing, deadbeat dads to start doing what they should have been doing all along, and unwed teenage girls to get married before they have children. The proposals in this volume aimed at these groups are simply more refined and sophisticated analyses of deterrence and rehabilitation. They suggest that the weight of evidence supports the conclusion that when we insist that these people achieve certain outcomes—ending drug abuse or avoiding unwed motherhood—we achieve more than when we merely try to help them cope.

Some readers may be willing to extend that argument to the homeless men and women claiming welfare benefits, although here the disagreement is likely to be stronger. Some hold that the homeless are either insane or indolent, while others believe that they are victims of a bad housing market or the loss of easy-entry jobs or a preference for being a vagabond. Some think unmarried mothers are seeking subsidies for free homes and fatherless families, but others suppose that they are pursuing an alternative lifestyle or are the victims of social oppression. The chief response this volume supplies to this disagreement is a practical one: paternalism makes, insofar as we can tell, these people better off no matter how they came to their present condition.

That is a useful but not ultimately conclusive answer. It is not conclusive because it does not tell us what we should do with someone who wants to be homeless or get welfare support but rejects the paternalism. It does not, in short, answer the "freedom and autonomy" argument. The answer most of us would give is a contract: if one wishes something from government, one must expect to do something in return. Just what that something might be is a matter of dispute, but the effort at welfare reform now under way in many states will test what that something should be. For some it is going to school, for others going to work, and for still others raising children decently.

In my view the chief goal ought to be the last. School and work are worthwhile activities, but the main reason we worry about poor unmarried women raising children is that children living in single-parent homes are likely to be much worse off than others. The evidence on this is now very clear.[5] Surely we wish to protect the next generation from neglect more than we wish mothers to work. Requiring work may reduce welfare rolls, but we are not certain that it improves children. There is, indeed, some evidence that it may help.[6] But the evidence that we know how to rescue children from neglectful or incompetent parents is very weak. One desirable feature of the welfare reform act of 1996 is that by requiring unmarried mothers younger than age eighteen to live with their parents or under some other form of adult supervision, we may discover state or private programs that make a difference. The ultimate goal of paternalism aimed at unmarried women on welfare should be to discourage the formation of single-parent homes, but if they form, to manage them through group homes, family shelters, and the like so as to improve the prospects of the children.

For homeless people seeking social assistance the argument is as simple as it is for welfare mothers: if you want help, you must do something in return. The something we want is an orderly life, a serious effort at avoiding drugs and alcohol, and a reasonable commitment to maintaining the quality of the supplied shelter. But for the homeless person who wants nothing from government except to be left alone, the argument is more difficult. Can we end homelessness involuntarily by, for example, committing those without homes to institutions? I doubt that we can move very far in that direction without making us not only deny the principle of personal freedom but ignore the lessons of history. There have always been and always will be voluntarily homeless people. For a society to deny that homeless life is acceptable is to impose more of a burden on people, including some confused people, than most of us will tolerate. "Let people who truly wish to live without homes do so."

Even so, we cannot avoid worrying about the voluntarily homeless, partly because we cannot not always be certain how voluntary that homelessness really is and partly because we naturally disapprove of people who defy the principles by which the rest of us live. Miles Shore begins his chapter by reminding us of how long (more than half a millennium) we have distinguished between "valiant beggars" and "impotent beggars" (or, in modern language, between the "deserving poor" and the "undeserving poor"). Most citizens today cling firmly to these principles, and for good reason: believing them justifies the hard work and personal forbearance of those who have helped create and sustain prosperity and freedom, whereas denying them implies that having a good character is unrelated to a maintaining a good society.

There are now and will always be people who are among the undeserving poor. They will be outcasts, dependent on charity. The principle of paternalism, rightly understood, is a statement of what we now think is the best way to sort the deserving out from among the undeserving poor. The work and behavior we demand of those who seek our help is one rough way of measuring just how voluntary their poverty may be. "If you wish our help, here is what you must do." There is no other way that will estimate as well who truly wants to be left alone.

Notes

1. Michael J. Sandel, *Democracy's Discontent: America in Search of a Public Philosophy* (Harvard University Press, 1996), p. 4.

2. John Stuart Mill, *On Liberty*, ed. David Spitz (Norton, 1975), pp. 10–11.

3. Sandel, *Democracy's Discontent*, pp. 5–6.

4. See James Lynch, "Crime in International Perspective," in James Q. Wilson and Joan Petersilia, eds., *Crime* (San Francisco: Institute for Contemporary Studies, 1995), pp. 11–38.

5. See, for example, Sarah McLanahan and Gary Sandefur, *Growing Up with a Single Parent: What Hurts, What Helps* (Harvard University Press, 1994).

6. Robert D. Plotnick, "Welfare and Out-of-Wedlock Childbearing: Evidence from the 1980s," *Journal of Marriage and the Family*, vol. 52 (August 1990), pp. 735–46.

Index

Abortion, teenage, 95, 96, 99
Academic achievement of U.S. students, 220, 225–26
Addiction. *See* Drug addiction
Administration as social policy, 20–21, 29
Administration of mandatory welfare employment programs, 61–63: coercive program implementation, 252, 266–69; diversion and direction as strategy, 65–67; high expectations philosophy and, 253–54, 268–69; institutional requirements for, 71–74; leadership in, 271–72; management strategies for, 262–66, 268–69; persuasive program implementation, 251, 254–62; reform through, 60–61; uses of structure, 64–65. *See also* Case management of mandatory welfare employment programs
Aid to families with dependent children (AFDC), 6–7, 39, 40–42; teenage parents receiving, 96, 97. *See also* Child support enforcement; Temporary Assistance to Needy Families (TANF)
Aid to needy, historical programs, 6–7
Alcohol abuse, 185, 186, 207, 281; treatment for addiction, 292
Alcoholics Anonymous, 282
Allen, Vernon, 314–15
Anxiety disorders, treatment, 322–23
Arrestee Drug Abuse Monitoring, 200
Assessment of paternalistic policy, 28–29; in mandatory work programs, 50–54, 67–70, 77–79(t)
Assessment of poor for mental disorders, 320–21
Association of Labor-Management Administrators, 281
Attributional Style Questionnaire, Seligman's, 319, 320, 321
Authority: in New York City homeless shelters, 172–74; of state in education, 222–26
Autonomy vs. dependency of citizens in democratic states, 340–43

Bane, Mary Jo, 135
Basic education skills acquisition, 221, 230, 235–36, 237, 239–42

Beck, Aaron, 319
Behavior: teenage sexuality, pregnancy, and parenting, 91, 92(t), 95–98; teenager values and, 90–95. *See also* Drug taking; Parents; Pregnancy
Behavioral requirements in paternalistic programs, 3–5, 7–9, 25, 339–40; duration of, and program effectiveness, 27–28; in New York City homeless shelters, 172–78; for teenage parents, 103–04, 111–14; work requirements, 40–50, 54–61, 266–69 *see also* Coercion; Mandatory work programs)
Behaviorism in classrooms, 221, 233, 235–36, 237, 239, 240
Borden Avenue Veterans Residence (BAVR), New York City shelter, 173, 174–78
Bornstein, Robert, 315–16
Breaking the Cycle program (Birmingham, Alabama), 215, 216
Bureaucracy, requirements of, in mandatory welfare employment programs, 72
Bush, George, administration, 13, 44, 216, 236

California, studies on effectiveness of welfare employment programs, 50–53
California Civil Addict program (CAP), 296–98
Callahan v. *Carey,* 161, 164, 167–68
Caring and coercion, integration of in paternalistic programs, 285–87, 294–95
Carroll, John B., 229
Carter, Jimmy, 12
Caseload: contracting out, 265–66; expanded paternalism and reduced, 75–76
Case management of child support enforcement programs, 144
Case management of mandatory welfare employment programs, 61–63, 71–74; contracting out, 265–66; creative strategies, 262–66; diversion and direction approaches, 65–67; help and hassle approaches, 61–63; leadership in, 271–72; monitoring systems, 63; most disadvantaged clients, 265
Caseworkers: coaching of welfare recipients, 260–62; creativity, 263–65
Chapter I program, 227
Character: democracy and, 331–33; politics of, 333–35; social policy and promotion of, 335–38
Children: in single-parent homes, 342; of teenage mothers, 92–94
Children First program, 131, 143–46, 150, 153, 154
Children's Aid Society Teenage Pregnancy Primary Prevention program, 100–01
Child support enforcement (CSE), 31–32, 130–60; divorce laws as self-administered, 137–38; fragile family concept and, 151–55; government involvement in, 138–42; nonresident father population diversity and, 135–37; overview, 132–35; paternalistic structure for, 142–51. *See also* Fathers, nonresident
Child Support Recovery Act of 1992, 132
Church charitable programs, 10
Civil rights movement, 14
Clinton, Bill, administration, 12, 44, 216, 238, 242
Coaching of welfare recipients in work programs, 260–62
Coalition for the Homeless, New York City, 163, 165, 167, 168, 170
Cocaine, 186, 199, 200
Coerced abstinence from drug taking by criminal offenders, 205–08; benefits and costs, 208–11; experiences with, 214–15; experimental approach to, 215–16; recent developments, 216; resistance to, 211–14

Coercion: caring and, in paternalistic drug and poverty programs, 285–87, 294–95; involuntary commitment of drug addicts, 296–98; levels in program for teenage parents, 111–14; mandatory treatment for mental disorders, 324–26; need for in paternalistic programs, 339–40; in welfare-to-work programs, 252, 266–69. *see also* Coerced abstinence from drug taking by criminal offenders
Cognitive therapy, 319
Coleman, James S., 228–29
Collins, Marva, 230
Community-based responsible fatherhood progams (CBRFP), 153
Community Service Society, New York City, 165
Comorbidity studies of mental illness and socioeconomic status, 309–13
Compulsory school attendance, 222–23, 224, 285–86
Conservatism, 22, 334; paternalism and, 11–13, 23
Consultants on Alcoholism, 281
Contracting out caseloads, 265–66
Core Knowledge Foundation, 240
Crime, 15, 16(t), 19; drug abuse and, 183, 185–86, 191, 199; teenage parenthood and, 94
Crime in the Making (Sampson, Laub), 294
Criminal offenders. *See* Offenders, criminal
Cuomo Commission report on homeless, 168–69, 171

Delpit, Lisa, 241
Democracy, 34; citizen autonomy vs. dependency in, 340–43; citizen character in, 331–33; politics of citizen character in, 333–35; promotion of citizen character by social policy in, 335–38; rights and policy in, 330–31; uses of paternalism in, 339–40; varieties of paternalism and, 249–50
Demonstration and service programs for pregnancy prevention, 99–101
Dependency. *See* Democracy; Welfare dependency
Dependent personality studies: policy implications for, 319–23; welfare dependency and, 315–19
Depression, treatment, 321–22
Diagnostic and Statistical Manual of Mental Disorders, 313
Dinkins, David, administration, 168, 171
"Direct instruction" classroom strategy, 221, 230, 235–26
Disease: drug addiction as, 212; poverty as, 283–85
District of Columbia Drug Court, 214–15
Diversion, reducing welfare caseload by, 65–67
Divorce, 136; child support enforcement and laws of, 137–38
Domestic violence, 153
Drug addiction, 32, 192, 193; civil commitment for, 296–98; crime and, 183, 185–86, 199; disease model of, 212; medical treatment, 287–96; as metaphor for poverty, 279–81; responsibility for, 282–83; self-help groups for overcoming, 298–300; social policy of prevention-enforcement-treatment, 200–03; treatment of, and treatment of poverty, 300–02. *see also* Drug policy
Drug addict-offenders, 198–200; coerced abstinence for, 205–16; current policies toward, 200–05
Drug diversion programs, 203–05
Drug Free Work Place Act of *1988,* 281
Drug policy, 32, 182–219; coerced abstinence programs as, 214–16; benefits and costs, 205–11; conceptual basis of paternalism and, 186–92;

Drug policy (*continued*)
drug diversion and drug courts as, 203–05; drug laws and, 194–97; drug taking and, 192–93; ineffectiveness for addict-offenders, 200–03; liberal vs. paternalistic, 182–84; paternalistic interventions and drug-involved offenders, 197–200; phenomenology and politics of drug problem and, 184–86; resistance to paternalistic, 211–14
Drug taking: crime and, 183, 185–86, 199; coerced abstinence, 205–16; in criminal offenders, 198–203; paternalism and, 192–93; social problems and, 184–86
Drug Use Forecasting (DUF) system, 200
Dunham, H. Warren, 308

Economics: antipoverty policy and, 28–29; lack of jobs and economic restructuring, 49–50; model applied to education, 226–27
Edmonds, Ronald, 229
Education, 33, 220–47, 337; academic achievement, 220; and consensus on new policies, 238–42; developmentalist philosophy in, 231, 232; effective instructional strategies, 227–31, 235–36; failure of economic model for, 226–27; limits of paternalism in, 223–26; paternalistic strategies in, 221, 229–31, 235, 240–43; progressivism in, 232–36, 241; prospects for reform, 242–44; reform, 220–21, 236–38; reform resistance of educational establishment, 231–34; and social programs for teenage parents, 106, 107(t); standards-based (outcomes-based), 236–38; state authority as paternalism in, 222–23
Education and training programs, 19; for teenage parents, 97, 100, 101–03, 106, 107(t)
Eldredge v. *Koch,* 168
Eligibility for welfare programs, 7–8; in New York City homeless shelters, 169–70
Ellwood, David, 135
Elmira Nurse Home Visiting Program, 102; outcomes, 105(t), 106
Employee assistance programs (EAPs) and paternalism, 279, 281, 282, 286, 301
Employment. *See* Work
Enforcement: and paternalism, 3–5; as policy toward drug-addicted offenders, 200, 201; social contract and supervision as, 5–6, 46; in welfare employment programs, 54–61. *See also* Behavioral requirements in paternalistic programs; Coercion; Sanctions
Engler, John, 12, 242
Equality of Educational Opportunity (Coleman), 228–29
Escalante, Jaime, 230, 236
Ettner, Susan, 311
Evaluation. *See* Assessment of paternalistic policy
Expectancy theory, 316

Family, fragile, 134–35, 151–55
Family planning services, 96, 98–101, 114
Family Support Act (FSA) of *1988,* 43, 46, 71, 96, 97, 139, 141, 147, 148
Faris, Robert, 308
Fathers, nonresident: child support and poverty, 140–41; diversity, 135–37; establishing paternity and, 140, 141–42; paternalistic programs for, 142–51; self-administered child support, 137–38; teaching responsible parenting and family building to, 152–55. *See also* Child support enforcement; Mothers; Parents
Federal Bureau of Investigation, 286
Federal Office of Child Support Enforcement (OCSE), 138–39

Federal Parent Locator Service, 133
Follow Through experimental program, 235
Fragile family concept, child support enforcement and, 134–35, 151–55
Freedom, social policy and cultural values for, 22, 23, 187; paternalism and, 71
Functionalist and structuralist explanations of homelessness, 164–67

GAIN program. *See* Greater Avenues for Independence (GAIN)
Gingrich, Newt, 13
Giuliani, Rudolf, administration, 161, 169, 170, 171–72
Goals: of paternalistic social policy, 3–5; of teenage parents, 92–94; of welfare recipients in work programs, 255–56
Goals 2000 program, 236, 238
Goodwill Industries, 144, 146
Government: authority in education, 222–23; limitations in education, 223–26; paternalistic programs directed by, 8–9; risk of underinvestment in welfare-to-work programs, 270–72
Great Depression, 7, 10
Greater Avenues for Independence (GAIN) welfare employment program (Riverside, California), 51, 52(t), 56, 59, 62, 72, 77(t); MDRC study of implementation, 252–54, 256, 258, 260–61, 263, 264, 266; sanctions, 266
Greenberg, Reuben, 222
Greenpoint Shelter, New York City, 173

Hamilton, Gerry, 144
Handler, Joel, 267
Hanushek, Eric, 229
"Harm" principle, John Stuart Mill's, 4–5
Harrison Act of *1914,* 287
Hasenfeld, Yeheskel, 267
Hayes, Robert, 167
Head Start, 227
Health services in public schools, 96, 100
Healthy Start program (Baltimore), 153
Help-and-hassle case management, 61–63
Heroin, 186, 199; medical treatment for addiction, 287–96
Herr, Toby, 258, 265
Hirota, Janice M., study of homeless shelter, 174–78
Hirsch, E. D., 236, 240, 242, 244
Hollingshead, Augustus, 308
Homeless men, 32, 161–81, 336, 342; exercise of authority in private shelters, 172–74; functionalist and structuralist concepts of, 164–67; New York City policy toward, 161–64, 167–69; occupied beds for, 172(t); operation of private shelters, 174–78; paternalism and privatization in programs, 170–74; paternalistic eligibility programs blocked for, 169–70; program shelters, 173–74
Homelessness, 19, 342
Homeless Services, New York City Department of, 171

Immerwahr, John, 239
Instructional educational practices, 221, 228–31, 235–36, 239–42

Jarvis, Edward, 307–08
Job Club workshops (Oklahoma), 257
Job Corps, 5, 101
Job Opportunities and Basic Skills Training Program (JOBS), 44, 97, 147; enforced participation in, 55; evaluation of, 55–56; innovative administration, 262–64; sanctions, 266; in Wisconsin, 53, 57–60, 62, 65–67, 69, 70, 73–74
Jobs, structural explanations for lack of, 48–50

JOBSTART program, 101
Job Training Partnership Act (JTPA), 48
Job training programs, voluntary, 47–48
Johnson, John, 239
Johnson, Lyndon, administration, 12; antipoverty policies, 305; educational policies, 226–28

Kane, Thomas, on welfare dependency, 316–18
Kearns, Utah, welfare employment program, 60, 63, 253, 264, 269
Kerner Commission, 14
Kessler, Ronald, 320; comorbidity study by, 309–13
Kozol, Jonathan, 227

Lamboy v. *Gross,* 168
Laub, John, 294
Law enforcement, 3; compulsory school attendance and, 222
LEAP program (Ohio Learning, Earning and Parenting), 102–03, 106, 222–23; mandatory nature, 103–04; outcomes, 104–08, 110–11
Learned helplessness, 316, 317, 318
Learnfare programs, 44, 66, 222
Leon, Andrew, 309
Liberalism, 22, 334; competence assumption underlying, 23–24; drug addiction and, 182–83; paternalism and, 11, 12; structuralist explanations of unemployment and, 48–50
Liebow, Elliot, 177
Long, Russell B., 138

McCain v. *Koch,* 168
Malin, Joan, 171
Mandatory treatment of mental disorders, 324–26
Mandatory work programs, 39–88; assessment of paternalistic approach in, 67–70; case management of, 61–63, 262–66, 268–69; client response, 64–67; coercion and pressure in, 252, 266–69; institutional conditions for, 71–74; paternalism in, 54–61; persuasive approach to implementing, 251, 254–62; success, 50–54; trends toward, 42–50; work problem in welfare and, 40–42
Manpower Demonstration Research Corporation (MDRC): Parent's Fair Share program and, 147–49, 151, 153; studies of mandatory welfare employment programs by, 50–53, 77–79(t), 252–54
Marijuana, 186, 207
Marine Corps, U.S., 298, 301
"Mastery learning" classroom strategy, 221, 230
Maternal and Child Health Services Block Grant, 98
Mazer, Milton, 320
Mediation services, family, 151
Medical model for paternalistic social programs, 279–80
Medical treatment for drug addiction, 287–96
Men's Services Program (Baltimore), 153
Mental illness, poverty and, 283–85, 307–13; mandatory treatment of, 324–26; policy implications for assessing and treating, 319–23
Methadone maintenance programs, 292, 295–96
Methamphetamines, 186
Midtown Manhattan Study on mental illness and socioeconomic status, 308
Mill, John Stuart, 4–5, 187–88, 193, 281, 302, 331
Mincy, Ronald, 135–36
Mismatch theory on job availability in inner city, 49–50
Monitoring in case management, 63
Moss, Philip, 156
Mothers: noncooperation in child support enforcement cases, 134, 140, 151; as recipients of AFDC, 40–42;

teenage, 92–94; in work welfare programs, 68. *See also* Parents; Teenage pregnancy and parenthood
Motivation, theories of, and welfare dependency, 316–18
Multnomah County (Portland), Oregon, Drug Testing and Evaluation Program, 214

Narcotics Anonymous, 298
National Commission on Excellence in Education, 220
National Comorbidity Study (NCS), 309–13
National Council of Teachers of Mathematics, 236
National Institute of Mental Health study of mental illness, 308–09
New Chance program, 101–02; mandatory nature, 104; outcomes, 104–08, 109–10
New York City: entitlement to shelter in, 161, 167–69; privatization of homeless shelters, 170–78, social policy toward homeless men, 161–64, 167–70;
New York City Commission on the Homeless (Cuomo Commission), 168–69, 171
New York Narcotic Control Commission (NACC), 296, 297
Nichols, Jeffrey, child support enforcement case against, 132–34, 139
Northeastern Oklahoma University A & M work program, 257–58

Obligations and responsibilities vs. rights, 21–23
Offenders, criminal: coerced abstinence from drug use, 205–16; paternalistic interventions with, 197–98; social policy toward drug-involved, 198–204
Ohio Learning, Earning and Parenting (LEAP), 102, 103–08, 110–11, 222–23
Other People's Children (Delpit), 241
Outcomes-based (standards-based) education (OBE), 236–38

Parents: dreams and realities for teenage, 92–94; limits of state authority and, 224–25; programs for teenage, 101–14, 119(t); welfare and teenage, 95–98. *See also* Child support enforcement (CSE); Mothers
Parent's Fair Share program, 147–49, 151, 153
Parole, substance abuse programs and, 282, 292, 293(t), 294
Pataki, George, 12
Paternal Involvement Project Demonstration program (Chicago), 154, 155
Paternalism, 1–38; advantages and disadvantages, 24–28; assessment of, in social programs, 28–35; assumptions of social policy and, 20–24; in child support enforcement, 5–6, 142–51; conceptual basis, 186–92; definition, 2; in drug addiction and poverty programs 279–81; drug policy and, 192–200, 205–16; education, state authority, and, 222–26; in education strategies, 221, 230, 235–36, 237, 239–42, 243; history of social policy and, 17–20; lack of assessment and research on, 28–29; in mandatory welfare employment programs, 50–61, 252–69; in New York City homeless shelter programs, 166, 169–78; old and new aspects, 6–9; political factors in turn toward, 11–13; potential in welfare programs, 74–76; privatization of social welfare and, 9–11; in programs for teenage pregancy prevention and teenage parent services, 98–114; psychological aspects of poverty and, 324–26; social contract idea and, 3, 5–6, 13, 46, 259; social goals and, 3–5; social problems and turn toward, 14–17;

Paternalism (*continued*)
traditional social policy vs., 3–6; uses in democratic societies, 339–40; varieties and approaches to implementation, 249–52
Paternity, establishing, 140–42, 152
Peck, Al, 175
Personality disorders, poverty and, 313–15; treatment, 323
Personal Responsibility and Work Opportunity Reconciliation Act (PRWORA) of *1996,* 9, 13, 45–46, 63, 71, 75, 76, 97, 152
Persuasion, paternalistic welfare-to-work programs using, 251, 254–62
Phoenix House, 298, 299
Pierce v. *Society of Sisters,* 224–25
Pinkerton, James, 13
Political climate: limitations on state authority in education and, 225; mandatory welfare employment programs and, 40–42, 46, 71–72; turn toward paternalism and, 11–13
Poor, defined, 2. *See also* Poverty; Welfare dependency
Poverty, 9, 14–20, 33–34, 279–304; assigning responsibility for drug addiction and, 282–83, 286–98; drug addiction as metaphor for, 279–81; child support enforcement and, 140–42; employee assistance programs (EAPs) as metaphor for paternalistic approach to, 279, 281, 282, 286, 301; integration of caring and coercion in paternalistic approach to, 285–87; involuntary civil commitment for addicts and, 296–98; mental illness and, 283–85; noncustodial fathers and, 140–42; paternalism and medical model for aiding, 279–81; paternalism vs. medical treatment of heroin addiction, 287–96; rates and age group, 17, 18(t); rates and employment, 42(t); self-help groups for drug addicts, and addiction metaphor for, 298–300; among teenage parents, 92–94; treatment of addiction and treatment of, 300–02
Poverty, psychological factors in, 33–34, 65, 305–29: mental illness, 283–84, 307–13; paternalism and, 324–26; personality traits and disorders as, 313–15; policy implications of, 319–23; psychology of welfare dependency, 305–07, 315–19; in welfare-to-work programs, 257–58
Pregnancy: prevention programs for teenage, 98–101, 106–08, 109(t), 111–14, 116–18(t); unplanned teenage, 91–92; unwed and work welfare programs, 68–69
Prevention: policy and drug addict-offenders, 200–01; of teenage pregnancy, 98–101, 106–08, 109(t), 111–14, 116–18(t)
Privatization of social programs, 9–11, 338; New York City homeless shelters, 170–78
Progressivism in education, 232–34; educational effectiveness and, 234–36
Project Match, 258
Project Redirection, 102; outcomes, 104, 105(t)
Project Renewal (New York City), 172, 177
Project Sentry (Lansing, Michigan), 214
Project Taking Charge, 99
Prospect theory, 189–90
Public opinion, 6, 13; public policy and, 334–35
Public policy. *See* Social policy

Quantum Opportunities program, 100

Race: academic achievement and, 220; social policy and, 22–23, 26
Rationality, individual, 187–92; drug taking and idea of, 192–93; less-than-rational action, 188–89, 190–91
Ravitch, Diane, 221, 232, 236

Reagan, Ronald, administration, 12, 43, 46, 47
Reciprocity of welfare recipients in work programs, 259–60
Redlich, Frederick, 308
Responsibility: for addiction and poverty, 282–83; obligations vs. rights, 21–23; of welfare recipients in work programs, 259–60
Rights: democracy and, 330–31; responsibilities vs., 21–23; to shelter in New York City, 161, 167–69; of welfare recipients, 46
Rutter, Michael, 229

Salvation Army, 163, 173, 174–78
Sampson, Robert, 294
Sanctions: in coerced drug abstinence programs, 205–08, 211, 212; in mandatory welfare employment programs, 59–60, 113, 266, 269
Sandel, Michael, 330
San Diego, California, AFDC welfare employment program, 51, 52(t), 72
Santa Cruz County, California, policy toward addict-offenders, 214
Saturation Work Initiative Model (SWIM) welfare employment program (San Diego), 51, 52(t), 56, 59, 72
Saxon, John, 236
Schizophrenia, treatment, 323
School effectiveness: Coleman report and, 227–31; consensus for reforms for, 238–42; "direct instruction" and, 221, 230, 235–36, 237, 239, 240; economic model for, 226–27; educational establishment resistance to reforms for, 231–34; progressivist philosophy and, 232–36; prospects for reforms leading to, 242–44; standards-based (outcomes-based) education and, 236–38
Schools: health services in, 96, 100; reforms in, 220–21, 236–38
Schools We Need and Why We Don't Have Them, The (Hirsch), 242
Self-Center program, 100
Self-help groups for drug addiction, 298–300
Self-interest: in educational establishment, 232; rationality and, in drug taking, 4, 24, 187–93
Seligman, Martin, on psychology of dependency, 318–19, 320
Sex education, 98–101
Sexual behavior, teenage, 90–98
Shelter, legal entitlement to in New York City, 161, 167–69
Sizemore, Barbara, 240–41
Skinner, B. F., 233
Sklar, Stanley L., 170
Slavin, Robert, 231
Smith, Marshall, 229
Social contract, paternalism and, 3, 5–6, 13, 46, 259
Social policy: administration of programs as, 20–21; competence assumptions underlying liberal, 23–24; disappointment in traditional, 17–20; on homelessness in New York City, 161–64, 167–78; privatization and, 9–11; promotion of character through, 335–38; psychology of poverty and, 319–23; public opinion and, 334–35; on teenage pregnancy and parenthood, 96–98; traditional versus paternalistic, 3–6. *see also* Democracy; Drug policy; Paternalism
Social problems, contemporary U.S., 14–17
Social Security Act, Title IV (D), child support enforcement and, 138–40
Social Services Block Grant, 98
Sorenson, Elaine, 132, 135–36
SPED program (Kearns, Utah), 60, 63, 253, 264, 269
Standards-based (outcomes-based) education, 236–38

State: citizen autonomy vs. dependency, 340–43; powers and limitations in education, 222–26
States: child support enforcement, 132–34; welfare reform and, 12, 74–75. *See also* Wisconsin
Stone, J. E., 230, 233
STRIVE, 5
Structuralist explanations of social problems: homelessness, 164–67; unemployment, 48–40
Success Express program, 99
Success for All program, 231, 240
Summer Training and Education program, 100
Supervision in social programs, 5–6; help and hassle approach, 61–63; monitoring in case management as, 63; persuasion and, 251, 254–62; pressure and, 252, 266–69; questions about, 29–35; uses of structure in, 64–65
Sylvan Learning Systems, 240

Teenage Parent Health Care Program, 102
Teenage Parent Welfare Demonstration, 102; coercion and enforcement, 111–14; mandatory requirements, 103; outcomes, 104–08, 111
Teenage pregnancy and parenthood, 31, 89–129; coercion and program effectiveness, 111–14; conflict between values and behavior, 90–95; discussion and conclusions on programs related to, 114–15; programs for prevention, 98–101, 116–18(t); programs for teenage parents, 101–08, 119(t); sources of information on programs for, 120–23(t); teenage sexuality, pregnancy, and parenting behaviors, 95–98; variation in program effectiveness, 108–11
Temporary Assistance to Needy Families (TANF), 39, 45
Third Street Program, New York City, 172
Thompson, Tommy, 12, 66, 73–74. *See also* Wisconsin
Tilly, Christopher, 156
Title IV (D) of Social Security Act, 138–40
Title X Family Planning program, 98
Treatment: drug-addicted criminal offenders, 200, 201–02, 210, 212–13; heroin addiction, 287–96; mental disorders and depression, 321–23
Trevino, Victor, 222

Underinvestment in welfare-to-work programs, 270–72
Unwed mothers, 68–69. *See also* Teenage pregnancy and parenthood

Values, 4; conflict between teenage behavior and, 90–95; toward education of children, 224–25; effect of paternalism on, 26; in sex education programs, 99, 100
Volstead Act of *1932,* 292
Vouchers, educational, 13

Walberg, Herbert J., 229
Watkins, Cathy L., 235
Way Home, The: A New Direction in Social Policy (Cuomo Commission report), 168–69, 171
Weissman, Myrna, 309
Welfare, 3; access to and eligibility for, 7–8; historical programs, 6–7; incentives to reduce pregnancies, 97–98; potential for paternalistic policy in, 74–76; programs for teenage parents receiving, 101–14
Welfare dependency: paternalism and, 324–26; policy implications of psychological factors in, 319–23; psychology of, 305–07, 315–19; reduction in employment programs, 50–61; teenage parents and, 90–91. *See also* Poverty; Welfare recipents

Welfare employment programs, 31, 39–88, 248–78, 336–37; assessment of paternalistic approach, 67–70; case management, 61–63; client response, 64–67; defined, 39; effects of paternalism on, 54–56; functioning of paternalistic, 57–61; historical move from voluntary to mandatory; 42–46; institutional conditions for paternalistic, 71–74; potential for paternalism applied to, 74–76; success of mandatory, 50–54; trends toward mandatory, 46–50; work requirements for welfare receipients in, 40–42. *See also* Welfare-to-work program implementation

Welfare recipients: caseworkers in mandatory work programs and, 61–63, 254–62, 266–69; goals of in work programs, 255–56; obligations and rights, 21–23; psychology of dependency in, 315–19; requiring work from, 40–42; reciprocity and responsibility in work programs, 259–60; response to mandatory welfare work programs, 64–67; rights, 46; self-respect in work programs, 257–58

Welfare reform, 1, 74–75; paternalism and, 74–76. *See also* Personal Responsibility and Work Opportunity Reconciliation Act (PRWORA) of *1996*

Welfare rights movement, 7–8

Welfare-to-work program implementation, 33, 248–78, 336–37; GAIN program as example, 252–54; management strategies, 262–66; paternalism with persuasion as strategy, 251, 254–62; paternalism with pressure as strategy, 252, 266–69; risk of underinvestment in, 270–72; varieties of paternalistic policies, 249–52

Wertheimer, Alan, 324

Wilson, James Q., 28

Wilson, Pete, 12

Wilson, William Julius, 49–50, 156

Wisconsin: Children First program, 131, 143–46, 150, 153, 154; contracting out administration of JOBS program, 266; Learnfare program, 44, 66, 222; mandatory employment programs and welfare dependency, 53–54, 57–60, 62, 65–67, 69, 70, 73, 75–76; Young Unwed Fathers Project, 146–47

Wiseman, Michael, 270

Work: enforcing requirements for, 42–46; poverty rates and, 42(t); and social programs for teenagers, 104–06; welfare recipients and, 40–42; work status, 41(t). *See also* Welfare employment programs; Welfare-to-work program implementation

Work and Responsibility Act of *1994*, 44

Workfare, 64, 266–69

Work Incentive Program (WIN) of *1967*, 43, 253; enforced participation, 54–55

Work incentives programs, 47

Work requirements, enforcement, 40–42, 57–61, 266–69: management strategies for, 268–69; performance associated with, 58–59; reasons for, 46–50; sanctions and, 59–60; trends, 42–46

Young Unwed Fathers Project, 146–47